REFERENCE GUIDES IN LITERATURE

Ronald Gottesman, *Editor*

Jack London:
A Reference Guide

Joan R. Sherman

G. K. HALL & CO., 70 LINCOLN STREET, BOSTON, MASS.

Library of Congress Cataloging in Publication Data

Sherman, Joan R
    Jack London : a reference guide.

    (Reference guides in literature)
    Includes index.
    1.   London, Jack, 1876-1916--Bibliography.
Z8514.6.S48   [PS3523.046]   016.813'5'2 76-54639
ISBN 0-8161-7849-6

This publication is printed on permanent/durable acid-free paper
MANUFACTURED IN THE UNITED STATES OF AMERICA

Contents

Introduction

There is no complete edition of London's writings nor even an incomplete "Collected Works." Macmillan's Sonoma Edition of 28 titles
in 21 volumes (1919) was the last such attempt by an American publisher. Moreover, a definitive canon of London's work does not exist.
Each year, scholars discover additional published and unpublished
stories, essays, articles, letters, plays and poems.[1] Most discour-
aging for those who wish to write about London's work is the fact
that of his 50 volumes (published 1900-1922) fewer than half are
available in any form outside of rare book rooms. Books in Print
(1975) lists 80 London items: 19 story anthologies, 40 editions of
novels, 8 editions of nonfiction, 2 plays, 1 poem, and 9 miscellaneous
(essays, memorabilia) items. This great number of entries attests to
the popularity of London with the general reader; however, among the
80 listings, there are only 21 of his original titles.[2] Duplication
of familiar titles, such as 17 editions of The Call of the Wild,
"beefs up" the total. A flurry of interest in London by publishers
in the 1960's brought many reprints in paperback, but only of the
perennially-popular titles.

In England in the 1960's, The Fitzroy Edition of the Works of
Jack London (London: Arco) offered 20 titles; and The Bodley Head
Jack London in four volumes reprinted five of his long works and many
stories, duplicating the Fitzroy selections for the most part. Thus,
in 1969, British Books in Print listed 21 of the original London
titles; but in 1974, all but two of the Fitzroy titles are missing
from the list, leaving, it seems, only nine London titles in print in
Great Britain.

London has fared better in non-English speaking countries, where
his popularity with publishers and the public has been extremely
strong since before World War I. The Woodbridge bibliographies
(1966.A6 and 1973.A7) and supplements in the Jack London Newsletter
document hundreds of book-length translations of London's stories and
articles in anthologies and magazines, and some 800 books, articles,
and reviews on London's life and works. Supporting this bibliographical documentation, many articles annotated in this Guide affirm
London's steady availability and readership abroad.

In Russia, where London remains the most popular foreign fiction-writer, 9 separate Collected Works (in 8 to 30 volumes each, totaling 164 volumes) plus over 130 single-volume anthologies and editions of his work were published in 1910-1961. In the past decade, a 5-volume collection in Georgian and two 12-volume Works in Armenian and Ukrainian were added (almost all London's writings are available in some of the 24 languages of the U.S.S.R. into which he has been translated). In Germany, London has been popular since about 1908, and he was first in readership there among American authors in 1918-1940. Three German Collected Works (44 volumes) appeared in 1926-1940 and an 18-volume Works was published in 1963-1970. London set new book-selling records in Sweden, reaching his height of popularity in 1907-1927 and placing far ahead of all American writers even in the early 1950's. Four Swedish editions of his Collected Works, in 15 to 30 volumes each, appeared in 1917-1963.

Bibliographies and articles in this Guide similarly attest to a flourishing London industry and loyal public in Poland, Finland, Hungary, Italy, Portugal, Spain, France, and South America. Publishing events of recent years in these and many other countries confirm this picture. In 1972-1973, London's work was translated into 20 languages. Among publications of the late 1960's-1970's are a 24-volume Danish Works, some two dozen volumes in Norwegian and the same number in Portugese. French publishers have been the most active in the Western world. Librairie Hachette published 13 titles in 1974-1975; and in 1975-1976, 22 volumes of the still incomplete "Collection 10/18" appeared, edited by Francis Lacassin, with extensive introductions, notes, bibliographies, and some primary materials not available in English editions (L'Appel de la Vie Series. Paris: Union Générale d' Éditions). Finally, France celebrates London's Centennial by devoting to him an entire issue of Europe (nos. 561-562 [January-February, 1976], 3-160); and five French publishers will reprint a total of 63 London titles in 1976.[3]

Clearly, London cannot have the readership and critical attention at home that he enjoys abroad until American publishers offer us textually-accurate, accessible reprints of his 50 volumes.

II. LONDON'S CRITICAL REPUTATION, 1900-1976

Jack London's reputation in America exemplifies the split between "high" and "low" culture. For three-quarters of a century, the "uncritical masses" have read and loved the "Kipling of the Klondike," while our literary establishment has scorned the "Barnum of the printed word." An incident recalled by Sinclair Lewis illuminates the issue. In Carmel in 1910, Lewis wrote, "the high literary point was watching Jack London read Henry James for the first time....Jack picked up James's The Wings of the Dove and, standing there, short,

Introduction

burly, in soft shirt and black tie, the Master read aloud in a bewildered way while Henry James's sliding, slithering, glittering ver-
biage unwound itself on and on. Jack banged the book down and wailed,
'Do any of you know what all this junk is about?' It was the clash
between Main Street and Beacon Street that is eternal in American
culture."[4]

When "the Master" published his forty-three books in the first
sixteen years of this century,[5] he faced critical standards established
by the New England Sages and their New York heirs in "The Age of Inno-
cence," "The Age of Decorum," "The Genteel Decades," "The Purple Cow
Period"--as the years from 1870 through the early 1900's were variously
called. The reigning conservators of culture, whose views permeated
criticism until World War I, tried to preserve in art the traditions
and values they saw progressively abandoned by an undiscriminating
public whose sensibilities were numbed by exploitative materialism,
ethics of scientific determinism, and a diet of sensational and sentimental fakery symbolized by P. T. Barnum's extravaganzas. The arbiters of literary taste in America were such elder poet-critics as
Thomas Bailey Aldrich, Richard Henry Stoddard, and E. C. Stedman;
academic and professional critics like George Edward Woodberry and
William Crary Brownell; and the editors of distinguished periodicals
for educated, well-to-do ladies and gentlemen, periodicals which re-
viewed London's work: <u>Atlantic Monthly</u>, <u>Bookman</u>, <u>Critic</u>, <u>Dial</u>, <u>Inde-
pendent</u>, <u>Nation</u>, <u>New York Times</u>, and <u>Outlook</u>.[6]

In varying degrees, these American taste-makers were Idealists
or Arnoldian humanists who demanded that literature emulate the
classical and renaissance masters, be finely crafted, have a serious
and ethical theme, and an underlying faith, preferably Christian, to
give it purpose. Beauty, morality, reason, discipline, decorum,
"sweetness and light" were their watchwords. Diverging from the Vic-
torian orthodoxies and romantic niceties of the traditionalists,
whom H. L. Mencken later called "the crepe-clad pundits, the bombastic
word-mongers of the <u>Nation</u> school" (1919.B5), were the moral and
psychological realists, principally William Dean Howells and Henry
James. From his "Chairs" at <u>Harper's</u>, Howells defined the novelist
as a "historian of feeling and character" who should reject the
"ideal grasshopper" and depict the "real grasshopper" with fidelity
to the simple, honest, and natural. But, Howells cautioned, since
the majority of American readers were young ladies, our writers must
"concern themselves with the more smiling aspects of life, which are
the more American." <u>Our</u> realists, he said, should study the "large
cheerful average of health and success and happy life." Although
Howells encouraged many pioneering realist and naturalist writers,
such as Frank Norris and Stephen Crane, much of his own highly influential fiction and criticism retained the prudish gentility, nostalgia for the past, and high moral idealism of Beacon Street.

A high moral tone, truthful representation of typical life, illumination of character above action, a "sense of the past" harmonized

ix

with the present, and avoidance of indecency and vulgarity--these were also the tenets of James, of his fiction which bewildered Jack London, and of his theoretical and practical criticism which London never read. Beacon Street critics applied to London's writings not only the "Genteel Tradition" principles but also Jamesian ideals. London's fiction, they pointed out, was neither moral, truthful, discriminating, well-proportioned, objective, subtle, peopled with "finely aware and richly responsible" characters, nor carefully designed.

A writer can no more choose the critical establishment of his time than he can choose his family, and London seems to have had bad luck with both. In his lifetime, literary reputations were adjudicated by these Beacon Street Americans and their models and teachers in England. Prestigious British journals which reviewed London's work included the Academy and Literature, Athenaeum, Bookman, Saturday Review of Literature, Spectator, and Times Literary Supplement. Throughout his career, with the exception of his earliest Klondike tales and The Call of the Wild, London received negative or, at best, mixed reviews from the literary elite on both sides of the Atlantic.

To be sure, there was another set of critics far from "the Boston offices of the Atlantic." London had many loyal supporters on the West Coast. Writers and editors such as George Wharton James, Charles Amadon Moody, Bailey Millard, Henry Meade Bland, and George Hamlin Fitch faithfully recommended London's work to readers of Out West, Overland Monthly, Sunset Magazine, Craftsman, the San Francisco Chronicle and Examiner, and other California-based periodicals.[7] In addition, London's work was noticed, sometimes enthusiastically, but often with negative or mixed feelings, by such literary and popular magazines as Arena, Argonaut, Current Literature, Forum, Life, Literary Digest, and Reader Magazine. But the positive verdicts of these men and periodicals established London as "the Master" only on Main Street; Beacon Street gave the nod to Henry James.

London's first collection of tales, The Son of the Wolf (1900), was favorably but not widely reviewed. It immediately evoked an enduring London critical vocabulary: Kiplingesque, muscular, strong, dramatic, frank, picturesque, original. For the stories in The God of His Fathers (1901) and Children of the Frost (1902) favorable reviews balanced mixed ones as the negative critical vocabulary emerged: coarse, disagreeable, sensational, immature, unpolished, inauthentic. The Academy and Literature sounded the cry that would echo for seventy-five years: London "cannot be called an artist....he is a vigorous story teller for the general public" (1902.B6). Although Beacon Streeters panned the structure, characterization, language, and thought of London's first novel, A Daughter of the Snows (1902), they joined Main Street critics to acclaim The Call of the Wild (1903) as London's finest work, a verdict which endures. Reviewers praised Call's imaginative and poetic realism, its grasp of animal and human psychology, and its dramatic story.

INTRODUCTION

Reception of The Sea-Wolf (1904) reveals the striking divisions of opinion that haunted evaluations of London's writing. Among major notices of this novel, six were positive, six negative, and ten mixed, with critics of all camps represented in each category. The New York Times admired this stirring romance and its majestic hero (1904.B24); Independent thought it might be the most important novel of the year (1904.B25); and Reader Magazine dubbed it "The Iliad of the Ocean" (1905.B7). But the Nation abhorred its "sickening brutality" and crude writing and thought it should be titled "Captain Outrageous" (1904.B29); and the San Francisco Call labeled The Sea-Wolf "butcher's meat, hacked, dripping, from the bones of realism" (1904.B43). Most often, such contrary verdicts prevailed within a single review of most London works; indeed, until this day the most frequently used word in London criticism is BUT: his work is thrilling BUT revolting; fresh BUT brutal; virile BUT exaggerated; forceful BUT superficial; vivid BUT unconvincing; passionate BUT clumsy; sincere BUT tedious; and on and on.

Until about 1906, many critics (of "highbrow," "middlebrow," and popular periodicals) excused as youthful folly London's lack of moral and intellectual strength, misuse of the English language, poverty of invention, and overbearing self-consciousness. But in 1905, through his national lecture tour, London's "revolutionary socialism" drew attention in the East. His political radicalism, added to the scandal of his divorce and re-marriage in 1905, well-publicized accusations of plagiarism and charges by President Theodore Roosevelt of "nature-faking" (1907) further alienated the Establishment. The critics' axes fell on Before Adam, Love of Life, and The Road (all 1907); bombs shattered The Iron Heel (1908), and the ten plagues of Egypt were loosed on Martin Eden (1909).

A few reviewers found Before Adam a daring and ingenious tour de force, but others vilified this "autobiography of a prehistoric baboon" for divesting humanity of its spiritual and moral nature, debasing our ancestors to apes. Kinder critics dismissed it as far-fetched, or pointless and jejune. The grim, unbalanced and unrelieved misery noted in Love of Life was also denounced in The Road, for several critics a sordid, unreliable saga of vicious, greedy hoboes. That London "should lead such a despicable existence is strange enough," said the Argonaut. "That he should tell his story with impertinent pride is still stranger" (1907.B30).

A majority of Beacon and Main Street critics found The Iron Heel unimaginative literature and unconvincing Socialism. It was called a pessimistic bore that would put an anarchist to sleep, or a dangerous tract to be condemned for fomenting social dissension. London is "so obsessed with a mania for blood and battle, that he reduces his own argument to absurdity" (1908.B8). Martin Eden received widespread attention but achieved neither critical nor popular success. A few leading periodicals praised London's truthfulness and courage in exposing himself to public view, and they noted the novel's "virility."

But most yawned, "Ho-hum" and "So what?" They sniggered at priggish Ruth, disclaimed sympathy for the egotistical hero, and expressed either delight or incredulity at Martin's dropping out of the port-hole.

After Burning Daylight (1910), gingerly accepted (with Adventure) as more "wholesome" than London's usual blood-spattered fare, or re-jected as maudlin clap-trap, interest in London's work gradually fell off among "high culture" journals, perhaps because they had already decided he was a writer to be judged only "by distinctively popular and unliterary standards" (1911.B11).[8] For example, for The Night-Born the Nation said: "These tales are all deliberately brutal in Jack London's worst and most popular manner....we begin to despair of his ever escaping his obsession for bunches of knuckles and buckets of blood" (1913.B11). London's alcoholic memoir, John Barleycorn, drew admiration for its brutal frankness, sincerity, and Prohibition-ist stance. Athenaeum recommended it as "instructive and wholesome especially in the hands of young laborers"; and added, "The lusty virility of the narrator is abnormal." London's other major work of 1913, The Valley of the Moon, received mixed comments: what was a refreshing "back-to-nature" gospel for some was an absurd "fairy dream" for others. By 1914, reviews had grown noticeably shorter, and critics were observing London's seeming lack of interest in his putatively machine-made fictions. The Mutiny of the Elsinore, said the Times, is "a perfectly corking potboiler [with a] general air of having been put together while you wait" (1914.B11). The noise level of such manufactures distressed New Republic, which suggested it would enhance London's art "if he could learn that to be effective it is not necessary to emulate the Fourth of July" (1914.B19).

For London's fantasy fictions of 1915, charges of vulgarity and shallowness mingled with approval for the Star Rover's imaginative comment on reincarnation and indictment of the prison system. Largely negative criticisms of The Little Lady of the Big House, added to scattered mixed reviews of the posthumous writings and essay-evalua-tions of 1917-1919 summarize London's virtues and failings at the end of his career. On the positive side, he was sympathetic to the underdog and frank and sincere in self-portraiture; he colorfully described fresh American landscapes and masterfully told stories of energetic struggle, dramatic adventures, and epic heroes; and he was a wizard of animal psychology. BUT: HE WAS NOT AN ARTIST. He wrote too much, too fast, and to titillate the masses. He never grew up emotionally or learned to think. His characters were psychologically and psychically incredible, his language hyperbolic and clumsy, plots trivial, themes banal, novels formless; his unassimilated ideas rigidi-fied the fictions which were less genuine than his life. London looked at life neither steadily nor as a whole, had no culture, no respect for civilization, and he created no values. Requiescat in Pace.

INTRODUCTION

In 1904, the 250 members of the National Institute of Arts and Letters had chosen thirty of their members as most distinguished in the arts to compose the new American Academy of Arts and Letters. They chose seven "most" eminent men who then chose the next eight, and so on. Among the first fifteen elected were Howells, E. C. Stedman, Thomas Bailey Aldrich, Mark Twain, Henry James, Henry Adams, Charles Eliot Norton (a Harvard scholar of Dante, Donne, and Carlyle), Thomas R. Lounsbury (a Yale professor), and Theodore Roosevelt. Larzar Ziff comments: "Had the election been held in 1890,...these same men would have entered the Academy....we are still in the Boston offices of the Atlantic."[9] Clearly, if this election had been held at any time before London's death, the results would have been identical (although a few of the worthies died shortly after 1904). In short, "high" literary standards in America and England remained essentially the same from 1890 to 1916; London published in these years and was judged by such standards; and when he died his rating as an artist among pre-eminent men of letters was zero.

Jack London died in 1916. So did Henry James, but only in his mortal parts. For sixteen years, while Americans of ordinary stamp had scarcely known James existed, London had been great "copy" especially for California periodicals which doted on his daily activities and printed his every pronouncement.[10] London's passing was mourned on both coasts as a loss to American literature; but as our literary history makes clear, there are two "American literatures," and only one would genuinely feel London's loss. The Outlook put it well:

> If environment and personal history are considered, Jack London's work is undeniably remarkable, and if he offended some tastes and failed to gain the approval of literary critics, he at least made himself one of the most popular story-tellers in recent American annals (1916.B32).

In the next fifty years, as Beacon Street brought hundreds of devotional books and articles to the shrine of Henry James's ART, Main Street erected monuments to London: Socialists established the Jack London Memorial Institute in San Francisco (1917); Oakland planted an oak tree (1917); Glen Ellen opened a Memorial Library (1923); the Native Sons of the Golden West put a bronze tablet at his Ranch entrance (1940); his widow presented the Snark's bell to a Liberty ship (1943); government officials dedicated Jack London Square in Oakland (1951); the California Historical Society commemorated his birthplace with a plaque (1953); and the United States Senate designated forty acres of the Beauty Ranch as the Jack London Historic State Park (1957, opened 1960).

In 1916, London's friend, Ford Madox Ford, saw it as a good sign that London was already loved "by the simpleminded" and that critics had not yet "described him as a 'classic'" (1916.B44). Ford's blessing remained in force, and it is not difficult to account for the benign

(and scornful) neglect of London by critics of the other American
literature from his death until our day. American critical movements
of the 1920's, intent on sweeping out the cobwebs of Puritanism,
Philistinism, Idealism, and Romanticism, brought intellectual excitement and reevaluations of American literature. A modern Battle of
the Books raged among critics of aesthetic and formalist persuasions
like Santayana, Huneker, Pound, and Eliot; "radical" historical and
social realists, led by Parrington, Brooks, and Mumford; early Freudian
and Marxist critics; and the New Humanist defenders of tradition led
by Babbitt and More. All deplored the sad state of contemporary culture, divided between "Highbrow" and "Lowbrow," with the masses wal-
lowing in a machine-dominated, materialistic, anti-intellectual speak-
easy. While critics searched for a cultural ideal, novelists of the
20's--Fitzgerald, Anderson, Dos Passos, Dreiser, Cather, Lewis, Hemingway, Faulkner, Wolfe--offered the public new fiction in place of the
sentimental melodramas, romances, and Westerns they consumed. With
innovative techniques and fine craftsmanship these novelists probed
man's inner life, his relation to society and the universe. The
literary tastes of Main Street had been changing since the War through
expanded formal education, public libraries, mass circulation of "cultural" magazines, the spread of serious drama, and the broadening experiences gained from automobile travel, radio, and motion pictures.
As their consciousness was raised, middle-class Main Streeters seemed
eager to move closer, financially and intellectually, to Beacon Street.

   These developments in criticism, fiction, and literary taste did
not enhance London's reputation. In the 1920's, H. L. Mencken offered
the most positive comment on him (though still studded with BUTS):
"The man, in truth, was an instinctive artist of high order, and if
ignorance often corrupted his art, it only made the fact of his in-
born mastery the more remarkable." London's ideas, Mencken continues,
especially his "jejune Socialism," spoiled his fiction and made him
greedy for money; he "sold himself into slavery to the publishers."
London, "at bottom, was no fraud....There was in him a vast delicacy
of perception, a high feeling, a sensitiveness to beauty. And there
was in him, too, under all his blatancies, a poignant sense of the
infinite romance and mystery of human life" (1919.B5). The "reevalu-
ation" of London started and stopped right there.

   Charmian London's The Book of Jack London (1921.A1) added the
weapon of biography to the critics' armament. Until then, their
primary focus had been on London's failings as an artist and moralist.
Now, however, in a more permissive critical atmosphere, the brave and
sordid details of London's rags-to-riches life, his fears, frustrations, prejudices, lust for money, and hatred of writing would per-
vade criticism and transform all his work into autobiography.[11] As
Lewis Mumford observed: "He had only to tell his life over again--
to make a story of it in the newspaper sense--to feed the romanticism
of the big urban populations" (1926.B7). In addition to the biographical, the historical and psychological modes of criticism became
fashionable, and both discovered London. Major critics saw him as

INTRODUCTION

the embodiment of the spirit of California, the West, and America of
his era; as both the product and chief interpreter of the frontier
movement, the economic forces of the Gilded Age, and the nineteenth-
century ideologies of Nietzsche, Darwin, Spencer, and Marx. This historical view, colorfully drawn by Fred Pattee (1922.B6) and endlessly
embroidered and expanded into our own time, created London the
journalist, which he was often called, merely a mirror of a place and
epoch, and London the "philosopher" and "propagandist." Other writers
of the 1920's put London on Freud's couch, and a splendid subject he
was. They diagnosed hysterical self-assertiveness, egomania, and
sado-masochism; later literary analysts added a father fixation, inferiority complex, manic-depression, paranoia, alcoholism, misogyny,
satyriasis, and homosexuality to his case history.

For the next three decades, London's work received little significant critical attention. In the 1930's, he was labeled a third-
rate writer, of interest only as a social phenomenon; his former
masterpiece, The Call of the Wild, was recommended "for an intelligent boy of eleven" (1935.B3). In 1932, Van Wyck Brooks cast London
into his ruined-by-Puritanism pot of writers, but he never rescued
London as he did Twain and James; rather, in every decade through the
1960's, Brooks embellished his image of London as the neurotic failure.
London's reformist writings attracted some well-known Marxist and
Socialist writers in this decade when art was viewed as an instrument
in the class struggle. Then, as now, opinions differed as to the
genuineness of London's commitment to the proletariat and the literary
and social value of his Socialist writings. Granville Hicks, the
establishment Marxist, denied that London's socialism had any effect
on his life or works (1933.B4).

Two book-length biographies of the thirties spread London's fame
on the world's Main Streets but had no effect on his Beacon Street
status. Irving Stone's best-seller, Jack London: Sailor on Horseback
(1938.A1), reinforced the non-artist reputation. Stone devotes to
each major work a one or two-line generalization of this fatuity:
"Karl Marx would have been pleased with The Iron Heel"; and Martin
Eden is "one of the greatest of all American novels." Joan London's
Jack London and His Times (1939.A1), although far superior factually
and artistically to Stone's novel, sandwiches the life between thick
slices of history and political science. She dwells on London's
hatred of writing and self-defeating pursuit of money and finds his
only lasting contributions to literature in The Call of the Wild and
books on "social themes."[12]

As "American Lit." gained ground in the universities, writers
compiled our literary histories and anthologies. Most of those who
noticed London repeated the litany of vices and virtues chanted in
the first decade of the century. For a new generation of students,
London remained "a kind of Tarzan in Marxist hand-me-downs" (1950.B6);
" a hack writer of genius" (1952.B7). In each of the three lean
decades, however, one seminal work on London did appear. Charles

Walcutt's analysis of London's fiction in relation to naturalism,
Darwinism, and the "superman" (1938.B6), and Philip Foner's essay on
the "rebel" writings (1947.A1) carved out areas of research that remained popular but have seldom been explored as well since. Maxwell
Geismar's (more influential) psycho-sexual critique of London committed the man and his fiction to the looney bin (1953.B1). But
Geismar unearthed a rich lode of archetypal and mythical themes in
London's nightmare worlds which later writers, notably Earle Labor,
have advantageously mined. Writers on London continue to favor the
most popular critical perspective of the 1950's, which was to treat
his life and writings as expressions of contradictions in America
between the individual and society, the wilderness and civilization,
Horatio Alger and Karl Marx, Darwin/Spencer and Marx, and Nietzsche
and Marx. Among other concerns that surfaced then and linger now
were his revolt from the genteel tradition, his kinship with Hemingway, and, prominent in the 1970's, his science fiction. Also, Clell
Peterson's tentative foray into London's symbolic imagination, and
Franklin Walker's research on the sources of his plots broke new
ground in the 1950's.

The 1960's brought gains in both the quantity and quality of
attention to London; however, such interest is not attributable to a
change of heart among academic and professional writers who shape
literary reputations. Since 1916, Beacon Street critics have indeed
left the confines of "the Boston offices of the _Atlantic_," but such
geographical dispersion has not diluted their hegemony which now re-
sides with a few dozen journals, presses, and professors of English.
For contemporary arbiters of taste, Henry James is more than ever
"the Master"; and Jack London is "a he-man Lafcadio Hearn or a Cro-
Magnon Henry Adams" (1960.B9); "He remains a splendid writer of books
for boys" (1973.B8).

It was other less-established writers who brought fresh insights
and approaches to London's work in the sixties: he is the precursor
of Jack Kerouac's hobo-wanderers, of Hemingway's cult of manliness
and direct style; he writes in the pastoral tradition of Twain and
Thoreau, or he renews the mythic quest-for-Eden motif of much American
writing. His complexity and rebelliousness, disassociated from Teddy
Roosevelt's era, are seen as essentially modern.[13] A few scholars in
the sixties (and seventies) offered close readings of London's individual stories and novels, explored his techniques or symbolic and
archetypal themes; and some examined his place in the traditions of
naturalism, tragedy, romance, and fantasy fiction. Several books devoted to London appeared in this decade. Richard O'Connor's _Jack
London: A Biography_ (1964.A2) may have set London's literary reputation back several decades. O'Connor adds no new facts to the life
(and perpetuates some apocrypha), and while dwelling on London's
sexual and financial escapades, he observes in passing that the excellence of _The Call of the Wild_ was an accident, that other works
were failures in one way or another; and, O'Connor concludes: "His
own life story, his consciously created legend, was an even greater

Introduction

artistic work than any he committed to paper." Thus the "hack writer of genius" portrait is sustained and circulated nationwide by a major publisher.

A more informed and balanced picture was Charles Walcutt's Minnesota pamphlet, Jack London (1966.A3), most significant, perhaps, because it brought London, fifty years after his death, into the mainstream of "American Writers." Unlike the O'Connor and Walcutt publications, two first-rate works of the 1960's enjoyed only limited circulation. Franklin Walker's Jack London and the Klondike (1966.A4), from a small press, is still not available in most libraries. A model of objective scholarship, it documents and illuminates London's Alaskan year and the fiction it generated. The major contribution to London studies, also published in a small edition and soon out-of-print, was Jack London: A Bibliography, compiled by Hensley C. Woodbridge, John London, and George H. Tweney (1966.A6; expanded: 1973.A7). This massive work, compiled over a period of seven years, remains the only book-length London bibliography to include both primary and secondary material in English and foreign languages. Although not "definitive," it is an indispensable research tool. Additional bibliographical guides to London's life, poems, plays, fiction, and science fiction have since appeared, and all are useful. The most notable undertaking, as yet unpublished, is Tony Bubka's thesis, "A Jack London Bibliography," which catalogues reports on London in Bay Area newspapers (1968.A1).

Three periodicals devoted to London were launched in the late sixties and early seventies. The Jack London Newsletter (1967-) offers a home to critical studies, bibliographical additions, and reviews; The London Collector (1970-) and What's New About London, Jack? (1971-), both issued irregularly, print writings by and about London and bibliographies, respectively.[14] Again, these publications circulate only among London "specialists," although the Newsletter, through its listings in the MLA Bibliography and other widely-consulted references, has gained exposure for London. Finally, London scholars welcomed Wolf House Books (Grand Rapids, Michigan), a private press devoted solely to publishing reprints of rare books and pamphlets about London, new collections of his writings, and critical monographs on his works.

Criticism of the 1970's reveals the magnitude of the task of justifying the ways of London to Beacon Street. Clearly, his earliest reputation as a writer of potboilers and juvenile thrillers, reinforced in every decade, remains strong. And today, alongside those who perpetuate the traditional image, many well-intentioned critics treat London as anything but a literary artist.[15] Too often, writers concentrate on his debt to nineteenth-century ideological heroes; or they interpret his fiction solely as autobiography, history, and sociology; or they contrast his vast popularity on the Main Streets of the world with his neglect by "blind" or "stupid" Beacon Street litterateurs. Such criticism which does not speak to the intrinsic

complexity of London's work, to whatever craftsmanship, depths of
thought and emotion, and universal values it _may_ offer does not help
distinguish his writing from merely journalistic or entertaining hack
work. Two books of the 1970's (and several articles) take more positive and rewarding avenues of criticism. Earle Labor's Jack London
(1974.A3), in the widely-known TUSAS series, is a compact but well-
balanced view of the man and his work. James McClintock's White
Logic (1975.A1), the first extended study of the short stories, examines London's development as a writer and his contribution to this
genre. Both critics stress London's "mythopoeic" vision, the American
and Jungian archetypes which pattern and vitalize his work, a direction
taken also by some shorter studies. Neither Labor nor McClintock
would claim "definitive" status for his book, but these volumes, with
the scholarship of the late 1960's, are admirable "firsts" in what may
become a London nascence.

Speaking of nascence, students of London may want to keep in
mind his very first press notice:

> Births. CHANEY. In this city, January 12, the wife of
> W. H. Chaney, of a son. (San Francisco Chronicle,
> 14 January, 1876, p. 4).

Jack London was born illegitimate. The burden of proving his literary
legitimacy rests heavily on his modern interpreters.

III. FORMAT, EXCLUSIONS, AND ANNOTATIONS

Entries are arranged chronologically, by year of publication.
Within each year, books, pamphlets, dissertations, and other writings
exclusively or principally about London are listed first (under "A.
Books"), followed by articles, reviews, and parts of books (under
"B. Shorter Writings"). Within each category, entries are alphabeti-
cal by author. I have read everything annotated in the Guide (and
the appended list of Poems); items not seen are marked (*) and their
sources given. I have not read the dissertations but have verified
all data I record.[16]

Each entry is numbered, and these numbers are used in the Index.
For example, a reference to 1905.B4 directs the user to the year 1905,
the "Shorter Writings" section, entry 4. The all-inclusive Index
alphabetically lists authors and titles of the secondary writings;
titles of London's works; and selected subjects: "Bibliography";
"Biography"; and "Criticism," divided into "General" and "Foreign."
Under the titles of London's books--a complete list of his works will
be found on pp. xxvii-xxviii--I index only articles and reviews which
deal exclusively with a single book and offer significant analysis of
it. Similarly, introductions to London's volumes are indexed under
their title only if they make substantial new critical contributions.
Under "Biography" I index major book-length treatments and articles

which either provide unique information or have influenced later
biographers. "Criticism--General" includes writings which discuss
several London works in some detail and present seminal ideas, or
which reflect a mode of evaluation typical of the period. I index
all substantive articles and parts of books on London's reputation
abroad under "Criticism--Foreign."

The reader should be aware that these indexing principles exclude a majority of the references from the subject categories, items
such as book reviews (anonymous and signed), biographical sketches,
dissertations, short critical pieces, and bibliographical addenda to
Woodbridge, 1966.A6 (principally those published in Jack London Newsletter) which were later included in Woodbridge, 1973.A7. Therefore,
to gain an overview of London's reputation, the student cannot rely
on the Index; he must "read" the Guide.

Without question, this work is not definitive. It excludes all
foreign-language materials except for a few articles available in
translation. Of secondary writings in English, I have left out perhaps thousands of book reviews and articles that lie still undetected
in periodical "morgues," library basements, and manuscript collections
in our fifty states and the British Empire.[17] In order to make the
Guide manageable and of greater value to literary researchers than to
biographers, I have deliberately excluded a few hundred articles and
parts of books which I did read. In this category are all reports on
London's day-to-day activities, many recollections by his admirers,
accounts of his work as a war correspondent and Socialist lecturer,
and obituaries. Omitted, too, are reports and reviews of motion pictures and television shows based on his life or works, student "study-
guides," and reviews of secondary books and of primary reprints that
did not offer independent literary evaluations. I exclude all articles
about Londoniana exhibits, auctions, donations to repositories, and
memorials to him.[18]

The Guide annotates some, but by no means all, "Introductions"
to London's works. I omit, for example, I. O. Evans's introductions
to The Fitzroy Edition volumes because they are extremely brief and
less "critical" than biographical. I generally exclude two categories
of "parts of books": histories of California and San Francisco and
guide books to the Bay area (and articles) which describe London's
ranch, Wolf House, the Park, and other landmarks; and anthologies of
American literature which give a biographical-bibliographical (and,
rarely, critical) introduction to their London selection. There are
perhaps three dozen of the latter excluded (dating from 1920-), but
none added data or criticism different from those in literary histories
and articles of each decade which I do include. Finally, many literary surveys and biographies of other writers merely mention London in
a list with others or give him a sentence or two in passing; his "name"
is ubiquitous. I omit most of such references.

Despite these many exclusions, this <u>Guide</u> may seem more "complete" than a <u>Reference Guide</u> in literature should be. I felt I ought to make known even slight or obscure items since this is the first annotated secondary bibliography for London. Because it is the first such <u>Guide</u>, and the materials included are generally not available to students, my annotations are more detailed than is usual. The press requires an objective, informative annotation, without evaluation. But it was truly said--in 1934--that more bad literature has been written about Jack London than he wrote himself; and in forty years, that quantity has quadrupled. Therefore, I annotate at length, allowing the book or article to reveal its own inconsistencies, false, foolish, or shop-worn data, and bias, as well as its substance.

Annotations are particularly detailed for the handful of full-length biographies. Readers should know that all biographical comment in writings to about 1921 derives from London's own essays, press releases he wrote (such as 1905.A1), his letters, fiction (principally <u>Martin Eden</u>), and such books as <u>The People of the Abyss</u>, <u>The Road</u>, and <u>John Barleycorn</u>. In addition to these, later secondary writings depend heavily on Charmian London's biography (1921.A1). After publication of Irving Stone's and Joan London's biographies (1938.A1; 1939.A1), and Joseph Noel's reminiscences (1940.A1), these, with the earlier sources were the basis for all comment on London's life and its relation to his works until very recently (the few exceptions to this rule are Indexed under "Biography"). Thus, when an annotation reads "Gives biography" it means the article contains only second-hand information.

I intend the extended annotations of biographies and major critical items to introduce the largely-unknown London to students and to disclose the great opportunities and need for original research and fresh assessment of the man and his works.

---

[1]James E. Sisson has compiled "The Non-Fiction of Jack London: A Chronological Bibliography" of 430 items, half of them previously unlisted anywhere. A volume edited by Sisson and Tony Bubka, <u>The Collected Poems of Jack London</u>, will appear in the summer of 1976 (Berkeley, California: Thorp Spring Press); it contains 31 poems, 20 of them previously unpublished. And Sisson is revising for publication "The Early Writings of Jack London" (103 leaves). For primary materials published since 1963 see the appended "Works by Jack London."

[2]In contrast, <u>The United States Catalogue Supplement</u> for 1912-1917 listed 40 different London titles in print.

Introduction

[3]Hensley C. Woodbridge has supplied the information on the most recent European publishing ventures. He describes the contents of _Europe_ in _JLN_, 9 (January–April, 1976), 57–59.

[4]Quoted by Mark Schorer, 1961.B13.

[5]Seven additional volumes appeared posthumously, 1917–1922.

[6]Among eminent editors/critics responsible for shaping London's reputation were Frederick Taber Cooper and Edward Everett Hale (_Bookman_, New York); William Morton Payne (_Dial_); Paul Elmer More (_Nation_); and Hamilton Wright Mabie (_Outlook_).

[7]London's partisans were aware of the East's literary climate. A photograph of London in the _San Francisco Chronicle_ was captioned: "His books are strong meat for the anemic generation that worships at the shrine of Henry James, but they will delight all people with red blood in their veins." (1903.B44).

[8]At this time, Philo M. Buck's critique of London, "The American Barbarian," stated the view of Matthew Arnold's heirs (1912.B13). The only earlier literary analysis was also largely negative (Garnett, 1907.B41).

[9]1968.B20, pp. 346–47.

[10]For example, Tony Bubka lists over 60 articles on London's marital troubles; 110 news reports related to the _Snark_ voyage; 165 items on London's lectures and speeches; and some 110 articles on his death, cremation, burial, and will—these in just 21 Bay Area newspapers. (1968.A1).

[11]London bears prior responsibility for creating the myths and "superman" legends of his life. Mrs. London admits basing her biography to 1897 on London's writings. But her work, in serial and book form, "authenticated" his myths and her fond additions.

[12]Since his death, London has been treated to three other kinds of biographies: the dramatically fleshed-out "soap operas," the pornographic "horse-operas," and "juveniles."

[13]Some of the best critical work on London has been done by graduate students. A very small but steady stream of Master's theses (47 of them in 1929-1972) and doctoral dissertations (some two dozen in America in 1935-1976) have been written. Less than a quarter of these generated published work.

[14]_Jack London Newsletter_, ed. Hensley C. Woodbridge, Department of Foreign Languages and Literature, Southern Illinois University, Carbondale, Illinois, 62901 (back issues may be ordered from Xerox University Microfilms); _The London Collector_, ed. Richard Weiderman,

1420 Pontiac Road, S. E., Grand Rapids, Michigan, 49506 (Wolf House Books is at the same address); What's New About London, Jack?, ed. David H. Schlottman, 929 South Bay Road, Olympia, Washington, 98506.

[15] London must share the blame for this state of criticism. Arthur Calder-Marshall, a friendly critic, describes him as "a writer of genius who denied even the nature of genius, an artist who thought of himself as a great politician, a great reformer, a great farmer, a great almost anything except writer" (1963.B7).

[16] Comprehensive Dissertation Index, 1861-1972; Dissertation Abstracts International (1973-1976).

[17] Some unpublished secondary bibliographies compiled by James E. Sisson suggest, in part, what is missing from this Guide: a 100-page bibliography on "Jack London and the South Seas"; one of 18 items on "Michael, Brother of Jerry and the Jack London Club"; one of 75 items on "Jack London and the University of California"; "Jack London Illustrators: A Bibliography," which lists 214 illustrators and the 305 London items they illustrated (1895-1975); and, with Tony Bubka, "Poetic Tributes to Jack London: A Bibliography" with 253 poems about London. Sisson is revising for publication "Jack London as a Dramatist" (54 leaves) and is checking some 500 radical magazines and newspapers published in London's lifetime for reports on his Socialist activities.

[18] For manuscript materials, see the appended "Manuscript Collections."

Acknowledgments

This guide is deeply indebted to three London scholars: to Hensley C. Woodbridge whose bibliographical works provided its foundation and whose encouraging correspondence proved invaluable; and to Russ Kingman and James E. Sisson who provided copies of materials from their London collections and answered my every inquiry with unfailing generosity and speed.

I am also grateful to Mrs. Hedy Seitz, in charge of the Inter-library Loan Office, and her staff at the Alexander Library of Rutgers University who acquired articles and books I needed to read. For the same contribution I thank Gilbert Cohen, Head of Reference, and his staff at the Dana Library of Rutgers University, and the staff of the Interlibrary Loan Office at Newark Public Library. I appreciate the freedom of access to the collections of the Newark Public Library granted to me by John R. Abram, Chief, Lending and Reference Department.

List of Abbreviations

ABC	American Book Collector
AL	American Literature
ALR	American Literary Realism
AmerS	American Studies
AR	Antioch Review
ASch	American Scholar
ASR	American-Scandinavian Review
BB	Bulletin of Bibliography
BNYPL	Bulletin of the New York Public Library
BuR	Bucknell Review
CanL	Canadian Literature
CE	College English
CEA	CEA Critic
DR	Dalhousie Review
ELT	English Literature in Transition (1880-1920)
EngR	English Record
HLQ	Huntington Library Quarterly
HSE	Hungarian Studies in English (L. Kossuth University, Debrecen)
JAmS	Journal of American Studies
JLN	Jack London Newsletter
KAL	Kyushu American Literature (Fukuoka, Japan)
L&P	Literature and Psychology (University of Hartford)
LHR	Lock Haven Review (Lock Haven State College, Pennsylvania)
LJ	Library Journal
MarkhamR	Markham Review
MFS	Modern Fiction Studies
MichA	Michigan Academician
MTJ	Mark Twain Journal
NCF	Nineteenth-Century Fiction
NY	New Yorker
OJES	Osmania Journal of English Studies
PBSA	Papers of the Bibliographical Society of America
QJS	Quarterly Journal of Speech
QNL	Quarterly News Letter (Book Club of California)
SAQ	South Atlantic Quarterly
SatR	Saturday Review
Serif	The Serif (Kent, Ohio)

SovL	Soviet Literature
SSF	Studies in Short Fiction (Newberry College, South Carolina)
SWR	Southwestern Review
TamR	Tamarack Review (Toronto)
TJQ	Thoreau Journal Quarterly
TLS	[London] Times Literary Supplement
TSB	Thoreau Society Bulletin
TUSAS	Twayne's United States Authors Series
WAL	Western American Literature
WN	A Wake Newslitter (Newcastle University College, New South Wales)
WR	Western Review: A Journal of the Humanities
WWR	Walt Whitman Review

Works by Jack London

E - Essays. N - Novel. NF - Non-fiction. P - Play. S - Stories.

The Son of the Wolf. Boston: Houghton Mifflin, 1900 (S).
The God of His Fathers. New York: McClure Phillips, 1901 (S).
Children of the Frost. New York: Macmillan, 1902 (S).
The Cruise of the Dazzler. New York: Century, 1902 (N).
A Daughter of the Snows. Philadelphia: Lippincott, 1902 (N).
The Call of the Wild. New York: Macmillan, 1903 (N).
The Kempton-Wace Letters (with Anna Strunsky). New York: Macmillan,
   1903 (NF).
The People of the Abyss. New York: Macmillan, 1903 (NF).
The Faith of Men. New York: Macmillan, 1904 (S).
The Sea-Wolf. New York: Macmillan, 1904 (N).
The Game. New York: Macmillan, 1905 (N).
Tales of the Fish Patrol. New York: Macmillan, 1905 (S).
War of the Classes. New York: Macmillan, 1905 (E).
Moon-Face and Other Stories. New York: Macmillan, 1906 (S).
Scorn of Women. New York: Macmillan, 1906 (P).
White Fang. New York: Macmillan, 1906 (N).
Before Adam. New York: Macmillan, 1907 (N).
Love of Life and Other Stories. New York: Macmillan, 1907 (S).
The Road. New York: Macmillan, 1907 (NF).
The Iron Heel. New York: Macmillan, 1908 (N).
Martin Eden. New York: Macmillan, 1909 (N).
Burning Daylight. New York: Macmillan, 1910 (N).
Lost Face. New York: Macmillan, 1910 (S).
Revolution and Other Essays. New York: Macmillan, 1910 (E).
Theft: A Play in Four Acts. New York: Macmillan, 1910 (P).
Adventure. New York: Macmillan, 1911 (N).
The Cruise of the Snark. New York: Macmillan, 1911 (NF).
South Sea Tales. New York: Macmillan, 1911 (S).
When God Laughs and Other Stories. New York: Macmillan, 1911 (S).
The House of Pride and Other Tales of Hawaii. New York: Macmillan,
   1912 (S).
Smoke Bellew. New York: Century, 1912 (S).
A Son of the Sun. Garden City, N. Y.: Doubleday, Page, 1912 (S).
The Abysmal Brute. New York: Century, 1913 (N).
John Barleycorn. New York: Century, 1913 (NF).

The Night-Born. New York: Century, 1913 (S).
The Valley of the Moon. New York: Macmillan, 1913 (N).
The Mutiny of the Elsinore. New York: Macmillan, 1914 (N).
The Strength of the Strong. New York: Macmillan, 1914 (S).
The Scarlet Plague. New York: Macmillan, 1915 (N).
The Star Rover. New York: Macmillan, 1915 (N). Published in England
 as The Jacket.
The Acorn-Planter: A California Forest Play. New York: Macmillan,
 1916 (P).
The Little Lady of the Big House. New York: Macmillan, 1916 (N).
The Turtles of Tasman. New York: Macmillan, 1916 (S).
The Human Drift. New York: Macmillan, 1917 (S;E).
Jerry of the Islands. New York: Macmillan, 1917 (N).
Michael, Brother of Jerry. New York: Macmillan, 1917 (N).
The Red One. New York: Macmillan, 1918 (S).
On the Makaloa Mat. New York: Macmillan, 1919 (S).
Hearts of Three. New York: Macmillan, 1920 (N).
Dutch Courage and Other Stories. New York: Macmillan, 1922 (S).
The Assassination Bureau, Ltd. (Completed by Robert Fish). New York:
 McGraw-Hill, 1963 (N).
Letters from Jack London. Edited by King Hendricks and Irving Shepard.
 New York: Odyssey, 1965.
Jack London Reports. Edited by King Hendricks and Irving Shepard.
 Garden City, N. Y.: Doubleday, 1970 (E; Articles).
Daughters of the Rich. Edited by James E. Sisson. Oakland, Califor-
 nia: Holmes Book Company, 1971 (P).
Jack London's Articles and Short Stories for the (Oakland) High School
 Aegis. Edited by James E. Sisson. Grand Rapids, Michigan: Wolf
 House Books, 1971 (S; Articles).
Gold (with Herbert Heron). Edited by James E. Sisson. Oakland,
 California: Holmes Book Company, 1972 (P).

Writings about Jack London, 1900 — 1976

1900 A BOOKS - NONE

1900 B SHORTER WRITINGS

1   ANON. "Books of the Week [The Son of the Wolf]." San Francisco Bulletin (29 April), p. 6.
     London has learned from Kipling, but he is not an imita-
tor. This "minstrel" of the White Silence is both dramatist and poet, exploiting his materials with a crisp,
clean, economic style, "an eye for situation, keen appreciation for the artistic side of man,...[and] sympathy
with nature." This is masterful, passionate writing.

2   ANON. "Fine Stories of the Far North by a New Writer [The
Son of the Wolf]." Literary News, 21 (May), 140-41.
     Where the "artisan" Norris failed, London the "artist"
succeeds in giving us "the real texture" of the Northland.
"Because he seems merely to be telling his story, not
going out of his way to belabor us with pages labeled
realism, [he] makes the actual impression [of the cold
and hardships] and leaves us wondering how he did it."
Reprinted from Town Topics (San Francisco).

3   ANON. "Jack London." Bookman (New York), 11 (May), 200-201.
     Tales in The Son of the Wolf are "striking examples of
word-painting." Although influenced by Kipling, they are
original.

4   ANON. [Jack London]. Bookbuyer, 20 (May), 277-78.
     A biographical sketch and portrait, both contributed by
London. Reprinted: 1900.B6.

5   ANON. "Son of the Wolf, The." Outlook, 65 (5 May), 88-89.
     London describes rough life skillfully. Brief.

6   ANON. "General Gossip of Authors and Writers." Current
Literature, 28 (June), 283-84.
     Reprint of 1900.B4.

1900

7   ANON. "Other Tales of the Frontier: <u>The Son of the Wolf</u>."
     <u>American Monthly Review of Reviews</u>, 21, no. 6 (June), 759.
        These "strenuous" tales differ sharply from our ordinary
     fiction. Brief.

8   ANON. "Jack London the Man (San Francisco, June 9)." <u>New York</u>
     <u>Times Saturday Review of Books and Art</u> (23 June), p. 420.
        "The Klondike has waited three years for its storyteller
     and interpreter" to set it in an "imperishable literary
     mold." In <u>The Son of the Wolf</u>, London catches the life
     and conflicts of the Far North with a sure touch, "strong
     dramatic power, a keen eye for character drawing and a
     natural gift for story-telling." Gives biography.

9   ANON. "Jack London's Tales of the Far North." <u>New York Times</u>
     <u>Saturday Review of Books and Art</u> (23 June), p. 420.
        In <u>The Son of the Wolf</u> London "combines accurate observa-
     tion with imaginative gifts....There is more than a trace
     of genius, together with much crude writing," refreshing
     frankness, and touches of poetic insight.

10   ANON. "The Lounger." <u>Critic</u>, 37 (August), 100.
        Biographical note and portrait.

11   ANON. "Literary Notes." <u>Public Opinion</u>, 29 (30 August), 281.
        Briefly notices "Sons [sic] of the Wolf" by "the son of
     a trapper and frontiersman."

12   EAMES, NINETTA. "Jack London." <u>Overland Monthly</u>, 35 (May),
     417-25.
        London's fiction derives from a childhood "cramped and
     embittered by omnipresent poverty," years of reading, ad-
     ventures as a sailor, a "secular evangelist" for Socialism,
     a tramp, and Klondike traveler. His writing uniquely com-
     bines fact, fantasy, "frank and wholesome sentiment" with
     spontaneous and felicitous expression. These, with "his
     assiduous application, his indomitable purpose,...give
     promise and prophecy of exceptional achievement."

13   FITCH, GEORGE HAMLIN. "What to Read." <u>San Francisco Chronicle</u>,
     <u>Sunday Supplement</u> (22 April), p. 24.
        London "is the Bret Harte of the Frozen North, with a
     touch of Kipling's savage realism and...disregard of the
     niceties of literary art." Written in a strong, simple
     style, the fascinating tales in <u>The Son of the Wolf</u> "reek
     of blood and sweat and fierce passions," giving him "a
     foremost place among American short story writers."

14 _____. "Some Phases of California Literature." <u>Impressions</u>,
     1, no. 7 (September), 113-14.
          Discusses several writers. London (in <u>The Son of the</u>
     <u>Wolf</u>) combines "the imaginative power and the dramatic
     force of Kipling" with his own sense of tenderness and
     heroism. His recognition may be slow "because of his bit-
     ter realism and his undisguised relish of savage human
     nature," but it is sure.

15 LATHROP, B. G. "Book Reviews." <u>San Francisco Sunday Call</u>
     <u>Magazine Section</u> (6 May), p. 4.
          The remarkable and compelling tales in <u>The Son of the</u>
     <u>Wolf</u> "are living breathing reproductions of scenes" he has
     experienced. "An Odyssey of the North" is the "most force-
     fully perfect of all." This is a book that will live; Gar-
     land and Kipling "have written no better."

16 L., C. F. Review of <u>The Son of the Wolf</u>. <u>Land of Sunshine</u>,
     12 (May), 351-52.
          The stories are "strong, elemental and unusually well
     poised." Despite occasional crudity and immature Anglo-
     Saxonism, they are "fine and muscular," well-crafted, and
     showing "very direct promise."

17 MAITLAND, LEROY OSBORNE. "Jack London and 'The Son of the
     Wolf.'" <u>National Magazine</u>, 12 (May), 50-53.
          London is a "modern argonaut" and "a revolutionaire of
     the extremist Karl Marxian type." His work compares well
     with Kipling's "in picturesqueness of phrase, terseness of
     expression, originality of imagery, graphic touch and depth
     of insight"; it reveals his belief in Anglo-Saxon supremacy.
     "An Odyssey of the North," the most notable story, is "su-
     perbly imaginative and tragic."

18 PRATT, CORNELIA ATWOOD. "Out of the East and the North."
     <u>Critic</u>, 37 (August), 162-63.
          Tales in <u>The Son of the Wolf</u> are strong and impressive.
     "His work is as discriminating as it is powerful; it has
     grace as well as terseness, and it makes the reader hope-
     ful that the days of the giants are not yet gone by."

1901 A BOOKS - NONE

1901 B SHORTER WRITINGS

1 ANON. "London, Jack," in <u>Who's Who in America, 1901-1902</u>.
     Chicago: A. N. Marquis, p. 695.

1901

London appears for the first time in this volume and in
all subsequent volumes through 1916-1917.

2   ANON. "General Gossip of Authors and Writers." <u>Current
Literature</u>, 30 (February), 223.
Quotes Howard V. Sutherland on London's promise to be-
come "a writer as forceful as Kipling."

3   ANON. "Collections of Short Stories: <u>The Son of the Wolf</u>."
<u>Literary World</u> (Boston), 32 (1 April), 55.
Brief favorable notice.

4   ANON. "Jack London's New Stories." <u>New York Times Saturday
Review of Books and Art</u> (1 June), p. 382.
Although there are many similarities to Kipling, London's
work lacks his "imagination, the idealism, the tenderness,
and the intellectual force." <u>The God of His Fathers</u>,
despite its crudeness and sensationalism, "shows the impulse of intense conviction" and does even a better job
for the Yukon than Harte did for California.

5   ANON. "More Novels." <u>Nation</u>, 73 (4 July), 15.
London has little to fear from comparison to Kipling.
The tales in <u>The God of His Fathers</u> "are vivid, concise,
and dramatic....sometimes coarse, generally disagreeable,
and always cynical and reckless." They have a "wild,
elemental savagery which is positively thrilling." Reprinted: 1901.B7.

6   ANON. "Book Reviews: Stories of Alaska." <u>Public Opinion</u>, 31
(25 July), 120.
In style, themes, and poor characterization of women,
London resembles Kipling, but he has a long way to go before he rivals Kipling's best work. London gives us
"stories, and they are short, but they are not short
stories....people of fastidious tastes are recommended
not to read 'The God of His Fathers.'"

7   ANON. "The God of His Fathers." <u>Literary News</u>, 22 (August),
236.
Reprint of 1901.B5.

8   ANON. "Jack London." <u>Mechanics' Institute Library Bulletin</u>
(San Francisco), 5, no. 8 (August), [1].
London's "vivid, concise and dramatic stories" belong
to "the literature of bone and sinew."

9 ANON. "Collections of Short Stories: The God of His Fathers."
   Literary World (Boston), 32 (1 August), 125.
      Brief favorable notice.

10 ANON. "Literature: The God of His Fathers." Independent, 53
    (8 August), 1868.
       In these admirable stories, London "gathers up every
    situation into his fists, squeezes the blood out of it
    upon the snow, scatters the bones of his heroes, and faces
    the next tragedy with astonishing nerve."

11 E.[ARLE], M.[ARY] T.[RACY]. "Fiction That is Talked About."
    Critic, 39 (August), 157-58.
       In spite of their "fairly Hogarthian" diction and lack
    of polish, the tales of The God of His Fathers "are all
    brave, and all have sanity, and are keenly, humorously
    alive to the relative importance of things, --the necessity
    for taking life philosophically and the wisdom of fighting
    for it."

12 LATHROP, B. G. "Writers of Books." San Francisco Sunday Call
    Magazine Section (14 July), p. 4.
       Tales in The God of His Fathers are not as good as those
    in The Son of the Wolf; they seem a little "written to
    order." London has a "natural genius" for spontaneous
    story-telling; however, he lacks "versatility." The tales
    are much alike, and when he strays from the Northland
    scene to civilization, "he sinks to the ordinary."

13 L., C. F. Review of (the story) "The God of His Fathers."
    Land of Sunshine, 14 (June), 480.
       It has "rude color," but the color is "stage 'makeup.'
    Its Indians are rather more than absurd." London foists
    the masks of one tribe on another and substitutes "Haida
    dugouts" for birch canoes. "In the name of decency in
    literature," expert opinion should be sought. Suggests
    consulting "the dean of all our Alaskan explorer-students,
    Wm. H. Dall of the Smithsonian." See Dall, 1902.B14;
    1903.B42; and see "L," 1903.B54.

14 P.[UTNAM], F.[RANK]. "Studies of Books and Their Makers: Who
    is the Foremost Living American Author?" National Magazine,
    14 (September), 693.
       In response, readers voted London in eighteenth place.

15 STRUNSKY, ANNA. "The God of His Fathers--Jack London." Im-
    pressions, 2, no. 4 (October), 59-60.
       He has caught the inner spirit and romance, the

1901

picturesqueness and poetry of the Klondike. He conveys
the "significance" of the dramatic conflicts between man
and nature, white and Indian by seeing them in broad
perspective and keeping them strongly bound to the fact of
life. There is greatness in this "classic," written by a
true "artist." Discusses several tales.

1902 A BOOKS - NONE

1902 B SHORTER WRITINGS

1   ANON. "Fiction: The God of His Fathers." Academy and Litera-
        ture, 62 (1 March), 220.
            In these "ensanguined narratives," characters return to
        the elemental and express themselves "with an exact, un-
        erring eloquence" matched only in Shaw's plays. "It would
        not be fair not to treat this book with some seriousness,
        but Jack London's loud and swaggering disregard for the
        simplest rules of realism is a temptation to jocosity....
        he writes on the whole very well and forcibly, [but] his
        eloquence is a fiery steed that sometimes runs away with
        him."

2   ANON. "Short Stories: The God of His Fathers." Athenaeum,
        3884 (5 April), 430-31.
            A volume "of exceptional merit" with "strongly dramatic
        stories."

3   ANON. "The Literary Colony of Piedmont." San Francisco
        Chronicle (3 August), p. 10.
            Gives biography.

4   ANON. "Recent Fiction: True Indians." New York Times Satur-
        day Review of Books and Art (25 October), pp. 724-25.
            Unlike the usual romanticized versions, London's Indians
        allow Children of the Frost to be "classed as an ethno-
        graphical study." He conveys his first-hand experiences
        with "wonderful dramatic expression....[and] holds a do-
        main which is quite his own by right of conquest." Gives
        details of several stories.

5   ANON. "Tales from the Northland." Out West, 17 (November),
        618.
            Death strides through the strong, "grim and tragic"
        stories of Children of the Frost. There are occasional
        notes of "fierce, triumphant, sardonic" laughter.

6 ANON. "New Novels: <u>The Son of the Wolf</u>." <u>Academy and Litera-</u>
   <u>ture</u>, 63 (8 November), 496.
       "We want analysis, not deification of the muscular ideal,
   and that is where Mr. Jack London fails." These are
   "healthy, breezy narratives of sensational incidents."
   "To the Man on the Trail" is the best because the "least
   theatrical." London "cannot be called an artist" like
   Kipling or Conrad; "he is a vigorous story teller for the
   general public.'

7 ANON. "<u>A Daughter of the Snows</u>: London's First Novel." <u>Argo-</u>
   <u>naut</u>, 51 (10 November), 322.
       It is a fast-paced novel of romance with "boisterous,
   rude strength....freshness and vigor." It should be
   popular.

8 ANON. "Notes on Novels." <u>Dial</u>, 33 (16 November), 330.
       "Mr. London is able to analyze savage motives and methods,
   and the great primal forces swaying mankind stand bare but
   not repellent" in <u>Children of the Frost</u>.

9 ANON. "An Unconventional Heroine." <u>New York Times Saturday</u>
   <u>Review of Books and Art</u> (22 November), p. 806.
       There are some incongruities here and it is not his best
   work; but <u>A Daughter of the Snows</u> gives a novel view of
   Dawson.

10 ANON. "London--A Daughter of the Snows." <u>Critic</u>, 41 (December), 582-83.
       This is "a species of immature problem novel, well
   seasoned with melodrama." It is neither new nor equal to
   his previous Klondike material. Brief.

11 ANON. "London--Children of the Frost." <u>Critic</u>, 41 (December),
   583.
       Here are fresh and colorful stories with "a Kipling-like
   pithiness and force." Brief.

12 ANON. "Notes on the Novels of 1902." <u>American Monthly Review</u>
   <u>of Reviews</u>, 26 (December), 760.
       With a "most attractive" but less than convincing heroine,
   <u>A Daughter of the Snows</u> conveys "a clear, bold picture" of
   Klondike life. Brief.

13 BROOKE, MARY CALKINS. "Three Books Apiece." <u>San Francisco</u>
   <u>Bulletin, Sunday Magazine</u> (2 November), p. 6.
       Review of <u>Children of the Frost</u> and <u>A Daughter of the</u>
   <u>Snows</u>. London told his friends his stories "were rot,"

and "from a literary standpoint, they are rather bad."
But there is so much happening in the fiction to compel
attention, that it's hard to form literary judgments.
They are "strenuous" tales.

14   DALL, WILLIAM H. "Jack London's 'Local Color.'" New York
Times Saturday Review of Books and Art (6 December), p. 871.
A letter. The writer was a "yukon pioneer of the sixties"
and spent many years living with and studying the natives.
"There is absolutely no local color or versimillitude in
Mr. London's stories." His "preposterous" Indians are "unlike any Indians whatsoever." He has mingled some superficial characteristics of a few tribes "in a ridiculous
hotchpotch" and made real people and scenes into fictitious
false ones. For exchanges in this controversy, see
1901.B13; 1903.B42; 1903.B54.

15   IRWIN, GRACE LUCE. "Current Books: The Kipling of the Klondike." Overland Monthly, 40 (December), 553.
A Daughter of the Snows is "full of thrilling situations,
fascinating picturesque figures, all made real and vivid."

16   LATHROP, B. G. "Books of the Week and Literary Chat." San
Francisco Sunday Call Magazine Section (9 November), p. 12.
The interest of A Daughter of the Snows lies in its
characters, setting, and suspenseful love story. Although
better than average fiction, it is not as good as London's
stories. The Children of the Frost tales are "more
finished as literary works" than his previous tales.

17   MacNAB, LEAVENWORTH. "A Book That Promises a Sensation."
Sunset Magazine, 10 (December), 167.
Announces The Kempton-Wace Letters, an "unusual" book
by London--the materialist view--and Strunsky--the
"idealist poet."

18   MOODY, CHARLES AMADON. "Telling What He Has Seen." Out West,
17 (December), 746.
A Daughter of the Snows has the compelling power of his
stories, power which comes from within the author, a "man
who has done things."

19   PUTNAM, FRANK. "Note and Comment." National Magazine, 17
(December), 390.
"The Kipling of the Klondike" has three new books of
fiction. Brief.

1903 A BOOKS - NONE

1903 B SHORTER WRITINGS

1   ANON. "Current Books [Children of the Frost]." Overland
        Monthly, 41 (January), 79.
            "No one writes of the Far North with more verve than...
        the Kipling of the Klondike." Brief.

2   ANON. "An Elemental Maid." Literary Digest, 26 (10 January),
        60.
            Despite faulty craftsmanship and some "absurdly polished"
        language, A Daughter of the Snows "throughout is splendidly
        virile,...the most vital presentation of Alaska that litera-
        ture has yet known." The heroine, "a magnificent Amazon,"
        blending the finest masculine and feminine traits, is a
        believable portrait of the new woman.

3   ANON. "Short Stories. Children of the Frost." Athenaeum,
        3925 (17 January), 77.
            They are "full of strange and graceless locutions, crude
        affectations, and astonishing misuse of 'dictionary words.'"
        London should "read a good deal of the masters of prose"
        before writing another book.

4   ANON. "London, Jack. Daughter of the Snows." Literary News,
        24 (March), 90.
            An "excellent record" of the strange and novel arctic
        life, with an interesting heroine. Reprinted from "Mail
        and Express."

5   ANON. "A Scientific Lover: The Kempton-Wace Letters." New
        York Times Saturday Review of Books and Art (27 June),
        p. 446.
            "The sex problem again." Nothing new is said here, nor
        is the old message reworded, nor "does the unnamed author
        infuse into either Wace or Kempton anything to give human
        personality or appeal." It "falls flat" as a story, is
        over-wordy as a discussion, and strikes "as trenching
        perilously on bad taste" as letters between men about a
        woman.

6   ANON. "Summer Fiction." World's Work, 6 (July), 3701.
            The Kempton-Wace Letters "is the best love story of the
        season," artistic and subtle. Brief.

7   ANON. "Books of the Weeks: The Call of the Wild." Outlook,
        74 (25 July), 762.

A fine dog story and description of life in the Far North. It is London's best work so far.

8   ANON. "Story of a Dog: Jack London's Newest Book, 'The Call of the Wild.'" New York Times Saturday Review of Books and Art (25 July), p. 512.
A book certain to be popular with men who love dog fights and others who appreciate a view of true dog standards, motives, and feelings. Offers detailed summary and excerpts.

9   ANON. "Chronicle and Comment: Jack London." Bookman (New York), 17 (August), 562–64.
Biography and portrait.

10   ANON. "The Evolution of Love and Marriage." Out West, 19 (August), 219–20.
The Kempton-Wace Letters "is sane, clean and stimulating," the only argument of its kind "at once so profound, so sweeping and so lofty as this."

11   ANON. "Notes on New Novels." Dial, 35 (1 August), 69.
In The Kempton-Wace Letters, "the debate is an unusual and profitable one, interesting from beginning to end, and full of sound philosophy and right reasoning."

12   ANON. "Literary Notes: Jack London at His Best." Argonaut, 53 (3 August), 72.
London is "prose poet" of the doctrine of evolution. In The Call of the Wild he tells the story of a noble dog "with fine imagination and poetic power....[It is] London's strongest and most virile work—thus far."

13   ANON. "The Books of the Week: Canine Atavism." Public Opinion, 35 (13 August), 217.
The Call of the Wild is probably as much concerned with human as with canine atavism. London's "style is frank and free and his drawing of life in the Northland is picturesque and impressive." Reprinted: 1903.B18.

14   ANON. "Literature: The Call of the Wild." Independent, 55 (13 August), 1933.
A "notable achievement" among nature books. The vivid personality of Buck has great human interest.

15   ANON. "Literature: The New Love." Independent, 55 (13 August), 1930–32.
Mr. Wace's "brutal, brilliant" epigrammatic style

resembles Charlotte Perkins Gilman's, making us wonder if
he is a lady. His "binomial theory of love will be a death
blow to fiction, to say nothing of its effect upon the
sexes in real life."

16   ANON. "Fiction: The Call of the Wild." Academy and Litera-
    ture, 65 (22 August), 169.
       A book of "force and individuality" which truthfully and
artistically conveys the natural psychology of the dog.

17   ANON. "The Call of the Wild." Athenaeum, 3957 (29 August),
    279.
       "It is an enthralling story, told ably, and with a
restraint and artistry." London's best work so far.

18   ANON. "Call of the Wild." Literary News, 24 (September), 258.
    Reprint of 1903.B13.

19   ANON. "London, Jack. The Call of the Wild." Literary News,
    24 (September), 280.
       Brief descriptive review.

20   ANON. "A 'Nature' Story: The Call of the Wild." Literary
    World (Boston), 34 (September), 22.
       A robust and original story "of the first rank." "If
you like dogs, you will like this book."

21   ANON. "Novel Notes." Bookman (London), 24 (September), 220.
       London writes with the "same directness,...vivid simple
realism,...[and] insight into the souls of men and beasts"
as Kipling. But The Call of the Wild is unique and "has
more than a touch of genius in the conception and the
writing of it."

22   ANON. "Views and Reviews." Comrade, 2 (September), 280-81.
       The Call of the Wild, an important and remarkable book,
shows London's wonderful insight into canine behavior.

23   ANON. "Sketch of Jack London." Publisher's Circular, 79
    (19 September), 265.
       Biography.

24   ANON. "Book Reviews: The Call of the Wild." Gunton's Maga-
    zine, 25 (October), 364-66.
       Although it is a strong picture of Arctic life, its re-
pulsive brutality, condoning of violence and crime un-
redeemed by moral result, and Buck's reversion to savagery
contrary to all reason and experience make the book "false

1903

    to art and to nature." It is "as disagreeable reading as can be found."

25   ANON. "Books and Writers." Sunset Magazine, 11 (October), [584].
        "By far the strongest work which has recently been done by a Western writer" is The Call of the Wild. Brief.

26   ANON. "Kempton-Wace--The Kempton-Wace Letters." Critic, 43 (October), 380.
        "In a somewhat highflown and impossible manner [the letters] contain some keen speculation." Brief.

27   ANON. "An Epic of the Dog." Literary Digest, 27 (3 October), 437.
        The Call of the Wild is a gripping dramatic story and "a piece of lasting literature." The details "are incredible," but no more so than in Homer.

28   ANON. "Recent Fiction." Nation, 77 (8 October), 287.
        The Call of the Wild is told graphically, forcefully, and "with simple directness." Gives plot summary.

29   ANON. "A Glance at the New Novels." American Monthly Review of Reviews, 28 (November), 633.
        The Call of the Wild is an "epic" story, "vital and true," whose sense remains permanently with you. Brief.

30   ANON. "The People of the Abyss." Literary News, 24 (November), 329-30.
        "Vivid and realistic" description of London's experiences, the book has "an interest akin to that of Mr. Jacob Riis's slum stories."

31   ANON. "East London: Jack London's Pictures of Life in Whitechapel and Shadwell." New York Times Saturday Review of Books and Art (7 November), p. 806.
        "A man with good nerves and a strong stomach may read with profit and not a little intellectual pleasure" The People of the Abyss. London is "an orator and a poet" whose skill with language and dramatic talent make the experiences very real. Gives excerpts.

32   ANON. "Notes." Nation, 77 (12 November), 384.
        "With an air that might become a Stanley or a Landor he now tells us all, and more than all, about--the East End of London!...describes it as Dante might have described his Inferno if he had been a yellow journalist." London's

statistics and proposed solutions for poverty in The People
of the Abyss are unrealistic.

33   ANON. "Books of the Year." Independent, 55 (19 November),
         2742.
            Mentions The Call of the Wild.

34   ANON. "Novels: The Call of the Wild." Saturday Review (Lon-
         don), 96 (28 November), 678.
            Both the story--of "a temperament which is neither human
         nor animal"--and the style "are delightful." Brief.

35   ANON. "London--The Call of the Wild." Critic, 43 (December),
         582.
            A "strong vital tale of a splendid sled dog....primeval
         earth nature that reddens one's blood as he reads."

36   ANON. "Views and Reviews." Comrade, 3, no. 3 (December),
         67-68.
            The People of the Abyss is a "vivid and harrowing" book
         of experiences personally-suffered. "It is the sickening
         but undeniably true account of a great city dying--rotting
         at its heart."

37   ANON. "Literature: London's Inferno." Independent, 55
         (24 December), 3063-64.
            London makes the misery of the East End real in The
         People of the Abyss. The book will add "to a reputation
         already deservedly high."

38   BASHFORD, HERBERT. "The Literary Development of the Pacific
         Coast." Atlantic Monthly, 92 (July), [1]-9.
            [London is mentioned on p. 8]. He "has exhibited a
         freshness and spontaneity of expression, a freedom from
         academic precision and restraint, that gives to his pic-
         tures the quality of work done at first hand."

39   B., F. "Reviews: A Daughter of the Snows." Reader Magazine,
         1 (February), 379-80.
            Although convincing in its nature description and pas-
         sages of "exquisite dramatic power," the novel is badly
         flawed by poor construction, crude characterization, self-
         conscious bombastic diction, and imitations of Kipling.
         London is a "writer of potentiality and promise."

40   BOYNTON, H. W. "Books New and Old: II." Atlantic Monthly,
         92 (November), 695-97.
            The Call of the Wild is a powerful study of "primitive

dog nature," clearly preserving the distinction between animal and human virtue but susceptible of being read as an allegory.

41 BROOKE, MARY CALKINS. "The Call of the Wild." San Francisco Bulletin, Sunday Magazine (23 August), p. 6.
    Buck's life should be read as an allegory. Men also have hidden depths of cruelty and greed, and they become "as wolfish and barbaric" as Buck when they scramble for wealth like the Alaskan goldhunters.

42 DALL, WILLIAM H. "From Readers: Jack London's Indians." New York Times Saturday Review of Books and Art (10 January), p. 26.
    To convey the romance and tragedy of a native people, the story "must flow within channels limited by" qualities unique to that region and its Indians' "social philosophy" and psychology. London's Indians "are melodramatic white men in their disguise." [Letter signed: "Smithsonian Institution, Washington, D. C."]. See 1901.B13; 1902.B14; 1903.B54.

43 DOUBLEDAY, J. STEWART. "Reviews: The Call of the Wild." Reader Magazine, 2 (September), 498-409.
    The philosophy of survival of the fittest, thrilling scenes of the Northland, and suggestions of eternal truths come from an author "at harmony with himself and nature." London's humanity and broad vision contribute toward making him "one of the most original and impressive authors this country has known."

44 FITCH, GEORGE HAMLIN. "New Books: Best Work of Jack London. The California Writer Produces a Great Book in 'The Call of the Wild.'" San Francisco Chronicle (2 August), p. 32.
    "Fierce, brutal, splashed with blood, and alive with the crack of whip and blow of club, it is yet a story that sounds the deep note of tenderness between man and beast, and that loyalty and fidelity that never falters." With dramatic and poetic power, London masters his materials and molds style to thought. Review accompanied by a photograph of London, captioned: "His books are strong meat for the anemic generation that worships at the shrine of Henry James, but they will delight all people with red blood in their veins."

45 HAILE, MARGARET. "Book Reviews: The Call of the Wild." Wilshire's Magazine, 62 (September), 90.
    A "clean, strong, stirring story, well told." Every

bit of it "is instinct with purpose, with meaning, with directed vitality." Summarizes novel.

46   HALL, GIFFORD. "'The Call of the Wild' and 'Of Both Worlds.'" San Jose (Sunday) Mercury and Herald (13 September), Editorial section, p. 6.
      Call is a masterpiece, with insights into mankind's "subtle yearnings" that amount to "clairvoyance." Geniuses like London cannot be confined by ordinary literary laws, for they write "on the eternal snows with pens of giant forestry rather than on paper with pens of steel." One reads this novel "as one reads wind-swayed forests or storm swept ocean."

47   HAMILTON, FANNIE K. "Jack London: An Interview." Reader Magazine, 2 (August), 278-83.
      "Great of mind, strong-hearted, of deep conviction and deep feeling, the problems of life have stirred him profoundly, yet always toward a sound and broad philosophy. The healthy and soul-bracing sentiments of his books are realities in the man." London is genuinely warm, "boyish, noble and lovable,...primitive, free and unhackneyed," a simple genius, at heart a poet, and an enthusiast for sociology. Gives biography, in London's own words.

48   HARKINS, E.[DWARD] F. "Jack London," in his Little Pilgrimages Among the Men Who Have Written Famous Books, Second Series. Boston: L. C. Page, pp. 235-51.
      "He has been so successful because he is gifted with a rare imagination and a well-cultivated mind, and because he himself,...had experienced the Northland gloom." His work to date is proof "that the artist is born, not made.... He is today the ablest writer of fiction in the far West." Gives biography and a plot summary of "In a Far Country." Reprinted: 1903.B49.

49   _____. "Little Pilgrimages Among the Men and Women Who Have Written Famous Books. No. 6. Jack London." Literary World (Boston), 34 (December), 337-39.

50   HAWTHORNE, JULIAN. "New Books: A Daughter of the Snow [sic]." Wilshire's Magazine, 62 (February), 84-87.
      The young writer has admirable aspirations and "too much vitality and good sense in him" not to profit by his mistakes in this "crude and incoherent" novel. He indulges in "fine writing and highfalutin"; his heroine is "a sort of Brunhilda brought down to our times,...a monster--a

15

thing contrary to nature--...utterly incredible and even inconceivable." She does and says things that "are unpleasant and actually vulgar." When Frona is out of the picture, London's "work is forcible, picturesque and interesting" as he draws the scenery and frontiers-men; but even in these areas, "he fatigues us with too much of a good thing." The novel fails, but the writer is welcome. "There is bone, fibre and sinew in Mr. London. If his good angels screen him from popular success, during the next few formative years of his career, he may do something well worth the doing, and do it well. But if he is satisfied with his present level of performance, there is little hope for him."

51 HOVEY, CARL. "Three Books of the Moment: Jack London's 'Children of the Frost.'" Bookman (New York), 17 (March), 83-84.
    Despite the unnatural language, crudity, and "claptrap" of some stories, others offer fresh materials treated simply, sincerely, and vividly.

52 HOYT, ELEANOR. "In Lighter Vein: A Daughter of the Snows." Book Buyer, 25 (January), 621-22.
    Less ably done than his powerful, original stories, the novel is melodramatic and the heroine unconvincing; yet, the book has "its vivid interest."

53 JACKSON, FLORENCE. "Current Books: Keynote of Character." Overland Monthly, 42 (September), 272.
    The Call of the Wild is a "thrillingly touching story... a book of great power and of intense interest." The inevitability of reversion to the primitive is not sufficiently proven.

54 L. [ONDON, JACK (?)]. "From Readers: Jack London." New York Times Saturday Review of Books and Art (3 January), p. 10.
    Mr. Dall is not an artist who selects detail with "a pictorial eye." "London's art is not realism, but is idealized realism;...artistically, London is an emotional materialist," and his vision is subjective not scientific. See 1901.B13; 1902.B14; 1903.B42.

55 MacENERY, P. H. "Jack London in Depths of the Literary Abyss." San Jose (Sunday) Mercury and Herald (18 October), p. 24.
    The People of the Abyss is an "epoch-making book,... [a] thoughtful and painstaking" essay on seamy life. With The Kempton-Wace Letters, however, London reaches "depths" of "dullness and morbidity" unparalled by the

worst dime novel. Its "lame philosophy" and sensationalism are unworthy of him; he writes better about dogs than matrimony.

56 MAURICE, ARTHUR BARTLETT. "Jack London. 'The Call of the Wild.'" Bookman (New York), 18 (October), 159-60.
    This is "far and away the best book" of London's, although not as good as Richard Harding Davis's The Bar Sinister. London invests Buck "with a humanity which he has failed to give to most of his men."

57 MILLARD, BAILEY. "London as Novelist." American Magazine Supplement of the San Francisco Examiner. (1 March), p. [10].
    A Daughter of the Snows has been kindly received by Eastern critics. London prefers writing short stories to novels because they pay better. He has two hobbies: socialism and kite-flying.

58 _____. "Jack London in the Slums. 'The People of the Abyss'-- His Greatest Work, About to Be Published, Tells with Sickening Realism the Tale of Wolfish Want in the British Capital." American Magazine Supplement of the San Francisco Examiner (22 November), p. [11].
    A "truly masterful work" which "treats of a vital subject in a vital way." Better than Jacob Riis or Zola, London makes a haunting appeal to the reader's sympathy with his strong realism.

59 [MOODY, CHARLES AMADON]. "The Use of Adversity." Out West, 19 (September), 321-22.
    The Call of the Wild "not only grips and holds the interest, but is of deep evolutionary significance....[the] world may listen with profit" to London.

60 MOODY, CHARLES AMADON. "The Underside of Prosperity." Out West, 19 (December), 685.
    The People of the Abyss is "a terrible indictment" of Christian Anglo-Saxon civilization. Brief.

61 PAYNE, WILLIAM MORTON. "Recent Fiction [The Call of the Wild]." Dial, 35 (16 October), 261.
    "A clever and appealing piece of work...which must rank high among animal stories."

62 RITCHIE, ROBERT W. "London's First Work." San Francisco Sunday Call Magazine Section (29 November), p. 7.
    Offers a "resume" of London's earliest writings for The

1903

High School Aegis (Oakland). His stories and sketches
first gained "respectful awe" from his classmates, then
shocked them with his anarchist tendencies. "Who Believes
in Ghosts," and even more, "One More Unfortunate" were his
best work for the Aegis and sure indications of the quality
of his maturer writings.

63 STILLÉ, KATE BLACKISTON. "The Call of the Wild." Book News
Monthly, 22 (September), 7-10.
With great force and feeling, London reveals the deepest
truths of life: "that the heights and depths of the universe are within the soul," that the savage in man can
swiftly overcome his moral nature. This "thrilling romance"
wakes us to real horrors of ourselves and bids us heed the
"Voice of the Divine" which is also within us.

64 W., H. G. "Book Reviews: The Kempton-Wace Letters." Wilshire's Magazine, 62 (July), 89-93.
Expresses amazement that the author can present both
sides so fairly and impartially. Wace's argument is powerful, but Kempton's voice "strikes the true note." The
letters "comprise a philosophy of being" for Socialists:
when mankind's material necessities are satisfied, "spiritual poverty" can then be abolished, and perfect love and
knowledge of God will prevail. Prints two letters in full.

65 WILLIAMS, CHURCHILL. "Red Blood in Fiction." World's Work,
3 (July), 3694-700.
London's work has "vigor and subtlety," but because it
is "nearly all so sombre" it lacks balance.

1904 A BOOKS - NONE

1904 B SHORTER WRITINGS

1 ANON. "London, Jack," in Who's Who, 1904. London: A. & C.
Black, p. 932.
Biographical sketch. London appears for the first time
in this volume and in all subsequent volumes through 1917.

2 ANON. "The Bookman's Table [The People of the Abyss]." Bookman (London), 25 (January), 188.
This "photographic study of the darker side of East-End
life" over-emphasizes and generalizes the horrors; but
with London's sympathetic understanding, it becomes "one
of the truest and most terrible indictments of civilization that any man has ever written."

3　ANON. "Notices of Books." Publishers' Circular, 80 (2 January), 11.
　　　The People of the Abyss "is vivid, truthful, and unexaggerated," although London is sometimes carried away by indignation. Brief.

4　ANON. "The Lounger." Critic, 44 (March), 197, 198.
　　　London would be writing for us if he had not gone to the Orient. Portrait.

5　ANON. "Briefer Notices: The People of the Abyss." Public Opinion, 36 (10 March), 315.
　　　"It is most refreshing to be told that the cockney slums have ours beaten." Brief.

6　ANON. "Jack London's 'People of the Abyss.'" Current Literature, 36 (April), 413-16.
　　　With sympathetic understanding, London offers realistic pictures of the East Enders, intelligent reasons for their plight, and original suggestions for remedy. "Nothing in recent literature is better calculated to bring these conditions home to the heart and conscience of the English-speaking race." Offers extensive excerpts.

7　ANON. "Jack London's Stories: The Faith of Men, And Other Stories." New York Times Saturday Review of Books, Part Two (21 May), p. 349.
　　　They suffer from monotony of subject (the Klondike) and of treatment (brutality). The best one, for its "geniality," is "The Marriage of Lit Lit."

8　ANON. "Literature: The Faith of Men, and Other Stories." Independent, 56 (26 May), 1203.
　　　London is the only storyteller "who can really swing the master's [Kipling's] style." He imitates like "an original genius."

9　ANON. "Fiction: The Faith of Men." Academy and Literature, 66 (28 May), 587.
　　　London "has a swinging style which gives life and vigour to his narrative....He makes us know the Klondike." In spite of the physical horror of the best story, "Bâtard," the book is entertaining.

10　ANON. "Short Stories: The Faith of Men." Athenaeum, 3998 (11 June), 748.
　　　These are strong stories, well-told.

11 ANON. "Eight Novels [The Faith of Men]." Nation, 78 (23 June), 501.
    "It seems regrettable that Jack London should employ his wide knowledge, keen insight, vivid powers of description, and trenchant vocabulary merely in order to make us plough through miles and miles of ice and snow" in the company of assorted gruesome, savage, and grotesque beings and actions.

12 ANON. "Novels: The Faith of Men, and Other Stories." Saturday Review (London), 97 (25 June), 822.
    Lacking originality and inventiveness, they are unattractive. London seems to have run out of subjects that Kipling and Wells could not handle better.

13 ANON. "Men and Women of the Outdoor World (Jack London)." Outing, 44 (July), [486]-87.
    "London's stories have taken a place in literature. His is a blunt, rough, forceful personality in American fiction." He has turned his adventures and hardships into romance. Gives biography.

14 ANON. "Personal and Miscellaneous Gossip." Argonaut, 55 (4 July), 9.
    W. L. Alden wants Jack to call himself John. See 1904.B42.

15 ANON. "A Daughter of the Snows." Athenaeum, 4005 (30 July), 140.
    This is not a novel; it lacks "craftsmanship...sustained power of thought....[and] skill in construction." The characters talk "sheer journalese."

16 ANON. "Fiction: 'A Daughter of the Snows.'" TLS (22 July), p. 229.
    "The story would have been fresh, vigorous, and manly but for this sort of Teuton priggishness [of the sermons and moral philosophy]...this air of inheriting the earth by virtue of superior strenuousness." London collapses "beneath the weight of his own seriousness."

17 ANON. "Fiction: A Daughter of the Snows." Academy and Literature, 67 (30 July), 81.
    This is not one of London's "happiest efforts. His picture of society in the Klondike is curiously unconvincing and unreal;...And yet the book has its moments, its brilliant descriptions, its exciting incidents."

18   ANON. "Novels: 'A Daughter of the Snows.'" Saturday Review
     (London), 98 (30 July), 145.
          London takes himself too seriously; he elaborates detail
     and intrudes "pseudo-philosophy" which detract from the
     vigor of the story.

19   ANON. "The Faith of Men." Catholic World, 79 (August), 691-92.
          "They are smart, well-told tales, with well-conceived
     plots and graphic characterizations."

20   ANON. "London--The Faith of Men." Critic, 45 (August), 190.
          The stories are very uneven in quality, some vivid and
     powerful, some indefensibly brutal or artificial in struc-
     ture. Brief.

21   ANON. "Novel Notes: A Daughter of the Snows." Bookman (Lon-
     don), 26 (August), 177.
          A novel "of powerful episodes, brilliant descriptive
     passages, and some few characters drawn with wonderful in-
     sight and ability, but the effect of the whole is somewhat
     patchy and disjointed."

22   ANON. "Wares in the Literary Shop: 'The Faith of Men.'" San
     Francisco Bulletin Sunday Magazine (21 August), p. 8.
          "Bold and strong" tales, some terribly relentless in
     their exposure of primitive emotions. London writes
     frankly of unconventional behavior which we falsely assume
     is absent in civilized men.

23   ANON. "Notices of Books." Publishers' Circular, 81 (27 Au-
     gust), 207.
          A Daughter of the Snows has "breadth and absence of
     artificiality," and a powerful heroine; however, "the
     local coloring too strongly predominates without relief of
     light and shade." Brief.

24   ANON. "The Sea-Wolf." New York Times Saturday Review of
     Books and Art (12 November), pp. 768-69.
          A "stirring and unhackneyed tale of life on the high
     seas, full of the seafaring spirit." It is a romance with
     "artistic and commercial" value. The minor characters are
     lifelike and Larsen is endowed "with a certain majesty"
     that his manner of death fails to match. Despite an
     "excess of brutality," this is "an ingenious and powerful
     story,...above the average alike in plan and execution."

25   ANON. "A Review of the Important Books of the Year." Inde-
     pendent, 57 (17 November), 1138.

1904

In originality and power <u>The Sea-Wolf</u> is probably the
most important novel of the year [29 novels briefly noted].

26   ANON. "A Review of the Season's Books: Fiction." <u>Outlook</u>,
          78 (3 December), 872.
          "Forcefulness, originality to the point of strangeness,
          thrill in story-interest" grip the reader of <u>The Sea-Wolf</u>.
          However, its brutality sickens, and the dog Buck was
          "vastly more real and even human" than Larsen.

27   ANON. "Other New Novels." <u>Public Opinion</u>, 37 (8 December),
          730.
          <u>The Sea-Wolf</u> fascinates and grips the reader. Larsen is
          "not quite convincing," and Maud is "colorless."

28   ANON. "New Novels: <u>The Sea-Wolf</u>." <u>Athenaeum</u>, 4024 (10 Decem-
          ber), 801.
          On the positive side, it is "full of incident and move-
          ment, compact of ingeniously contrived situations,...[and
          a] consistent study of character." London shows "a ten-
          dency to exaggeration, a sort of riotous rejoicing in his
          own virility and enthusiasm." This is his best book.

29   ANON. "Recent Fiction [<u>The Sea-Wolf</u>]." <u>Nation</u>, 79 (22 Decem-
          ber), 507.
          "Never has sickening brutality been more gloatingly de-
          scribed than in this story....Yet the conception is at
          least novel and powerful" and might be admired except for
          the "strained exaggeration" of the horror and love passages,
          the "longwidedness" and "exasperating tricks of speech."
          Perhaps the novel is a parody, "in which case 'Captain
          Outrageous' would be a more fitting title."

30   BLAND, HENRY MEADE. "Jack London." <u>Overland Monthly</u>, 43
          (May), 370-75.
          Biographical sketch. London's close friend Louis Bond
          was the prototype of Stanley Price, and Bond's dog was the
          model for Buck. The striking features of London's career
          are his "tenacity" and ability to turn his romantic life
          into books. In his work there is a "growing sympathy with
          humanity....hatred of sham and pretense." He conveys the
          triumph of moral right and a sense of "infinite aspiration."

31   COCKERELL, T. D. A. "London on London." <u>Dial</u>, 36 (1 January),
          11-12.
          <u>The People of the Abyss</u> is a straightforward and readable
          book. Advertising this serious work as entertaining fic-
          tion "does Mr. London a great injustice." Offers excerpts
          and compares the English to Alaskan Indians.

32 COOPER, FREDERIC TABER. "The Sea-Wolf." Bookman (New York),
    20 (November), 219.
        This is "another Moran of the Lady Letty without Frank
    Norris's epic strength, and with much more grimness and
    brutality....one needs strong nerves to read" it to a
    finish.

33 _____. "Some Recent Fiction." World's Work, 9 (December),
    5654.
        "In 'The Sea-Wolf' Jack London preaches the same doctrine
    that a flabby man may be made virile by a vigorous life;...
    [it] is the strongest book" he has written.

34 FITCH, GEORGE HAMLIN. "Noteworthy New Novels." San Francisco
    Chronicle, Sunday Supplement (13 November), p. 8.
        London "is the strongest American romance writer of to-
    day." We hope he will not lose his joy in storytelling to
    become "the preacher and tractarian" that Kipling now is.
    The Sea-Wolf is a "powerful romance," but it lacks the
    "fine spiritual quality" of The Call of the Wild. Only a
    "mawkish" love affair relieves the "repellent realism,"
    and although Larsen is real in his savagery, he is unbe-
    lievable as a scholar. This second part of the story is
    unconvincing and seems unrelated to the first part.

35 HODDER, ALFRED. "The Clan and the Boss." Critic, 44 (March),
    217-18.
        The People of the Abyss reveals London's shock and dis-
    tress, but he objectively conveys the East End experience
    "with much sprightliness and accuracy."

36 KERFOOT, J. B. "The Latest Books." Life, 44 (22 December),
    650.
        Larsen "alone saves the story from the commonplace."
    The Sea-Wolf is unhappily "an artistic failure after many
    artistic successes." Brief.

37 LOUGHEAD, FLORA HAINES. "The Call of the Tame: an antithesis.
    The Call of the Wild. Buck, the St. Bernard, gently born
    at San Jose, answers the Call of the Wild and becomes
    leader of the Alaskan wolves. The Call of the Tame. Bones,
    the Mahlemiut, bred of the Wolf in Alaska, answers the
    Call of the Tame and becomes a household pet at San Jose."
    San Francisco Chronicle, Sunday Supplement (4 December),
    p. 3.
        Gives plot summary of London's novel and compares the
    lives of Buck and Bones.

1904

38   MARSH, EDWARD CLARK. "Jack London's 'People of the Abyss.'"
        Bookman (New York), 18 (February), 647-48.
            London went into the slums not out of love for mankind
        but for adventure and materials for a book. His life
        there, with sovereigns sewn in his clothes, was not authen-
        tic. His stories may be entertaining, but in no way is
        this book the semi-scientific work it pretends to be.

39   MILLARD, BAILEY. "New Book by Jack London: Some Remarkable
        Strong Stories of Arctic Life in 'The Faith of Men.'"
        San Francisco Examiner (26 June), p. 52.
            London is a remarkable teller of stories "of point and
        purpose, wonderfully realistic and full of Kiplingian
        fire." There are many serious realistic tales in this
        volume, strong, gripping revelations of "the essence of
        things."

40   _____. "Here Come the Holiday Books: Stories of the Season
        for Young and Old." San Francisco Examiner (11 December),
        Editorial section, p. 78.
            Brief comment on The Sea-Wolf.

41   MOODY, CHARLES AMADON. "The Lady and the Tiger." Out West,
        21 (December), 586.
            The Sea-Wolf is London's "most powerful, and most un-
        pleasant work." It must be read to appreciate its "life
        and vigor."

42   P., R. S. "Communications: 'Jack' or 'John' London." Argo-
        naut, 55 (25 July), 51.
            Jack is London's real name and he should go on using it.
        Response to 1904.B14.

43   RITCHIE, ROBERT W. "Books of the Day: London Deals in Bru-
        tality." San Francisco Sunday Call Magazine Section
        (4 December), p. [10].
            The Sea-Wolf replaces "the spiritual" with "gross
        materialism," raising questions of the aesthetic value of
        a novel which condones "the ugly, the sordid, the brutal."
        This book does not raise London's well-earned reputation;
        it is "butcher's meat, hacked, dripping, from the bones
        of realism."

44   S., R. M. "Reviews: The Faith of Men." Reader Magazine, 4
        (August), 351.
            These tales "were not worth the original printing in
        the magazines, much less gathered into book form." London
        should return to "dogs and wolves."

45   STONE, FRANK F.   "Wilshire, Jack London, and The 'Pauper
        Workers of Europe.'"   Wilshire's Magazine, 63 (May), 237-41.
        The People of the Abyss, although a "masterly and, in
     most respects, luminous picture of certain aspects of life
     among the London poor," creates too sharp a contrast be-
     tween the workers of England and America. The Londoner,
     with his low wage, can eat and live better than the higher-
     paid American. It is dangerous to flatter American workers
     into thinking they are so well off that they do not need
     Socialism. Describes the commodities, prices, and recrea-
     tion available in London.

1905 A BOOKS

1   ANON. Jack London. A Sketch of His Life and Work. With
        Portrait. New York: Macmillan, 15 pp.
           Biographical and critical sketch. Reprinted: 1971.A1.
        Revised and enlarged: 1908.A1.

1905 B SHORTER WRITINGS

1   ANON. "Literature." Pacific Monthly, 13 (January), 72.
           The Sea-Wolf is "a big breezy sea story, superbly
        written, with London's virile, full-blooded style at its
        best." He is now writing a play "at the request of Ethel
        Barrymore."

2   ANON. "The Season's Notable Fiction: By Well-Known American
        Authors." American Monthly Review of Reviews, 31 (January),
        115.
           London remains "entirely impartial" as he depicts the
        struggle between the "'overman'" and his opposite in The
        Sea-Wolf. "We are told of the two, and of their fight
        for life, with swift directness, with sincerity and
        strength."

3   ANON. "Literature: A Nietzche Novel." Independent, 58
        (5 January), 39-40.
           In The Sea-Wolf "the ethical theorem is developed by
        argument and illustration with a symmetry and completeness
        rare even in a serious treatise." London apparently be-
        lieves that moral action is "a blind instinct developed by
        the necessities of interracial struggle." The thesis of
        his novel is correct, "that altruism must conquer egoism
        in the end."

4   ANON. "Fiction: <u>The Sea-Wolf</u>." <u>Academy and Literature</u>, 68
     (7 January), 14.
         "It streams blood from beginning to end....London shouts
     at us from its pages in no uncertain voice. Certainly he
     will be heard, but it is not great art....it serves no
     good purpose to rake over filth and garbage....we must pro-
     test against this picture of rampant inhumanity and bru-
     tality."

5   ANON. "Jack London at Berkeley." <u>Argonaut</u>, 56 (30 Jaunary),
     70.
         London's exhortation to the students to support the
     revolutionary aims of the Socialist party was political
     propaganda that should not be sanctioned by a state-
     supported institution. <u>See</u> Wheeler, 1905.B50.

6   ANON. "About New Books: <u>The Sea-Wolf</u>." <u>Canadian Magazine</u>,
     24 (February), 384-85.
         A "thrilling story." Gives plot summary and excerpts.

7   ANON. "Reviews: <u>The Sea-Wolf</u>." <u>Reader Magazine</u>, 5 (February),
     378-79.
         This is the "high water mark" of London's power; he has
     outdone himself "in the cruelty, the peace, the awfulness,
     the beauty of the sea." Larsen is a compelling character
     in a story that "cuts down to the raw of human nature."
     For the reader with strong nerves, "the Iliad of the Ocean"
     is here.

8   ANON. "The Knave: How Jack London Stands in the World of
     Letters." <u>Oakland Tribune</u> (4 February), Second section,
     p. [13].
         Denounces San Francisco critics who attack London for
     his "phenomenal success." Quotes Julian Hawthorne: London
     "is hearty, genial, honest, simple,...[he] inspires strong
     liking from first to last"; he is honest and true to his
     convictions.

9   ANON. "Notices of Books." <u>Publishers' Circular</u>, 82 (18 Febru-
     ary), 180.
         <u>The Sea-Wolf</u> is "the best novel we have read for some
     time....a clever, artistic, and enthralling book." Brief.

10   ANON. [Jack London]. <u>Current Literature</u>, 36 (April), 408.
         Biographical sketch. A photograph of London is the
     frontispiece of this issue.

11   ANON. "The Lounger." Critic, 46 (May), 397, 399.
         War of the Classes is "very personal, very egotistical,
      very entertaining....[and] Utopian."

12   ANON. "Novel Notes: The Sea-Wolf." Bookman (London), 28
         (May), 69.
         A strong, psychologically acute study, often unpleasant
      to read but "written with verve and rush on every page."

13   ANON. "Jack London Socialist: War of the Classes." New York
         Times Saturday Review of Books and Art (6 May), p. 291.
         Discusses the essays. The most interesting are those on
      the scab and the tramp.

14   ANON. Review of War of the Classes. San Francisco Sunday Call
         Magazine Section (7 May), p. 23.
         "Socialism has a clever advocate" in London. Discusses
      the essays in detail.

15   ANON. "The Latest Call of the Wild." Oakland Tribune (11 May),
         p. 8.
         In War of the Classes London mistakenly identifies workers
      and trade unionists with Socialists. His "call" for revo-
      lutionary destruction of the government turns men into dogs,
      as we've seen in the Chicago riots, dogs "tearing at the
      throat of society." London seems ambitious to become "the
      Marat of a Socialist uprising in this country."

16   ANON. "Literature: War of the Classes." Independent, 58
         (25 May), 1190-91.
         Lists contents. "Some of Mr. London's best and most
      lasting work is to be found in these pages."

17   ANON. "The Game." New York Times Saturday Review of Books
         and Art (17 June), p. 394.
         London's "Rooseveltian joy in the strong play of muscles
      makes him an ideal man" to treat this theme; it is done
      with "vigor and picturesqueness."

18   ANON. "Mr. Jack London's New Novel." Publishers' Circular,
         82 (24 June), 696.
         The Game is a truthful and "intensely graphic portrayal
      of the prize ring," its values, and its participants.
      Brief.

19   ANON. "Literary Notes: London's Fine Strong Story." Argonaut,
         56 (26 June), 455.
         The Game is "a tremendously good story," robust, vivid,
      and exciting; but the heroine is unconvincing.

1905

20   ANON. "Literature: The Game." Independent, 58 (29 June),
        1480.
            With a "beautifully written" love story and vividly
        described fight scenes London convinces the reader that
        "the delight of contest and the joy of triumph, is worth
        the sacrifice of love and home and family."

21   ANON. "List of New Books and Reprints." TLS (7 July), p. 220.
        Notices The Game.

22   ANON. "Books of the Week. Game (The)." Outlook, 80 (29 July),
        837.
            London's "stories are never lacking in power, dramatic
        quality, and picturesqueness, but his love for the strenuous
        and the tragic has led him to end his story in a way that is
        fairly brutal." Brief.

23   ANON. "New Novels: The Game." Athenaeum, 4057 (29 July), 138.
            This is neither a novel nor literature but "simply a
        clever journalistic account," a book with "much margin, a
        good deal of allegorical illustration of the vignette type,
        and something under two hundred small pages of big print."
        It gives the public "sheer street-bred sensuality" and
        "short measure" for its money.

24   ANON. "Recent Fiction and the Critics: The Game." Current
        Literature, 39 (August), 218.
            Gives excerpts, mostly favorable, from periodical re-
        views; these range from "the very best thing" London has
        done to a book with no relation to literature.

25   ANON. "Fiction: The Game." Academy, 68 (5 August), 809.
            "Mr. Shaw's Cashel Byron was much more convincing....
        [Fleming] is altogether too noble, and unselfish, and
        pure-minded." The description of the fight is well done
        and the prose forceful; but prize-fighting should not be
        glorified.

26   ANON. "The Prize Ring." New York Times Saturday Review of
        Books and Art (12 August), p. 528.
            The Game does not convince in truthfulness to life.
        The story of the fight is "vivid and thrilling." The novel
        succeeds as a pretty and sad love story with real lovers.
        [In a letter to this section of the Times (2 September,
        p. 574), London insiste The Game is true-to-experience.]

27   ANON. "Book Reviews." Public Opinion, 39 (19 August), 252.
            The Game leaves a reader "high and dry, empty-handed and
        unsatisfied, upon the sands of misfortune." Brief.

28   ANON. "Novels: 'The Game.'" Saturday Review (London), 100
         (19 August), 252.
            London's work since The Call of the Wild lacks inspira-
         tion. This is "good journalism."

29   ANON. "London--The Game." Critic, 47 (September), 285.
            "It is of the most banal and ordinary stamp, utterly
         lacking in the dramatic power" of his previous work.
         Brief.

30   ANON. Review of War of the Classes. Annals of the American
         Academy of Political and Social Science, 26, no. 2 (Sep-
         tember), 412.
            "It is an interesting, thought-provoking volume, to be
         read and pondered, but truths and half-truths are so inter-
         woven that it is scarcely a safe guide." Brief.

31   ANON. "Jack London's First Play." Current Literature, 39
         (October), 435-46.
            The Great Interrogation, written with Ada Lee Bascom,
         has been "enthusiastically received" in San Francisco.
         Gives plot summary and critical comment from San Francisco
         papers.

32   ANON. Review of The Great Interrogation. Sunset Magazine, 15
         (October), 597-98.
            It is a "play of strong emotions, and scored a big hit."

33   ANON. "Comment on Current Books." Outlook, 81 (4 November),
         579-80.
            Tales of the Fish Patrol is good reading for boys and
         others. Brief.

34   ANON. "The Season's Books: Novels and Tales." Outlook, 81
         (25 November), 712.
            Mentions The Sea-Wolf, The Game, and Tales of the Fish
         Patrol. "At his best he is vigorous, picturesque, and
         powerful." Brief.

35   ANON. "Persons in the Foreground: Jack London, Apostle of the
         Primitive." Current Literature, 39 (December), 673-74.
            "At once passionate idealist and brute materialist,"
         London incarnates the restless spirit, with something of
         Byron and Gorky added. Gives biography; quotes London's
         essays and Julian Hawthorne.

36   ANON. "Topics of the Times: Criticism and Hydraulics." New
         York Times (4 December), p. 8.

Poses a question about "Love of Life": How can you bail
dry "a little pool connecting with a big pool, without
bailing out all the water in the big pool in the course
of the operation?" The mistake in this episode, the likes
of which Kipling never made, requires an explanation; "and
knowing Mr. London's ingenuity, we can almost hope it will
be adequate."

37 ANON. [Jack London]. <u>San Francisco Chronicle</u> (22 December),
p. 6.
    An editorial critical of London's socialism; his 7,000,000
"avowed enemies of society" should go somewhere else.

38 BRITT, JIMMY. "Jimmy Britt reviews 'The Game,' Jack London's
story of the ring: Tale of pugilist is true to the life.
Thrilling description of a battle within the roped en-
closure moves champion to words of high praise for author.
Worthy to referee the coming contest." <u>San Francisco
Examiner</u> (27 August), Editorial section, p. 46.
    A thrilling story "with the intensity of a real contest."
London shows true insight into the life, mind, and conver-
sation of a fighter, and the technical aspects of the ring.
It is "an epic on pugilism."

39 BROOKS, ROBERT C. "Eight Books of the Month: London's 'The War
of the Classes.'" <u>Bookman</u> (New York), 22 (September),
61-64.
    It lacks originality and logical coherency, but the
work's "forcefulness and literary merit" recommend it as
"an effective textbook for the socialist propaganda."
Discussion of the tramp and scab shows some inconsistency
and confusion. Offers detailed analysis and rebuttal.

40 COOPER, FREDERIC TABER. "The Individual Note and Some Recent
Books." <u>Bookman</u> (New York), 22 (September), 35-36.
    In <u>The Sea-Wolf</u> London "is by instinct a realist of such
brutal strength that at times he is repellent. Yet even
when you shrink from him, you are forced to concede his
power." <u>The Game</u> is a "very nearly flawless story" of its
kind. Reading it "is quite as good, or quite as bad" as
seeing a fight.

41 EAMES, NINETTA. "Haunts of Jack London." <u>Cosmopolitan</u>, 40
(December), [221]-30.
    While his bungalow is being built on the Sonoma ranch,
London lives nearby with friends in a "wildwood haunt...
brotherly with Nature and human hearts, working aye for
larger ends, his thoughts so plainly in tune that men

catch them on the quick, and are held and moved imperiously to join in the primal harmony." London works in the morning, then swims, or rides through the village with his "trail-worn husky." "Imagination in him generates the strong, the pictorial and the heroic as inevitably as the sun and soil bring forth oak and sequoia."

42 EMERSON, EDWIN, JR. "When West Meets East." Sunset Magazine, 15 (October), 515-30.
     Discusses Western correspondents in the Russian-Japanese War. According to various editors, London was a good correspondent, eager for news and able to write an exciting story, but he was over-emotional and he loathed the Japanese.

43 FITCH, GEORGE HAMLIN. "Books for Summer Reading." San Francisco Chronicle, Sunday Supplement (18 June), p. 8.
     The Game is finely detailed and true-to-life. It will "please thousands."

44 McEWEN, ARTHUR. "Jack London J. [sic] on the Constitution." San Francisco Bulletin (16 March), p. 8.
     Comments on London's "to hell with the Constitution" remark. Finds admirable the "revolutionary ardor which burns in the generous heart" of this young man, the same manly spirit which "chucked the tea overboard in Boston." His strong language is useful to shock people into realizing that their "blind veneration" of the Constitution is superstition.

45 PAYNE, WILLIAM MORTON. "Recent Fiction." Dial, 38 (1 January), 16.
     When The Sea-Wolf focuses on development of Van Weyden's character, the psychological aspects obscure the narrative of adventure. Although "not a pleasant tale to read," it has "a certain fascination...and fairly grips the attention in its culminating passages."

46 RICH, AMY C. "Books of the Day: The Sea-Wolf." Arena, 33 (April), 452-53.
     A strong and original romance with outstanding characterization of "primal man in all his savagery." It is not recommended to the general reader, for its morbidity and gloom neither serve a useful lesson nor strengthen "moral and intellectual vigor."

47 ROBERTSON, PETER. "A Play by Jack London: 'The Great Interrogation' at the Alcazar is Received with Impressive Interest." San Francisco Chronicle (22 August), p. 4.

1905

"Gracefully constructed--...with some virile and telling
speeches." The plot is less than original and the ending
"maudlin."

48   STEVENS, ASHTON. "Alcazar Audience Demands Speech of Author:
First Production is a Memorable Event in O'Farrell Street
and Results in Riotous Calls for the Gifted Writer." San
Francisco Examiner (22 August), p. 3.
The Great Interrogation "has the grip of real drama....
[It] is as vivid as a blow between the eyes. It is indeed
a rich hour." Gives lengthy review, with cartoons of the
play's characters and London titled, "A Great Success is
Jack London?"

49   _____. "Jack London, Dramatist--An Interview: Jack London Reveals Himself Gradually in the Hum of a Newspaper Office."
San Francisco Examiner (27 August), Editorial section,
p. 47.
"Irresistably, he is a straightway man....He is Socialist
without being freak, and where most fellows have theories,
Jack London has first-hand information." London discusses
The Great Interrogation, his other plays, realism in fiction, the English language, and future plans.

50   WHEELER, BENJAMIN IDE. "Dr. Wheeler, Jack London, and
Socialism." Argonaut, 56 (6 February), 87.
The President of the University of California writes:
"We seek the man and not the subject" from among those who
have achieved the right to be heard. This is a response
to 1905.B5.

1906 A BOOKS

1   [IRVINE, ALEXANDER]. Jack London at Yale. Edited by the State
Secretary of the Socialist Party of Connecticut [Alexander
Irvine]. Westwood, Mass.: Connecticut State Committee;
Ariel Press, 28 pp.
Essay by Irvine, "Jack London at Yale," pp. [3]-11.
Irvine arranged "Comrade London's" appearance at Yale on
January 26, 1906. London spoke for two hours to "a hundred
professors and ten times as many students; many hundreds of
workingmen; many hundreds of citizens." He spent the rest
of the evening chatting with interested students. Section,
"Press Comments and Remarks," pp. [12]-28, includes: "Jack
London to Yale Men: Lecture on Socialism in Woosey Hall.
University Ideals Clean and Noble but not Alive. Indict-
ment Against the Capitalist," reprinted from Yale Alumni

Weekly (31 January, 1906); "London's Lecture," reprinted
from Yale Alumni Weekly (n.d.); also reprints 1906.B5,
with a "Note," Irvine's response to this editorial; "The
Gospel of Londonism," reprinted from The Register (New
Haven) (27 January, 1906), an editorial approving London's
preaching "in the very citadel of conservatism" and stressing
the need for economic reform. Irvine's essay reprinted:
1910.B24; pamphlet reprinted: 1972.A2. See Forrey, 1976.B4.

1906 B SHORTER WRITINGS

1   ANON. "Jack London," in The National Cyclopaedia of American
    Biography. Volume 13. New York: James T. White, 133-34.

2   ANON. "They All Wear Red to Hear Jack London." New York
    Times (20 January), p. 2.
       Reports lecture on "The Coming Crisis" in Grand Central
    Palace. Quotes speech in part.

3   ANON. "Jack London the Socialist--a Character Study. When
    and Why the Author of 'The Call of the Wild' Became a Con-
    vert and Propagandist. His Literary Methods and Aims."
    New York Times (28 January), part 3, p. 6.
       London's movement from "a poet" to a "revolutionary
    socialist" imperils his literary career. He is "wearing
    the weave of his nature threadbare with this cause,...
    sacrificing the best of him to the worst of him." Quotes
    London on his Socialism and writing.

4   ANON. "Jack London at Harvard and Faneuil Hall." Arena, 35
    (February), 187.
       London's lectures in December (1905) were popular. Brief.

5   ANON. "Class War." New York Times (1 February), p. 8.
       Editorial. "Mr. Jack London's Socialism is bloody war....
    a destructive Socialism. He glories in it." He "must be
    commended for his courage and for his honesty" in stating
    the nature and aims of his cause in the Yale address. Re-
    printed: 1906.A1. Response by Sinclair: 1906.B47.

6   ANON. "Topics of the Times: Advertising for Jack London."
    New York Times (10 February), p. 8.
       The "exceedingly foolish" announcement by the Derby Neck,
    Connecticut, library that London's books will be banned is
    "good advertising for some good books." London's crazy
    talk about the Constitution has nothing to do with his
    stories which are "of somewhat unusual excellence as
    literature."

1906

7   ANON. "Shall Jack London's Books be Blacklisted?" Public
     Opinion, 40 (24 February), 41-42.
         A majority of the press comments on banning London's
     books in Derby Neck, Connecticut, "is decidedly against
     London." [The banning was widely reported in Bay Area
     newspapers which generally supported London; see Bubka,
     1968.A1.]

8   ANON. "Short Stories: Tales of the Fish Patrol." Athenaeum,
     4087 (24 February), 229.
         "Mr. London's style has of late shown marked signs of a
     chastening process. He progresses. His gift for descrip-
     tion and for easy narrative is undeniable."

9   ANON. "Editorials: The Quick and the Dead." Independent, 60
     (1 March), 521-23.
         London's essay, "What Life Means to Me," is a "self-
     revelation of an American gifted with the divine fire"
     which penetrates deeply into our lives with "insight of
     genius." A fascinating and masterfully written story, it
     is to our materialistic society what the Gospel of St.
     Matthew was to the Roman world.

10 ANON. "'Tales of the Fish Patrol.'" Saturday Review (London),
     101 (17 March), 338.
         Exciting tales of perilous seas and poachers. London
     makes excellent use of personal experience.

11 ANON. "Fiction: Tales of the Fish Patrol." Academy, 70
     (24 March), 287.
         Such tales, "monotonous in theme and wholly without magic
     of style...appeal to the large unlettered public that is
     content to find in excitement its adequate reward."

12 ANON. Review of Tales of the Fish Patrol. Out West, 24
     (April), 330.
         "Recommended for boys of from seven to seventy." Brief.

13 ANON. "Partisans and Historians in Social Science." Dial, 40
     (1 May), 297.
         In War of the Classes London's "style betrays the hunter's
     eagerness and thirst for blood." He offers some "valuable
     suggestions" and vividly paints "the sentiments which are
     gathering force in cities"; we should heed these.

14 ANON. "The Author of 'White Fang.'" Outing Magazine, 48
     (June), 361.
         An exciting, well-motivated story, told with "a fine

sense of proportion." London has "the touch of genius to
handle these big passions." Gives biography. [White Fang
is serialized here, May-October.]

15   ANON. Review of Tales of the Fish Patrol. Spectator, 97
      (21 July), 98.
      Brief note.

16   ANON. "Jack London." Publishers' Circular, 85 (15 September),
      309.
      Brief biographical note.

17   ANON. "Literature: Moon-Face, and Other Stories." Independent,
      61 (20 September), 698.
      Most of them "are horrible without being thrilling."

18   ANON. Review of Moon-Face and Other Stories. New York Times
      Saturday Review of Books (29 September), p. 596.
      These tales are nearly all below London's usual level of
      work, which at its best is "vigorous, human, the real
      flesh and blood souls of men and women molded in Rodinesque
      style and pulsing with the hot blood of primitive passions."

19   ANON. "Comment on Current Books: Moon-Face." Outlook, 84
      (October), 337.
      Brief notice.

20   ANON. "London, Jack. Moon-Face, and Other Stories." Literary
      Digest , 33 (6 October), 474.
      They show London's "dramatic quality and virile powers
      of expression....freshness and originality...a sort of
      primitive vigor and pulsing life that lifts them above the
      average." There are faults of exaggeration, "cocksureness,"
      and use of slang.

21   ANON. "Recent Fiction: Moon-Face, and Other Stories." Nation,
      83 (11 October), 308.
      "These stories present Jack London at his shallowest,
      but by no means at his worst. Everything in them, even
      their brutality, is subordinated to a trivial ingenuity of
      plot."

22   ANON. "Our Booking-Office." Punch, 131 (17 October), 288.
      The Cruise of the Dazzler is a "breezy book, redolent of
      the sea,...a surging story" to please a boy and his father.

23   ANON. "Fiction: Moon-Face." Academy, 71 (20 October), 399.
      "They are terse, virile to the verge of brutality, and

1906

> they grip the mind. The language is fresh and convincing,
> ...[but] we miss in these the power of The Call of the
> Wild and The Sea-Wolf."

24   ANON. "Our Library Table." Athenaeum, 4121 (20 October), 477.
        London's hasty rate of writing does not produce good
        literature. His early work showed great promise, but The
        Cruise of the Dazzler has the "flat strenuousness of a
        'penny dreadful'....and has no real study of character."
        The stuff of Moon-Face "is all handled carelessly and lacks
        sincerity of purpose. In places it is irritating and bad."

25   ANON. "Literature: Animal Stories." Independent, 61 (1 Novem-
        ber), 1055-56.
        London understands animal psychology, and his convincing
        tale is as good in workmanship as anything in this field.
        An illustration from White Fang, p. 1054.

26   ANON. Review of White Fang. Argonaut, 59 (10 November), 223.
        "A thoroughly interesting study."

27   ANON. "Jack London: 'White Fang' is Another Tale of the Primi-
        tive Forces of Nature." New York Times Saturday Review of
        Books (17 November), p. 764.
        "His vigorous incisive style, unconventionality, and
        sympathetic understanding of nature" and of animals make
        this the best thing since The Call of the Wild. London
        creates an "enthralling hero" in a "splendid story."

28   ANON. "Current Fiction: White Fang." Nation, 83 (22 Novem-
        ber), 440-41.
        "As a biographer of wild animals he has hardly an equal."

29   ANON. Review of Scorn of Women. New York Times Saturday Re-
        view of Books (24 November), p. 778.
        "It is much like other recent plays in the manner of its
        intrigue and the quality of its sentiment and humor."

30   ANON. "The Season's Books." Outlook, 84 (24 November), 710.
        White Fang offers convincing psychology and striking
        drama. "No stronger piece of work in this field has
        appeared." Brief.

31   ANON. "In the Realm of Bookland." Overland Monthly, 48
        (December), 502.
        "Moon-Face" is evidently plagiarized from Norris's "The
        Passing of Cock-eye-blacklock" (1903). For this "literary
        crime" London should be condemned.

32   ANON. "In the Realm of Bookland." Overland Monthly, 48
     (December), 503.
       White Fang is "readable to those who like animal stories."
     Brief.

33   ANON. "Drama." Nation, 83 (6 December), 490.
       Scorn of Women offers more dialogue than action, "and
     the dramatic motive is chiefly conspicuous by its absence."
     The setting and incidents "freshly evoke the Yukon atmo-
     sphere and the piece is entertaining reading."

34   ANON. "Novelists and Cave-dwellers. Parallel Passages in the
     Stories by Stanley Waterloo and Jack London." Argonaut,
     59 (8 December), 285.
       There are similarities between The Story of Ab and Before
     Adam in the episodes of escape from the wild pigs and the
     hyena, in portrayal of "the man-animal," and elsewhere.
     London denied plagiarism, claiming he wrote Before Adam as
     a reply to the "unscientific" work of Waterloo. [This
     controversy received a great deal of press coverage, most
     supporting the plagiarism charge.]

35   BLAND, HENRY MEADE. "Jack London: Traveler, Novelist and
     Social Reformer." Craftsman, 9 (February), 607-19.
       Biography. London's complex personality was formed by
     the rough characters he met in his travels and by the
     natural beauties of California. He is a dreamer and social
     reformer, aware of the "profound tragedy of life" and
     fascinated by the evolutionary history of the race. He
     "came to dress the dead skeleton of scientific philosophy
     with all the finest colorings of Life" and found remedies
     for modern struggles, symbolized by the struggles of primi-
     tive men, in socialism. London's art has four qualities:
     realism, tragedy, the music of lyric poetry, and "suggestive-
     ness." He is "the ideal of strenuous Americanism," of spon-
     taneous individualism.

36   COOK, MAY ESTELLE. "Nature Books for the Holidays." Dial, 41
     (1 December), 389.
       White Fang ends happily; therefore its cruelty will be
     forgiven by the reader. London's understanding of animal
     psychology "seems almost uncanny."

37   COOL, UNA H. H. "Jack London's Play Makes an Unworthy Book."
     San Francisco Call (16 December), Magazine section, p. 5.
       London's "last foolishness," Scorn of Women, is "cheap,
     weak and poorly done. London would better stick to his
     last."

1906

38 COOPER, FREDERIC TABER. "The Note of Untruth and Some Recent Books: 'Moon-Face.'" Bookman (New York), 24 (November), 247.
  In London's work "the physical life lords it insolently over the spiritual and moral life." He is at his best when he writes frankly of man as "human animal."

39 FITCH, GEORGE HAMLIN. "A Batch of New Novels." San Francisco Chronicle, Sunday Supplement (11 November), p. 9.
  "London has never done better work than in the last half" of White Fang.

40 FLOWER, B. O. "Placing Jack London's Books Under the Ban." Arena, 35 (April), 435.
  The action of the Derby Neck library was "hasty and ill-considered."

41 HORWILL, HERBERT. "Present Day Tendencies in Fiction." Forum, 38 (September), 547-49.
  White Fang, a brilliant study in animal psychology, creates the impression of a "first-class popular scientific lecture." Dramatic power is confined to the chapters in which humans appear. London implies analogies between animals and humans in conditioning--to eat or be eaten-- and environmental pressures.

42 KERFOOT, J. B. "The Latest Books [Moon-Face and Other Stories]." Life, 48 (6 November), 544.
  "From a magazine standpoint they are Art. From a London standpoint they are potboilers." Brief.

43 _____. "The Latest Books [White Fang]." Life, 48 (22 November), 606.
  "A fascinating fiction." Brief favorable review.

44 LARKIN, EDGAR L. "Within a Literary Botanical Maze: A Day Filled with Wonderful and Fascinating Things--A Visit with Jack London and Luther Burbank." San Francisco Examiner (25 September), p. 16.
  Describes spending the night in London's den and exploring his workshop. [This reminiscence by Larkin appears in slightly revised form in several periodicals of 1906 and again in 1916.]

45 MOSS, MARY. "Notes on New Novels." Atlantic Monthly, 97 (January), 49.
  The Game is an attractive but too idyllic novelette. Brief.

JACK LONDON: A REFERENCE GUIDE

46   SANDBURG, CHARLES [CARL]. "Jack London: A Common Man." To-
        morrow, 2, no. 4 (April), 35–39.
            Gives biography. A remarkable "common man" who fights
        for the well-being of other common men and agitates against
        the system, London also writes masterpieces such as The
        Sea-Wolf and The Call of the Wild, the "greatest dog story
        ever written." "If he were not a Common Man, I would call
        him a Great Man." Reprinted: 1972.B30.

47   SINCLAIR, UPTON. "The Call of the Wild. Jack London Put an
        'If' on the Condemned Constitution." New York Times
        (5 February), p. 8.
            A letter to the editor. By omitting "qualifications,"
        the editorial [1906.B5] gives a wrong impression. In con-
        text, the red flag symbolizes "the Brotherhood of man" not
        war; Socialists are the "party of Constitutional agita-
        tion," they oppose "redistribution of wealth," and many of
        them are as courageous as London.

48   WILLIAMS, P. S. "Jack London, Lecturer." Overland Monthly,
        48 (October), 247–50.
            London is a popular unprofessional lecturer, who does
        not care for the work. He is "a ready, unpretentious
        talker, and has an engaging smile which quite captivates
        the ladies." Informally attired, he reminisces, reads his
        works, and occasionally expounds his socialism, which he
        takes very seriously.

1907 A BOOKS - NONE

1907 B SHORTER WRITINGS

1   ANON. "The Novels of the Season." American Monthly Review of
        Reviews, 35 (January), 128.
            White Fang is "ferociously picturesque." Brief.

2   ANON. "Recent Fiction and the Critics: White Fang." Current
        Literature, 42 (January), 111.
            He returns here to "a vein original and unique to him-
        self." Gives excerpts from critical reviews.

3   ANON. "Our Booking-Office [Moon-Face]." Punch, 132 (2 January),
        18.
            "Quite remarkably good" stories, resembling the popular
        themes of Kipling, Wells, and Poe. "I venture to commend
        him to magazine editors who are anxious to reduce their
        lists of contributors."

1907

4 ANON. "White Fang." Mother Earth, 1, no. 2 (February), 44-48.
Shares with The Call of the Wild the theme: "environment
is the principal thing, it wakens or puts to sleep whatever element of heredity responds to it. This is good
socialism." The novel shows "poverty of invention" and
excessive brutality. Offers detailed summary.

5 ANON. "Shorter Notices of Books: 'White Fang.'" TLS (8 February), section 6, p. 46.
Although "original and powerful in matter and treatment,"
the novel is weakened by emphasis on the law of tooth and
claws, by "precosities and affectations of diction," and
by vain attempts to imitate Kipling.

6 ANON. "New Novels: White Fang." Athenaeum, 4137 (9 February),
161.
"Full of interest, movement, and vivid description....
[but] packed full of absurdly precious idioms, literary
cliches, and pompous little mannerisms." London used to
write better.

7 ANON. "Novels: Moon-Face and Other Stories." Saturday Review
(London), 103 (9 February), 178.
Stories lack quality and imagination, are "tiresome imi-
tations." Brief.

8 ANON. "Novels: White Fang." Spectator, 98 (9 February), 219-20.
Description of the pursuit and brutal fighting is first-
rate; but the anthropomorphic psychology is less than convincing.

9 ANON. "Against Jack London." New York Times Saturday Review
of Books (23 February), 109.
Reports Egerton R. Young's charge of plagiarism. See
1907.B31.

10 ANON. "Moon Face." Catholic World, 84 (March), 833-34.
Tales "of varying interest and merit."

11 ANON. "Jack London's Idea of Primitive Man." New York Times
(9 March), 145.
Summarizes Before Adam. "A remarkable achievement,...
dumfounding" in concept. London has "builded a romance of
the unknown ages,...and endowed it with poignant reality."

12 ANON. "Some Good Novels of Early Spring: 'Before Adam.'"
San Francisco Chronicle, Sunday Supplement (10 March),
p. 9.

A vivid sketch, "thrilling as an episode of real life."
Brief.

13   ANON. "Literature: Evolutionary Fiction." Independent, 62
      (14 March), 620-21.
         Although "decidedly ingenious," Before Adam is "but
      another animal story" without imagination. It does not
      convince or interest a reader.

14   ANON. "Fiction: 'White Fang.'" Academy, 72 (16 March), 274.
         "There is quality in his work....from the immense pleasure
      which he takes in telling his tale. It is as apparent as
      his fluency, and is infectious....It is a capital story,
      marred a little by the brutality of detail" in the bulldog
      fight.

15   ANON. "Comment on Current Books." Outlook, 85 (23 March),
      718-19.
         Before Adam is "a sort of literary tour de force ably
      done and curiously fascinating."

16   ANON. "Prehistoric Romance." Bookman (New York), 25 (April),
      115-16.
         Resemblance of Before Adam to The Story of Ab is "glaringly
      obvious" although the works differ in "temperament." Lon-
      don's is "less a novel of human beings than of missing links."

17   ANON. "The Way of Letters: Jack London Again." Canadian Maga-
      zine, 28 (April), 614-15.
         Before Adam is a "work of the imagination that out-
      Darwins Darwin....The work is pretty well done" and enter-
      taining but not poetical as it might have been.

18   ANON. "A Guide to the New Books: London, Jack. Before Adam."
      Literary Digest, 34 (20 April), 639.
         London's "unbridled imagination" has created "a fairy-
      tale of science" and "the autobiography of a prehistoric
      baboon....the whole forming a narrative of surpassing in-
      terest for a boy of twelve."

19   ANON. "Literature and Art: An Attempt to 'Place' Jack London."
      Current Literature, 42 (May), 513-14.
         "He is one of the most widely read and widely discussed
      writers in America, and easily the foremost in importance
      among the writers of the West." Quotes Garnet, 1907.B41.

20   ANON. "Virtue and Consistency." Bookman (New York), 25 (May),
      228-31.

Before Adam is a dull, unconvincing "hybrid thing of human psychology and lower animal life which has been done before and done better." Tired of the matter of London's plagiarism, we print these articles: prints 1907.B13 (of 14 March) and another almost identical to it from an un-named source (dated 23 March).

21 ANON. "A Review of the Season's Fiction: Dual Personality." American Monthly Review of Reviews, 35 (June), 762.
 Brief summary of Before Adam.

22 ANON. "President Versus Nature Fakir. A Wordy War is Waged over the Accuracy of Animal Stories." Argonaut, 60 (8 June), 728.
 Theodore Roosevelt says London knows nothing about the fighting habits of wolves or lynxes (in White Fang). [Re-ports of this "nature-faking" controversy are widespread: for West Coast articles, see Bubka, 1968.A1.] See Clark, 1907.B34, 1907.B35; Roosevelt, 1907.B44, 1952.B5.

23 ANON. "New Stories of the Frozen North: Jack London's Volume Shows Human Passion at White Heat in the Arctic." New York Times Saturday Review of Books (5 October), p. 594.
 For those safely lodged at home "there is grim fascina-tion in the human tragedies" depicted in Love of Life. Analyzes "A Day's Lodging."

24 ANON. "Three Recent Plays: Scorn of Women." Spectator, 99 (5 October), 461.
 "His plays are as original as his novels, and of a simi-lar quality."

25 ANON. "Current Fiction: Love of Life by Jack London." Nation, 85 (17 October), 353.
 "The usual London thing: wolf-dogs and miners and Indians; starving and freezing and killing." Brief.

26 ANON. "Comment on Current Books." Outlook (26 October), 450.
 Love of Life offers "grim stories....unrelieved pictures of misery." Brief.

27 ANON. "London, Jack. Love of Life and Other Stories." ALA Booklist, 3 (November), 202.
 The stories are "all good, some of them of distinctive merit."

28 ANON. "A Guide to the New Books: London, Jack. Love of Life, and Other Stories." Literary Digest, 35 (2 November), 655.

London "has intensified his method of presenting a scene in simple, forceful language that makes one forget the telling and realize the vision with inward sight."

29   ANON. "Jack London on the Road." New York Times Saturday Review of Books (28 December), p. 861.
     The Road "is the sordid Odyssey of a hobo....written with Mr. London's usual command of clear, incisive English and powers of terse vivid description....the form is the form of realism, but the spirit of [sic] that of sentimentalism." London confuses the real tramp with "Nietzche's blonde beast."

30   ANON. Review of The Road. Argonaut, 61 (28 December), 433.
     "That a man of the author's unquestionable powers should lead such a despicable existence is strange enough. That he should tell his story with impertinent pride is still stranger." Brief.

31   BOSWORTH, L. A. M. and JACK LONDON. "Is Jack London a Plagiarist?" Independent, 62 (14 February), 373-76.
     Proves the "marked similarities between The Call of the Wild and Egerton R. Young's My Dogs in the Northland (1902) by comparing parallel passages. Prints London's reply to the charge.

32   BUCHANAN, AGNES FOSTER. "Story of a Famous Fraternity of Writers and Artists." Pacific Monthly, 17 (January), 65-83.
     London is a member of San Francisco's "Coppa Crowd." Gives biography.

33   CHENEY, SHELDON. "Some California Book-Plates." Sunset Magazine, 18 (February), 332-36.
     London's bookplate, the wolf's head with snowshoes and his name, was designed by E. J. Cross.

34   CLARK, EDWARD B. "Roosevelt on Nature Fakirs." Everybody's Magazine, 16 (June), 770-74.
     As an example of the "false natural history" being fostered as realism in fiction, Roosevelt said of the fight between White Fang and the bulldog: "Reading this, I can't believe that Mr. London knows much about the wolves, and I am certain that he knows nothing about their fighting, ...This thing is the very sublimity of absurdity," as is the lynx tearing to pieces the dog-wolf. See 1907.B22; 1907.B35; 1907.B44; 1952.B5.

1907

35 CLARK, EDWARD B. "Real Naturalists on Nature Faking." Every-
body's Magazine, 17 (September), 423-27.
A symposium of opinions sparked by Roosevelt's remarks
(London's name not mentioned).

36 COLBRON, GRACE ISABEL. "Six Books of the Month: Jack London's
'White Fang.'" Bookman (New York), 24 (February), 599-600.
In all his works, London pours out his "vivid, virile
personality." He is always alive and "delightfully the
same." This fascinating story is "full of blood and death,
rough, rugged strength, horror and beastliness, passing
glimpses of kindliness and love."

37 NO ENTRY.

38 COOPER, FREDERICK TABER. "The Novelty of Plot and Some Recent
Books: 'Before Adam.'" Bookman (New York), 25 (April),
183-84.
"It would be impossible to debase even the prehistoric
man any further and have him retain a vestige of humanity."
We wonder if the book "is not a romance of prehistoric
chimpanzees rather than our own progenitors."

39 CORYN, SIDNEY G. P. Review of Before Adam. Argonaut, 60
(23 March), 538.
Its "autobiographical basis" and farfetched premise are
weaknesses. It strikingly resembles The Story of Ab.

40 DUNN, ALLAN. "The Sailing of the Snark." Sunset Magazine, 19
(May), 3-9.
Describes the Snark and trip plans in detail.

41 GARNETT, PORTER. "Jack London--His Relation to Literary Art."
Pacific Monthly, 17 (April), 446-53.
London attains "felicity of expression" in The Kempton-
Wace Letters but elsewhere lacks subtlety and "charm," that
combination of nobility and beauty generated by "the aesthetic consciousness." London's usual style is compact,
forceful, masterful in vocabulary, pictorially vivid; but
he is strident as a "brass band," and given to hysterical
or histrionic ranting. The absence of "poetic quality" is
due to "an arrested development on the idealistic side of
his nature." He will be remembered "as a philosopher and
a propagandist rather than as a literary artist....His sincerity, his keen perception, his skill as a weaver of
tales, and his mastery of a vigorous idiom have given him
a high place among writers of his time, and America as well
as the West may well be proud of him."

42   KERFOOT, J. B. "The Latest Books." Life, 49 (4 April), 490.
         Before Adam is an "ingenious tale" with interesting
      "psychological suggestions." Brief.

43   MARCHAND, J. "Jack London's 'Love of Life.'" Bookman (New
      York), 26 (December), 419.
         The stories are characteristic of London's work in theme,
      style, and characterization, with the good points of
      "strength, aliveness, vividness of colouring." "A Day's
      Lodging" is "admirable as a bit of soul-painting."

44   ROOSEVELT, THEODORE. "Nature Fakers." Everybody's Magazine,
      17 (September), 427-30.
         Amplifies his comments on "reckless untruth" in nature
      writing. Under "Story-Book Beasts," mentions London's
      lynx and wolf. See 1907.B22; 1907.B34; 1907.B35; 1952.B5.

45   SMITH, HARRY JAMES. "Some Recent Novels." Atlantic Monthly,
      100 (July), 125-26.
         Before Adam "occasionally stirs our curiosity" and admi-
      ration for London's ingenuity, but it never gains our
      sympathy. Like dozens of other novels, it stresses "ma-
      teriality"; London divests "humanity of its human attri-
      butes," of spirituality and personality, in an inversion
      of the romantic.

1908 A BOOKS

  1   ANON. Jack London: Who He Is and What He Has Done. New York:
      Macmillan, 16 pp.
         Cover title of the pamphlet is Jack London: His Life and
      Literary Work; the essay itself, pp. 5-16, is titled,
      "Jack London, A Sketch of His Life and Work." Biography
      and criticism. Revised and enlarged text of 1905.A1. Re-
      printed: 1972.A1.

1908 B SHORTER WRITINGS

  1   ANON. "Books: Jack London's 'Love of Life.'" Sunset Magazine,
      20 (January), 299.
         London seems convinced that strength lies in "coarse and
      cruel" language and subjects. These stories will "make a
      direct appeal" only to "readers of the grotesque, the
      horrible and the utterly dispiriting."

  2   ANON. "Literature: Love of Life." Independent, 64 (9 January),
      104-105.

London has the distinctively "monstrous mind" and a "savage genius" at home in the Arctic where life is an agonizing battle to the death.

3   ANON. "The Way of Letters: Experiences of a Real Hobo." Canadian Magazine, 30 (February), 386-87.
The Road generates sympathy for hoboes through London's "graphic and entertaining" description of his experiences.

4   ANON. "Literature: The Road." Independent, 64 (20 February), 421.
There is some doubt about London's sincerity and accuracy, but the book is interesting.

5   ANON. "Current Fiction." Nation, 86 (19 March), 264.
"We have little more regard for him as a man of letters than for his 'comrade' in Socialism, Mr. Sinclair; but [The Iron Heel]...is interesting as a sign of the times." Being "a trifle bloodthirsty," London invites us to wallow through three hundred years of gore.

6   ANON. "Books of the Day: The Iron Heel." Arena, 39 (April), 503-506.
"From a literary and imaginative point-of-view, [it] is one of his greatest works of fiction." However, his hopelessness and pessimistic view of the poor "make his book a detriment rather than a help to the cause of social justice in our day."

7   ANON. "Short Stories: Love of Life, and Other Stories." Athenaeum, 4198 (11 April), 448.
They exhibit the "savage intensity" of his imagination and grip the reader.

8   ANON. "Literature: Socialistic Storm and Sunshine." Independent, 64 (16 April), 865.
"Jack London is a boy bucaneer....so obsessed with a mania for blood and battle, that he reduces his own argument to absurdity" in The Iron Heel.

9   ANON. "Recent Fiction and the Critics: The Iron Heel." Current Literature, 44 (May), 570-71.
London "dips his pen in blood" for this dynamic socialist tract. Gives excerpts from reviews.

10   ANON. "The Way of Letters: A Socialistic Bloodcurdler." Canadian Magazine, 31 (May), 91.
The Iron Heel "is entirely problematical and conjectural, ...[but it] contains food for contemplation."

11   ANON. "New Novels: Before Adam." Athenaeum, 4204 (23 May),
        633-34.
        London's astonishing recreation of an imaginary past is
        not eclipsed by Kipling or Wells. Its "vividness and
        verisimilitude" are so strong that "a modern man winces"
        reading it.

12   ANON. "A Review of the Season's Fiction: Some American Novels
        of Note." American Review of Reviews, 37 (June), 760.
        Brief note on The Iron Heel.

13   ANON. "Our Booking-Office [Before Adam]." Punch, 134 (3 June),
        414.
        London's theory of racial memory is more interesting than
        this "very plain (and short) tale from the tree-tops. Mr.
        London gets fewer words on to a page than anybody I know.
        His ancestor must have been an economist with the nuts."

14   ANON. "Notices of Books." Publishers' Circular, 88 (13 June),
        773.
        In Before Adam, London's "almost cruel powers of descrip-
        tion are used with great forcefulness." Brief.

15   ANON. "Comment on Current Books." Outlook, 89 (20 June), 388.
        The Iron Heel is "not a pleasant book to read; as a work
        of fiction it has little to commend it; and as a Socialist
        tract it is distinctly unconvincing." Brief.

16   ANON. "Novels: Before Adam." Saturday Review (London), 105
        (20 June), 793-94.
        There is little pleasure in this story, resembling
        Hobbes in its theme. Brief.

17   ANON. "Fiction: Before Adam." Academy, 74 (27 June), 934.
        London "has told a somewhat difficult story with a con-
        siderable amount of vigour...[without] violating the proba-
        bilities. He has also compassed the original feat of
        writing a novel without dialogue."

18   ANON. "A New Novel by Jack London." Overland Monthly, 52
        (July), 89.
        We cannot agree with London's prophecy of bloodshed in
        The Iron Heel. His "strong, virile style" is admirable.

19   ANON. "Jack London's Great Novel, 'Martin Eden': Editorial
        Announcement." Pacific Monthly, 20 (August), 145-50.
        London knows how "to achieve the great end of the finest
        art in literary creation....viz: to stir the emotions; and

he has written nothing that stirs them so profoundly" as this "epic." It will inspire and encourage those who battle fate for self-fulfillment. Gives excerpts and biography. [Martin Eden is serialized here, beginning in September.]

20 ANON. "Novels: Love of Life." Saturday Review (London), 106 (1 August), 149-50.
The tales are "readable and interesting" because of the wild Arctic setting and London's direct, picturesque style.

21 ANON. "Chronicle and Comment: Jack London at Sea." Bookman (New York), 28 (September), 5.
"While the socialists are gloating over the grewsome [sic] picture of the impending social struggle...in The Iron Heel, and the powers that be are fixing his status once for all in the class of undesirable citizens, the irresponsible London" calmly cruises the South Seas.

22 ANON. "Before Adam." Bookman (London), 35 (October), 57.
London recreates "a crude and naked world" of primitive people "and tells their tale daringly, graphically, and with a subtle narrative skill."

23 ANON. "Christmas Reading: The Iron Heel." Athenaeum, 4233 (12 December), 757-58.
"As a forecast of the possibilities of the future it is sufficiently harrowing....we commend the book to all who are troubled by the present inequalities of opportunity, work, and recompense for it." Brief.

24 ANON. "Notices of Books." Publishers' Circular, 89 (12 December), 838.
Portrayal of the struggle in The Iron Heel is "ruthless and terrible," well-documented with facts, and earnest. It is a book "to be reckoned with." Brief.

25 BIERCE, AMBROSE. "Small Contributions." Cosmopolitan, 45 (July), 220.
Notes "Colonel" London's "accuracy and moderation" in describing the mob riot in The Iron Heel. After this "cheerful incident" and three centuries of controversy, the Brotherhood of Man arrives with "its gallant author in receipt of a comfortable pension."

26 COOL, UNA H. H. "'The Road.'" San Francisco Sunday Call Magazine Section (9 February), p. 6.
It destroys the "picturesqueness...in the tramp's life.

It reveals the hobo as a dirty, lying, stealing, conscience-less wretch intent only on avoiding work and keeping his stomach filled at the expense of anyone, however poor, who will feed him." London was this "burly tramp," beggar, and criminal, stealing from "helpless people," along with the rest of the "contemptible, vermin infested brutes." My disillusionment is complete.

27 _____. "'The Iron Heel.'" San Francisco Sunday Call Magazine Section (5 April), p. 6.
"Seriously considered as a sociological study...[it is] pernicious, incendiary, and nearly anarchistic. Otherwise it may seem even amusing." London "poses as the fanatic preaching the gospel of discontent and hatred"; he takes us through "a sea of blood" and fails to convince us that socialism will indeed be realized. The book has "literary excellence."

28 CORYN, SIDNEY G. P. "New and Notable Novels: The Iron Heel." Argonaut, 62 (18 April), 256.
In "the mantle of the prophet and under a thin veil of weak romance," London writes this terrible book "that could anaesthetize the average anarchist in half an hour." Everhard is an "intolerable maniac" and a "tiresome wind-bag."

29 HALE, EDWARD E., JR. "The Hobo in Theory and Practice." Dial, 44 (16 May), 301-302.
The Road combines "very considerable knowledge" of tramp life with the "obvious unreliability" of autobiography from one who admits he frequently "lied for his own advantage." The qualities of London and his fellow hoboes seem entirely "vicious," self-seeking and greedy.

30 PAYNE, WILLIAM MORTON. "Recent Fiction." Dial, 44 (16 April), 247.
The Iron Heel is a dull and unimaginative tract. Since it and Sinclair's The Metropolis "have a mischievous in-fluence upon unbalanced minds,...fomenting social dis-sension and arraying class against class," they deserve "the severest condemnation."

31 RICH, AMY C. "Books of the Day: The Road." Arena, 39 (January), 124.
It is not pleasant reading but it carries "a tremendous lesson" and will help the "social revolution" for human rights.

1909

1909 A BOOKS - NONE

1909 B SHORTER WRITINGS

1   ANON. "Novels: The Iron Heel." Saturday Review (London), 107
     (23 January), 114.
          "The interest of the book lies in its analysis of current
     political and social conditions in the United States." The
     triumph of the oligarchy is unconvincing. Brief.

2   ANON. "Bernard Shaw in Fact and Fiction: London's New Book."
     San Francisco Bulletin (9 October), p. 16.
          Martin Eden is a pretty poor book. It ranges from
     "vociferous" to overly romantic, it too lavishly praises
     Martin and builds him into a Nietzschean superman, it shows
     poor taste in portraying still-living people, and it goes
     "to woeful length" about Martin's writing problems. "Some
     of London's descriptions show flashes of genius as of old.
     It is unfortunate that he had not inspiration enough to
     leave a few flashes of silence between."

3   ANON. "The New Books." Outlook, 93 (16 October), 361.
     Martin Eden is "tedious."

4   ANON. "A Self-Made Author." New York Times Autumn Book Number,
     Part I (22 October), p. 631.
          Martin's melodramatic suicide leaves the reader dry-
     eyed. London is "quite at sea" when he writes about
     ordinary respectable society. "If you don't like the
     rules of society, don't play the game."

5   ANON. "Current Fiction: Martin Eden." Nation, 89 (28 October),
     406-407.
          Readers will recognize the autobiographical elements and
     may be "stirred piquantly by its daring adumbrations of
     various well-known proper names. But nothing actionable!"
     Gives plot summary.

6   ANON. "Literature: Martin Eden." Independent, 67 (28 October),
     980-82.
          Martin, devoted to the doctrines of survival of the fit-
     test and Nietzschean supremacy of the strong, remains a
     selfish egoist despite his "Promethean struggle" to become
     an educated man. He earns no sympathy from the reader.
     We respect London for arguing against his own beliefs and
     showing their failure. "Few saints, bourgeois or other-
     wise, could have accomplished it."

7   ANON. "Notes: Reviews." Craftsman, 17 (November), 232.

Martin Eden is a significant book which returns to London's earlier direct and vigorous style. Brief.

8   ANON. "London, Jack. Martin Eden." ALA Booklist, 6 (December), 92.
    "Reminiscent of the author's own experiences and voices his individualistic creed."

9   ANON. "Recent Fiction and the Critics." Current Literature, 47 (December), 695-96.
    Martin Eden is an autobiographical "sensational novel" whose ending is overly pessimistic. Gives plot summary and excerpts from reviews.

10 BOYNTON, H. W. "Recent American Fiction." New York Times Autumn Book Number, Part II (23 October), p. 648.
    Martin Eden is "likely to create the most stir" this season because of its autobiographical content. London's sharp, contemptuous criticism of editors and the public "steers close to the actionable. It is not a very sane or well-balanced book, but there is much wholesome truth in it."

11 COOL, UNA H. H. "Martin Eden. Jack London's New Novel." San Francisco Sunday Call Magazine Section (5 December), p. [7].
    It is "the best work from a literary point of view" that London has done. All London's theories are put into the mouth of the hero, whose transformation is rather incredible, as is his attraction for Ruth. This heroine, "small mentally, morally, physically," will interest men readers but be disbelieved by women. The ending of the novel is "inartistic and unnecessary."

12 COOPER, FREDERIC TABER. "Primordialism and Some Recent Books: Martin Eden." Bookman (New York), 30 (November), 278-80.
    London is "out of his element" when he portrays higher types of humanity and the delicate workings of heart or brain. Despite good graphic descriptions of the sordid life, "there is much that is unspeakably bad" here: "grotesque exaggeration of Martin's difficulties with his publishers; his snarling rebellion against the slowness of his progress,...[and] the complete fiasco" in the portrait of Ruth Morse.

13 HARRIS, FRANK. "How Mr. Jack London Writes a Novel." Vanity Fair, 82 (14 April), 454.
    Accuses London of taking the idea and "almost every word" for Bishop Morehouse's speech in The Iron Heel from Harris's

1909

"The Bishop of London and Public Morality" (1901). Gives comparative extracts. [This controversy is widely reported in Bay Area newspapers; see Bubka, 1968.A1.] See 1909.B14; 1909.B15.

14 _____. "Mr. Jack London: Knave or Fool. Or Knave and Fool?" Vanity Fair, 83 (28 July), 102-103.
        Prints London's reply to charges in 1909.B13. Reiterates charge, points out London's "extraordinary stupidity," and asks to be paid for the pages stolen, "at the very least a sixtieth of what he [London] got" for The Iron Heel. Demands London send him the article he claims to have taken seriously as a news story. See 1909.B13; 1909.B15.

15 _____. "Mr. Jack London Again." Vanity Fair, 83 (27 October), 519-20.
        Prints London's response to 1909.B14. Harris accepts the source article (from The Socialist Voice) but insists London "is content to profit by his own blundering misuse of other men's work....That Mr. Jack London was deceived hardly affects the ethics or the aesthetics of the question." Besides, he has not paid for the use of the material. Harris will forgive London if he stops writing books like The Iron Heel and returns to his better "first-hand experiences of life." See 1909.B13; 1909.B14.

16 MARKHAM, EDWIN. "Bookland: Reviews and Notes." San Francisco Examiner (25 December), p. 10.
        Martin Eden is London's "best novel--his story richest in the wisdom of the heart." The style is vigorous and splendid. Martin's life "is a little epic of noble purpose and possibility."

17 M., M. "Jack London." The Lone Hand (Australia) (1 February), pp. 366-71.
        An interview in Australia. London was "American" in all of his actions, a splendid arguer "on every subject that appeals to man," and an eloquent non-stop talker. Quotes at length from London's autobiographical essays.

18 PAYNE, WILLIAM MORTON. "Recent Fiction." Dial, 47 (16 November), 386.
        "It is just as well" that Martin Eden drops out of the porthole. London fails to "invest his hero with the attributes that awaken sympathy"; rather, Martin's "turbulent egotism" and "defiance of the collective wisdom of mankind" keep the reader from mourning his death. Luckily, he "is not to live and make miserable the heroine" who is

"far more worth while than the man who has outgrown her in his own conceit."

19   "VALDON." "Our Artistic Workers: Mr. Jack London." The Australian Photographic Journal (20 March), pp. 70–74.
         An interview with London at the Hotel Australia, c. February-March.

1910 A BOOKS - NONE

1910 B SHORTER WRITINGS

1   ANON. "A Guide to the New Books: London, Jack. Martin Eden." Literary Digest, 40 (22 January), 155.
         An autobiographical novel, passionate in convictions. "He touches the rock bottom of human experience which he describes in vivid, picturesque word-painting."

2   ANON. "London, Jack. Lost Face." ALA Booklist, 6 (April), 303.
         "Seven vigorous, clean-cut stories."

3   ANON. Review of Lost Face. New York Times Saturday Review of Books (2 April), p. 183.
         Unforgettable, although not enjoyable tales which emphasize the savage rather than the noble in man.

4   ANON. "Current Fiction: Lost Face." Nation, 90 (21 April), 403.
         "If we no longer go to public hangings, we need not feel the deprivation acutely." Brutality, torture and horror are a staple of popular fiction, and London is a master of this school. He "seems to us the victim of a disease of the fancy."

5   ANON. "Literature [Lost Face]." Independent, 68 (5 May), 986-87.
         Stories "in which suspense and physical agony play a large part,...Mr. London's genius lies in canine psychology." Brief.

6   ANON. "Jack London, Revolutionist." New York Times Saturday Review of Books (28 May), p. 302.
         Revolution and Other Essays combines "destructive criticism,...muscular literary style....with a habit of reckless and inflammatory assertion, of wholly unproved and untrue statement." The book "is well worth reading" as entertainment alone, not as serious economics.

1910

7 ANON. "Briefs on New Books." <u>Dial</u>, 49 (1 July), 17.
   In <u>Revolution and Other Essays</u> London "does a service in
   calling renewed attention, in language idiomatically forceful, to some of the defects and injustices of the existing
   social order."

8 ANON. "New Novels: Mr. Jack London's Novel." <u>Manchester</u>
   <u>Guardian</u> (England) (13 July), p. 5.
   <u>Martin Eden</u> is "a rough-hewn piece of work, but it has
   power and a large measure of sincerity." "Violence and
   excess" in diction and improbable characters and conclusion
   mar the novel.

9 ANON. "Fiction: 'Martin Eden.'" <u>TLS</u> (14 July), pp. 253-54.
   A "moving, a passionate, and evidently a sincere book"
   despite its clumsy language, "straining after effect,"
   excessive introspection, and Martin's incredible infatua-
   tion with the "pale prig of a girl."

10 ANON. "New Novels: Martin Eden." <u>Athenaeum</u>, 4317 (23 July),
   93.
   "The tale is vigorous, exhilarating and arresting." The
   hero's rapid growth and suicidal end are improbable.

11 ANON. "Notices of Books." <u>Publishers' Circular</u>, 93 (13 August),
   199.
   <u>Martin Eden</u> is a "powerful and brilliant study," with
   one jarring note: the paltriness of the heroine. "One
   hesitates to apply the word <u>great</u> to any modern novel, and
   yet it is the only one that sums up our impression of this
   book."

12 ANON. "London, Jack. <u>Revolution, and Other Essays</u>." <u>ALA</u>
   <u>Booklist</u>, 7 (September), 22.
   Not as valuable as his fiction, but written in his "most
   robust and assertive style."

13 ANON. "Our Booking-Office [<u>Martin Eden</u>]." <u>Punch</u>, 139 (14 September), 198.
   He applies the "whip of scorn" unsparingly to newspaper
   men and tells Martin's struggles with strong realism.
   Since Martin drowns himself at the end, one wonders why
   London didn't simply write a "scathing satire" on contemporary culture instead of the novel.

14 ANON. "Novels: Martin Eden." <u>Saturday Review</u> (London), 110
   (22 October), 522.
   Unevenly written, but with some brilliantly expressionistic

scenes, the novel incisively preaches against "the tendency of America to hold 'making good' the summum bonum." The "revelation of American types of society is cunningly revolting."

15   ANON. "Burning Daylight." New York Times Saturday Review of Books (5 November), p. 522.
        It is untrue to life in the homes or cities of ordinary Americans. "The present yarn, with its claptrap title and its maudlin mixture of false sentiment, tawdry heroics and abysmal ignorance of conventional ways" proves that London writes better about dogs than about men and women. "It is in short, Twaddle with the T sharp."

16   ANON. "Current Fiction: Burning Daylight." Nation, 9 (10 November), 443-44.
        Daylight's act seems "inevitable and suitable....this is by all odds the most interesting, as well as the most wholesome long story Mr. London has written." Gives plot summary.

17   ANON. "Notable Books of the Year [Burning Daylight]." Independent, 69 (17 November), 1091-92.
        It shows progress that London and his heroes now prefer the "good woman" to the mate-woman. And "if he grows in grace," he may yet offer "a proper moral man for a hero... [in a] great piece of fiction."

18   COLBRON, GRACE ISABEL. "The Eternal Masculine." Bookman (New York), 32 (10 October), 157-59.
        London leads the newly developing "masculine school in fiction" which truthfully and strongly portrays contemporary conflicts in "straight out from the shoulder" style. In Burning Daylight he achieves "objectiveness" and success as a storyteller of this new type. For response to Colbron, see 1911.B1.

19   CONNERS, MOLLIE. "Around the Literary Table: London's Essays." Oakland Tribune (1 May), p. 8.
        Revolution and Other Essays "carries to the world in general many a message from California." A "charming study" is "The Golden Poppy." Quotes from this essay.

20   COOL, UNA H. H. "'Revolution.'" San Francisco Sunday Call Magazine Section (5 June), p. [7].
        "By none of the recognized tenets of literary tradition" can this book be called essays. The pieces range from vindictive to silly to the egocentric. "They are boyish

and unbalanced frequently and lack literary finish, but they reflect a personality more interesting than shown in any of his previous work." Gives excerpts and discusses a few.

21 _____. "'Burning Daylight.'" San Francisco Sunday Call Magazine Section (18 December), p. [7].
Daylight is London's typical "barbarian [who] is perfect physically and can do everything just a little better than his comrades." Dede Mason is the best woman London has created, "a real human being and everything she does is meritable--except the scorning of the thirty millions." This is London's "most sympathetic work."

22 CORYN, SIDNEY G. P. "Books and Authors: Martin Eden." Argonaut, 66 (15 January), 40.
A real novel, with traditional structure and a forward-moving plot. London describes Martin's efforts "with imagination, pathos, and force." Flaws in the novel include its autobiographical intent and the author's self-pitying and egotistical recriminations against editors.

23 FITCH, GEORGE HAMLIN. "'An Admiral's Log,' and Other Books." San Francisco Chronicle, Sunday Magazine (20 March), p. 6.
The stories of Lost Face have graphic power and force charged with the "fierce struggle for life."

24 IRVINE, ALEXANDER. From the Bottom Up: The Life Story of Alexander Irvine. New York: Doubleday Page, pp. 250-55.
Recounts arrangements for London's talk at Yale (1905). Revised text of 1906.A1.

25 KERFOOT, J. B. "The Latest Books." Life, 55 (21 April), 728.
When we measure our response to the stories in Lost Face against our response to London's 1901-1902 volumes, we less readily "accept gratuitous brutality as strength." Brief.

26 MARTIN, JOHN. "Books on Social Ills [Revolution and Other Essays]." Survey, 24 (10 September), 830.
"London, with a primitive energy developed in the wilderness, rages over the oppression of the poor...in a manner immature, almost boyish." Brief.

27 PAYNE, WILLIAM MORTON. "Recent Fiction." Dial, 49 (16 November), 384.
Burning Daylight "is deliciously and glaringly absurd, and done in the crudest of colors, but it has the merits

of swift action and forcible expression, and is, on the
whole, rather better work than the author has been giving
us of late."

1911 A BOOKS - NONE

1911 B SHORTER WRITINGS

1   ANON. "Recent Fiction and the Critics: Burning Daylight."
     Current Literature, 50 (February), 224.
          "The fact that Jack London worships brute strength as an
     end of itself is essentially a feminine characteristic."
     A response to Colbron, 1910.B18.

2   ANON. "Jack London's Latest Collection of Stories Dealing with
     the Primitive Passions." New York Times Review of Books
     (19 February), p. 88.
          When God Laughs succeeds "in almost exact proportion to
     the native horror of the raw material" which London handles
     to produce a "hot choking sensation in the gorge." He shows
     skill and strength here that was utterly lacking in the
     novels. "He should stick to his last."

3   ANON. "When God Laughs." Nation, 92 (23 February), 194.
          "Crude energy and the unblinking record of harsh or even
     brutal fact are the earmarks of this writer." Only "The
     Apostate" strikes a true note which we wish he would repeat.

4   ANON. "New Novels: Adventure." Athenaeum, 4351 (18 March),
     300.
          A "brisk, and bright and individual" story with a "stark,
     virile" hero. The "feminine element" seems out of place.

5   ANON. "Reviews of New Books: [When God Laughs]." San Fran-
     cisco Bulletin (25 March), p. 9.
          The best of them are "The Apostate," "Just Meat," and
     "A Piece of Steak." Describes these stories.

6   ANON. "Seven Plays by Americans." New York Times Review of
     Books (26 March), p. 169.
          Theft is London "at his worst." Sensationalism prevails,
     "dialogue and incidents are crudely framed" and stage
     directions "amateurishly complex."

7   ANON. "Current Fiction: Adventure." Nation, 92 (30 March),
     318.
          A novel "frankly in the realm of the agreeably

1911

preposterous....Gory details are not lacking," but it is
"a milder type of romance" than London's usual.

8   ANON. "Theft: Jack London's Latest Attempt." Dramatist, 2
     (April), 156-57.
          London violates every principle of play construction.
     "The whole book is a confusion of episode, atmosphere and
     prattle."

9   ANON. "The Theory of Heroes and Some Recent Novels: 'When God
     Laughs.'" Bookman (New York), 33 (April), 195.
          "Just Meat" and "The Chinago" are unforgettable; the rest
     are not.

10   ANON. Review of Adventure. Argonaut, 68 (1 April), 201.
          London depicts the heroine as a perfectly efficient man.
     His women "are either Amazons or they are silly." This is
     "a fascinating story" with "ethnological value."

11   ANON. "Jack London's 'Adventure'; A Good Story if Judged by
     Distinctively populaar [sic] and Unliterary Standards."
     New York Times Review of Books (2 April), p. 185.
          London's talent lies with short stories; he "declines
     to a very rude apprentice when he tries to enlarge his
     canvas to novel size." This heroine is a figure out of
     melodrama, and the whole is of popular magazine quality.

12   ANON. "Novels: Adventure." Spectator, 106 (15 April), 569.
          Mentioned.

13   ANON. "London, Jack. Adventure." ALA Booklist, 7 (1 May),
     397.
          "A conventional tale of adventure set against well
     handled and new scenery."

14   ANON. "Novel Notes [Adventure]." Bookman (London), 40 (June),
     143-44.
          London holds the idea "that women are the real rulers of
     the world, and Joan is far and away the 'best man'" in
     this enjoyable book.

15   ANON. "Some of the Season's Best Fiction." American Review
     of Reviews, 43 (June), 758.
          Adventure is milder and less didactic than London's
     usual work. Brief.

16   ANON. "New Novels: Burning Daylight." Athenaeum, 4363
     (10 June), 653.

The hero is "an extravagant creation." The novel is picturesque and not quite convincing, but it will confirm London's rank "as the most forceful writer of fiction in his country."

17 ANON. "Notices of Books." Publishers' Circular, 94 (10 June), 884.
    A larger-than-life hero "moves through the world like an elemental force, and the reader loves him." Burning Daylight is another "noble and inspiring" work of London's.

18 ANON. "Our Booking-Office [Burning Daylight]." Punch, 140 (21 June), 489.
    With excellent points: a "super-being" hero, a Klondike setting, and fine descriptive writing, "the book remains one that is quite worth anybody's while to read for himself. Yes Sirs! Every time!"

19 ANON. "The Animal Story." Edinburgh Review, 214 (July), 108-11.
    The Call of the Wild and White Fang reassert the forgotten power of the wilderness, its immensities, solitudes, and elemental forces which call men back to their primordial being.

20 ANON. "The New Books." Outlook, 98 (8 July), 552-53.
    The Cruise of the Snark is an "animated...interesting and unusual" narrative.

21 ANON. "Literary Notes." Independent, 71 (13 July), 100.
    Mentions The Cruise of the Snark.

22 ANON. "Briefs on New Books." Dial, 51 (16 July), 54.
    The Cruise of the Snark is well-told with an "abundance of sufficiently unusual adventure."

23 ANON. "Jack London's Correspondents." Bookman (New York), 33 (August), 567-69.
    Describes application for a berth on the Snark.

24 ANON. "The Cruise of the Snark." Nation, 93 (17 August), 146.
    It does not communicate the joyfulness of the voyage that London claims for it. Gives summary.

25 ANON. "London, Jack. The Cruise of the Snark." ALA Booklist, 8 (September), 23.
    The "style is animated," but the chapters "are disconnected and lack unity."

1911

26 ANON. "Pacific Personalities: A Creator of Pacific Literature."
    Mid-Pacific Magazine, 2 (September), 291.
    Biography of London.

*27 ANON. "Jack London Can Gloat over His Enemies: Author Gets His
    Revenge on Timothy Muldowney and Judge Samuels." San Fran-
    cisco Examiner (15 October), p. 79.
    London makes them villains in his story "The Benefit of
    a Doubt." Cited in Bubka, 1968.A1.

28 ANON. "Fiction." Academy and Literature, 81 (28 October),
    539.
    Although Burning Daylight is "probably the best he has
    written," it shows "that absence of sense of proportion
    and idea of perspective" common to all American writing.
    The book has value as a description of life in the North,
    "as a convincing criticism of American finance," and for
    London's "literary skill, the intellectual conviction, the
    breadth of vision."

29 ANON. "London, Jack. South Sea Tales." ALA Booklist, 8 (De-
    cember), 174.
    Stories "full of dramatically told, but not always con-
    vincing nor pleasant adventure."

30 ANON. "Fiction for the Fireside Season." New York Times Re-
    view of Books (31 December), p. 860.
    South Sea Tales are all "virile and none of them vicious."
    The human good and bad are exposed with a directness "that
    is positively uplifting."

31 COOL, UNA H. H. "'Theft.'" San Francisco Sunday Call Magazine
    Section (1 January), p. [7].
    London's "rampage" of reformism in four acts offers im-
    possibly vulgar and exaggerated characters among its vil-
    lains and only one honest man, who is a fool. "The grand
    climax will draw a laugh from the reader if he is not too
    disgusted to finish it....It's a pretty little play."

32 _____. "'The Cruise of the Snark.'" San Francisco Sunday Call
    Magazine Section (23 July), p. [7].
    London tells the story to "bring out the excitement of
    the cruise, its fun and exhilaration, as well as its mo-
    ments and days of breathless danger." Quotes sections.

1912 A BOOKS - NONE

1912 B SHORTER WRITINGS

1 ANON. "Jack London's Stories." New York Times Review of Books (21 April), p. 248.
   In The House of Pride London shows both the "gruesome" and "romantic" aspects of leprosy, and the "essential elements in Hawaiian life." In the form of a novel these scattered and unrelated incidents would have made a deeper impression.

2 ANON. "Literary Notes." Independent, 72 (23 May), 1120.
   Tales in The House of Pride are "too fragmentary." Brief.

3 ANON. "London, Jack. The House of Pride, and Other Tales of Hawaii." ALA Booklist, 8 (June), 411.
   In most stories, "effective but somewhat hackneyed use is made of the tragic literary possibilities of leprosy."

4 ANON. "Picked Fruit: A Study in Current Fiction." American Review of Reviews, 45 (June), 761.
   Mentions The House of Pride.

5 ANON. "Literature: A Son of the Sun." Independent, 72 (6 June), 1277.
   London has a painter's eye for color contrast but "a taste more savage than refined....those who have so far been unimprest [sic] by his genius will probably yawn over this installment of sudden death and startling language."

6 ANON. "London, Jack. A Son of the Sun." ALA Booklist, 9 (September), 37.
   "They are adventurous and full of local color."

7 ANON. "The Barbarian in Jack London." Literary Digest, 45 (5 October), 564.
   Excerpts from Buck, 1912.B13.

8 ANON. "The New Books: Smoke Bellew." Outlook, 102 (12 October), 320.
   Readers will be attracted to the strong story-telling. Brief.

9 ANON. "Smoke Bellew." New York Times Review of Books (20 October), p. 612.
   "Mr. London is like Robert Louis Stevenson, inasmuch as women aren't particularly in his literary line....[but] when he does write about women he does it stirringly."

1912

10 ANON. "Short Stories: South Sea Tales." Athenaeum, 4441
(7 December), 690.
A chronicle of excessive violence, brutality, death, and
horrors.

11 BASHFORD, HERBERT. "South Sea Tales: Jack London's Latest
Volume of Splendid Stories." San Francisco Bulletin
(13 January), p. 14.
"Tense and virile" stories, each bearing the "unmistakable
London touch which is so strongly individual as to defy
imitation." Describes some tales.

12 _____. "'Smoke Bellew.'" San Francisco Bulletin (5 October),
p. 19.
London likes to take "city-bred youths into the frozen
north" where they bring out their manly qualities. He is
at his best depicting "scenes of strife and such heart-
breaking struggles against the inevitable....[This] is a
story pulsing with life." Describes tales.

13 BUCK, PHILO M., JR. "The American Barbarian." Methodist Review, 28 (September), 714-24.
London's fictional heroes are Barbarians, as defined by
Matthew Arnold and popularized, in more genial form, by
Kipling. Resembling our Teutonic ancestors, these indi-
vidualistic, primitive supermen combat nature that is "all
crude, mysterious, harsh, full of primeval unrest, force,
and elemental rage," unsoftened by civilization. They
cherish only physical and external virtues, gamble at life,
play the game of war against nature with some success but
fail when they assert their individualism against "a set-
tled social order." Martin Eden and Elam Harnish lose
faith in mankind, then in themselves, and they cease to be
men because they lack "true culture": knowledge of self
and the world, and the power "'to see life steadily and to
see it whole'" in order to actively make culture prevail
for others. London's stories stimulate Americans' virtues,
but to excess: "our love of the strenuous life, our generosity, our courage, our coolness;...also our worst vices--
our thoughtless, reckless, inconsequential energy, our
love of blind conflict, our man and institution-baiting,
our love of change, our caprice, our so-called reform and
progressiveness." Because of all this, London "is probably
the most popular author in America to-day. But it is also
because he lacks true culture" that he fails to achieve
greatness. Excerpted in 1912.B7; reprinted: 1961.A1.

14 COOL, UNA H. H. "'The House of Pride.'" <u>San Francisco Sunday Call Magazine Section</u> (5 May), p. [7].
    One of London's best books, showing his deep knowledge and understanding of Hawaii. The title story is first-rate, clever and artistic. Gives excerpts.

15 E.[DGETT], E.[DWIN] F.[RANCIS]. "Of Many Novels." <u>Boston Evening Transcript</u> (23 October), p. 24.
    <u>Smoke Bellew</u> lacks the originality and sincerity of previous works. Brief.

16 GARNETT, PORTER. "Adventures of a Meat Eater ('Smoke Bellew,' by Jack London)." <u>San Francisco Sunday Call Magazine Section</u> (13 October), p. [7].
    This is not a novel but "a series of adventurous incidents" all told "graphically and with a rugged humanism and rough humor." The hero does not "emerge as a personality"; the book seems an entertaining "journal of an explorer." Gives details of stories.

17 [JAMES, GEORGE WHARTON]. Review of <u>When God Laughs</u>. <u>Out West</u>, NS 3 (February), 144-45.
    Brief favorable review.

18 _____. Review of <u>A Son of the Sun</u>. <u>Out West</u>, NS 4 (September), 211.
    London's "wonderful powers of perception, absorption and imagination" are best shown in these powerful stories, "the most vivid conceptions of the South Seas that have ever been written."

19 JAMES, GEORGE WHARTON. "Jack London: Cub of the Slums, Hero of Adventure, Literary Master and Social Philosopher." (Part I). <u>National Magazine</u>, 37 (December), 476-91.
    Using excerpts from London's writings, gives a detailed account of his life, philosophy, and interpretation of his work. With a "fertile and brilliant" imagination, London often develops stories from incidents or characters he finds in newspapers; and since he is also "a profound philosopher and humanitarian," all his works have purpose. Part II: 1913.B44.

20 LIEBERMAN, ELIAS. <u>The American Short Story</u>. Ridgewood, N. J.: The Editor, pp. 16, 150-57.
    Stories in <u>The Son of the Wolf</u> impressively describe the White Silence which releases men's basic instincts and necessitates cooperative efforts and harsh justice among men. These are needed to combat Nature's destructiveness.

1912

"All in all, we are indebted to Jack London for the vivid
subjective delineation" of this Northern world.

1913 A BOOKS

1   JOHNSON, MARTIN E. Through the South Seas With Jack London.
      Introduction and Postscript by Ralph D. Harrison. New
      York: Dodd, Mead, 380 pp.
        Chosen as a crew member of the Snark from among hundreds
      of applicants, Johnson lived with the Londons for three
      months before the sailing. They were "one big happy
      family....both amiable Bohemians." Describes the Snark:
      dimensions, construction, accessories, furnishings, sup-
      plies taken on board; discusses the problems and mishaps
      encountered before sailing. With Jack's writing gear, 500
      books, and a "talking machine" with 500 records on board,
      the $30,000 boat sailed on April 23, 1907.
        During the 27-day stormy voyage to Hawaii, all were sea-
      sick, flooding and gasoline leaks ruined tools and pro-
      visions, the dynamo and engine broke down, and the boat
      would not heave-to. Nevertheless, London wrote for two
      hours every day: "He writes it [a story] just once, and
      never goes over it to change it." Describes arrival in
      Pearl Harbor, changing of crew members, and overhauling
      the Snark. Discusses history of the Hawaiian Islands,
      current population and customs, the Londons' visit to
      Molokai, the Leper Island--leprosy was London's "hobby."
      Discusses history of leprosy, fictions, facts, and clini-
      cal details.
        They sailed to the Marquesas. Jack, writing Martin Eden,
      explained he had named his hero Martin for Johnson and
      Eden after "an old friend." On board they enjoyed fishing
      contests and suffered from bad weather. Marooned in the
      doldrums without fresh water, London, "almost dead with
      thirst himself,...went into his cabin and wrote a sea
      story about a castaway sailor that died of thirst while
      drifting in an open boat." Johnson's shipboard diary re-
      printed here, in part.
        Discusses the climate, vegetation, natives, customs, and
      history of the Marquesas and Typee valley, Society Islands,
      Polynesia, the Samoas, and Melanesia; also, their meetings
      with Ernest Darling and Helene of Raiatea, and Robert Louis
      Stevenson's life in Apia. In mid-November, 1908, all were
      suffering from yaws and malarial fever (and Jack from a
      painful skin disease as well). They abandoned the Snark
      and sailed on the Makambo for Sydney, Australia. All were
      broken-hearted at having to give up their cruise. Re-
      printed: 1972.A3.

1913 B SHORTER WRITINGS

1   ANON. "Books of the Day--Short Stories by Jack London: The
      Night Born." Boston Evening Transcript (26 February),
      p. 22.
        They evidence "the observant eye, the keenness of mind,
      the swiftness of verbal movement, the knowledge of the
      world" that make London a master of fiction.

2   ANON. "A Son of the Sun." Bookman (London), 44 (Spring),
      "Spring Supplement," 32.
        "An iridescent fabric steeped in the intense colours and
      perfumes of the tropics, and thickly studded with clearcut
      gleaming gems of adventure....[It is] certain to be one of
      the most widely read adventure stories of the year."

3   ANON. "In the Realm of Bookland [The Night Born]." Overland
      Monthly, 61 (March), 304-305.
        "Mighty good stories," vivid and absorbing.

4   ANON. "London, (Jack), A Son of the Sun." Athenaeum, 4454
      (8 March), 282.
        These seem autobiographical yet are "not more convincing
      than the average clever writer's" imaginative inventions.
      Brief.

5   ANON. "By South and North." New York Times Review of Books
      (9 March), 123.
        "The Night Born" is very well done, "brightened by little
      gleams of poetry and romance." "To Kill a Man" is the most
      artistically constructed story.

6   ANON. "Shorter Reviews: Stories by Jack London." San Fran-
      cisco Call (10 March), p. 7.
        "The Mexican" will probably be considered the best story
      in The Night Born. "It is better than several, any one of
      which might have been the best had it been written with
      the integrity of form and diction which Mr. London has
      sometimes shown in his work." Describes several stories.

7   ANON. "Our Booking-Office [A Son of the Sun]." Punch, 144
      (26 March), 251-52.
        London "is a Polynesian Encyclopedia, and he presents
      his knowledge to the public" in these high quality adven-
      tures.

8   ANON. Review of Smoke Bellew. Out West, NS 5 (March-April),
      214-15.

It "breathes the great big vast life of the open," with characters who are vital "creators of the heroic epoch of a nation's life." Here is proof of London's fame as a "word-wizard."

9 ANON. "London, Jack. The Night-Born." ALA Booklist, 9 (April), 344.
   Stories "less brutal but also less vital than" earlier tales.

10 ANON. "The New Books: Night Born (The)." Outlook, 103 (19 April), 863-64.
   The savage bravery of London's "unmoral" heroes inspires admiration and repulsion. His heroines are heartlessly cruel. London "knows how to write."

11 ANON. "Current Fiction: The Night-Born." Nation, 96 (1 May), 443.
   "These tales are all deliberately brutal in Jack London's worst and most popular manner....we begin to despair of his ever escaping his obsession for bunches of knuckles and buckets of blood."

12 ANON. "In the Realm of Bookland." Overland Monthly, 61 (June), 616.
   Briefly notices The Abysmal Brute.

13 ANON. "Literature and Art: A Tireless Romancer." Current Opinion, 54 (June), 490-91.
   If London would take time to think he might become a great storyteller instead of a "popular romancer." [Brief review of The Night Born.]

14 ANON. "'John Barleycorn' and Others." San Francisco Evening Post (2 June), p. 8.
   It has attracted more readers than anything since The Call of the Wild because it honestly reveals London's "own subjective experiences."

15 ANON. "The Abysmal Brute." Boston Evening Transcript (11 June), part 3, p. 4.
   It will in no way sustain London's reputation. With only traces of his former powers, "it is trivial in plot, weak in execution and scarcely worthy as a whole of the reportorial capacities of a skillful penny-a-liner." London offers "the grape juice of melodrama."

16   ANON. "The New Books: Abysmal Brute (The)." Outlook, 104
         (14 June), 345.
            "As an exposé of the evils of present-day prizefighting
         the story has points and one does not mind its fantastic
         improbability."

17   ANON. "Fiction. London (Jack), Smoke Bellew." Athenaeum,
         4472 (12 July), 37.
            A "striking" story with a "monotonously infallible hero."
         Brief.

18   ANON. "Our Booking Office [Smoke Bellew]." Punch, 145
         (16 July), 79.
            London can depict physical struggle and fatigue so well
         that it leaves the reader exhausted. He has all writers
         beat for "tales of endurance and for sheer breathtaking
         adventure."

19   ANON. "Jack London Writes a Libretto: Novelist Tries Musical
         Comedy." San Francisco Examiner (1 August), p. 7.
            In collaboration with C. P. Clement (music by Edward
         Gage), London wrote "Babylonia." It concerns the adven-
         tures of "Billy Wilson, a dynamite drummer" who is trans-
         ported back thirty centuries by drinking an elixir.

20   ANON. "Books of the Day--Jack London Confesses: Jack London
         Athirst." Boston Evening Transcript (20 August), p. 18.
            John Barleycorn seems an imaginative and ingenious fic-
         tional creation with only occasional verisimilitude.

21   ANON. "The New Books: John Barleycorn." Outlook, 104
         (23 August), 964.
            "The self-revelation is brutally frank." Brief.

22   ANON. "Notes." Nation, 97 (28 August), 190.
            John Barleycorn is "a disconcertingly frank record of
         his life....[that] will please the prohibitionists and
         suffragists."

23   ANON. "Reviews of New Books: London, Jack. The Abysmal Brute."
         Literary Digest, 47 (6 September), 390.
            His greatest power is in the portrayal of "man spelled
         with a capital 'M,' virile, rugged, and direct." This is
         a "thrilling and dramatic story."

24   ANON. "Prize Ring Romance." New York Times Review of Books
         (7 September), p. 461.
            The unbelievable hero of The Abysmal Brute is "an

1913

engaging young fellow," and the tale is wholly implausible, but one would like to believe it.

25   ANON. "Is Jack London's 'White Logic' Real Logic?" San Fran-
      cisco Bulletin (17 September), p. 6.
          An editorial. John Barleycorn is "one man's experience
      supremely well told." Its major argument against drinking
      is that alcohol destroys man's illusions, which sustain
      his will to live. With alcohol man sees "the real truth--
      the futility and utter unimportance of all we do or are."
      London might find an even greater truth in the lives of
      those "occupied with sacrifice and service" to others.

26   ANON. Review of John Barleycorn. Overland Monthly, 62 (Octo-
      ber), 414.
          A graphic work, the "most entertaining" of autobiographies
      against alcohol.

27   ANON. Literature and Art: 'John Barleycorn.'" Current Opinion,
      55 (October), 269-70.
          "Mr. London knows the drinking game as few know it, and
      he interprets the drinker's psychology with almost uncanny
      power." Gives excerpts from the work and reviews.

28   ANON. "London, Jack. The Abysmal Brute." ALA Booklist, 10
      (October), 70.
          "A breezy tale."

29   ANON. "London, Jack. John Barleycorn." ALA Booklist, 10
      (October), 70.
          "A strangely frank confession....[and] strong and effec-
      tive plea for prohibition."

30   ANON. "The New Books: The Adventure Path and Drinking." In-
      dependent, 76 (2 October), 36-37.
          He describes forcefully and frankly the rough and reck-
      less road of a heavy drinker in John Barleycorn.

31   ANON. "The Hundred Best Books of the Year." New York Times
      Review of Books (30 November), p. 665.
          John Barleycorn should be judged as "a human document....
      its sincerity is indisputable, and its interest."

32   AKED, C. F. "A Book for Every Citizen." San Francisco Examiner
      (3 October), p. 22.
          John Barleycorn is a "vivid and palpitating human docu-
      ment" by "this big brother of our own with his prize-
      fighter's jaw and philosopher's forehead, with his

instincts of a caveman and aspirations of a poet." It is
the finest plea for Prohibition in memory.

33 BARRY, JOHN D. "Ways of the World: 'John Barleycorn': The
      Autobiography That Is Bound to Win Recognition as One of
      Jack London's Greatest Literary Achievements." San Fran-
      cisco Bulletin (29 September), p. 6.
        As a literary achievement and for showing "that drinkers
      are not born, but made" it is sure to become a "classic"
      document. It places London "among the great leaders and
      inspirers of contemporary thought. It shows fine intellec-
      tual and moral courage." Gives detailed description.

34 BULLIS, HELEN M. "Jack London: His 'Valley of the Moon' a
      Pioneer Story." New York Times Review of Books (9 November),
      p. 607.
        Writing as a "press agent" and "preacher," London glori-
      fies California and Saxon stock in a novel that "spreads
      like a rich quarter section under partial cultivation."
      It is "a man's size book, containing a man's size idea....
      If only Mr. London would not write...so much like Mr. Man-
      in-a-Hurry!"

35 CONNERS, MOLLIE E. "Around the Library Table [John Barley-
      corn]." Oakland Tribune (17 August), p. 5.
        "It is one of the most effective sermons that has ever
      been preached....He simply gives an absolutely truthful
      account of his own life--of his failures--his defeats"
      and his trials with alcohol, all "to save the souls of
      young men." It belongs in every home. Gives extensive
      excerpts.

36 _____. "Around the Library Table [The Valley of the Moon]."
      Oakland Tribune (23 November), p. 9.
        It is the very best thing London has written, with splen-
      did characters and scenery. He sings of "California the
      great, the glorious, the golden....Perhaps it is a good
      thing for the Eastern reader to see the difficulties of
      the Anglo-Saxon race in California when it has to live up
      in a struggle with the Orient." Gives extensive excerpts.

37 E.[DGETT], E.[DWIN] F.[RANCIS]. "Books of the Day--Jack Lon-
      don's Latest Novel." Boston Evening Transcript (8 Novem-
      ber), part 3, p. 8.
        The Valley of the Moon "is the epitome of his style, his
      theories and his genius." He subordinates Socialism to
      art and treats industrial turmoil, romance, and foreigners'
      displacement of native Californians realistically. A novel
      "for all thoughtful readers."

1913

38   FITCH, GEORGE HAMLIN. "Some of the Last Books of Summer:
       'John Barleycorn.' A Spirited Story of His Fight Against
       Drink by Jack London." San Francisco Chronicle (17 August),
       Sunday Magazine, p. 6.
            An imaginative autobiography which makes the saloon and
       drinking sound more attractive than evil. Men will like
       this "cross-section of life, laid bare with the frankness
       of Rousseau."

39   _____. "The New Spiritual Revival and Other Books: 'The Val-
       ley of the Moon.'" San Francisco Chronicle (16 November),
       Dramatic Section, p. 22.
            An interesting novel with much "practical political
       economy" and real life characters. Brief.

40   GOODHUE, E. S. "Jack London and Martin Eden." Mid-Pacific
       Magazine, 6 (October), 359-63.
            London dictated Martin Eden to Charmian who typed it
       while sitting on the lanai of Dr. Goodhue's Pearl Harbor
       bungalow. Martin, like London, is "a very human, tender-
       hearted lad with a large vision cruelly narrowed by the
       vicious circle of circumstances." The press attacks Lon-
       don for his divorce and charges him with plagiarism be-
       cause they resent his courageous denunciation of editors
       and reviewers in the novel. He is a man of "purity," and
       although he borrows materials, he shapes them into personal
       patterns.

41   HALDEMAN-JULIUS, EMANUEL. "The Pessimism of Jack London."
       Western Comrade, 1 (June), 90-92.
            Account of an interview with London in Los Angeles. He
       looked no more than thirty, had a "magnificent body," and
       spoke colloquial ordinary English. In all, he was "an
       open, frank fellow." London is a pessimist because his
       "liver is out of order." Reprinted: 1917.A1.

42   HOLLY, F. M. "Some of the New Spring Novels: The Night Born."
       Publishers' Weekly, 83 (22 March), 1142.
            Good stories, some of them "classics in their way."
       London's work stirs readers with his "bigness, his daring,
       and his power to create and magnify physical beauty and
       strength."

43   HUBBARD, ELBERT. "John Barleycorn." San Francisco Examiner
       (5 September), p. 22.
            A classic confessional work with "grip and punch." Ana-
       lytical and entertaining, "as a study in psychology....

[it] will be new a hundred years from now....a monument to the man who wrote it."

44 JAMES, GEORGE WHARTON. "Jack London: Cub of the Slums, Hero of Adventure, Literary Master and Social Philosopher." (Part II). National Magazine, 37 (January), 682-96.
        Personal reminiscences of a visit to London's ranch; describes Wolf House. "His home life today is a very beautiful one, and his devotion to his wife, as also to his art, sincere and true." Part I: 1912.B19.

45 [JAMES, GEORGE WHARTON]. Review of Smoke Bellew. Out West, NS 5 (March-April), 214-15.
        It fixes London's fame "as a word-wizard and delineator of strong characters." The adventure "breathes" the great outdoors and heroic pioneer life. Describes stories.

46 _____. Review of The Night Born. Out West, NS 6 (September), 148.
        A book full of primitive power and "artistic excellence."

47 KILMER, JOYCE. "John Barleycorn: Mr. London's Graphic Story of Personal Experiences." New York Times Review of Books (24 August), p. 445.
        A frank and "interesting story--perhaps the most vivid and compelling narrative he has ever written....an arraign-ment and a plea" for recognition of the destructive powers of alcohol. "A distinguished achievement, a book surely destined to a high place in the world's esteem."

48 M., A. N. "New Novels [Smoke Bellew]." Manchester Guardian (England), (16 July), p. 5.
        "Mr. London does not know moderation and he exults in danger and labour....his real and considerable talent is for descriptions of physical exertion and strain and their effects in the evolution of manhood."

49 TRIDON, ANDRE. "The Curse of Sociability." New Review, 1, no. 22 (November), 916-18.
        "London never liked booze...but he can't get along with-out it." John Barleycorn reveals that he drinks to be sociable. It's not the alcohol but the people around him, demanding "the miserable, boresome fetish of sociability," who have killed London's creative imagination and vocabu-lary. When he frees himself of the need to be sociable, we will once more have "the London we idolized,...who stood before us as an example of simple virility in life and in art."

1914

1914 A BOOKS - NONE

1914 B SHORTER WRITINGS

1   ANON. "Fiction: The Valley of the Moon." Athenaeum, 4497
           (3 January), 11.
               London has grasped "the essential traits of humanity" in
           this "essentially American,...breezily" written novel.

2   ANON. "Our Booking-Office [The Valley of the Moon]." Punch,
           146 (7 January), 19.
               The novel is "really two stories--one grim, one pleasant,
           and both brilliantly successful."

3   ANON. "Jack London's Call to the Land." Current Opinion, 56
           (March), 212-13.
               The Valley of the Moon contains "many autobiographical
           touches."

4   ANON. "Recent Reflections of a Novel Reader." Atlantic
           Monthly, 113 (April), 494.
               If The Valley of the Moon is not true, it ought to be.
           It is "a chapter from the pilgrimage of our nation back to
           the land,...the most refreshing its author has written,
           and even if over-roseate, it is really practical."

5   ANON. "Jack London's Stories." New York Times Review of Books
           (14 June), p. 270.
               Stories in The Strength of the Strong are of uneven quali-
           ty. "The Sea-Farmer" and "Samuel" are exceptional, with
           "Samuel" being "simple, and human, and dreadful, all at
           once, as life is....it is perhaps the finest and most
           moving story that he has ever written."

6   ANON. "The New Books." Independent, 78 (14 June), 491.
               The Strength of the Strong mentioned.

7   ANON. "Socialists and Rebels." Nation, 99 (2 July), 7.
               London's letter from Mexico shows a non-Marxian individ-
           ualistic and capitalistic spirit. London is more fascinated
           by Socialism's promise of revolution than reconstruction.

8   ANON. "Our Booking-Office [John Barleycorn]." Punch, 147
           (29 July), 119.
               "Alcoholic memoirs" for anyone interested in the prac-
           tical or theoretical aspects of drinking.

9   ANON. "The Drink Question." <u>Athenaeum</u>, 4527 (1 August), 149.
    In <u>John Barleycorn</u> London blames alcohol when he should
    blame himself for misusing it. "Though far from edifying,
    ...[it] should prove instructive and wholesome especially
    in the hands of young laborers. The lusty virility of the
    narrator is abnormal."

10 ANON. "Reviews of New Books: London, Jack. <u>The Strength of</u>
    <u>the Strong</u>." <u>Literary Digest</u>, 49 (1 August), 199.
    Stories in London's "original and unconventional" style
    which are "all rugged, vivid, and interesting."

11 ANON. Review of <u>The Mutiny of the Elsinore</u>. <u>New York Times</u>
    <u>Review of Books</u> (20 September), pp. 386-87.
    The Captain is unconvincing, but Mr. Pike and other
    "picturesque and catastrophic figures" are very real and
    terrible. This "perfectly corking potboiler" abounds in
    "purple patches," sentimentalism, and a "general air of
    having been put together while you wait." It offers "the
    real wildness and savor of the sea...the thrill of adven-
    ture."

12 ANON. "The New Books." <u>Independent</u>, 80 (5 October), 26.
    Mentions <u>The Mutiny of the Elsinore</u>.

13 ANON. "London, Jack. <u>The Mutiny of the Elsinore</u>." ALA Book-
    list, 11 (November), 122.
    "A cruel and brutal story" with unusually good descrip-
    tion of the sea and fiendish characters.

14 ANON. "Notes on New Novels [<u>The Mutiny of the Elsinore</u>]."
    <u>Dial</u>, 57 (1 November), 342.
    "Mr. London's real object is to revel in sailing a ship
    around the Horn with a crew of devils; and in that he
    admirably succeeds."

15 ANON. "Books of the Autumn." <u>Independent</u>, 80 (16 November),
    243.
    <u>The Mutiny of the Elsinore</u> is "a stirring sea-tale....
    Good reading!" Brief.

16 ANON. Review of <u>The Mutiny of the Elsinore</u>. <u>Argonaut</u>, 75
    (28 November), 364.
    Elements of "a sub-human brutality and of a hellish
    cruelty" dominate. The novel "is wholesome although
    bloody."

1914

17   ANON. "Current Fiction." Nation, 99 (3 December), 654.
      The Mutiny of the Elsinore is "vigorous as usual."
      Brief.

18   ANON. "The New Books." Outlook, 108 (9 December), 846.
      The Mutiny of the Elsinore is an "exciting, excessively
      brutal tale of a sea voyage." Brief.

19   ANON. "Mere Adventure." New Republic, 1 (26 December), 28.
      The "fighting of brutal men" is the interest of The
      Mutiny of the Elsinore. "There might have been a bigger
      interest....but Mr. London only feebly touches it....it
      would enhance his art if he could learn that to be effec-
      tive it is not necessary to emulate the Fourth of July."

20   ASHMUN, MARGARET. Modern Short Stories. New York: Macmillan,
      pp. 333-36.
      Gives brief biography and prints "To Build a Fire."

21   BLAND, HENRY MEADE. "'John Barleycorn' at the Plough." Sun-
      set, The Pacific Monthly, 33 (August), 347-49.
      London is planning a book on scientific agriculture for
      which he reads extensively, and he plans a research trip
      to the Orient. His ranch and writing, both extremely well-
      organized pursuits, are flourishing.

22   COOPER, FREDERIC TABER. "The Dearth of Ideas and Some Recent
      Novels: 'The Valley of the Moon.'" Bookman (New York), 38
      (February), 541-42.
      This novel is "an object lesson in London's chief faults:
      exaltation of the animal side of human nature; idealization
      of agrarian success--"It is all a fairy dream, a new Eldo-
      rado." Here is proof for rating Norris's work higher than
      the best of London.

23   _____. "Summer-Time Fiction: 'The Strength of the Strong.'"
      Bookman (New York), 39 (August), 679.
      A varied collection whose title story "while cleverly
      done, is rather tedious, blatantly unreal, and...quite un-
      important." However "The Unparalled Invasion" is an
      "amazing and delicious piece of extravagance."

24   E.[DGETT], E.[DWIN] F.[RANCIS]. "Books of the Day--Stories by
      Jack London." Boston Evening Transcript (10 June), part 3,
      p. 4.
      "It is a pity that Mr. London cannot forget his Socialism,"
      preached in two stories, and write tales with universal
      values like the others in The Strength of the Strong.

25 _____. "Books of the Day--Jack London at Sea: The Mutiny of
the Elsinore." Boston Evening Transcript (30 September),
part 2, p. 24.
It is drawn from experience, is picturesque in detail
and characterization. "Never before with all his fertility
of invention has Mr. London let himself go so unrestrainedly."

26 JAMES, GEORGE WHARTON. Review of The Abysmal Brute. Out West,
NS 7 (April), 233.
A "wonderful piece of literature." London's exposé of
corruption in prize fighting shows great courage.

27 LEWIS, SINCLAIR. "The Relation of the Novel to the Present
Social Unrest: The Passing of Capitalism." Bookman (New
York), 40 (November), 280-86.
Mentions London's opposition to private ownership.

28 MARCHAND, J. "Nine Books of the Month: Jack London's 'The
Mutiny of the Elsinore.'" Bookman (New York), 40 (November), 324-25.
This shows "a new phase" in London's development with
emphasis on "thought, character-study [and] motivation"
rather than action. He uses a "mosaic method" to construct
a "modern world in miniature" on the ship.

29 MARKHAM, EDWIN. California the Wonderful. New York: Hearst's
International Library, pp. 363-64.
"A storyteller by inspiration," London writes with
dramatic vitality directly from his romantic experiences.

30 PAYNE, WILLIAM MORTON. "Recent Fiction." Dial, 56 (1 January),
25.
In the first half of The Valley of the Moon, London is
"the impassioned advocate of socialism and the exalter of
men with red blood in their veins"; then, he appeals as
the "preacher of the simple life." This is his "most
wholesome book, as well as the most interesting, and his
new gospel of 'back to nature' is a far more acceptable
one than the sordid and violent socialistic gospel that he
has hitherto mainly dinned into our ears."

31 VALE, CHARLES. "John Barleycorn." Forum, 51 (January),
146-54.
"Nothing so frank and sincere, and therefore clean and
beautiful, has been written for a long time." Its vivid
and dramatic pictures of life have the great depth and
universal significance for mankind which only an inspired
poet and genius can offer. Gives extensive excerpts.

1915

1915 A BOOKS

1 LONDON, CHARMIAN KITTREDGE. The Log of the Snark. New York: Macmillan, 496 pp. Published as Voyaging in the Wild Seas; or A Woman Among the Head Hunters (A Narrative of the Voyage of the Snark). London: Mills & Boon, 456 pp.

Describes the Snark's voyage from April 25, 1907, through October 15, 1908, with a brief epilogue.

Because dishonest builders made the Snark two feet shorter than specifications, she refused to heave-to, and her parts and fittings rotted away and broke in use. Otherwise, except for infestation by insects, an occasional storm, and an incompetent captain who was replaced, the voyage was by turns idyllic and exciting. On shipboard they read Conrad, Stevenson, and Melville; fished; played poker; boxed daily; Jack became an expert navigator and, for a long stretch, was the "god-like skipper" of the ship: "I'd rather see my husband navigate and sail his boat than write the greatest book ever written. It is living life, whereas writing is but recording life, for the most part. Jack himself always insists that he wishes he had been a prizefighter." Jack worked on many stories and essays, and the novels Martin Eden and Adventure at sea and wherever they landed, writing 1000 words in "two hours of creation" every morning. On such islands as Tahiti, Bora-Bora, and the Samoas, the Londons were royally lodged and entertained by both native and colonial rulers with gala feasts, ceremonial dances, song-fests, and gifts. They bought souvenirs, explored active volcanoes, made a pilgrimage to Stevenson's Vailima home and tomb and to Melville's Typee, which had become a decayed "unholy jungle" inhabited by only a dozen wretched diseased natives. On German Samoa, London's lecture, "Revolution," provoked long discussions.

In the Spring of 1908, Jack and other crew members developed ulcerated sores which he treated with intermittent success; in June, he diagnosed his own fistula, later operated on in Australia. In July, London contracted malaria, "bush-poisoning," and a rare tropical skin disease. To recover from these ailments, he spent five weeks in a hospital in Sydney. Here he sold the Snark "for a mere fraction of her cost" and returned to California. Reprinted: 1925.A2.

1915 B SHORTER WRITINGS

1 ANON. "Our Booking-Office [The Mutiny of the Elsinore]." Punch, 148 (20 January), 59.

"The disgusting thing about the book is that the author

gives to its most horrific episodes a cold and calculated air of truth." This is "what one might call an active, open-air book."

2   ANON. "Fiction: The Mutiny of the Elsinore." Athenaeum, 4555 (13 February), 140.
     London "deals with the abnormal, the super-man, the super-woman, and the super-beast," never with the ordinary. And he admires only "the virile and the full-blooded." Here is a curious Nietzschean emphasis, wonderful descriptions of weather, and "nauseous details of the bestial cruelty of sailors."

3   ANON. "Fiction and Satire." New York Times Review of Books (23 May), pp. 193-94.
     Unlike Patrick MacGill, "London is more interested in himself as an observer than in what he observes."

4   ANON. "The Scarlet Plague." New York Times Review of Books (23 May), p. 194.
     It takes courage to write yet another novel set in the future, and this one is conceptually shallow. Gives plot summary; "And there you are."

5   ANON. "The New Books: Scarlet Plague (The)." Outlook, 110 (2 June), 285.
     "Mr. London has never done a truer or more consistent piece of imaginative work."

6   ANON. Review of The Scarlet Plague. Argonaut, 76 (19 June), 401.
     "An entirely admirable piece of descriptive writing."

7   ANON. "Notes on New Novels [The Scarlet Plague]." Dial, 59 (24 June), 31.
     London "seems determined to prove that fiction can be stranger than fact,...It is difficult to be sympathetic with such a story; the realities are sufficiently ghastly nowadays."

8   ANON. "Current Fiction." Nation, 101 (1 July), 17.
     The Scarlet Plague has "a sort of off-hand vividness; the writer himself is not particularly interested in it, and, indeed, it lacks even such human quality as belonged to The Iron Heel."

9   ANON. "Fiction: The Jacket." Athenaeum, 4579 (31 July), 77.
     Two remarkable aspects are its revelation of the horrors

1915

of prison life in America and the hero's separation of
spirit from body and subsequent reliving of former identi-
ties.

10   ANON. "Current Fiction: The Scarlet Plague." American Review
      of Reviews, 52 (August), 255.
         Brief notice.

11   ANON. "Fiction: The Jacket." Spectator, 115 (28 August), 280.
         London "has gone too far....he has overstepped the bounds
      of sensationalism and borders on literary indecency. The
      horror is unrelieved from beginning to end,...it does seem
      to us most pitiful that Mr. London should so abuse his
      brilliant gifts as to estrange even his truest admirers."

12   ANON. "Novel Notes: The Jacket." Bookman (London), 48 (Sep-
      tember), 178.
         "Mr. London's astonishing versatility has never been
      better displayed than in the vivid glimpses he affords"
      of Standish's lives. As an indictment of the prison system,
      a stirring adventure, and an imaginative comment on rein-
      carnation, it is a "distinct success."

13   ANON. "A World of Dreams in Leading Novels." New York Times
      Review of Books (17 October), p. 389.
         London "has done something original in 'The Star Rover,'
      and done it supremely well." The idea of reincarnation
      and plea for prison reform are worked out well. "The book
      will not suit all tastes for there are painful things in
      it; but it has imagination, skill, freshness, and must
      stand with the best of this author's works."

14   ANON. "Current Fiction [The Star Rover]." Nation, 101 (4 No-
      vember), 548.
         The favorite theme of this "professional strong man of
      American fiction" is "brute strength, plus human will--
      whether to conquer or endure." He sees all men as brutes
      beneath a civilized veneer. His imagination "is singularly
      narrow and vulgar."

15   ANON. "Fiction: Lost Face." Athenaeum, 4594 (13 November),
      346.
         "The collection as a whole is distinctly interesting."

16   ANON. "What America Reads...Stories to Taste." Independent,
      84 (15 November), 270, 272.
         The Star Rover "is necessarily fragmentary, but the con-
      sistency of viewpoint, that of a man diseased in mind and

body, is rather remarkable. But in piling horror on horror, Mr. London overshoots his mark and numbs the mind into disbelief."

17 ANON. "London, Jack. The Star Rover." Wisconsin Library
        Bulletin, 11 (December), 371.
        "A man's book, without any sentiment, but much virility
        and some unpleasant realism." Brief.

18 ANON. "Notes on Current Fiction." American Review of Reviews,
        52 (December), 765.
        Brief note on The Star Rover.

19 ANON. "Two Sprees a Year as Statutory Limit." New York Times
        (3 December), p. 1.
        The National Defense Association's "'No Drunkard Bill,'"
        coming before the New York legislature, is a fine plan "for
        the abolition of drinking," says Jack London, a Vice-presi-
        dent of the NDA.

20 BASHFORD, HERBERT. "The Latest in Literature: The Strength of
        the Strong." San Francisco Bulletin (2 January), part 2,
        p. 10.
        These tales are marked by the same "vigor and virility...
        boldness of treatment and an originality of conception"
        that characterize London's work.

21 _____. "'The Scarlet Plague.'" San Francisco Bulletin
        (5 June), p. 10.
        Gives plot summary. It is "a flight of the imagination--
        a picture of social chaos....told in Mr. London's usually
        vigorous style."

22 COLBRON, GRACE ISABEL. "Jack London's 'Scarlet Plague.'"
        Bookman (New York), 41 (July), 566-67.
        London tries to prove that "only brawn...and the ability
        to perform the more primitive forms of labour" endure when
        civilization fails. It is discouraging that "this prince
        of American storytellers couldn't have made a better story
        of it."

23 E.[DGETT], E.[DWIN] F.[RANCIS]. "Books of the Day--A Jack
        London Romance: Jack London the Prophet." Boston Evening
        Transcript (15 May), part 3, p. 8.
        Gives plot summary of The Scarlet Plague. Hopes now
        London will return not to "his dumb animals, his sea
        wolves, his gold-diggers or his Socialists," but to charac-
        ters like Martin Eden. "Despite his romantic wanderings,
        he has in him the making of a great realist."

1915

24   FITCH, GEORGE HAMLIN. "California Books and Authors," in
     History of California. Edited by Zoeth Skinner Eldredge.
     Volume 5. New York: Century History Co., [487]-502.
        Discusses many California authors, and London briefly,
     pp. 499-500. He "is in a class by himself....If London
     had a finer nature, if his imagination could free itself
     from the physical, he would write novels for all time. As
     it is, he is far and away the most powerful writer Cali-
     fornia has produced."

25   M., W. A. "Jack London on a Far Journey." Boston Evening
     Transcript (13 October), p. 22.
        The Star Rover "stirs our wonder, fascinates us with days
     and deeds." Its "tremendous" concept reveals London's vast
     knowledge in many areas. It is actually a series of short
     stories held together by the personality of the hero. Of-
     fers extensive summary and excerpts.

26   PHELPS, WILLIAM LYON. The Advance of the English Novel. New
     York: Dodd, Mead, pp. 282-84.
        "To read a book like White Fang is to feel like a canni-
     bal, crunching bones and bolting blood. Yet Jack London
     is a man of letters; he has the true gift of style, so
     rare and so unmistakable; if he would forget his social
     and political creed, and lower his voice, he might achieve
     another masterpiece" like The Call of the Wild. Same, re-
     printed: 1929.

1916 A BOOKS - NONE

1916 B SHORTER WRITINGS

1   ANON. "The Little Lady of the Big House." Annual Register
     (London), NS, part 2, p. 115.
        "This is a beautiful story set in beautiful and unusual
     surroundings. The characters are drawn with great insight
     and power, and Dick Forest,...is a most lovable hero."

2   ANON. "In Realm of Bookland: 'The Little Lady of the Big
     House.'" Overland Monthly, 67 (March), 262.
        London brings "all his powers of construction, of visuali-
     zation, and of imagination" to notable characters and a
     problem plot.

3   ANON. "Love Tangles Between Two Coasts." New York Times Re-
     view of Books (9 April), p. 129.
        A superman, and a superwoman, and a third party create

the love problem which "finds its solution in tragedy--
tragedy which a singular lack of discrimination on the part
of the author steeps in bathos." The Little Lady of the
Big House lacks important incidents; it has colorful descriptions and "many, many pages of discussion."

4   ANON. "New Novels: 'The Little Lady of the Big House.'" TLS
        (27 April), p. 202.
            "Mr. London has written the efficient man's fairy tale,
        and if the efficient man would have no time to revel in
        it, we others can and do."

5   ANON. "London, Jack. The Little Lady of the Big House."
        Athenaeum, 4605 (May), 243.
            The characters, psychologically and physically unreal,
        evoke neither belief nor pity from the reader.

6   ANON. "Plays and Pageants." American Review of Reviews, 53
        (May), 634.
            The Acorn-Planter "is a fine and a beautiful play--a
        call to the world of men to awaken and know that construc-
        tive effort is the highest duty man can realize." Brief.

7   ANON. "Our Booking-Office [The Little Lady of the Big House]."
        Punch, 150 (3 May), 150.
            London's "superstrenuous beings" are too "energetic"
        for "Capuan ease" and tend to become melodramatic. He
        should return "to the muscle-grinding."

8   ANON. "Jack London--Protean." Boston Evening Transcript
        (6 May), part 3, p. 8.
            The Little Lady of the Big House is a "glamoured" and
        illogical disappointment. "He has made his people lie
        throughout all the pages...he has called them strong and
        made them weak."

9   ANON. Review of The Little Lady of the Big House. Argonaut,
        78 (6 May), 308.
            A thinly disguised autobiography with some improbabili-
        ties. We hope Easterners will not accept this novel as
        typical of California life.

10   ANON. "Readable Novels: The Little Lady of the Big House."
        Spectator, 116 (13 May), 609.
            Mentioned.

11   ANON. "London, Jack. The Little Lady of the Big House."
        Literary Digest, 52 (20 May), 1461-62.

1916

London is at his best describing the big, virile things
of nature. Here he paints "with broad sweeps, brilliant
colors, highlights, and deep shadows" unconventional situations and an unusual hero. His skill with women characters
is less convincing.

12   ANON. "Jack London at His Worst." Independent, 86 (22 May),
      305.
          The superhuman characters of The Little Lady of the Big
      House "are so thoroly [sic] incredible that they are in-
      teresting." Brief.

13   ANON. "The New Books: A California Forest Play." Independent,
      86 (29 May), 343.
          With music The Acorn-Planter would "make an effective
      production. It is good reading, too." Brief.

14   ANON. "London, Jack. The Little Lady of the Big House." ALA
      Booklist, 12 (June), 430.
          An entertaining view of California life with an inter-
      esting love triangle.

15   ANON. "Novels for Summer Reading: The Little Lady of the Big
      House." American Review of Reviews, 53 (June), 760.
          "The strain on the reader's sense of the probable is in-
      tense. But it is a brilliant novel, like its predecessors
      from the same pen." Brief.

16   ANON. "Current Fiction." Nation, 102 (15 June), 647-48.
          London's earlier romantic and adventurous work had a
      special appeal. "He has done pretentious things since
      then, has featured himself in print as a prophet, a propa-
      gandist, a philosopher. But the old theme of primitive
      hero against the world always surfaced." The Little Lady
      of the Big House "does not achieve reality or sincerity...
      [or] the enervated voluptuousness of his model." The only
      idea in the story is "that of a helpless impulse of poly-
      andry in the modern woman."

17   ANON. "The Acorn-Planter: A California Forest Play." New
      York Times Review of Books (13 August), p. 320.
          It is "well constructed, and the songs and recitatives
      are written with an intelligent appreciation of Indian
      feeling....In the right setting it would make a very pretty
      spectacle" and surely be popular among pacifists.

18   ANON. "Our Booking-Office [The Night Born]. Punch, 151
      (16 August), 132.

"The freshness and fertility of Mr. London's imagination" create original exciting stories that are "a delightful relief from the fiction connected with the War."

19   ANON. "American Verse." Nation, 103 (17 August), 151-52.
      The Acorn-Planter is "of cyclic duration yet of stationary effect." The combination of simple prose and familiar meters leaves the question of a purely poetic gift in a possibly fortunate abeyance."

20   ANON. Review of The Turtles of Tasman. New York Times Review of Books (22 October), p. 439.
      With their great variety of subject, mood, and treatment, some of these should appeal to everyone.

21   ANON. "Recent Publications [The Turtles of Tasman]." New Republic, 9 (11 November), 55, 57.
      "When Mr. London thinks of De Maupassant and the form-perfect French, he becomes just uninterestingly imitative. When he thinks of other American writers, he becomes clumsily humorous or sentimental. But when he writes of Alaska or the Klondike or the sea as he knows it and loves it, his stories have the qualities for which he is still famous."

22   ANON. "The New Books: Frivolous and Grave." Independent, 88 (20 November), 330.
      The Turtles of Tasman is "a literary remnant counter." Brief.

23   ANON. "Jack London Dies Suddenly on Ranch." New York Times (23 November), p. 13.
      Brief biography. His experiences "have all been brilliantly built into his many works of fiction."

24   ANON. "London's Early Mentor Gives Warm Praise." San Francisco Bulletin (23 November), p. 7.
      Frederick Irons Bamford recalls London's love for Browning, Whitman, his conversion to socialism and loyalty to friends.

25   ANON. "He Pictured the Life He Lived." New York Times (24 November), p. 12.
      An editorial. The mystery remains of "how or why" London became a writer. He had the power to photograph and create at once. We admire the "excellencies of his style," his "imaginative" realism, "amazing powers of observation and interpretation," and the "plausibility" and strength of his writing. "By Jack London's death American letters

1916

suffer a heavy loss, as by his life they incurred a heavy debt."

26   ANON. "Jack London--An Uncompleted Life." <u>San Francisco Bulletin</u> (24 November), p. 6.
       An editorial. London's major interest in his later years was farming. He postponed writing the "masterpieces" of maturity until his ranch was successful, and that day never came.

27   ANON. "Some Short Stories by Jack London." <u>San Francisco Call</u> (25 November), Magazine Section, p. 13.
       When London follows his "natural bent" and writes from experience, he strikes "the deeper emotions, principles and impulses of action" better than anyone. <u>The Turtles of Tasman</u> is "well worth reading."

28   ANON. "Jack London." <u>Nation</u>, 103 (30 November), 502.
       A man of "abounding and winning vitality," London was more genuine than his fictional characters. His early work, particularly <u>The Call of the Wild</u>, was his best, conveying his impulsive love of life, the "simple elements of struggle, of human endurance and loyalty and sacrifice." Later, academic generalizations, formulaic characters, and sophisticated ideas rigidified his work. Foreigners admire London's "primitive strength" as typically American. "A creative artist he was not."

29   ANON. "Eastern Estimates of London's Genius." <u>California Writers' Club Quarterly Bulletin</u>, 4, no. 4 (December), 10-11.
       Excerpts of reviews from New York, Chicago, and other newspapers.

30   ANON. [Jack London]. <u>New York Times Review of Books</u> (3 December), p. 534.
       An editorial. There is no doubt about the "precocity" and "originality" of London. The "virile spirit" of his fiction, "preaching of a gospel of outdoor, strenuous living," seems his "most effective contribution to the literature of his period" at home and the cause of a developing "London cult" abroad.

31   ANON. "'Musty' Books." <u>San Francisco Bulletin</u> (4 December), p. 6.
       An editorial. It is better to put life's substance into developing the "art of talking well" than into books which die. "Jack London himself, the apostle of first

hand inspiration, could find nothing better to do with his experiences than to turn them into books."

32 ANON. "Jack London." Outlook, 114 (6 December), 742, 745, (758 portrait).
    Gives biography. "He affected scorn of literary grace and gentle sentiment, and yet there are passages in some of his books which show that he was not always rough and violent in feeling....If environment and personal history are considered, Jack London's work is undeniably remarkable, and if he offended some tastes and failed to gain the approval of literary critics, he at least made himself one of the most popular story-tellers in recent American annals."

33 ANON. "Jack London." Literary Digest, 53 (9 December), 1537-38.
    Excerpts from New York newspapers evaluating London's work.

34 ANON. "A Long Distance Interview with Jack London. (In Pursuit of a Fugitive Poem.)" Silhouette (Oakland), 1 (December 1916-January 1917), 70.
    A request to "America's Greatest Fictionist," who no longer writes poetry, for his "The Worker and the Tramp," a villanelle. Poem printed here, p. 71. Reprinted: 1970.B2.

35 BASHFORD, HERBERT. "Around the Reading Lamp: The Acorn-Planter." San Francisco Bulletin (18 March), part 2, p. 10.
    "He has encroached upon the province of the lyrist and smites his lyre with the assurance of one who feels that the muse has bestowed upon him her richest gifts....Perhaps he may be classed with the Imagists, who bear the same relation to poetry as the Futurists bear to art.... We would not care to lend Poet London too much encouragement, however, lest, like Thomas Hardy, he might be tempted to forsake prose for verse, which would be in the nature of a catastrophe in Western letters."

36 BLAND, HENRY MEADE. "Jack London." Book News Monthly, 34 (March), 292-94.
    Out of his romantic life-experiences, all of them "a search for his sorrowfully regretted lost youth," London created his books and his ranch. He has drifted away from Socialism but remains a political idealist, a philosophical materialist, and an acute chronicler of human nature. Describes London ranch, workshop, and home.

1916

37   BLAND, HENRY MEADE. "Hail and Farewell to Jack London." Cali-
        fornia Writers' Club Quarterly Bulletin, 4, no. 4 (Decem-
        ber), 3.
            In October, London told Bland he planned "to complete
        and perfect his farm" and retire to Hawaii. London's
        literary goal was "to make the ideal and the real harmonize."

38   C.[ARRUTH], C. W. [Jack London]. California Writers' Club
        Quarterly Bulletin, 4, no. 4 (December), 6.
            An editorial. Critical appraisals of London's work
        stress its vitality and "red-blooded" quality while
        mourning the "great loss to literature in his untimely
        death."

39   FOLLETT, WILSON. "Sentimentalist, Satirist, and Realist:
        Some Recent Fiction." Atlantic Monthly, 118 (October),
        495.
            The Little Lady of the Big House "reproduces merely the
        facund [sic]--nay, glib--erotomania of three persons...
        whose very continence is a mere voluptuous refinement upon
        desire." Brief.

40   FORD, FORD MADOX. See Hueffer, Oliver Madox.

41   HALE, EDWARD E. "Recent Fiction." Dial, 60 (6 January), 30.
            The structure and plot of The Star Rover are built on
        the idea of "supremacy of mind over body," and the book's
        dominating concept is the transmigration of souls.

42   _____. "Recent Fiction." Dial, 60 (11 May), 473.
            London is a master of imaginative details, "the complete
        filling out of an idea." "All this is exciting and ex-
        hilarating at first, but in the course of time...it be-
        comes rather tedious." After the first few pages The
        Little Lady of the Big House is certainly not interesting.

43   _____. "Recent Fiction." Dial, 61 (2 November), 353.
            The Turtles of Tasman is a characteristic collection
        showing London's "infinite variety" of subject, "terse
        vigor," and philosophy of adventure.

44   HUEFFER, OLIVER MADOX. "Jack London: A Personal Sketch."
        New Statesman, 8 (2 December), 206-207.
            London "was the ideal yarn-spinner--his spoken stories
        were even better than his written--...[and] he was per-
        fectly unconscious of it. Like Peter Pan, he never grew
        up, and he lived his own stories with such intensity that
        he ended up believing them himself." London's self-defined

romanticism "bubbled out in his books, and it is on that
lack of effort that his claim to fame will probably rest.
...I have very little doubt that he simply burnt his life
out by his enjoyment of it....As a writer, I believe that
also he will not grow old quickly. It is a good sign
that, already, he is loved--as is perhaps no other contemporary writer--by the simpleminded....It is another
hopeful sign that critics talk of him contemptuously, or
with a mild tolerance, and that no one has yet described
him as a 'classic.'" Reprinted: 1917.B37.

45   MACMILLAN COMPANY, THE. "Jack London and His Work. A Sketch
     of the Life of the Author of 'The Star Rover.'" Silhouette
     (Oakland), 1 (December 1916-January 1917), 71-73.
         Biography and appreciative comment on his work.

46   MIHAN, LEO B. "The Genius of Jack London." Bohemia (San
     Francisco), 1, no. 6 (15 December), 167-70.
         London "saw all the modern world as Blake saw his in-
     ternal world and cosmogony." His strong, vital, often
     "creative art" reflected the "Western mind" of his time.
     "He preferred to be Jack London instead of, like Conrad,
     a second-rate Dostoiffski [sic]."

47   MILLARD, BAILEY. "Jack London, Farmer." Bookman (New York),
     44 (October), 151-56.
         Describes London's ranch, crops, buildings. London com-
     ments on his ranching goals and accomplishments.

48   M., W. A. "Jack London: A Recent Collection of Characteristic
     Short Stories." Boston Evening Transcript (8 November),
     p. 6.
         Stories in The Turtles of Tasman show London's usual
     sound psychology and "clearly-flowing, acid-biting
     English."

49   SCOTT, RUPERT. "Some Novels of the Month: 'The Star Rover.'"
     Bookman (New York), 42 (February), 720.
         There is a freshness in the treatment of this old theme
     which shows originality and power. But London's "evolu-
     tion is more an outer evolution than an inner one." The
     blond superman still reigns supreme.

50   SINCLAIR, UPTON. "A Sad Loss to American Literature." Cali-
     fornia Writers' Club Quarterly Bulletin, 4, no. 4 (Decem-
     ber), 3-4.
         "He is and will remain one of the great revolutionary
     forces in American letters. His work is a bugle call to

the American soul, especially to the youth of the people
seeking a way to freedom and justice." London's best works
were his Socialist writings. [This eulogy appears under
various titles in 1916 and 1917.]

51 STERLING, GEORGE. "George Sterling in High Tribute to Jack
London." San Francisco Examiner (27 November), p. 3; as
"Sterling's Tribute to Jack London." California Writers'
Club Quarterly Bulletin, 4, no. 4 (December), 7; and under
various titles in several California papers in November
and December.
Describes burial of London's ashes. "Jack London had
gone--...had turned his back on mortality with much of the
splendid and dramatic quality of his accustomed life,...
and he died smiling triumphantly." London's greatness will
yet be recognized by America; "a genius so flaming, so passionate, so sincere and catholic is not to be circumscribed
by the bourns of prejudice and nationality." Reprinted:
1975.A4.

52 STOY, E. "Personality of Jack London." Wasp, 74 (2 December),
1, 14.
Gives biography. London's genius was "a restless in-
toxication with life" which drove him to seek big experiences that became part of his "epic" fiction. His theme
was the struggle between life and death. He portrayed
only "two types of mind, his own, and the primitive." A
simple philosophy, "that death ended all," and pessimism
characterize his work. London "gave to the west its fullest
and strongest expression in literature."

53 WALLACE, JAMES. "'The Aegis' Published Jack London's First
Stories." Weekly Aegis (8 December), 2 pp [unnumbered].
Describes the stories and sketches, with excerpts, con-
tributed to the Oakland High School Aegis, and London's
life c. 1895-96.

54 WOLFE, FRANK E. "Jack London." Western Comrade, 4, no. 8
(December), 21.
"Our comrade has passed and the world will long turn in
the lathe of time before the workers shall have a champion
of his equal." Brief.

1917 A BOOKS

1 HALDEMAN-JULIUS, EMANUEL. Jack London. Girard, Kansas:
[Appeal to Reason], 16 pp.

Contains "The Pessimism of Jack London," pp. [1]-7, a reprint of 1913.B41; and two essays unrelated to London.

2   [LIVINGSTON, LEON RAY]. From Coast to Coast with Jack London, "By A-No 1, The Famous Tramp." Erie, Pennsylvania: A-No 1 Publishing Company, 136 pp.

In 1894, in New York City, they formed a hobo comradeship, and their friendship lasted until London's death. Recounts sixteen "adventures" of their trip from New York to Nevada, such as brushes with the law, cadging meals, and dangers faced riding the rails. Reprinted: 1969.A2.

3   LONDON, CHARMIAN KITTREDGE. Our Hawaii. New York: Macmillan, 359 pp. Published as Jack London and Hawaii. London: Mills & Boon, 1918, 314 pp.

This is Charmian's diary of May 21-October 7, 1907; March-July, 1915; December 23, 1915-July 26, 1916. Describes the Hawaiian Islands: geography, history, agriculture, flora and fauna, museums, monuments; the Hawaiian people: their food, music and dance, language, clothing, sports, religion. Discusses the Londons' experiences with Alexander Hume Ford, Louis von Tempski, Alice Roosevelt Longworth; London's thoughts on justice, editors, "nature-faking," the "physics of a breaking wave," and his love for Hawaii. The Londons' activities on the islands included swimming, riding, sightseeing, surfboarding, writing, canoeing, card-playing, repairing the Snark, and socializing "with the best of Hawaii's white citizenship," with the royal family, and (on July 2-6, 1907) with the lepers of Molokai. On their final visit to Hawaii, London was ill and sedentary, unable to eat, and depressed by the course of the War. Revised edition: 1922.A1.

4   MOSBY, C. V. A Little Journey to the Home of Jack London. St. Louis: Front Rank Press, 18 pp.

"If he ever wrote a poor short story it never saw the light of day. Everything that came from his pen was a classic in its line." London's creative imagination, interest in psychology, passionate living, socialism, his happy choice of a second wife--"When the domestic skies were darkest, Charmian came to him like the cow moose comes out of the Canadian wilds in answer to the call of her lordly mate"--; these and his vision, energy, and pioneering action and work in harmony with Nature, made him a successful writer and rancher of immortal fame. Reprinted: 1972.A5.

1917

1917 B SHORTER WRITINGS

1   [ABBOTT, LEONARD D.]. "Jack London's One Great Contribution
    to American Literature." Current Opinion, 62 (January),
    46-47.
        The Call of the Wild is "his chief claim to immortality."
    Gives excerpts of reviews from periodicals.

2   ANON. "London, Jack. The Turtles of Tasman." ALA Booklist,
    13 (January), 177.
        Stories on a variety of subjects.

3   ANON. "Some Recent Short Stories [The Turtles of Tasman]."
    Nation, 104 (4 January), 19.
        "Here above all is that exultation in youth, strength,
    red blood, maleness,...the rather wistful utterance of
    that creed by one who feels that time is flying."

4   ANON. "Recent Fiction [The Turtles of Tasman]." Literary
    Digest, 54 (3 March), 565.
        A variety of "appealing" stories. Brief.

5   ANON. Review of The Human Drift. New York Times Review of
    Books (11 March), p. 88.
        "A varied collection of material." Briefly described.

6   ANON. "Our Booking-Office [The Strength of the Strong]."
    Punch, 152 (4 April), 232.
        Uncharacteristic essay-stories, neither "defiantly
    propagandistic" nor "joyously adventurous," but a series
    of "social pictures."

7   ANON. "Journalization." New York Times Review of Books
    (8 April), p. 128.
        An editorial. Estimates from Russia all note the "'truly
    American'" nature of London's "work and genius." Andreyev
    admires his "strength and originality"; Kuprin ranks him
    with Kipling; Volsky cites London's primitiveness, vitality,
    and particularity; but Chukovsky believes him "greatly
    overrated." Gives brief quotations from Russian critics.

8   ANON. "Jerry of the Islands." New York Times Review of
    Books (22 April), p. 158.
        "The story suffers a good deal from excess verbiage. A
    severe course of blue-penciling would have improved its
    strength, beauty, and appeal." But the reader who perse-
    veres "will be well repaid. For Jerry is one of the

dearest of dog-creatures,...and Mr. London has written his
story with penetrating and loving sympathy and understanding."

9 ANON. "Briefs on New Books." Dial, 62 (3 May), 404.
   In The Human Drift "London portrays himself: the man of
   action, the lover of adventure, the self-made philosopher,
   who is not afraid of danger or death." The sketches reveal "what a multum in parvo his life was--a pitiful short-
   ness packed full by his boyish eagerness."

10 ANON. "Notes." Nation, 104 (10 May), 583.
   "The author's characteristic emphasis of mystery, with
   his insistence upon it as a healthful, rewarding aspect of
   life" connects the pieces in The Human Drift.

11 ANON. "The New Books: Jerry of the Islands." Outlook, 116
   (16 May), 116.
   Brief mention.

12 ANON. "London, Jack. The Human Drift." ALA Booklist, 13
   (July), 440.
   Lists contents.

13 ANON. "The New Books: From the Novelists." Independent, 90
   (9 June), 474.
   The Human Drift is "odds and ends." Brief.

14 ANON. "New Novels: Jerry of the Islands." TLS (26 July),
   p. 356.
   "This story is authentic London....[the killing] is
   scientific, cold-blooded, and inevitable....[and] heredity
   is at the bottom of it all." But London strikes a new
   note here in expressing "the gentler emotions" of mutual
   love between master and dog.

15 ANON. "Our Booking-Office [Jerry of the Islands]." Punch,
   153 (1 August), 85.
   It will be welcomed by readers who share London's "sympathetic understanding of his hero."

16 ANON. Review of Jerry of the Islands. Athenaeum, 4621 (September), 471.
   "As a protracted dog yarn, the story is quite pleasant
   reading." Brief.

17 ANON. "A Dog Story: Jerry of the Islands." Saturday Review
   (London), 124 (29 September), 251.
   London had "a real insight into dog nature."

1917

18   ANON. "London, Jack. Jerry of the Islands." ALA Booklist,
      14 (November), 60.
         "The story shows the life and color of the islands and
      makes Jerry all dog though sometimes more than human."

19   ANON. Review of Michael, Brother of Jerry. New York Times
      Review of Books (25 November), p. 490.
         This is unpleasant reading "which people should have
      forced upon them." Michael will "appeal to all dog-lovers."

20   ANON. "Red Blood: Gore and Ichor." Nation, 105 (13 December),
      666-67.
         London could not see the difference between the strong
      man's blood and "the visible red blood torn in torture
      from shrieking flesh, for which he had a morbid and lamen-
      table fondness." Despite his sincere love of dogs "part
      of him gloated over the spectacles of their torments."

21   ANON. "A Jack London Dog Story: Michael, Brother of Jerry."
      Boston Evening Transcript (19 December), part 2, p. 8.
         The novel illustrates London's plea to eliminate animal
      acts from the stage. Although the work of other writers
      of the school he founded will outlive his, a "magnetism"
      distinguishes his fiction.

22   [BAGGS, MAE LACY]. "The Real Jack London as Revealed in
      Hawaii." Current Opinion, 62 (January), 23.
         Excerpts of an article from the New York Sun; expanded
      text: 1917.B23.

23   BAGGS, MAE LACY. "The Real Jack London in Hawaii." Overland
      Monthly, 69 (May), 405-10.
         Impressions of the Londons in Waikiki, early in 1915.
      London's "life was one long attempt to convince the world
      through his pen that the conditions which produced his
      pitiful beginnings were all wrong. His method was chiefly
      to show up every man as a primitive, with primitive pas-
      sions--brutes." He, therefore, was "indifferent to social
      amenities," was self-conscious and diffident with upper-
      class people, and a "playful" joker. His stories, typed
      by his Japanese secretary, were always subjected to
      Charmian's revisions, as was his behavior. He "was a
      man's man, therefore, a woman's man. More than that, he
      was a child's man." London loved Hawaii because "life
      here was virtually without effort."

24   BARRY, JOHN D. "Personal Qualities of Jack London." Overland
      Monthly, 69 (May), 431-32.

London liked to be with ordinary people, enjoyed the retirement of his ranch, reading aloud, and seeing photographs of himself.

25   BELTON, GEORGE R.   "'The Call of the Wild,' a Plagiarism?"
     Reedy's Mirror, 26 (16 March), 182-83.
        A letter to the editor. London admitted copying "in
     better literary style" a book written by a Canadian
     missionary.

26   BERENBERG, DAVID F.   "Reviews and Comment: Essays by Jack London.   'The Human Drift.'" New York Call (24 June), p. 15.
        "A Wicked Woman" and "The Birth Mark" are very poor work.

27   BOYNTON, H. W.   "Some Stories of the Month." Bookman (New
     York), 45 (July), 536.
        London "was the type of man whom babies bored and embarrassed, but, by a familiar paradox of the male nature,
     he had no end of sentiment to bestow on dogs." Jerry's
     ability to count and to speak seem miraculous, but Jerry of
     the Islands is a good story.

28   COLBRON, GRACE ISABEL.   "Jack London: What He Was and What He
     Accomplished." Bookman (New York), 44 (January), 441-51.
        London's "zest of life" characterizes his fiction which
     is best when intensely subjective, sincerely showing life
     as he saw it, "as a wonderful, glowing, pulsing, colourful
     thing." Short stories are his best work because they are
     most analogous in form to the "sketchiness and evanescent
     quality" of his life experiences; his novels "are merely
     short stories in longer form." London successfully portrayed men like Larsen, "the culmination of mere animal
     joy of living plus a brain," but he failed to make his
     women characters convincing. He was not a realist but a
     romantic. His later novels suffer from padding, and his
     non-fiction, inspired by the "emotional radicalism" he
     called socialism, "are wonderful bits of writing" but
     offer no constructive solutions to world problems. London sincerely sympathized with victims of economic oppression, but he did not understand economics. Offers biography and London's philosophy from his writings.

29   DARGAN, E. PRESTON.   "Jack London in Chancery." New Republic,
     10 (21 April), "Spring Literary Review," part 2, 7-8.
        "The key-note of this writer was apparently an autobiographical realism with a taste for virile adventure....
     he admired and portrayed types that could steer, mush,
     drink, box and overcome. And his types were nearly always

1917

Jack London himself, transposed to a heroic key." Philo-
sophically he glorifies strength, the common people, and
Socialism. "Socialists say that London has set back the
cause at least five years." John Barleycorn, his "chief
document and probably his greatest book....contains his
best, his only thinking; it gives us the true philosophy
of alcohol and rough living." "London remains a clever
short story writer,...Realistic, forthright, and very personal, his manly figure looms as the Klondike of our soil.
...But he has few contacts with civilization and none with
civilized literature which, presumably, is still to come."

30   E.[DGETT], E.[DWIN] F.[RANCIS]. "Books of the Day--Jerry of
     the Islands: Jack London Tells His Last Tale." Boston
     Evening Transcript (28 April), part 3, p. 6.
          Further indication of London's expert, unbounded "knowl-
     edge of and sympathy with" animals; an imaginative and
     realistic story which brings London's work "to a fitting
     though untimely close."

31   FORD, ALEXANDER HUME. "Jack London in Hawaii, Rambling Remi-
     niscences of the Editor." Mid-Pacific Magazine, 13
     (February), 117-27.
          They were close friends from 1907, when they met in
     Hawaii. There, London wrote his 1000 words every morning;
     then he "longed to be a boy again." He romped with chil-
     dren on the beach, mixed well with people of all ages,
     and enjoyed water sports. London claimed he would never
     write "smutty" fiction, and he would rather get "one cent
     a word more" for a novel than have it "live forever."
     Jack was an "unconventional" man, who "loved humanity
     more than he loved himself, his work, or life itself."

32   FORD, FORD MADOX. See Hueffer, Oliver Madox.

33   FORDER, HERB. "Jack London: A Man of a Thousand Lives."
     Pearsons, 37 (March), 230-33.
          They met in a London pub (1902), and London described
     his method of writing The People of the Abyss. Many years
     later, they met in Los Angeles where London, who "was
     hiding from his creditors," said he was "rich in pure un-
     diluted gall and optimism" and in friends but burdened
     with a large mortgage and dependent relatives. For The
     Sea-Wolf he used the yarns of Captain Jock McLean whom he
     had "cultivated" in Vancouver, B. C. The Valley of the
     Moon and The Little Lady of the Big House "were written
     to order, built to fit the policy of an extremely popular
     periodical. That's all that can be said for them."

London was a paradoxical man who crowded eighty years of
living into half that time.

34   FRENCH, HAROLD. "The Cruises of 'Bay-Pirate Jack.' What a
       St. Nicholas Story Did for Jack London." St. Nicholas,
       44 (July), 848-50.
          Gives biography, in fictionalized form, of London and
       the Razzle-Dazzle. A story in this magazine (November
       1884) showed London the error of his oyster-pirate life;
       he reformed, joined the Fish Patrol, and went on to publish
       stories in St. Nicholas.

35   FRIEDLAND, L. S. "Jack London as Titan." Dial, 62 (25 January),
       49-51.
          London, "who is rejected by the literary élite in his
       own country, has been hailed as a mighty prophet in Russia,"
       where "action, power, personality" are worshipped. Russian
       writers and critics admire his strong, fresh, uniquely
       American style and subjects, his primitivism and manliness,
       and concern for "social programmes" rather than aesthetic
       values in literature.

36   HERVEY, JOHN L. "Jack London and O. Henry: A Parallel."
       Reedy's Mirror, 26 (2 March), 134-36.
          These writers, who today are "the most powerful formative
       influences" in the short story field, had parallel careers:
       their early work appeared in magazines, they wrote prolifi-
       cally and led romantic, legendary lives. Unlike O. Henry,
       London courted fame, held a "self-created" grudge against
       society, saw life as a "cosmic tragedy" and "ranged the
       illimitable spaces of undiscovered countries and all but
       unknown worlds." There is, however, a certain monotony
       about his work, an absence of true women and of mastery of
       the novel form. London's writings, especially The Call of
       the Wild, will outlast O'Henry's.

37   HUEFFER, OLIVER MADOX. "Jack London: A Personal Sketch."
       Living Age, 292 (13 January), 124-26.
          Reprint of 1916.B44.

38   JAMES, GEORGE WHARTON. "A Study of Jack London in His Prime."
       Overland Monthly, 69 (May), 361-99.
          Discusses London's origins, philosophy, early and later
       life, socialism, and works; material is taken largely from
       London's writings, interviews and James's previous articles:
       1912.B19; 1913.B44. "He will be regarded not only as a
       master writer of fiction, but as a keen philosopher, rug-
       gedly, but none the less earnestly, bent on helping upward
       and forward his fellow-men."

1917

39 KERFOOT, J. B. Review of <u>Jerry of the Islands</u>. <u>Life</u>, 70
    (5 July), 22.
        The yarn states London's "favorite thesis: the relation
    between primitive instincts and the upward urge." Brief.

40 LANE, ROSE WILDER. "Life and Jack London." <u>Sunset, The
    Pacific Monthly</u>, 39 (October), 17-20, 72-73; (November),
    29-32, 64-66; (December), 21-23, 60, 62, 64, 66-68.
        A popularized dramatically rendered biography; includes
    excerpts from London's writings; with many photographs.
    Continued: 1918.B10.

41 LANGDON, BEATRICE. "Mrs. Jack London's 'Log of the Snark.'"
    <u>Overland Monthly</u>, 69 (May), 447-50.
        Itinerary and details of the <u>Snark</u> voyage from C. London,
    1915.A1.

42 LAY, WILFRED. "'John Barleycorn' Under Psychoanalysis." <u>Book-
    man</u> (New York), 45 (March), 47-54.
        London's spiritual and intellectual development were
    arrested in childhood; therefore he retained the infantile
    qualities of Sadism--he delighted in shocking people--and
    of Masochism--he enjoyed his own misery and thoughts of
    death. London is revealed as "an active type of homo-
    sexual" by "taking extreme satisfaction out of men's com-
    pany, and exalting man's purely physical performance"; by
    his inability to appreciate women except as animals or to
    portray them realistically; by seeking always to "impress
    the reader with his virility"; by prodigious drinking to
    prove manliness; and by taking to the sea and the road to
    escape from a responsible "full life." London intensified
    his pleasure "to its uttermost limit" where it became "the
    pain of the Long Sickness, which is pleasure exhausted."
    This excessive extraversion, "aimless running up and down
    upon the face of the earth," not balanced by introversion
    which gives life to the soul, brought him destruction and
    death. It is unfortunate that London failed to develop
    beyond adolescence. "Had he stayed on land and received
    a social education, he might have become a great cultural
    writer."

43 LEWIS, OSCAR. "Jack London's California." <u>Book News Monthly</u>,
    35 (June), [367]-69.
        Nearly one-half of London's books are located, wholly
    or in part, in the San Francisco Bay area. Identifies and
    describes places, events, and buildings so located in the
    works.

44   M.; A. N.   "Jack London's Strength."   Manchester Guardian
     (England) (16 February), p. 3.
        The Strength of the Strong is "a volume of uncommon in-
     terest" which deepens the regret that London died while
     "his powers were fresh...developing and refining....he
     could make of physical exertion a symbol of spirit."

45   MARSHALL, L. RUDIO.   "Mrs. Jack London's Viewpoint."   Overland
     Monthly, 69 (May), 400-404.
        Describes a visit to the ranch where Charmian explains
     Jack's ambitions for it and his accomplishments.

46   MILLARD, BAILEY.   "Valley of the Moon Ranch: A Recent Visit
     There."   Overland Monthly, 69 (May), 411-15.
        Describes the ranch; London talks about it.

47   MITCHELL, THEODORE C.   "Introduction," in his edition of The
     Call of the Wild.   Macmillan's Pocket American and English
     Classics.   New York: Macmillan, pp. vii-xxxi.
        Discusses the geographical setting of the novel; Klondike
     history; placer-mining; the dog in mythology and literature;
     life in the Klondike; London's life and broad range of
     writings.   London is "typically American" and "the literary
     representative of his age."   Critics recognize his strengths:
     his "'barbarian' curiosity, alertness, concreteness, and
     zest of struggle and conquest"; his skillful, sympathetic
     portrayal of nature's vastness and society's victims; his
     clear style, plausibly-rendered characters and action, and
     the frankness of his self-portraits.   However, "the more
     thoughtful critics feel...[he] fell short of greatness."
     He lacked Harte's simplicity and Kipling's "literary re-
     straint," as well as breadth of subject and characteriza-
     tion, and objectivity.

48   PEASE, FRANK.   "Impressions of Jack London."   Seven Arts, 1
     (March), 522-30.
        At the "beer bust" described in John Barleycorn, London
     awed the young men with his persuasive socialism and the
     "overpowering and protean charm" of his personality.   Lon-
     don was born to command others and should have become a
     political leader; but his milieu forced him to channel his
     egoism into autobiographical writings.   His work is not
     "fine art": it is too personal and too limited by his ob-
     session with science; it is unsophisticated and omits the
     "three aristocratic principles: culture, selection, sim-
     plicity."   As "both moralist and immoralist" in John Bar-
     leycorn, London fails to be "a creator of values, which is
     what a literary man should be."

1917

49   PRICE, ARTHUR. "London's Sea Tales Are Assailed." San Fran-
        cisco Examiner (26 September), p. 20.
            Lincoln Concord said London wrote "landlubberly" sea
        stories, "all false--and rot besides." But London really
        did know the sailor's life and he stressed its brutality
        because this part was meaningful to him as a "reporter of
        life."

50   SINCLAIR, UPTON. "About Jack London." Masses, 9 (November-
        December), 17-20.
            From their first exchange of letters in 1902, through
        correspondence (and two meetings) until London's death,
        "there existed a suppressed controversy" between Sinclair
        and London of "self-discipline versus self-indulgence; or,
        as Jack would have put it...asceticism versus self-expres-
        sion." Such conflicting attitudes towards alcohol and sex
        limited their friendship. London planned to write a book
        about his sexual experiences "revealing his tragic disil-
        lusionment, his contempt for woman as a parasite and a
        snare." But from the beginning, he dreamed and wrote of
        a higher type of "strong, free, proud" mate-woman and con-
        tinued to write about her "long after he had ceased to be-
        lieve in it himself. I have often thought that this ne-
        cessity of writing about sex in a way that was utterly in-
        sincere was the main cause of that contempt for his own
        fiction which London was so swift and vehement to pro-
        claim." His real feeling about women surfaces only in
        Martin Eden. In this novel, as in The Sea-Wolf and The
        Mutiny of the Elsinore, he intends to show the defeat of
        the "red-blooded superman," but the "Nietzschean all con-
        querer has conquered London's imagination, in spite of his
        reason and his conscience," and he fails to make the moral
        clear. The People of the Abyss and Socialist essays make
        London "one of the great revolutionary figures of our his-
        tory." He was a generous, honest, and tenderhearted man;
        "a man with a magnificent mind, and a giant's will....he
        was a man of action....he had a love of truth that was a
        passion, a hatred of injustice that burned volcanic fires.
        He was a deeply sad man, a bitterly, cruelly suffering
        man....one of the greatest writers and one of the greatest
        souls that America has given to the world." Revised text:
        1925.B3.

51   STELLMANN, LOUIS J. "Jack London--The Man." Overland Monthly,
        70 (October), 385-87.
            Describes London's life on the ranch and his ideals.
        Revised text: 1917.B52.

52 _____. "Jack London, Super-boy." <u>Sunset, The Pacific Monthly</u>,
 38 (February), 42, 81.
  Essentially the same as 1917.B51.

1918 A BOOKS - NONE

1918 B SHORTER WRITINGS

1 ANON. "London, Jack. <u>Michael, Brother of Jerry</u>." <u>ALA Book-
 list</u>, 14 (January), 132.
  Describes plot.

2 ANON. "Our Booking-Office [<u>Michael, Brother of Jerry</u>]."
 <u>Punch</u>, 154 (13 February), 112.
  "The author's sincerity and skill make this tale...in-
 tensely moving. When Mr. Jack London died, animals lost a
 very true friend and the world of letters a spirited
 writer."

3 ANON. "Fiction: London (Jack). Hearts of Three." <u>Athenaeum</u>,
 4635 (November), 485.
  This is "novelized kinematograph film." Brief.

4 ANON. "Latest Works of Fiction: <u>The Red One</u>." <u>New York Times
 Editorial Section and Review of Books</u> (10 November),
 pp. 3-4.
  The title tale is "powerful, imaginative, it grips the
 reader's interest and impresses itself on his memory....
 [It is] poetic in its conception, bitter in its irony,
 vivid, instinct with life and with color." The other
 tales are not bad.

5 ANON. "In Various Worlds [<u>The Red One</u>]. <u>Nation</u>, 107 (23 November), 628.
  "London's fancy tarried to the last." Brief.

6 ANON. "The War Has Laid Basis for Better-Informed Prophecy."
 <u>San Francisco Examiner</u> (13 December), p. 18.
  In "The Human Drift" London described the perpetual movements in search of food which he felt would in time be
 accomplished without war. His optimism was premature.

7 [DOUGLAS, GEORGE]. "Books of the New Year: 'Michael,' A Dog
 Story that Shows Jack London at His Best." <u>San Francisco
 Chronicle</u> (13 January), Editorial, Book Review...Section,
 p. 2E.
  A sympathetic and memorable story.

1918

8 E.[DGETT], E.[DWIN] F.[RANCIS]. "Books of the Day--The Red
   One; Jack London and His Essence of Humanity." Boston
   Evening Transcript (30 November), part 3, p. 6.
       "He saw life in terms of fiction, and fiction in terms
   of life, and the extent of his imaginative labors during
   his brief period of popularity is amazing....He wrote too
   much for his own good....but he wrote not a little that
   was marvelously fine and that may likely endure." These
   stories masterfully analyze primitive life; "they are of
   the veriest stuff of humanity."

9 HOMANS, JAMES E., ed. Appleton's Cyclopaedia of American
   Biography. Revised edition. Volume 8. New York: Press
   Association, 454.
       Biography and bibliography.

10 LANE, ROSE WILDER. "Life and Jack London." Sunset, The
   Pacific Monthly, 40 (January), 34-37, 62-64; (February),
   30-34, 67-68; (March), 27-30, 64-66; (April), 21-25, 60,
   62; (May), 28-32, 60, 62, 64, 66, 68, 70, 72.
       A continuation of Lane, 1917.B40.

11 RANKIN, THOMAS E. American Authorship of the Present Day.
   Ann Arbor, Michigan: Wahr, p. 23.
       London "remains unequalled in his special field."

12 TRENT, WILLIAM PETERFIELD, et al., eds. Cambridge History of
   American Literature. Volume 2 (of 3 volumes). New York:
   Macmillan, 391, 392, 393. [Essay in which London is
   discussed is written by Fred Lewis Pattee.]
       London gave the masses what they demanded: sensation,
   strangeness, action, melodrama. "Force undoubtedly he
   had and freshness of material, but, lacking poise and
   moral background and beauty of style, he must be passed
   as an ephemeral sensation." Reprinted: 1922.B7. Same,
   reprinted in CHAL, volume 2, 1936; and in CHAL, 3 volumes
   in 1, 1943. See 1921.B6.

13 VOLLMER, CLEMENT. The American Novel in Germany, 1871-1913.
   Philadelphia: International Printing Company, pp. 36, 39,
   78-79.
       A bibliography of London's works published in German to
   1914; lists 10 items.

14 WILLIAMS, HAROLD. Modern English Writers: Being a Study of
   Imaginative Literature, 1890-1914. London: Sidgwick &
   Jackson, pp. 477-78.
       London "was by gift a writer of the brief sketch and

short story....he was no novelist." His tales, uneven in
quality, "relate to wild and savage, to vagrant and curious
life." "The style is sometimes ugly" and beset by "exaggerated language." He does "wonderfully realistic painting
of the landscape, colour, and atmosphere" in the Alaskan
tales where he is an unrivaled "artist in words." Same,
in third edition, revised, 1925.

1919 A BOOKS - NONE

1919 B SHORTER WRITINGS

1   ANON. "Jack London's Tales of Hawaii." New York Times Review
     of Books (16 November), p. [649].
         On the Makaloa Mat gives a "fascinating picture" of old
     and modern island life. With great variety of subjects,
     the tales are colorful and well-written. Describes con-
     tents in detail.

2   ANON. "Three Careers." Nation, 109 (29 November), 693.
         "He wrote himself out for lands and houses....he more
     and more substituted gesture for impulse and mere violence
     for the superb gusto and freshness of his youth." A col-
     lection of his finest stories should be published, in-
     cluding some from this volume, On the Makaloa Mat, which
     is "as a whole, mellow and deeply felt."

3   ELLSWORTH, WILLIAM W. "Jack London," in Golden Age of Authors.
     Boston: Houghton Mifflin, pp. 97-102, 109.
         Biography, and a letter by London.

4   FRANK, WALDO. Our America. New York: Boni & Liveright,
     pp. 34-38.
         London's background was "the background of America: He
     had gone back to primal stratum: stolen and labored and
     adventured....He pierced the American myths." But nothing
     of his passionate experience entered his writing whose
     burden "was an infantile romanticism under which he de-
     liberately hid his own despair." Typically, John Barley-
     corn "reveals no trace of self-consciousness, no suggestion
     of the sanctity of art, no hint of the values of life."
     London, like America (and because he wrote in America) was
     "over-extraverted"; he lacked "inner fire," avoided present
     reality, and remained a child. Same, reprinted: New York:
     AMS Press, 1972.

1919

5   MENCKEN, H.[ENRY] L.[EWIS]. "Jack London," in his Prejudices,
     First Series. New York: Knopf, pp. 236-39.
       "The man, in truth, was an instinctive artist of high
     order, and if ignorance often corrupted his art, it only
     made the fact of his inborn mastery the more remarkable."
     London's ideas, especially his "jejune Socialism," spoiled
     his fiction and made him greedy for money; he "sold him-
     self into slavery to the publishers." But "at bottom, [he]
     was no fraud....There was in him a vast delicacy of per-
     ception, a high feeling, a sensitiveness to beauty. And
     there was in him, too, under all his blatancies, a poignant
     sense of the infinite romance and mystery of human life."

6   SILVER, GRACE V. "Jack London's Women." Overland Monthly,
     74 (July), 24-28.
       He gave us "the most wonderful series of pen portraits
     of modern women ever drawn." They are of two kinds: the
     "mate-women," comrades, co-workers, homemakers, and de-
     voted lovers, such as Saxon, Dede Mason, and Lizzie Con-
     nolly, all "vivid incarnations of Charmian Kittredge."
     The second type, the "parasite," is a woman who gives love
     only in return for economic support, such as Ruth Morse
     and Maud Brewster. The latter may seem artificial, but
     they are true-to-life "artificial products of an arti-
     ficial social system, crippled daughters of a soul-
     destroying civilization." London's popularity among men
     comes in large part from his portraits of mate-women,
     "the ideal woman consciously or unconsciously in the
     minds of millions of men."

1920 A BOOKS - NONE

1920 B SHORTER WRITINGS

1   ANON. "Jack London and Oklahoma." Historia, 8, no. 5
     (1 January), 6-7.
       Mr. Ham Gardener, who "accompanied London on his tour
     of the South Seas in 1912 [sic]," donated a large collec-
     tion of souvenirs London accumulated on the voyage to the
     Oklahoma Historical Society. Gives biography.

2   ANON. "New Books and Others: 'On the Makoloa Mat'; Jack Lon-
     don's Volume Contains Some of the Best of His Hawaiian
     Tales." San Francisco Chronicle (18 January), Editorial--
     Music--Features Section, p. 2E.
       These "dramatic and colorful tales," written in London's
     "mature, spontaneous style," reveal his love and apprecia-
     tive sympathy for the Hawaiians.

3   ANON. Review of <u>Revolution and Other Essays</u>. <u>Athenaeum</u>,
        4701 (4 June), 749.
          "Squalid and heartrending pictures of destitution in the
        United States." London's "faith was in the working-class."

4   ANON. "Our Booking-Office [<u>Island Tales</u>]." <u>Punch</u>, 159
        (25 August), 159.
          Examples of "his art in one aspect of its best," a highly
        successful recreation of "the lotus-leisure of perpetual
        afternoon" in the South Seas. We suffer a great loss in
        London who "could put such jewelled loveliness on to the
        printed page."

5   ANON. "The Book of the Week: Jack London's Last Tales."
        <u>John O'London's Weekly</u>, 3 (4 September), [601]-602.
          <u>Island Tales</u> give romantic pictures of larger-than-life
        primitive men, and other stories are ironically comic,
        cynical, or sentimental. They bear no relation to real
        life but give reading pleasure.

6   ANON. "The New Books: <u>Hearts of Three</u>." <u>Outlook</u>, 126
        (10 November), 470.
          Brief mention.

7   ANON. "Latest Works of Fiction: <u>Hearts of Three</u>." <u>New York
        Times Book Review</u> (26 December), p. 24.
          An amusing and "refreshingly frank" work.

8   B., L. "New Fiction." <u>Freeman</u> (New York), 2 (1 December),
        285.
          <u>Hearts of Three</u> resembles a moving-picture scenario by
        Charles Goddard. It "is a novel with a wealth of action,
        piled up without discrimination."

9   BOWEN, EDWIN E. "Jack London's Place in American Literature,"
        <u>Reformed Church Review</u>, 4th series, 24, 306-15.
          Gives biography. London's short stories, notably the
        Klondike tales, are his best work. He sometimes "sacri-
        ficed quality to quantity," portrayed life inaccurately
        or incompletely, lacked polish and the ability to create
        flesh and blood women. His fiction and socialist writings
        succeeded when they were most subjective, reflecting Lon-
        don's romantic, emotional nature, his love of life, and
        sympathy for the underdog. The "virility and dramatic
        power" and the originality of his tales make them a "mar-
        vellous achievement" which critics have undervalued.

1920

10   CONNELL, SARAH. "Stories from the Files: Jack London Wooed
        Fame Through the Overland Monthly: An Appreciation of the
        Virile Californian in His Varieties." Overland Monthly,
        76 (October), 65-71.
           London's early hard life, adventures, and indefatigible
        labors produced a large quantity of sincere, vital, and
        interesting work. "There are at least a dozen of the short
        stories that ought to endure as long as the language it-
        self....there is every reason to believe that his master-
        piece was yet to come."

11   HILL, MURRAY. "Murray Hill on His Travels." Bookman (New York),
        52 (December), 349-55.
           The original of Wolf Larsen was a "professional smuggler"
        well-known around San Francisco. Phineas Frolic, a Nor-
        wegian sculptor, insisted on meeting London after he read
        The Sea-Wolf. "Gambling with London the sculptor won a
        cow and three goats."

12   HOLLIDAY, ROBERT CORTES. "A Pal of Jack London," in his Men
        and Books and Cities. New York: George H. Doran, pp. 232-44.
           Mentions London's meeting with Phineas (Finn) Frolic, the
        sculptor.

13   McCABE, JOSEPH, comp. A Biographical Dictionary of Modern
        Rationalists. London: Watts & Company, pp. 455-56.
           Brief biography.

14   M.[ANSFIELD], K.[ATHERINE]. "Hearts are Trumps." Athenaeum,
        4713 (27 August), 272.
           "Here was a genial, warm-blooded fellow, who liked a
        name to be a name, a snowstorm to be a snowstorm and a man
        to be a hero." He never became a real adventurer and rebel
        because "his heart went to his head and he was carried
        away by passions"; then he smothered his simplicity "under
        a torrent of puffed-up words." London's best work was
        White Fang. Island Tales are "machine-made, ready-to-
        read," of average magazine quality, and heavy with senti-
        mentality. London's "salvation lay in wolves, snow, hard-
        ship and toil." Reprinted: 1930.B8.

15   SINCLAIR, UPTON. "The Press and Jack London," in his The
        Brass Check, A Study of American Journalism. Pasadena,
        California: Author, pp. 341-43.
           The press frequently misquoted and vilified London for
        his radical activities.

16   WILLIAMS, BLANCHE C. "Jack London," in her <u>Our Short Story</u>
      <u>Writers</u>. New York: Moffat, Yard, pp. 256-77.
      "A short story critic and a short story lover will pro-
      nounce Jack London engaging, thrilling, and satisfactory.
      The critic of literature,...will declare him at best a
      third-rate writer." He was a superior story-teller, a
      "raconteur" who pioneered "in marking our unexplored geo-
      graphical areas" and in developing new and often shocking
      "radical or refreshing" style. Admirable are the "clear-
      ness and vividness of narrative action....his sense of the
      dramatic and picturesque....his amazing fertility and his
      wide range of subject matter," all unified by his "interest
      in sociology, and evolution [which] is usually not obtru-
      sive." On the other hand, he blunders in academic and
      philosophic areas, avoids "the realm of pure spirit" and
      all subtlety, and he creates no living characters. Same,
      reprinted: Essay Index Reprint Series. Freeport, N. Y.:
      Books for Libraries, 1969.

1921 A BOOKS

1   LONDON, CHARMIAN. <u>The Book of Jack London</u>. 2 volumes. New
     York: Century, 841 pp. Published as <u>Jack London</u>.
     2 volumes. London: Mills & Boon. Serialized in part:
     <u>Century Illustrated Magazine</u>: "The Sailor on Foot and
     Rod," 101 (March), 545-55; "Briton Blood and Gypsy Instinct,"
     102 (May), 105-11; "Jack London as a Boy," 102 (June), 287-
     93; "Jack London: Man and Husband," 102 (July), 443-52;
     "Jack London's Last Day," 102 (August), 599-606.
     Volume I covers 1876-1904; the life to c. 1897 is from
     London's autobiographical essays, such works as <u>The Road</u>
     and <u>John Barleycorn</u>, and from "conversations" with Charmian
     in later years.
     [Origins-1882]. Describes London's pride in his Anglo-
     Saxon breed, his titled British ancestors. His parents
     were John London of Pennsylvania, a Civil War hero and
     father of eleven children by his first wife, and Flora
     Wellman, an upper-class woman of predominantly British
     stock. London was born in "a large and not inelegant"
     house. Throughout his life "his excessive sensibilities"
     caused him acute mental and physical suffering; and his
     ambitions drove him "to superactivity," bringing on
     "weariness of heart and brain." At such times, he exag-
     gerated the poverty, hunger, lovelessness, and trials of
     a childhood which actually was far from a poor one.
     [1883-1893]. At the age of seven, he drank himself un-
     conscious; at eight, he read and loved Ouida's <u>Signa</u>; he

built a model of the Alhambra after reading Irving. A
"spiritually lonely" child, he read voraciously and dreamed
a lot, which made him a misfit in school. His most cherished
comrade was his father John. In adolescence, "there was im-
planted in him a second nature of protest and rebellion,"
and he came to love the sea with a passion that endured all
his life. The Queen of the Oyster Pirates became his, but
he did not lose his head over her. "As always, a woman's-
man, still women never interfered with his playing the
man's game....he succeeded in spite of petticoats." London
decided there would be no alcohol aboard his boats; ashore,
Johnny Heinhold opened a charge account for him in his
saloon. From age 16 to 21, he "must have committed nearly
every <u>natural</u> crime in the calendar, save disloyalty and
murder." To him, disloyalty was "the only real sin." He
shunned "<u>unnatural</u> crimes." As early as age 17, money became only "a means to an end, or to many ends. Money
brought larger life, and life to the full, was all his
goal." After his visit to Yokahama "he nourished an ad-
miring respect for these...brilliant-minded sub-Mongolians"
and their women. London "did not drink. He did not want
to drink. He never in his whole life wanted to drink for
drink's sake." He fell in love with Haydee, adored her
with a "mysteriously holy, passionless, clean" love, "as
if for an angel or a bird."
   [1894-1897]. Resenting the exploitation of his "manifest
and enviable muscle," London took to the road and enjoyed
"this great picnic of irresponsibility." He met and so
admired his uncle Ernest Everhard that he used the name
"for one of his own favorite characters." The many hoboes
who were failures he saw as "hereditary inefficients," the
cultured tramps fired his ambition for education, and he
felt "brother-love" for all the unloved men, a love which
eventually broke his heart. Because of his outrageously
unjust jail conviction, London never expressed patriotic
support for America until Mexico and Germany threatened.
He became a high school student and a Socialist, met the
"Lily Maid of Britain" [Mabel Applegarth], whose "unlike-
ness to him" made him worship her; and he attended the
University of California. For a year and a half, busy
with the "Lily Maid" and his studies, he "never took a
drink."
   [1897-1898]. Describes London's adventures in the
Klondike from Fred Thompson's journal, London's writings
and diary of June, 1898 (printed here in full), and a
recollection of W. B. Hargrave.
   [1898-1903]. Prints letters, in part or in full, with
little commentary: London's to the "Lily Maid,"

Cloudesley Johns, Anna Strunsky, and one from Strunsky (1919) describing her friendship with Jack.

[1900-1902]. Ninetta Eames, Charmian's aunt, arranged her first meeting with Jack in the Spring of 1900: "I met a pair of fathomless sea-blue eyes, and experienced a sudden and unexpected impact of his mental and physical vitality." Discusses London's marriage to Elizabeth (Bess) Maddern: "His idea of adding a member to the household was born of the moment." His reasons for this "abrupt and loveless union" may have related to his feelings for Anna Strunsky. "The Crowd" and numerous celebrities enjoyed Wednesday parties in the Piedmont bungalow, "all good, and clean, and wholesome" fun.

[1903]. "Desperate for funds," London accepted a flat $2000 from Macmillan for The Call of the Wild and $700 for serial publication in the Saturday Evening Post. He was under great strain and terribly unhappy. "Much suffering he concealed in the solitude of a leafy study on a mossy shelf down the bank....He caught at a wild unthought-out suggestion for a northern trip without an ending--and not without a companion. Largely owing to restlessness, he renounced the steamer voyage as lightly as he had conceived it." But he desired freedom, recognized "a boundless mistake in his arrogant youth," and, although he deeply loved his daughters, he moved to an apartment in Oakland.

[1904]. Discusses London as correspondent in the Russo-Japanese War; prints his letters to Charmian.

Volume 2: Autumn, 1904-November, 1916.

[1904-1905]. Discusses London's divorce from Bess; an idyllic summer with Charmian at Glen Ellen; purchase of a 129-acre farm. Prints London's letters to publishers and to Cloudesley Johns. Jack despised the emotion of jealousy. Although he "charmed women of all classes" and women "have died for love of him," he never allowed them to interfere with his life. He could not "abide a stupid woman." He bought love only "in the course of laying his curiosity. A passion with him, must be mutual, else worthless." London "saw the primitiveness in all life, in himself"; but he did not live it, for he was "delicate," sensitive to beauty, sympathetic and generous; "his materialism incarnated his idealism, and his idealism consecrated and transfigured his materialism." Jack had a "missionary mind" and loved to shake people out of complacency. "He cared almost not at all, except as it might affect his market, or his authority, for public opinion of himself or his books." The greatest virtue of this "protean man-boy" was his "surpassing lovableness."

[1905-1906]. Prints London's love letters to Charmian.

Describes their marriage; London's lecture tour; their
trips to Jamaica, Cuba, and New York City; planting a vine-
yard and orchard on the Ranch; charges of plagiarism [Be-
fore Adam]; the problem of London "doubles"; the San Francisco earthquake; London's writing habits, and his quarrel
with Bierce over Sterling.

[1907-1909]. Prints London's correspondence with magazines concerning the Snark voyage. Describes the Manyoungi
incident: "Will God have some beer?"; their continual entertaining of friends at the Ranch; Jack's diet of "'ten-
minute'" wild ducks and Liebfraumilch. Prints London's
letters to Sterling and Johns and excerpts from his notes
and essays, all concerning the Snark voyage. During the
Snark trip, London wrote "the equivalent of more than
eight full volumes." Describes their experiences in South
and Central America on the homeward journey from Australia;
improvements and additions to the Beauty Ranch; London's
justification for Martin Eden's suicide.

[1910-1911]. When their daughter Joy died 38 hours after
birth, Jack went into Oakland where he suffered an "unpro-
voked attack" in a saloon [Muldowney's] which he had entered to use the lavatory. Eliza's search of real estate
records revealed "that the Hebrew police judge who dared
to sit on the case, was in truth owner of the resort."
The press vilely distorted Jack's part in this affair.
Discusses a sailing trip on the Roamer; planning of Wolf
house; hospitality at the Ranch and notable guests; Jack's
generosity to young writers; the nightly "ceremonial" pro-
visioning of his bedside table; a four-horse driving trip;
Jack's notes for future works. "I marvel to think of his
eternal patience with pain; probably he was never, for
years at a time, free from pain or at least discomfort."

[1912]. Describes a winter trip to New York City; a
voyage around Cape Horn on the Dirigo during which Jack
caught albatrosses and pulled teeth for the crew. While
typing John Barleycorn, Charmian was shocked "at the content of Jack's mind....with regard to his past,...[and] by
a realization of the restlessness and deep-reaching melancholy he suffered from the frustrations of his dearest
ambition--victorious fatherhood of my children."

[1913]. This "bad year" brought deaths of friends and
farm animals, a lawsuit over copyright to The Sea-Wolf
movie rights, losses in a fraudulent Mexican land scheme,
destruction of Wolf House by arson: "The razing of his
house killed something in Jack, and he never ceased to
feel the tragic inner sense of loss." Jack did everything
in a large way. By temperament, he "was a Builder of
books, of houses, of roads, of soil, of things that would

outlast merely temporary use." He loved to be called
"Farmer"; he was "really far more interested in introducing
farming into Sonoma County and the country at large than he
was in leaving behind masterpieces of literature." Discusses London's accomplishments and plans in farming, animal raising, building, and soil conservation. Gives excerpts
from his essays and letters.

[1914-1915]. Describes failure of a grapejuice company
venture; London's six-week stay in Mexico; a trip to Hawaii;
the loss of Nakata. "He never ceased to maintain that he
hated to write--he had to drive himself to do it."

[1916]. London's resignation from the Socialist party
and responses to it; his letters supporting the rightness
of World War I. "Jack's life is the story of a princely
ego that struggled for full expression, and realized it
only in a small degree." He discovered Freud and Jung,
applied their insights to himself and other people, and
this probing brought him greater unhappiness and disillusionment with humanity. Through his last year, he seemed
to be "running away from himself," willing his destruction.
Tired, under great strain, overweight, suffering from
pyorrhea, rheumatism, uremia, and dysentery, he ignored
physician's orders to diet and exercise, and he had a
"physical and nervous breakdown." Describes their last
evening together and the futile efforts of many persons
to rouse London from his coma. Nothing could save Jack.
"He was, I see it, setting the last fleeting effort of
his life, of his reasoned will, against rehabilitation of
that life and will." Charmian "preferred to remain away
from a funeral which represented Jack's idea so little,
but which I felt should be accorded to his daughters and
their mother." Includes bibliography, pp. 397-414.

1921 B SHORTER WRITINGS

1   GOODMAN, HENRY. "Faith and Jack London." Bookman (New York),
    54 (September), 13-16.
        A short story.

2   [LONDON, CHARMIAN]. "Jack London as His Wife Charmian Knew
    Him." Current Opinion, 71 (November), 645-48.
        Excerpts from 1921.A1.

3   _____. "After Klondike Gold, with Jack London." Literary
    Digest, 71 (5 November), 37-38, 40-41.
        Excerpts from 1921.A1.

1921

4   PERRY, BLISS. The American Spirit in Literature. New Haven:
      Yale University Press, pp. 243-44.
        "His books are very uneven, but he wrote many a hard-
      muscled, clean-cut page....[His] formula was that at bot-
      tom, every man is a brute."

5   VAN DOREN, CARL. The American Novel. New York: Macmillan,
      pp. 266-70.
        London's books, most of them autobiographical, propagan-
      dized for socialism, and "he wrote always under the obses-
      sion of physical energy" and evolutionary struggle. "As
      he had a boy's glee in conflict, so he had a boy's insensi-
      bility to physical suffering." For popularity and money
      he wrote too much, never attaining the early excellence of
      The Call of the Wild with its "fine sensitiveness to land-
      scape and environment, a robust, moving genuine current of
      poetry." Same, reprinted: 1922, 1924. Essentially the
      same, reprinted: The American Novel: 1789-1939. New York:
      Macmillan, 1940, pp. 237-40.

6   TRENT, WILLIAM PETERFIELD, et al., eds. Cambridge History of
      American Literature. Volume 3 (of 3 volumes). New York:
      Macmillan, 94. [Essay in which London is discussed is
      written by Carl Van Doren.]
        "He carried the cult of 'red-blood' to its logical, if
      not ridiculous extreme." Same, reprinted in CHAL, volume 3,
      1936; and in CHAL, 3 volumes in 1, 1943. See 1918.B12.

1922 A BOOKS

1   LONDON, CHARMIAN. Our Hawaii (Islands and Islanders). New
      and revised edition. New York: Macmillan, 439 pp. Pub-
      lished as The New Hawaii. Containing My Hawaiian Aloha
      by Jack London. London: Mills & Boon, 1923, 270 pp.
        Revised editions of 1917.A3, with biography the same and
      writings by London added.

1922 B SHORTER WRITINGS

1   ANON. "A Reviewer's Notebook." Freeman (New York), 4
      (4 January), 407.
        [A review of 1921.A1.] London's early work, characterized
      by "typically American glorification of the will," a "bra-
      zen style," and "swagger of incidents" best reveals the
      "abnormal self-assertiveness" which made him fail as an
      artist.

2   GARNETT, EDWARD. Friday Nights: Literary Criticisms and Appre-
    ciations, First Series. New York: Knopf, pp. 256-60.
        Burning Daylight, although "written with literary skill
    and conviction," exaggerates and generalizes the charac-
    ters, reducing their vitality and unique humanity to stan-
    dardized cliches. Harnish "is an American superman" and
    Dede Mason talks "like a syndicate of American women as
    reported by a news agency." The novel is valuable for its
    information on Yukon pioneering and "as a smashing criti-
    cism of American business ideals."

3   JORDAN, DAVID STARR. The Days of a Man. Volume 1. Yonkers-
    on-Hudson, N. Y.: World Book Company, 460.
        London took Jordan's "university extension course on
    Evolution....[and] became in some degree an intellectual
    disciple." Jordan invited him to read his Alaskan stories
    at Stanford.

4   MANLY, JOHN MATTHEW and EDITH RICKERT. Contemporary American
    Literature: Bibliographies and Study Outline. New York:
    Harcourt Brace, pp. 37-38, 223-24.
        London conquered "new domains of action and emotion for
    the short story....His reputation lives on chiefly in
    Germany and Russia....His influence survives in no repu-
    table writer." Gives biography and lists works. Same,
    revised edition: 1929.

5   MUMFORD, LEWIS. "Jack London." New Republic, 30 (29 March),
    145-47.
        [A review of 1921.A1.] "Her hero, if not a Chocolate
    Soldier, turns out to be a Gingerbread Superman." Lon-
    don's real life was far more drab and conventional than
    the myths about him. "What is lovable and attractive in
    London seems to remain over from" his years through ado-
    lescence. Afterwards "he hardened into a self-conscious,
    aggressive, dogmatic, 'economic man'; this whole phase was
    devoted to the 'game' of literature....London turned out
    to be a red-blooded prig." In exchange for comfort and
    security he abandoned his art and ran away from "the self
    of an artist." After Martin Eden, the man himself disin-
    tegrated; "he relapsed into mud pies." London rationalized
    "his inferiority complex as Anglo-Saxonism,...his slavish
    attempts to win the pecuniary favors of the big magazines
    as 'survival of the fittest.'" His "philosophy and science
    is a superstitious rigamarole." London failed to find new
    values and as an artist to create new values: "the recog-
    nition of this failure probably killed the man."

1922

6   PATTEE, FRED LEWIS. "The Prophet of the Last Frontier," in
     his Sidelights on American Literature. New York: Century,
     pp. 98-160.
         "Whatever one may think of his literary product, one can
     but admire the pluck and perseverance that brought his
     final success. No one ever succeeded with heavier odds,
     and no one with more of toil." London's work was wide-
     ranging in subject, uneven in texture and content. "To
     read Jack London through is to emerge in confusion: a
     swift-running film of vignette-like pictures; hobbies
     furiously ridden;...everywhere antithesis: soap-box shrill-
     ness and harmonious music; poverty of style and sonorous
     ornateness;...always superlatives and exaggerations in
     wild riot." All his work is autobiographical, his charac-
     ters idealized self-portraits and "demigods, the unsung
     heroes of a heroic age now put into epic setting." Most
     convincing are his Indian women, "his only addition to the
     gallery of original characters in American fiction." Lon-
     don's techniques include Kipling-like "startling pictures,"
     "Bret Harte paradoxes," "Defoe-like concreteness" of detail.
     After the early Alaskan fiction, theorizing and propaganda
     overburden his work; the novels are episodic and poorly
     constructed, and his range narrowed to the gross or sensa-
     tional surfaces of life. London's materialistic and indi-
     vidualistic temperament, and lack of humor and restraint,
     made him a masterful journalist of primitive action but
     kept him from major artistic accomplishment. He did, how-
     ever, try to convey a larger cosmic motif, to find a
     meaning and purpose for life itself; and he emerges as the
     interpreter and voice of California and the Pacific North-
     west that enriched the entire United States. London also
     embodied the age's international spirit in his ethics,
     goals, and language: he was "the most widely representa-
     tive American literary figure, the more arresting literary
     voice during the decade preceding the war." He prophesied
     the savage tyranny of men and nations that lay beneath
     civilized veneers and supremacy of the strong in battles
     for survival. He "can be but a temporary disturbance,"
     for his philosophies, pseudoscience, and escapist solu-
     tions are fallacious and out-dated. Of his writings, "a
     few fragments from his novels, a dozen or two of his short
     stories that are wholly American in scene and spirit, and
     The Call of the Wild may survive their day. Gives biogra-
     phy. Abridged and revised: 1923.B4; abridged: 1930.B10.

7   TRENT, WILLIAM PETERFIELD, et al., eds. A Short History of
     American Literature. New York: G. P. Putnam's, pp. 335,
     336, 337.

JACK LONDON: A REFERENCE GUIDE

Reprinted: London: Cambridge University Press, 1924.
Both are reprints of 1918.B12.

1923 A BOOKS

1   [TICHENOR, HENRY MULFORD]. Life of Jack London. Ten Cent
    Pocket Series No. 183. Edited by E. Haldeman-Julius.
    Girard, Kansas: Haldeman-Julius Company, 53 pp.
       A biography based on and illustrated by extensive quo-
    tations from London's writings (novels, essays, and non-
    fiction) and from published articles about him. London
    was a romancer, a Socialist, and a materialist. "A versa-
    tile writer, with a broad range of mind; turning to any
    field of thought that came to his vision; drawing his own
    conclusions of life, of society, of time and eternity;
    restless as the sea he loved so well; ever in the storm,
    seemingly certain that all voyages ended in shipwreck,...
    No man ever hurried through life faster than Jack London."
    He wrote about the tragic side of life and man's subcon-
    scious and recorded his own life in Martin Eden.

1923 B SHORTER WRITINGS

1   HANEY, JOHN LOUIS. The Story of Our Literature. New York:
    Scribner, pp. 258, 359.
       Brief biography and bibliography.

2   KENNEDY, ANNEBELLE. "Maxim Gorky and Jack London: A Compara-
    tive Study." Life and Letters (Girard, Kansas), 2, no. 4
    (December), 3-6.
       They had in common a poverty-stricken childhood, hard
    work at menial jobs, self-education; both were individual-
    ists, Socialists, tramps; their early work was their best,
    and their heroes expressed a Nietzschean philosophy. Un-
    like the later Gorky, whose emotions and social conscious-
    ness matured, London remained an egocentric until he died
    "a bitter cynic." For his solitary heroes, battling nature
    and other men, the active struggle is all; his women
    characters are unreal and unconvincing. London's second-
    hand knowledge outweighed his originality and social in-
    sights. Both men symbolize their countries during the
    periods of their creativity.

3   O'BRIEN, EDWARD J. The Advance of the American Short Story.
    New York: Dodd, Mead, pp. 187-90, 193, 197, 302.
       London had tremendous "vitality and curiosity," a unique
    "forceful style and epic subject-matter." But "the blight

1923

of commercialism ruined a fine artist." He wrote "down to
an undiscriminating public" which cherished the brutal
ethics of urban and business life and sought escape "from
its own inhibitions" in melodrama and romantic adventure.
Same, in revised edition: St. Clair Shores, Michigan:
Scholarly Press, 1972.

4   PATTEE, FRED LEWIS. The Development of the American Short
     Story: An Historical Survey. New York: Harper, pp. 316,
     343-44, 347-53, 356, 373.
        "One's first impulse is to dismiss him with a line. His
     crudeness, his unrevised prolixity and chaotic story struc-
     ture, his red-flag socialism...his cave-man philosophy,...
     wild dreams of adolescence--all of this seems hardly ma-
     terial for permanent literature." But he must be reckoned
     with as "the product of a literary condition in America."
     London could make intensely alive and dramatic a single
     episode, create atmosphere and an "underrunning motif," and
     write in a distinctive "nearly poetic style." His stories
     "have the quality of sagas." The Call of the Wild is "an
     epic dream of the heroic age of the North." "Jack London-
     ism,...was antisentimentalism,...a call of the wild, a pro-
     phet cry in the soft decade before the German deluge." Re-
     vised and abridged text of 1922.B6.

5   ROMM, CHARLES, comp. "American First Editions: A Series of
     Bibliographic Check-lists." Edited by Merle Johnson and
     Frederick M. Hopkins. Number 33. "Jack London, 1876-1916."
     Publishers' Weekly, 103 (12 May), 1463-64.
        Lists fifty volumes, three miscellaneous pieces by Lon-
     don; and six books about him. Reprinted, slightly revised:
     Johnson, 1929.B7.

6   TULLY, JIM. "The Baffled Greatness of Jack London." The
     Literary Digest International Book Review, 1 (June), 18-19,
     80.
        Personal reminiscences. London was a dynamic, generous,
     intellectually gifted rebel, a great story-teller, and the
     "first really great vagabond writer" of America. But fame
     and wealth came too early and killed the artist in him.
     He conformed to editorial and public tastes, propagandized,
     and became a "bourgeois citizen and owner of land." Lon-
     don "was greater than anything he ever wrote, as are many
     writers in America....Though he did not express the great
     things in his life, he felt them, nevertheless. He died,
     baffled and beaten." Revised: 1925.B5.

1924 A BOOKS - NONE

1924 B SHORTER WRITINGS

1   FRANCE, ANATOLE. "Introduction," in The Iron Heel. Sonoma
     edition. New York: Macmillan, pp. xiii-xvii.
          London was like Everhard, a revolutionary Socialist from
     the working class, a courageous, wise, great-souled, gentle
     man. He rightly showed us "our faults and our imprudences"
     in this novel. We must struggle to make Everhard's cause
     succeed. [This introduction is reprinted in many later
     editions of The Iron Heel.]

2   GALANTIERE, LEWIS. "American Books in France." American Mer-
     cury, 2 (May), 97-102.
          The ordinary Frenchman sees America through the eyes of
     London and Curwood. Brief reference.

3   GRAHAM, STEPHEN. "Jack London." The English Review, 33 (May),
     732-37; The Literary Review of the New York Evening Post
     (26 January), sec. 3, pp. 469-70.
          London was America's Gorky and Wells, and he achieved
     remarkable success abroad. "London loved himself." His
     women characters express his nearly hysterical feminine
     self-admiration. Through such exalted verbal extravagances,
     he "made emotional discoveries of new continents; at times
     he flared up with the philosophical genius of a Coleridge."
     With intuitive understanding, London presented the ideal
     spirit of California and of America, "the ideal of a clean,
     straight man, every bit white, a St. Paul or Jesus Christ
     in the boxing ring,...a man of the people,...a captain of
     men." He exaggerated and burlesqued the ideal in Daylight,
     Billy Roberts, and Martin Eden. His habit of imputing
     philosophical ideas to such heroes as Larsen and Daylight
     is "inartistic and nauseating....much of London's writing
     ought to be judged as journalism rather than as literature."
     If he had curbed his alcoholism, "he would have been less
     neurotic and emotional and written finer books." London
     "is a living writer for young men and the unfinished Ameri-
     ca....He is a man with a bugle; an awakener,...a man
     standing on a slag-heap, sword in hand and pointing with
     his sword." Gives biography. Reprinted: 1930.B5.

4   _____. [Note.] SatR, 1 (13 September), 109.
          Although "wholly inferior as an artist [to Conrad], he
     nevertheless presented life with inspirational power."

1924

5   HINDUS, MAURICE G. "American Authors in Russia." <u>SatR</u>, 1
    (16 August), 50.
        London, Sinclair, O. Henry, and Burroughs are "the idols
    of the Russian reading public now," and they are destined
    "to wield a more profound influence over Russian social
    and literary life than any official American" agency or
    envoy.

6   LEWIS, AUSTIN. "Jack London." <u>Labor Unity</u> (San Francisco)
    (27 November), p. 4.
        London had great vitality, power, strength, an athlete's
    grace, and a charming smile. The promise of his early
    work was not fulfilled because the bourgeois values and
    society "seduced and traduced him." London knew nothing
    about the "machine proletariat," and "revolt, not revolu-
    tion...formed the basis of his socialistic thinking."
    Nietzsche affected him profoundly; and his experience in
    the East End of London had "ineradicable" and depressing
    effects on him. He lost faith in the people, became a
    "magazine celebrity," lost desire for bourgeois success,
    and began to die.

7   LONDON, CHARMIAN. "How Jack London Would Have Ended Eyes of
    Asia: His Wife, Charmian London, Tells How the Famous
    Writer Spent His Last Days on His Last Novel." <u>Cosmopoli-</u>
    <u>tan</u>, 77 (October), 78-79, 124, 126, 128, 130-31.
        London had thought about the novel, with its theme of
    interracial marriage, for ten years. He completed the
    first half the day before he died and left notes on the
    rest. Mrs. London completes the story here.

8   MORRELL, ED. <u>25th Man: The Strange Story of Ed. Morrell, the</u>
    <u>Hero of Jack London's 'Star Rover.'</u> Montclair, N. J.:
    New Era, pp. 367-69.
        In 1912, Morrell gave "the immortal" London his dungeon
    experiences of "mind projection," later used in <u>The Star</u>
    <u>Rover</u>. In this novel, London "hurled the most damning in-
    dictment ever recorded against our whole iniquitous Ameri-
    can Jail system." "A strange bond of love, which he often
    mentioned to our mutual friends, existed between us until
    his death." [London is mentioned in the "Introduction"
    by Dr. Raymond S. Ward and in the "Author's Preface," both
    unpaged.]

1925 A BOOKS

1   LANE, ROSE WILDER. <u>He Was a Man</u>. New York: Harper, 380 pp.

Published as <u>Gordon Blake</u>. London: Harper, 380 pp.
A fictionalized biography of "Gordon Blake," incorpora-
ting incidents, highly embellished, from London's life.

2   LONDON, CHARMIAN KITTREDGE. <u>The Log of the Snark</u>. New York:
     Macmillan.
          Reprint of 1915.A1.

1925 B SHORTER WRITINGS

1   MONTENEGRO, ERNESTO. "Horacio Quiroga, Literary Kin of Kip-
     ling and Jack London." <u>New York Times Book Review</u> (25 Oc-
     tober), p. 10.
          Concerns Quiroga's work; mentions London's name.

2   PRENTICE, J. H. [sic] [J. A.]. "Stork Soliloquies: 'Jack Lon-
     don, 1876-1916.'" <u>Overland Monthly</u>, 83 (January), 41.
          The bird's brief biography.

3   SINCLAIR, UPTON. "Supermanhood," in <u>Mammonart</u>. Pasadena,
     California: Author, pp. 363-72.
          Revised text of 1917.B50, essentially the same.

4   VAN DOREN, CARL and MARK VAN DOREN. <u>American and British
     Literature Since 1890</u>. New York: Century, pp. 50-52.
          As a "socialist and revolutionist," London resented and
     hoped for the overthrow of established society. His fic-
     tional subjects were limited to the warfare among men,
     society, classes, and nature. <u>The Call of the Wild</u>, al-
     though sentimentalized, "exhibits a fine sensitiveness to
     natural beauty, a robust, moving, genuine current of poetry,"
     and power derived from "something autobiographical." Lon-
     don's later work is inferior because he wrote too fast and
     became obsessed with "primitive emotions," violence and
     suffering. With Crane and Norris, he made it possible for
     novelists to deal with subjects other than "the surface
     lives of respectable Americans."

5   TULLY, JIM. "The Failure of Jack London." <u>Story World and
     Photo-Dramatist</u>, 6, no. 8 (February), 11-12, 30, 32.
          Revised text of 1923.B6, largely the same.

1926 A BOOKS

1   PAYNE, EDWARD BIRON. <u>The Soul of Jack London</u>. Edited by
     Felicia R. Scatcherd. London: Rider & Company, 142 pp.
          Payne, second husband of Charmian's aunt, Ninetta Eames,

was London's intimate friend for many years. London's belief that life was a "desperate game" of continual conflict
together with his materialistic-mechanistic philosophy
shaped his life and works. He found writing an "irksome
task," preferring to engage in dangerous adventures, but
he wrote to ascend the socio-economic ladder. London dis-
trusted metaphysics, rejected the idea of "spontaneous
creative genius" and all opinions other than his own.
His Socialism was elitist, a program that would bring happiness to physically and intellectually select Anglo-Saxons
and extinction to lesser breeds. Since by nature he was
an idealist, the war between his scientific code and spiritual instincts brought on his "long sickness." In 1920 a
psychic brought Payne a story "which she believed had come
to her directly from Jack London's mind"; and she reported
"conversations" with London which in style, subject, and
personal detail were most probably London's own. In these
communications from the other world [printed here], London
decried his continued craving for alcohol, his inability
to produce, via the psychic, an artistic novel, and his
enduring egotism which sustained earthly ambitions. Volume
includes a "Prefatory Letter" by Sir Arthur Conan Doyle
and a "Foreword" by David Gow. Reprinted: 1933.A1.

1926 B SHORTER WRITINGS

1   ABBOTT, LEONARD D. "Foreword," in his edition of London's
        Essays of Revolt. New York: Vanguard Press, pp. 3-6.
          His works, particularly Martin Eden, expressed his life.
        "The motive of all is escape from the commonplace rou-
        tine....to open up new worlds to the human spirit." To
        read London "is a mental adventure of the most bracing
        sort....almost everything that he wrote is worth reading,
        and at his best he is unsurpassed."

2   ADAIR, WARD. Vital Messages in Modern Books. New York:
        Association Press, pp. 12-22, 86-93.
          In White Fang, London offers "the great truth that
        while resistance can go far, it has well-defined limits,"
        a truth especially valuable to men in "middle life." The
        Call of the Wild dramatizes "atavism of the soul" as well
        as physical reversion.

3   CHUBB, EDWIN. "Jack London, The Yarn-Spinner," in his Stories
        of Authors: British and American. New York: Macmillan,
        pp. 374-79.
          "Neither steadily nor as a whole did he look at life."
        Quotes from John Barleycorn and Hueffer, 1916.B44.

4   HOUCK, CALVIN B. "Jack London's Philosophy of Life (In Two
     Parts)." Overland Monthly, 84 (April), 103-104, 120;
     (May), 136-37, 141, 147, 149.
         Biography and "philosophy" taken largely from London's
     writings, with Houck's commentary. London's "great-great-
     grandfather was Sir William London who fought in Washington's
     army." London was a "beautiful and precocious child" who
     miraculously survived the poverty, injustices, and manual
     labor which stunted his growth and made him a "materialist."
     The central theme of his work is survival of the fittest.
     "Blood runs red throughout all his stories. The eternal
     desire to live is portrayed most powerfully in each one of
     them."

5   MOTT, FRANK LUTHER. "Introduction," in his edition of The Call
     of the Wild, and Other Stories. Modern Reader's Series.
     New York: Macmillan, pp. v-xxxvii.
         Discusses in detail London's life and notices his works.
     A "dynamic and picturesque romanticism" dominated him as
     man and author, and his works must be judged as romance.
     He was a great story-teller, masterful with settings and
     dramatic action. His heroes are self-projections; only
     one, Buck, is truly convincing and real. Much of London's
     work "is unmistakably excellent, and some small part of
     it of enduring value." This introduction is reprinted in
     various editions of The Call of the Wild to date.

6   MULLIN, GLEN H. "Introduction," in The Road. The Rogue's
     Bookshelf. New York: Greenberg, pp. ix-xviii.
         While vividly and dramatically painting the tramp as a
     social problem and a human being, London glorifies him-
     self as "a picaresque hero surviving by virtue of superior
     strength and wit....[The Road] symbolizes youth in quest
     of adventure."

7   MUMFORD, LEWIS. The Golden Day: A Study in American Experience
     and Culture. New York: Boni & Liveright, pp. 246-50.
         "He had only to tell his life over again--to make a
     story of it in the newspaper sense--to feed the romanticism
     of the big urban populations....London became a sort of
     traveling salesman of literature, writing to his market,
     offering 'red blood' and adventure." With his self-defined
     Socialism he mingled beliefs in imperialism and Nordic
     supremacy, faith in personal success and the Superman.
     London's gallery of superman-heroes "was the social plati-
     tude of the old West, translated into a literary epigram."
     He "held a mirror up to society," and like Dreiser, he re-
     corded only the dullness and brutality of the passing

1926

scene. Same, reprinted: Boston: Beacon Press, 1957, pp. 125-27.

8   TULLY, JIM. "Light Reading." SatR, 3 (28 August), 70.
     The Road is "the epitome of London's weakness as a
     writer and a man." He leaves out the real truth about
     tramps: "poor Jack was the most wretched prostitute that
     ever walked down an alley of literature for money. As de-
     fiant as a sophomore about social conditions, he worried
     about the poor and died wealthy....He lacked pity, sympa-
     thy, and irony. He never wrote a moving story of men in
     pain....He was really a more highly gifted journalist."

1927 A BOOKS - NONE

1927 B SHORTER WRITINGS

1   AUSTIN, MARY. "George Sterling at Carmel." American Mercury,
     11 (May), 65-72.
     London thought women preferred "the tenth share in a
     man of distinction to the whole of an average man. Women
     flung themselves at Jack, lay in wait for him." Sterling
     adopted London's feelings for socialism and Nordic suprem-
     acy. Jack's buying of plots from others "was chiefly a
     generous camouflage for help that could not be asked or
     given otherwise." Reprinted: 1932.B1.

2   BRAYBROOKE, PATRICK. "The Unexpected," in his Peeps at the
     Mighty. Philadelphia: Lippincott, pp. 113-29.
     London was "a writer of hurricane force....who combined
     a very sound common sense with an extraordinary power of
     writing terrific melodrama." His story "The Unexpected"
     [analyzed here] offers "drama, deep psychology and grim
     horror."

3   BRODY, ALTER. "Jack London via Moscow." Nation, 25 (28 De-
     cember), 740.
     Reviews Venture by Max Eastman in which several London
     motifs are recognizable.

4   CONRAD, JOSEPH. "To Ernst Bendz [letter of March 7, 1923]."
     in G. Jean-Aubrey. Joseph Conrad, Life and Letters.
     Volume 2. Garden City: Doubleday, Page, 295-96.
     Conrad heard he was regarded in Sweden "as literarily a
     sort of Jack London." He "sympathized much with the warm
     and direct talent" of London but is not at all like him
     "temperamentally, mentally, and as a prose writer."

5   LONDON, CHARMIAN. "As I Knew Him." <u>Overland Monthly</u>, 85
        (December), 360-61.
            A tribute to Sterling; notes his friendship with London.

6   RUTTER, FRANK. <u>Since I Was Twenty-Five</u>. Boston: Houghton
        Mifflin, pp. 123-25.
            Rutter, the first British editor to publish London's
        stories, serialized his "Tales of the Far North" in <u>To-day</u>.

7   SCOVILLE, SAMUEL, Jr. "Boys and Books." <u>SatR</u>, 4 (12 November),
        304.
            Mentions <u>The Call of the Wild</u> as a book to attract 12-
        to 16-year-old boys to reading.

8   SINCLAIR, UPTON. <u>Money Writes</u>. Long Beach, N. Y.: Author,
        pp. 35, 49-50, 77, 159, 160, 163, 169.
            "He came among us as a young god, a blonde Nordic god
        with a halo about his head." Sinclair's article on London,
        illustrating "the devastating effects of alcohol upon
        genius," was rejected by Mencken's <u>American Mercury</u>.

*9 WICKERSHAM, JAMES. <u>A Bibliography of Alaskan Literature</u>.
        Volume 1. Fairbanks: Alaska Agricultural College and
        School of Mines, 231-34.
            Cited in Woodbridge, 1966.A6.

<u>1928 A BOOKS - NONE</u>

<u>1928 B SHORTER WRITINGS</u>

1   CHISLETT, WILLIAM. <u>Moderns and Near Moderns</u>. New York:
        Grafton Press, pp. 109-11.
            Contrary to their poor critical reputation, London's
        works have value: sympathy with the weak, influence for
        freedom abroad, acknowledgement of "culture in others,"
        and pioneering psychological insights.

2   COLEMAN, CHRYSE D. "The Jinx Ship." <u>Sunset: The Pacific
        Monthly</u>, 60 (January), 35, 75-76.
            <u>The Saucy Lass</u>, a schooner owned by London, was the
        model for the <u>Ghost</u> in <u>The Sea-Wolf</u>. The ship became a
        rum-runner, <u>Hakadate</u>, until confiscated by the U. S.
        Government in 1926.

3   DAVIS, MALCOLM J. "Highways to Heaven." <u>SatR</u>, 4 (10 March),
        664.
            Mentions <u>Essays of Revolt</u> with other "vanguards of the
        social revolt."

1928

4   DICKINSON, ASA DON. <u>The Best Books of Our Time, 1901-1925</u>.
      Garden City: Doubleday, pp. 183-85.
        Chosen "according to a consensus of expert opinion,"
      London ranks 17th among favorite authors with 61 endorse-
      ments. Five of his novels received endorsements, and <u>The</u>
      <u>Call of the Wild</u> ranks 11th among all books rated.

5   FOERSTER, NORMAN. <u>The Reinterpretation of American Literature</u>.
      New York: Harcourt Brace, pp. 156-58.
        Like Robert Herrick, London combined sociological realism
      with faith in liberalism.

6   G., J. "J. G. [letter to] The Reader's Guide." <u>SatR</u>, 5
      (6 October), p. 197.
        Includes <u>Martin Eden</u> and <u>John Barleycorn</u> in a list of
      biographies showing pains of authorship.

7   GRAHAM, BESSIE. <u>The Bookman's Manual: A Guide to Literature</u>.
      New York: Bowker, pp. 468-69.
        Brief biography and bibliography. The same entry appears
      in editions through 1958.

8   MARBLE, ANNIE R. <u>A Study of the Modern Novel, British and</u>
      <u>American Since 1900</u>. New York: Appleton, pp. 246-51.
        "His radiant personality impressed all who knew him; he
      scorned models and wrote his stories--far too rapidly and
      too hastily--in a distinctive spirit and style." Gives
      biography.

9   MICHAUD, REGIS. <u>The American Novel Today: A Social and Psycho-</u>
      <u>logical Study</u>. Boston: Little, Brown, pp. 4, 110, 167.
      Mentions London.

<u>1929 A BOOKS - NONE</u>

<u>1929 B SHORTER WRITINGS</u>

1   ANON. "Jack London," in <u>Who Was Who...1916-1928</u>. London:
      A & C Black, p. 641.
      Biography.

2   ANON. "Italy Bans Books of Jack London." <u>San Francisco</u>
      <u>Chronicle</u> (10 August), p. 4.
        For promoting delinquency among its youth, Italy bans
      works of London, Tolstoi, Turgenev, Gorky, and Dostoievsky.

JACK LONDON: A REFERENCE GUIDE

3 de CASSERES, BENJAMIN. The Superman in America. Chapbook No.
   30. Seattle: University of Washington Book Store, p. 26.
   Mentions London.

4 DOYLE, A.[RTHUR] CONAN. "The Alleged Posthumous Writings of
   Great Authors." Bookman (New York), 66 (December), 342-49.
   Summarizes London's communications via a psychic woman
   to Edward Payne (See 1926.A1). "I accept Jack London's
   return as being a genuine one." Revised: 1930.B3.

5 GRATTAN, CLINTON HARTLEY. Bitter Bierce. Garden City:
   Doubleday, pp. 41-42, 273.
   Bierce got drunk only once, at the age of seventy with
   London.

6 GRATTAN, C.[LINTON] HARTLEY. "Jack London." Bookman (New
   York), 68 (February), 667-71.
   London's fiction expressed and was limited by his need
   to prove manliness, sadistic pleasure in mastering and
   punishing others, and masochistic pleasure in recording
   his physical and intellectual sufferings. As a man of
   action, he felt "learning was a fraud and a delusion";
   ideas were true and valuable only if workable. He could
   never "assume a saving skepticism" for he lacked the capacities to view the world with awe, to deal with abstrac-
   tions, and to comprehend primitive psyches. His fiction,
   concrete and organic in structure and style, is weak in
   conveying mental activities and matters of sex and love
   because London was enslaved to the editors. He wrote
   only for money and "to realize his personality through
   literature, not in literature." To solve internal conflicts, he tried to return to a frontier or agrarian past
   or to "the wild." "A great deal that London wrote was
   trash, but certain short stories and The Call of the Wild
   belong to permanent literature."

7 JOHNSON, MERLE DEVORE. "Jack (John Griffith) London," in his
   American First Editions. New York: Bowker, pp. 318-22.
   Lists 52 volumes by London; collections containing first
   appearance of his writings; and 6 secondary works. Second
   and Third Editions (1932, 1936), revised and enlarged by
   Jacob Blanck, are essentially the same. Revised and enlarged: 1942.B6.

8 JOHNSON, MERLE [DEVORE]. High Spots of American Literature:
   A Practical Bibliography and Brief Literary Estimate of
   Outstanding American Books. New York: Bennett Book
   Studios, pp. 51-52.

1929

Lists The Call of the Wild, Before Adam, and John Barleycorn among first editions of American "literary landmarks"--
the "great and readable books."

9   LEISY, ERNEST. American Literature: An Interpretative Survey.
    New York: Crowell, pp. 208-209.
        "His reputation once established [by The Call of the
    Wild], London poured forth with journalistic abandon tale
    after tale dealing with 'red blooded' supermen, indulging
    in fights and rejoicing in storms. But his pen was too
    headlong....he most truly represents the prevailing taste"
    of the decade before World War I.

10 McWILLIAMS, CAREY. Ambrose Bierce: A Biography. New York:
    Boni, pp. 204, 284-86.
        London's attitude towards Bierce's scientific and philo-
    sophic knowledge is "amusing."

11 RUSSAK, MARTIN. "Jack London, America's First Proletarian
    Writer." New Masses, 4, no. 8 (January), 13.
        The "most popular writer of the American workingclass,"
    London was a true proletariat by birth and viewpoint. He
    showed "absolute class solidarity, and revolutionary pas-
    sion," and he hated the bourgeoisie. The "spirit of the
    wobbly--...heroic, fiery, and adventurous--will live for-
    ever in the pages of his rebel stories." His work "was
    a phase of the class struggle," and he was a better writer
    than any bourgeois writer of his time.

12 SPRAGUE, ROGER. "Contrast as Device." SatR, 6 (26 October),
    320.
        A letter to the editor. In the chapter on Coronation
    Day in The People of the Abyss, "we find the element of
    contrast raised to the nth power."

1930 A BOOKS - NONE

1930 B SHORTER WRITINGS

1   CAIRNS, WILLIAM B. A History of American Literature. Re-
    vised edition. New York: Oxford University Press, pp. 484,
    487-88, 490, 505, 525, 548.
        In The Call of the Wild, his best work, brutality is
    integral to the tale, and he shows "real feeling for the
    natural scenery." Later, hasty writing, greater brutality,
    and propaganda weaken the writings. Same, reprinted: New
    York: Johnson Reprint, 1969.

Jack London: A Reference Guide

2   COTTRELL, GEORGE W. and HOXIE N. FAIRCHILD. Critical Guide.
    New York: Columbia University Press, pp. 376-77.
        Wolf Larsen is "the most complete embodiment of the Lon-
    don ideal."

3   DOYLE, ARTHUR CONAN. The Edge of the Unknown. New York: Put-
    nam's, pp. 141-46.
        Essentially the same as Doyle, 1929.B4.

4   GERBAULT, ALAIN. In Quest of the Sun: The Journal of the
    'Firecrest.' Introduction by Charmian London.   Garden
    City: Doubleday, pp. 6, 110, 198.
        Mentions London and the Snark.

5   GRAHAM, STEPHEN. "Jack London," in his The Death of Yesterday.
    London: Ernest Benn, pp. 53-61.
        Reprint of 1924.B3.

6   KRUPSKAYA, NADEZHDAK. Memories of Lenin. Translated by E.
    Verney. New York: International Publishers, pp. 208-209.
        Two days before Lenin's death, his wife read to him Lon-
    don's "Love of Life." "That tale greatly pleased Ilyich,"
    and he asked the next day for more; but this story was
    "saturated with bourgeois morals....Ilyich smiled and dis-
    missed it with a wave of the hand. That was the last time
    I read to him."

7   McWILLIAMS, CAREY. "A Letter from Carmel." SatR, 6 (4 Janu-
    ary), 622.
        Account of the Carmel writers and artists. The "spirit
    of the place...is rather roughly outlined" in The Valley
    of the Moon.

8   MANSFIELD, KATHERINE. "Hearts are Trumps," in her Novels and
    Novelists. London: Constable, p. 246.
        Reprint of 1920.B14.

9   PARRINGTON, VERNON LOUIS. The Beginnings of Critical Realism
    in America, 1860-1920. Volume 3 of the 3-volume Main
    Currents in American Thought: An Interpretation of Ameri-
    can Literature from the Beginnings to 1920. New York:
    Harcourt Brace, pp. 198, 325, 352, 368, 406.
        London was "a man of strong vital energy with a philoso-
    phy shaped by Darwin, Spencer, and Nietschze." The Sea-
    Wolf is "the frankest statement in American literature of
    the unbridled will-to-power, egoistic, amoral." London's
    work "lacks restraint and finish."

1930

10   PATTEE, FRED LEWIS. "Jack London," in his <u>The New American
        Literature</u>. New York: Century, pp. 121-43.
            Abridged text of 1922.B6. Omits most quotations from
        London's works, some biography, a discussion of <u>The Road</u>,
        sections on literary style and method and on London as a
        national and international voice. Criticisms and conclu-
        sions remain the same. Adds a primary bibliography. <u>See</u>
        also Pattee, 1923.B4.

11   PHOENICIAN, THE. "The Phoenix Nest." <u>SatR</u>, 7 (11 July), 968.
            The manuscript of "Poppy Cargo" was discovered on Lon-
        don's ranch; it was just published in <u>Physical Culture
        Magazine</u>.

12   SINCLAIR, UPTON. "Is This Jack London? [Part I]." <u>Occult
        Review</u>, 52 (December), 394-400.
            In July, 1930, in Los Angeles, Mr. and Mrs. Sinclair
        attended a séance at which Arthur Ford's "spirit called
        'Fletcher'" claimed to be with London. London said he was
        helping Sinclair to write fiction and sent his love to
        Charmian. Sinclair believes genuine telepathy occurred.
        Part II: 1931.B11. Abridged: 1941.B7; reprinted: 1968.B16.

<u>1931 A BOOKS</u>

1   BAMFORD, GEORGIA LORING. <u>The Mystery of Jack London: Some of
        His Friends, Also A Few Letters; A Reminiscence</u>. Oakland,
        California: Author, 255 pp.
            London was "the most interesting figure in California
        literature; he was also the most interesting of my many
        friends, and the most talked of man of my large acquain-
        tance, over a long period of years [1895-1916]." In
        1890-93, "his family was in a state of extreme poverty,
        also in a wretched state of mind." London lived in
        "squalor of an aggravated type," but he had "a real home."
        His writings emphasized "the bad influences" and minimized
        or forgot the good, although he suffered only "the ordinary
        vicissitudes of life." Describes London's life in Oakland,
        1895-99, and friends who encouraged his literary and so-
        cialist pursuits. By 1899 London "was an educated man,"
        but he "was still a primitive by deed, as well as his
        written word." He was a "Revolutionist" and an "Anarchist"
        with "a leaning toward Nihilism." London showed "weakness
        of judgment" by his admiration for Spencer and "his con-
        tempt for...Ralph Waldo Emerson." He had "no interest in
        painting and almost none in sculpture" or classical music.
        London's first story seems "a narrative poem that hints

at the heights reached by Coleridge." The Call of the
Wild exerted "a power and a mystery indescribable"; The
People of the Abyss "served no purpose and was not literature."
"Any effort to fathom him or to rationalize him will be
very elusive to all but a limited few;...only those who
knew him." Volume includes 16 inscriptions by London in
his first editions to Frederick Irons Bamford; and 52 letters from London to F. Bamford, May 6, 1902-March 7, 1916.
Reprinted: 1969.A1.

1931 B SHORTER WRITINGS

1   BLANKENSHIP, RUSSELL. American Literature as an Expression of
     the National Mind. New York: Holt, pp. 551, 566-68.
        London, "the bar-room Socialist," was a "proletarian of
     vigorous, untrained intellect....[he] never realized a
     fraction of his power" to become a naturalist or spokesman
     for the workingclass. Instead, he wrote for money and "to
     please the bourgeoisie."

2   BRIDGE, JAMES HOWARD. Millionaires and Grub Street: Comrades
     and Contacts in the Last Half-Century. New York: Bren-
     tano's, pp. 200-204.
        Bridge, as editor of the Overland Monthly, in 1898 bought
     "To the Man on the Trail" for the top price of $25. He
     ordered six more stories and told London, "Your work is
     worth more than we can pay for it." Reprinted: 1932.B2.

3   [COREY, WILLIAM A.] An Ex-Atheist. "Atheist Jack London,
     Who Prayed Only to Man: His Forlorn California Estate, and
     the Grave that is Hard to Find." The Sunday School Times
     (14 February), pp. 91, 94.
        A lesson on the transitoriness of worldly things, with
     the anti-Christian London and his ranch as examples.
     Describes tour of Glen Ellen and conversations with Lon-
     don's neighbors and barber.

4   _____. An Ex-Atheist. "An Atheist's Hero: Jack London's Own
     Description: Is His Book 'Martin Eden' Disguised Autobiog-
     raphy?" The Sunday School Times (14 March), pp. 151-52.
        Corey devotes three lessons to London [see: 1931.B3;
     1931.B5] because his "destructive influence was, like his
     fame, world-wide." London's life and writings were fasci-
     nating, but his erroneous philosophy doomed him to unhap-
     piness. Martin Eden relates "this brilliant man's spiri-
     tual downfall and death."

1931

5   [COREY, WILLIAM A.] An Ex-Atheist. "The Atheist Describes
        John Barleycorn: Jack London Speaking for Himself in One
        of His Famous Books." The Sunday School Times (28 March),
        pp. 183, 186.
            A lesson on the evils of drink and the philosophy of
        materialistic monism.

6   DOBIE, CHARLES CALDWELL. "Literature of the Pacific Coast,"
        in American Writers on American Literature. Edited by
        John Macy. New York: Liveright, pp. 415, 420, 421.
            Mentions London.

7   GOLDMAN, EMMA. Living My Life. Volume I. New York: Knopf,
        227, 468-69.
            Goldman met London in 1897 and in 1909 after having read
        most of his works. She was impressed by his exuberant
        youth, "creative spirit," and love for and understanding
        of humanity.

8   HART, JEROME A. In Our Second Century: From An Editor's Note-
        book. San Francisco: Pioneer Press, pp. 164-65, 168.
            Describes meeting of London and Bierce in Bohemian Grove.
        Same, reprinted: New York: AMS Press, 1970.

9   [McDEVITT, WILLIAM]. "We Entertain an International Visitor:
        A San Francisco Book Store Made Famous in Berlin." Biblio-
        Ana (San Francisco), 3, no. 1 (January), 6-7.
            Excerpt from Paradies Amerika by a German visitor; and
        comment on London's first story.

10 MARKHAM, EDWIN. "Introduction: A Glance at Literary California,"
        in his compilation of Songs and Stories. Los Angeles:
        Powell, pp. 16-17.
            London's writings "register a vibration of spirit that
        carries intense light and heat." The Call of the Wild,
        "his masterpiece....carries an accompaniment of beauty and
        poesy that conspires to make it a classic."

11 SINCLAIR, UPTON. "Is This Jack London? [Part II]." Occult
        Review, 53 (January), 10-14.
            Annotation given under Part I, 1930.B12. Abridged:
        1941.B7; reprinted: 1968.B16.

12 VIERECK, GEORGE SYLVESTER. "The Ghost of Jack London: Sinclair
        Lewis Becomes the Central Figure in a Literary Mystery."
        Liberty, 8 (10 October), 15-18.
            Considers London's motives for purchasing plots from
        Lewis: "Did he buy the plots partly to assist young Lewis,

partly to assuage a secret biological or post-alcoholic
fear that he had reached the end of his creative rope?"
Quotes Lewis and Charmian London on the plot-sales; prints
Lewis plot, "Mr. Cincinnatus, A Novelette," and excerpts
from John Barleycorn.

1932 A BOOKS

1   LEWIS, SINCLAIR. Sinclair Lewis on the Valley of the Moon.
    Cambridge, Massachusetts: Harvard University Press, 5 pp.
        Finds a curious resemblance between London's novel and
    Gold by Steward Edward White. London's native Americans
    originally lose out to "the shrewder Japs, Dalmatians,
    Greeks, and what not," but with the gallantry of their
    forefathers, they go onward. This pamphlet was issued in
    an edition of 100 copies, privately distributed by Harvey
    Taylor. Reprinted: 1974.A5.

1932 B SHORTER WRITINGS

1   AUSTIN, MARY. Earth Horizon. Boston: Houghton Mifflin,
        pp. 299-304.
            Reprint of 1927.B1.

2   BRIDGE, JAMES HOWARD. "Millionaires and Grub Street." Over-
        land Monthly, 90 (May), 116.
            Reprint of 1931.B1.

3   BROOKS, VAN WYCK. Sketches in Criticism. New York: Dutton,
        pp. 248-52.
            London was a "Red-Blood...the most neurotic of men" whose
        sense of inferiority drove him to "an abnormal self-asser-
        tiveness," a compulsive "passion to beat the enemy at his
        own game" and to "dazzle the reader" with a "brazen...
        noisy style" and unnecessarily violent, shocking incidents.
        His "egomania" drove him to dominate and succeed, "and for
        this reason, as he knew very well himself, he failed as an
        artist." His life, works, and Mrs. London's account seem
        to prove that his greatest fear "was to look himself in
        the face."

4   CALVERTON, VICTOR. The Liberation of American Literature.
        New York: Scribner, pp. 419-24, 427.
            London was the "last literary figure who was able to re-
        tain something of the energy and vigor of the frontier
        force" because he believed in socialism, which made him
        "an anti-militarist, an internationalist, a feminist, and

an advocate of a proletarian revolution." His inner conflict between individualism and socialism remained unresolved, and his fiction in late years became "tawdry and
shallow." London's radical writings had a lasting, significant effect on America and the world.

5   CHAMBERLAIN, JOHN. Farewell to Reform: The Rise, Life and
    Decay of the Progressive Mind in America. Second edition.
    New York: John Day, pp. 33, 177, 179, 186-92.
        "In every way," London inspires considerably less respect
    than Sinclair." London was theatric, spent his great
    earnings on himself, and diluted socialism (which gave him
    "the ego-soothing feeling of high danger") with cynical
    individualism. However, his vigorous and "hard-hitting"
    radical pamphlets influenced thousands. The Iron Heel,
    "a cogent simplified, and very effective exposition of the
    theory of surplus production and surplus value,...does not
    convince as a prophecy; it remains an interesting pamphlet
    of an interesting time."

6   DICKINSON, T. H. The Making of American Literature. New York:
    Century, pp. 647-48.
        "His career is marked with action, struggle against temp-
    tation, strong social feeling...and understanding of nature."
    The "autobiographical element is the strongest motive and
    the greatest limitation of his work."

7   GARLAND, HAMLIN. My Friendly Contemporaries: A Literary Log.
    New York: Macmillan, p. 81.
        Mentions The Sea-Wolf.

8   HAWKES, EDITH GRANGER. "Jack London: A Brief Sketch of His
    Life." Overland Monthly, 90 (May), 109-10, 122, 125.
        Biography from C. London, 1921.A1, with brief excerpts
    from critical articles.

9   KELLOGG, BYRD WEYLER. "Treasures from the Snark's Cruise."
    Overland Monthly, 90 (May), 113-14.
        Describes the London collection of South Seas curios.

10 KNIGHT, GRANT C. American Literature and Culture. New York:
    Long & Smith, pp. 121, 378, 426, 436-39, 446, 482.
        "He made a fetish of derring-do....[He] was never sure
    of himself; never sure whether he was novelist, short
    story writer, or agitator." His tales of adventure will
    last, but he "founded no school, and his importance in
    American literature is steadily waning." Gives biography.

11 LEWISOHN, LUDWIG. Expression in America. New York: Oxford
    University Press, pp. 317, 324-26.
        "He was a better writer; he had far more creative power;
    he had a greater flexibility of mind and a more liberal
    heart" than Frank Norris. London's best works are "the
    sound, concrete, restrained, and moving" The People of the
    Abyss; the "sincere, plain, pathetic" John Barleycorn; and
    "his ablest full-length novel," The Sea-Wolf. In the lat-
    ter, the reader gains "sadistic joy" and satisfies "his
    lust for ferocity" by identifying with Larsen; and he ful-
    fills "unconscious homoerotic wishes" from the Larsen-Van
    Weyden relationship.

12 LONDON, CHARMIAN. "My Husband--An Old Contributor." Overland
    Monthly, 90 (May), 106-107, 120.
        Describes the connections of Charmian and Jack to this
    magazine and the compilation of an introduction to this
    "Jack London issue" by members of the League of American
    Penwomen, Sonoma County Chapter.

13 [McDEVITT, WILLIAM]. "Jack London--A Foreword." Book Col-
    lecting for Love or Money (San Francisco), 4, no. 8 (n.d.),
    1, 8.
        London "was a pioneer--always out near the front, in
    life, in economics, in ethics." He will become a symbol
    to America of "the original Native Son; a portent of a
    newer generation; the 'Man on the road'; the Pal on the
    Trail; the eternal traveler, the ongoer, the forward
    marcher."

14 MARCOSSON, ISAAC F. David Graham Phillips and His Times.
    New York: Dodd, Mead, pp. 300-301.
        Describes an unsuccessful meeting of London and Phillips.

15 MURPHY, CELESTE G. "Library Collected by Jack London Reveals
    Thirst for Knowledge." Overland Monthly, 90 (May), 111-12,
    120.
        Describes London's reading and his "notable collection
    of 15,000 books." Material here derived principally from
    C. London, 1921.A1 and London's letters.

16 MURPHY, CHESTER G. "Jack London's Valley of the Moon," Over-
    land Monthly, 90 (May), pp. 117, 126.
        A recollection of London on his "ranch of glorified pig-
    pens."

17 WALKER, FRANKLIN. Frank Norris, A Biography. New York:
    Doubleday, pp. 128, 164, 238, 255, 298.
        Mentions London.

1933

1   PAYNE, EDWARD BIRON. The Soul of Jack London. Second edition.
    Kingsport, Tennessee: Southern Publishers, 136 pp.
        Reprint of 1926.A1 with a preface by Ninetta Eames Payne.

1   BOAS, RALPH P. Social Backgrounds of American Literature.
    New York: Little, Brown, pp. 184, 195-96, 197-99.
        London gained popularity for a life and fiction that
    exemplified romantic adventure, the "strenuous life," and
    "the law of club and fang."

2   CARGILL, OSCAR, ed. The Social Revolt: American Literature
    from 1888 to 1914. New York: Macmillan, pp. 623-25.
        Summarizes London's life and works. The Call of the
    Wild, "the most poetic study of atavism in literature,
    gave him an international audience, 1903."

3   DELL, FLOYD. Homecoming: An Autobiography. New York: Farrar
    & Rinehart, p. 283.
        London repudiated Socialism's ideals after Mexico and
    died "a tired cynic."

4   HICKS, GRANVILLE. The Great Tradition: An Interpretation of
    American Literature Since the Civil War. New York: Mac-
    millan, pp. 188-96, and passim.
        "Two-thirds of London's books are ignored, and most of
    the others slip towards oblivion." Spencer's doctrines of
    survival of the fittest and of atavism influenced his
    Alaskan fiction. "We find the primitive man, who is also
    the superman of Nietzsche's dreams, in the guise" of Lar-
    sen, Eden, Daylight, Roberts, and Standing. Ernest Ever-
    hard, "merely the superman in red," and the others are
    Jack London "as he felt himself to be." Although he
    claimed his work supported socialism, and he was sincere,
    his socialism never affected his personality, outlook, or
    writings. He was driven by desire for wealth and power,
    he preached Anglo-Saxon supremacy and return to the soil,
    and noted the stupidity of the poor--all non-socialist
    ideas. "It was on the egotistic level that his books were
    conceived"; and the one character he could depict "is so
    much a product of his dreams, so nearly a personal myth,
    that we cannot find it convincing." London's works,
    created in haste, lack "a subtle and dignified style."
    They do have vigor, evocative description, and "the relief
    of vicarious adventure....[in] a dreamland of heroic op-
    portunity." Same, revised edition, 1968.

5   KUNITZ, STANLEY J., ed. Authors Today and Yesterday. New York:
    H. W. Wilson, pp. 415-18.
        "He wrote as he lived, at an intense pitch and in a
    highly colored style, lavish with superlatives....His sto-
    ries dealt with the primitive, they glorified brute force."
    Gives biography.

6   LONDON, CHARMIAN KITTREDGE. "Jack London and Sonoma County,"
    in Singing Years: The Sonoma County Anthology of Poetry
    and Prose. Santa Rosa, California: Press Democrat Pub-
    lishing Company, pp. 106-108.
        An introduction to "Brown Wolf." London recognized the
    region "as his Promised Land," worked hard to fulfill his
    "agrarian vision" on the Ranch, and made Sonoma County the
    setting of many stories and novels.

7   PALMER, FREDERICK. With My Own Eyes. Indianapolis: Bobbs-
    Merrill, pp. 96, 237-39, 241-42, 293.
        Palmer knew London in the Yukon, Mexico, and at the
    Russo-Japanese front. London "fairly hated the Japanese.
    ...[he] was the most inherently individualistic, and un-
    Socialist of all the Socialists I have ever met,...a philo-
    sophical anarchist. Although cheery and kindly,...he pre-
    ferred to walk alone in aristocratic aloofness, and always
    in the direction he chose."

8   W.[HIPPLE], T.[HOMAS] K. "London, Jack," in Dictionary of
    American Biography. Edited by Dumas Malone and Allen John-
    son. Volume 11. New York: Scribner's, 370-72.
        His most important works are the fictions laid in the
    Far North. "Almost all his writing,....has to do with one
    motif--the primitive, and above all, reversion to savagery.
    His insistence is constant upon the importance of brute
    force....[which] shocked and thrilled his readers." Lon-
    don is "still read as a master of swift and vivid action
    and adventure." He himself "was a man of abnormal sensi-
    tiveness, both physical and emotional....He was generous
    and sympathetic;...a man alert, ardent, and alive." Gives
    biography.

1934 A BOOKS

1   GAER, JOSEPH, ed. Jack London: Bibliography and Biographical
    Data. Monograph No. 1, California Literary Research
    Project. San Francisco: California Relief Administration,
    45 pp.
        Mimeographed. In four sections, plus an index: 1) lists

1934

fiction, non-fiction, essays, and reviews by London with
publication place and date of first appearance; 2) a biographical sketch; 3) selected critical estimates (unidentified); 4) lists 27 secondary references. Reprinted:
1970.A2.

1934 B SHORTER WRITINGS

1 HARTWICK, HARRY. "Men with the Bark On," in his The Foreground
    of American Fiction. New York: Century, pp. 67-84.
       Offers biography, brief summaries of London's works and
    excerpts from writings of Huxley, Spencer, Haeckel, and
    Nietzsche. The Sea-Wolf is "his most typical novel"; the
    "conclusion is flabby with sentiment, and worse than the
    lubricity he tried so hard to avoid." "In Norris and Lon-
    don naturalism reached the depth of mawkish melodrama" and
    might be called "romanticism going on all fours." London
    pioneered in popularizing scientific ideas, far-away
    places, and socialism. "More bad literature has been
    written about London...than he wrote himself....What his
    enraptured critics have neglected to observe is that Jack
    London's worst enemy was Jack London. He desired only two
    things: to be thought a rough, VIRILE MAN, and to have
    power as represented by money." Same, reprinted: New York:
    Gordian Press, 1967.

2 LENORMAND, H. R. "American Literature in France." SatR, 11
    (27 October), 244.
       London's adventure novels are "enormously popular" in
    France. White Fang has influenced Constantin-Weyer.

3 SYMES, LILLIAN and TRAVERS CLEMENT. Rebel America: The Story
    of Social Revolt in the United States. New York: Harper,
    pp. 202, 220, 232-33.
       "London was Rousseau's Noble Savage crossed with Nietzsche's
    Blond Beast....more of an anarchist than a socialist."

1935 A BOOKS - NONE

1935 B SHORTER WRITINGS

1 ANON. "London, Jack (John Griffith London)," in The Columbia
    Encyclopedia. New York: Columbia University Press.
       Biography and bibliography. London appears in all sub-
    sequent editions to 1974.

2   HATCHER, HARLAN. Creating the Modern American Novel. New
    York: Farrar and Rinehart, pp. 17, 26-27, 46.
        Martin Eden is a good autobiographical novel; The Iron
    Heel is "no better than later attempts to fictionize"
    labor-capitalist conflict. The naturalistic fiction of
    Norris and London illustrates the latent bestiality of man
    and survival of "only the ruthless." Same, reprinted:
    New York: Russell and Russell, 1965.

3   LOVEMAN, AMY. "The Clearing House." SatR, 12 (1 June), 20.
        Recommends The Call of the Wild "for an intelligent boy
    of eleven."

4   MURPHY, CELESTE G. "Jack London in Sonoma Valley," in her The
    People of the Pueblo; or, the Story of Sonoma. Sonoma,
    California: W. L. and C. G. Murphy, pp. 264-69.
        Biography. This "literary genius," beloved by all his
    neighbors, found "peace and inspiration" in the Valley,
    where his ranch was "the pride of the countryside." Same,
    reprinted: Portland, Oregon: Binfords & Mort, 1948.

*5 TAYLOR, HARVEY. "The Jack London Bibliography." With notes
    from the Cresmer Collection. Introduction by Dr. C. J.
    Cresmer. Preface by Charmian London. Typescript. Los
    Angeles, California, n.d.
        Cited in Tweney, 1974.B30.

6   WOODWARD, ROBERT H. "Jack London's Code of Primitivism."
    Folio, 18 (May), 39-44.
        The Sea-Wolf is two books: "the first an incomplete,
    naturalistic study of character"; the second, from the
    arrival of Maud, a melodramatic romance. Naturalistic
    elements include shaping of character by past environment
    (Larsen, Van Weyden, Mugridge) and reshaping by present
    environment (Johnson, Leach); adaptation to more primitive
    levels of behavior to insure survival (Maud and Van Weyden);
    and primordialism, as embodied in Larsen, a reasoning brute.
    Larsen is a Nietzschean superman only in the sense that
    "Milton's Satan is a superman." London did not fully de-
    velop these naturalistic elements and the novel's serious
    philosophical import; therefore, The Sea-Wolf "is remem-
    bered as a red-blooded adventure of sea life and as senti-
    mental melodrama."

1936 A BOOKS

1   POPE, MARGARET I. "Jack London: A Study in Twentieth Century

Values."
Ph.D. dissertation, University of Wisconsin.

1936 B SHORTER WRITINGS

1 BOYNTON, PERCY. Literature and American Life. New York: Ginn,
pp. 653, 718, 746, 754, 755, 756-57, 759, 892.
London's "extraordinary energy dissipated itself in a
life of adventure...and in a life of violent social protest." His mass-produced books generally lack distinction.

2 COWLEY, MALCOLM, ed. After the Genteel Tradition: American
Writers Since 1910. New York: W. W. Norton, pp. 116, 214,
260.
Mentions London. Same, reprinted: Gloucester, Massachusetts: Peter Smith, 1959.

3 FREEMAN, JOSEPH. An American Testament. New York: Farrar and
Rinehart, pp. 313, and passim.
Mentions London and his socialism.

4 GENTHE, ARNOLD. As I Remember. New York: Reynal and Hitch-
cock, pp. 49-50, 62, 64, 69, 74-75.
Genthe frequently photographed London and received inscribed first editions from him. London "had a poignantly
sensitive face. His eyes were those of a dreamer, and
there was almost a feminine wistfulness about him. Yet at
the same time he gave the feeling of a terrific and uncon-
querable physical force."

5 QUINN, ARTHUR H. American Fiction: An Historical and Critical
Survey. New York: Appleton-Century, pp. 541-45, 720, 765.
Among the flaws in London's work are sentimentality;
confusion of two narrative voices in White Fang; description of primitive man in Before Adam "not as he was or
thought, but as London gave him thoughts and emotions";
"unnatural" dialogue and a trite love situation in The
Sea-Wolf; and an absurd climax in The Iron Heel--London
is weakest in "sociological propaganda." Some of his
works show virtues of sincerity, sympathy for the underdog, and a journalist's close observations. The Call of
the Wild is attractive because of its "direct forcible
style, the celebration of primitive force, and the new
setting of Alaskan gold fields." "It is almost certain
that his vogue is passing, for there is something imperma-
nent in the very nature of the literature of violence."

6   TAYLOR, WALTER. A History of American Letters. New York:
     American Book Company, pp. 315-18, and passim.
         London was "distracted from true naturalism by his love
     of vigorous action." He was both a "materialistic prole-
     tarian" and a "frontiersman." In The Call of the Wild,
     "his masterpiece," beauty and brutality merge in "a strong,
     rhythmical, semi-poetic style." Although London glorifies
     "sheer strength and cunning," his philosophy was "collec-
     tive," as demonstrated in the defeat of Larsen and Eden.
     To literature "he brought the raw brutality of the primi-
     tive struggle for existence....the battle cry of the pro-
     letariat," and reemphasis on "the physical basis of life."

1937 A BOOKS - NONE

1937 B SHORTER WORKS

1   LOGGINS, VERNON. I Hear America: Literature in the United
     States Since 1900. New York: Crowell, pp. 253-63, 311, and
     passim.
         "He was many things—but primarily a propagandist for the
     principles of Karl Marx....[Americans] were dead to the
     message of his tales—...that every man true to himself is
     a materialist, that the church is maintained by the capi-
     talists as a blind for pillage, that priests who preach
     metaphysics are drones clustering greedily about the honey
     vats, that government as we know it is no government, and
     that the inevitable next step in human progress is the
     establishment of the communistic state." Offers various
     interpretations of "Londonism" by traditionalists, Russians,
     and average Americans. "Martin Eden is of all the books
     the most autobiographical and realistic and the richest in
     Londonism....Russia sees it as a sincere picture of the
     fundamental weaknesses in the capitalistic system....Jack
     intended the book to be interpreted according to Russia."
     The Call of the Wild allegorizes "anthropological and social
     truths." London "was a genius—one of the best equipped
     propagandists the modern world has known." Gives biography.

2   McCLOE, C. J. Lucifer at Large. New York: Longmans, pp. 21,
     26-27.
         Wolf Larsen is "one of the best examples of Nietzschean
     supermen in our fiction."

3   SHIELDS, ART. "Jack London's Alaska Claim." (New York) Daily
     Worker (2 May), pp. 1, 9.

The Iron Heel heartened striking gold miners in Nome
during World War I.

4   WARFEL, HARRY R., et al., eds. The American Mind: Selections
     from the Literature of the United States. New York: Ameri-
     can Book Company, pp. 1004-1005.
     London's fifty volumes "suffer from feverishness and
     over-writing." Brief biography.

1938 A BOOKS

1   STONE, IRVING. Sailor on Horseback: The Biography of Jack Lon-
     don. Cambridge, Massachusetts: Houghton Mifflin, 338 pp.
     London: Collins, 327 pp.
     Serialized as "Sailor on Horseback: The Life of Jack
     London." Saturday Evening Post, 210 (25 June), 5-7, 30,
     32-33, 36, 38; 211 (2 July), 16-17, 47, 49-52; 211 (9 July),
     16-17, 53-54, 56; 211 (16 July), 20-21, 51-54, 57; 211
     (30 July), 16-17, 30-33; 211 (6 August), 14-15, 63-66; 211
     (13 August), 20-21, 61-66; 211 (27 August), 16-17, 48-50,
     53-54; 211 (3 September), 16-17, 39-40, 42-44. *Excerpted
     in The Passing Show, 7 (15, 22, 29 October; 5 November);
     cited in Woodbridge, 1966.A6.
     [Life]. Son of Flora Wellman, "black sheep" of her
     family, a neurotic woman and a spiritualist, and William H.
     Chaney, "a full-blooded Irishman," writer, astrologer, lin-
     guist, and an improvident woman-chaser. Jack was physically
     the "spit and image" of Chaney and inherited his "brain and
     character." As a boy, Jack "suffered from frequent nervous-
     ness and was occasionally on the verge of a breakdown."
     With John London he hunted and fished; their mutual love
     and trust transcended the family's life of "poverty and de-
     feat." Jack sold newspapers, did odd jobs, saved his pen-
     nies to buy small boats and became "one of the most expert
     small-boat sailors" on the bay. At age fifteen, he bought
     the Razzle Dazzle and raided oyster beds with Mamie, queen
     of the oyster pirates who had fallen in love with him at
     first sight. After several months, he joined Young Scratch
     Nelson on the Reindeer, made as much as $180 a night, and
     "when times were dull, he drank, he got drunk...[one] night
     he consumed more than two quarts." After one three-week
     drunk, he attempted suicide by drowning. He was a deputy
     for the Fish Patrol for nearly a year; a boat-puller and
     seal-skinner on the Sophie Sutherland; mill-hand; coal
     passer; and, as "Sailor Kid," then "Frisco Kid," he took
     to the road, where he "developed the art of spontaneous
     story-telling" to be a successful beggar and enjoyed the

danger of riding the rails. Realizing he needed an education to live by his brains, at age nineteen he entered the
freshman class at Oakland High School; he also got false
teeth to replace his rotten ones and bought the first
toothbrush he had ever owned. The Henry Clay Debating
Society, which he joined, appreciated his "clear and logical" thinking, his humor, sea stories, and passion for
socialism, which, to Jack "was a system of human, historical, economic logic, as irrefutable as the multiplication
table." He transmuted his internal "quarrel with the
world: his illegitimacy" into the socialist's "overthrowing
of the predominant class of society by the subservient
class." After five weeks at cramming school and twelve
weeks studying at home, he passed exams and entered the
University of California where he "enjoyed his work hearti-
ly." He left school because he had to support his family
and worked in a laundry until he left for the Klondike.
In the Yukon, he conquered the problem of portage over
Chilkoot Pass, designed two boats, earned $3000 for taking
boats through the rapids, and "spent a delightful winter"
gathering materials for fiction and arguing about socialism
in a cabin at Steward. He prospected on the Henderson, had
fun in Dawson City, got scurvy, and came home "without a
penny in his pocket." London wrote many stories, and when
a few had been accepted, he and Mabel Applegarth confessed
their love for one another and decided to be engaged for a
year. He read voraciously, searching for a personal philosophy. "He was honest, he was courageous, he could think
straight, and he had a profound love for truth." London
"conceived of himself as a superman, able to conquer all
obstacles, a giant who would end by ruling (teaching,
leading, directing) the masses....All his life he remained
an individualist and a socialist; he wanted individualism
for himself...and socialism for the masses." Jack "saw
himself as a fish out of water" in society; he rebelled
against conventionality and sentimentality, believed in
reason and science. "The backbone of his life was socialism" combined with "Haeckel's monism, Spencer's materialistic determinism, and Darwin's evolution." He determined to make literature "smell of life....[to] play
his part in destroying organized religion, in destroying
organized capitalism, and in converting sex...into the
scientific play of selective forces engaged in perpetua-
tion of the species."
   Jack married Bessie Maddern "on an impulse"; she proved
to be "loyal, devoted, gentle, intelligent," a true help-
mate; but she could not share the wild ranges of exultation
and despair on which Jack burned to live. Deeply in debt

and despondent, he moved to the country where he entertained "no less than a hundred people a week" in his Piedmont home. In 1903 he "renounced all obligations to [sexual] abstinence," believing that sex "was a purely sensory experience." Caught in the grip of a "shattering compulsion" for Charmian Kittredge, he left home; for two years "the lovers met secretly once or twice a week" and exchanged torrid love letters. When he returned from his stint as correspondent in the Russo-Japanese War, "Jack entered one of the most unhappy and unproductive periods of his life....Both his body and mind went soggy and stale" as family, marital, and creative problems mounted. In 1905, his lecture tour was cut short by the scandal of his "theatrical rush" into marriage with Charmian. He invested $30,000 in the Snark. "Robbed, ridiculed, cried over, given up for a hopelessly romantic idiot," London, with his amateur crew, sailed for the South Seas in 1907. After a few months, he found himself "in Tahiti with sixty-six dollars in the world" after having spent $104,000 in the previous four and a half years.

Forced by illness to abandon the Snark, the Londons returned to their ranch. "He thrived and gloried in being... the benevolent patriarch" to thousands of people at Glen Ellen on whom he practiced "all sorts of ridiculous practical jokes." When Jack needed to get away from family and obligations, he went drinking in Glen Ellen and Santa Rosa saloons. Thoughts of his illegitimacy made him melancholy; he suffered from "recurrent depressions,...not more than five or six a year."

In 1913, he provided a living for "five hundred human souls....earning seventy-five thousand dollars a year from his writing and spending a hundred thousand. Everything he owned was heavily mortgaged, including his future." By mail or in person, "half of all the money Jack earned was given to other people." He answered an average of 10,000 letters a year, gave helpful criticism to other writers, and in business "he was equally generous and honest." With the loss of Wolf House, he lost his faith in humanity. Problems and disappointments mounted rapidly: the Millergraph company went bankrupt; he failed to gain the friendship of his daughters; he realized that Charmian "was still a child, preoccupied with infantile details"; his pigs caught pneumonia and other prize animals suddenly died; his vast eucalyptus forest was good only for firewood; the public tired of his work; "he was torturing himself with the fear of going insane." London had affairs with several women, drank heavily, and suffered physical ailments; "he held out only one hope for himself: that he would find a mature, genuine woman whom he could love, who would love

him, and give him a son." His resignation from the Socialist party in 1916 "dealt the party a severe blow and
himself a death blow."

Dr. Allan Thomson "found Jack in a state of narcosis"
and treated him for morphine poisoning. The doctor claimed
that Charmian insisted Jack's death "should not be ascribed
to anything but uremic poisoning." His body was cremated
on the night he died. "He was childlike in his desire to
play," hated traditional people and ideas, "despised money
...and squandered it to show the world how little he was
its slave....He was independent, self-willed,...moody,
volatile, often ornery, pig-headed, tempestuous, sadistic.
...had great personal courage....He worshipped beauty and
nature." London believed in humanity and devoted himself
to "bringing mankind an intelligent civilization."

[Works]. The Son of the Wolf "was like a time-bomb
blowing open the new century." London brought the short
story "home to the common people." A Daughter of the
Snows showed his Anglo-Saxon racism and inability to portray realistically "any woman above the working class."
The People of the Abyss is "one of the world's classics
about the underprivileged." The Call of the Wild, written
in "thirty glorious labor-laden days," is a "beautiful and
moving dog story, carrying with it the thrill of first-
rate literature." In The Sea-Wolf, an overnight sensation,
"he made the battles of the mind as exciting as the Irish
bricklayers' free-for-all in Weasel Park in the later The
Valley of the Moon, no mean accomplishment." Before Adam
"was a brave attempt to popularize Darwin and Wallace."
The Iron Heel "paid his debt to his master,...Karl Marx
would have been pleased with The Iron Heel." Martin Eden
is "perhaps the finest novel he ever wrote, and one of the
greatest of all American novels." He was broken-hearted
over the poor reception it got. The excellence of Love of
Life indicates that some men "who write for money can
create literature." Burning Daylight, at once "proletarian writing and art," reinstated him in favor with the
public. John Barleycorn and The Valley of the Moon "are
not among the best he has done but stand shoulder to
shoulder with the finest novels written in America." "For
pure death-appeal, breathlessness of suspense, musical
lyricism of writing, and profound human sympathy, The Star
Rover is a magnificent literary accomplishment." The
Little Lady of the Big House "developed into a love tri-
angle written with all the flowery sentimental hyperbole
of the nineteenth century, a book so artificial, strained,
and exaggerated that the reader is stunned" by disbelief.
Reprinted: 1947.A3; 1960.A1.

1938

1938 B SHORTER WRITINGS

1   ANON. "Jack London: A Suicide? No! Says Daughter." San Fran-
     cisco Chronicle (8 September), p. 11.
     Joan London's denial based on London's last letter to
     her, printed here.

2   ANON. "Jack London." Scholastic, 33 (5 November), 23.
     Brief note on his life and work.

3   CARNEGIE, DALE. "Dale Carnegie's 5-minute Biographies: He Rode
     the Rods to Fame." San Francisco Chronicle (6 February),
     Sunday Magazine, part 2, p. [2].
     Biography.

4   HAVERLAND, STELLA. "Jack London's Debt to Books and Libraries."
     Pacific Bindery Talk, 10 (April), 135-38.
     Discusses influences on London's intellectual development
     of Ina Coolbrith and Frederick Bamford, and London's reading
     which included classical and modern fiction, history, eco-
     nomics, philosophy, and poetry. Gives biography.

5   HINKEL, EDGAR JOSEPH, ed. Bibliography of California Fiction,
     Poetry, and Drama. United States WPA Project. Oakland,
     California: Alameda County Library, Volume 2: 209-12;
     Volume 3: 70.
     Mimeographed. Lists works by London.

6   WALCUTT, CHARLES CHILD. "Naturalism and the Superman in the
     Novels of Jack London." Papers of the Michigan Academy
     of Science, Arts and Letters, 24, 89-107.
     The brutal experiences of London's youth conditioned his
     response to Spencer and Darwin. Although his fiction
     promulgates the philosophies of materialism, determinism,
     atavism and glorification of physical strength and the will
     to power, he modifies these with moral idealism which as-
     sumes an ordered universe, the triumph of justice, and the
     validity of spiritual values. In A Daughter of the Snows,
     Frona is "the higher woman, the superwoman with perfect
     body and piercing intellect," an example of the Nietzschean
     ideal. Atavism and naturalism are represented in Corliss
     and the cowardly St. Vincent, respectively, and materialism
     in the Alaskan background; but structurally, the novel "is
     built around acts of free will and based upon an implicit
     faith in a moral order" which at the end prevails. In The
     Call of the Wild, no conflict exists between animal and
     ethical nature because Buck is a dog; however, the sense
     of the "moral rightness" of Buck's love for Thornton moves

the novel into the ethical sphere. In <u>The Sea-Wolf</u>, Larsen, "a mixture of egotism, cruelty, 'atavism,' and disillusion-ment, is not a genuine Nietzschean superman," nor is the novel naturalistic. It is flawed in plot and structure, for conflict between moral idealism and egoism is avoided; Larsen, central to the first third of the book, in a "worse than inept" switch is abandoned for Van Weyden, "spokesman and hero [who] stands for the ethical point of view." With the novel as a love story, Larsen "is an elaborate <u>decora-tion</u>." London's naturalism is limited by the imposition of his code of ethics on his characters, plots, and struc-tures. His attempt to combine materialism with "moral propriety...wrenches nearly all of London's novels into strange and illogical patterns." Revised text: 1956.B13.

7   WHIPPLE, T. K. "Jack London--Wonder Boy." <u>SatR</u>, 18 (24 Sep-tember), 3-4, 16-17.
        Review of Stone, 1938.A1. Biographers should not be de-luded by London's romanticized self-portraits. He was "a precocious boy, with an excellent physique and a brilliant mind,...as a man he was eminently, even excessively, so-ciable, generous, kind, and likable;...he had the writer's gift with words, the literary genius,...[and] a genius for self-deception." London wasted his potential greatness; "he never did the work he was meant for, and his own life ended in failure" because "the regressive myth of the primi-tive, barbaric hero" ruled him and drove him out of civi-lized society. London's "intrinsic literary value is not great; mainly he is of interest as a social phenomenon," manifesting the "two-facedness" of America: its individual-ism and collectivism. London was about ten percent so-cialist and ninety percent individualist. Attitudes of the Gilded Age and of the frontier, and myths of the lower middle class contributed to his "peculiar and paradoxical literary blend." Valuable qualities of his work are its social consciousness, criticisms of sterile American cul-ture and business, and perhaps his advocacy of "physical stamina, physical courage and endurance and hardihood," which we may have need of. Reprinted: 1943.B5.

1939 A BOOKS

1   LONDON, JOAN. <u>Jack London and His Times: An Unconventional Biography</u>. New York: Doubleday, 391 pp.
        Interchapters give details of historical events and movements, c. 1850-1917. London's parents were Flora Wellman, "a closemouthed

woman," and William Chaney, a quarrelsome, self-taught,
restless wanderer, "an egotist of the first water," six
times married and always bankrupt. London was wet-nursed
by "Mammy Jenny" Prentiss and raised by the kindly John
London who married Flora in 1876. The family's endless
moving around until "Johnny" was ten brought him "first a
terrifying feeling of insecurity, and finally indifference
to home and home ties," as well as "a hatred of country
life." In Oakland, London became a voracious reader, discovered drama, had dreams alternately of glory and failure,
made friends with Frank Atherton, sailed his small skiff,
finished eighth grade, and worked in Hickmott's cannery.
He hated this work, and with $300 borrowed from Mammy
Jenny, he bought the Razzle Dazzle, complete with a girl.
After several months of earning $25 a day and drinking
heavily when on shore, he became a deputy fish patrolman
for a while. But "his drunken decision to commit suicide
one night...is significant of the extent of his disorienta-
tion" and dissatisfaction with life.

After seven months as an able-bodied seaman on the Sophia
Sutherland, he returned to Oakland, worked in a jute mill,
and won first prize in a story contest. "Acutely percep-
tive, naturally articulate, he must have sought words
hungrily long before he consciously recognized his need."
London found himself "in love with love," but was shy with
girls. "He was to study and master much in his life, but
knowledge and understanding of women would always elude
him." After a job shoveling coal in a power plant, he took
to the road in pursuit of Kelly's Industrial Army, and when
the movement fell apart, London deserted and hoboed on his
own through parts of the States and Canada. From these
road experiences, he learned contempt for the law and respect for its strength, consciousness of class and property
distinctions, and the need to sell "the products of his
brain." The "softer environment" of Oakland High School
and hostility of his classmates gave him "a tragic sense
of social inferiority" which "permanently warped his judge-
ment" and made him defiantly assert his differentness
through dress, manners, radical activities and publications
in the Aegis. He made friends with Frederick Bamford, and
Fred Jacobs introduced him to the middle-class world of
Ted and Mabel Applegarth and Bess Maddern. He fell in
love with Mabel, "idealized and worshipped her." But "the
more he saw of what he later was to call the parlor floor
of society, the more poignantly he remembered the cellar."
In 1896, he joined the Socialist party and entered the
University of California, which he left after a few months,
feeling contempt for the students and professors. At this

time, he learned that John London was not his father, and
Chaney denied his paternity. Jack was deeply shocked and
hurt and remained sensitive about his illegitimacy all his
life.

He spent a year in the Klondike for adventure and to
gather materials for his writing. He admired the simple,
free, and noble pre-civilized life there, realized that
capitalism had corrupted inherently beneficial civilization, and decided to regain the simplicity by a return to
nature. But he could never achieve this goal: "Until the
end of his life, he sought with growing desperation to
reconcile his revolutionary principles and belief in the
class struggle with his personal desires and preferences."
With the defeat of his principles, "preference ruled,
brilliantly rationalized, but transparent finally even to
himself."

On his return to Oakland, Jack attacked his writing with
"a purely professional attitude," studied other writers'
work, practiced style, built vocabulary, kept a bookkeeping
system of submissions and rejections, and established a
routine of writing a thousand words a day, six days a
week. He was to become the last American writer to cele-
brate the frontier and the first to battle for social justice. Darwin, Spencer, Nietzsche, and Marx had little
effect on his writing; but the Anglo-Saxonism of Benjamin
Kidd profoundly affected his thinking. He unskillfully
applied what he understood of socialism and evolution to
current problems or wrote to please an audience which re-
garded the frontier as "vicarious escape from urban life."
The Call of the Wild, to him "a lucky shot in the dark,"
became a best seller. In the novel he flees "to a world
of his own devising, a clean, beautiful, primitive world."
He did not realize that the story of Buck, like Larsen's
and Eden's, celebrated individualism and repudiated socialism; when he later "realized the truth it was too late."
He wrote The Iron Heel, "reaffirming his faith in the ultimate achievement of socialism, but ruthlessly placing
the overthrow of capitalism three long centuries ahead
and,...exaggerating the weakness of the working class and
the overwhelming strength of its oppressors." He turned
down several opportunities to write in support of social
reform for "fear lest his income be jeopardized by his
radicalism." His late work had little merit, except for
portions of The Star Rover and a few stories.

London married Bess Maddern (1900) for comradeship and
children; they called one another "Mother-Girl" and "Daddy-
Boy." Although he was publishing successfully, he became
restless, moody, and depressed from the pressures of work

he disliked, the slowness of fame, and burden of debts.
His experiences in the East End of London weakened his
faith in both socialistic solutions and in civilization
itself. With critical acclaim (1903) came hordes of "intellectual bohemians and bourgeois pseudo intellectuals"
to feed his vanity. He acquired a life-long friend in
Sterling; "it seems probable that the emotional interplay
which continued between them for a number of years revealed this latent homosexuality of which neither was
aware." Jack found a mate-woman in Charmian Kittredge,
who as his wife "exerted little influence over him either
for good or for evil." In 1904, as Hearst correspondent
in the Russo-Japanese conflict, he showed "scorn and
loathing of the Japanese," but he returned with a Korean
valet, the first of many Oriental servants. The next year,
he purchased 129 acres, the beginnings of his 1500 acre
estate near Glen Ellen, and he embarked on a three-month
lecture tour, cut short by criticism of his divorce and
remarriage (1905) and his ostentatious living.
  "Failure, disappointment, frustration and bitterness--
these were the dominant themes in the closing years" of
his life, brought about by expensive ventures of the Snark
and agricultural experiments, the burning of Wolf House,
his failure to have a son or be close to his daughters,
his "hatred of writing," several charges of plagiarism,
waning of popularity with the public, and his movement
away from socialism. He took a lethal dose of a pain-
killing drug: "Who could say whether it had been with
suicidal intention, or merely an overdose miscalculated
in the midst of his agony?" "Aside from The Call of the
Wild, his reputation rests most securely today on the handful of books he wrote on social themes....Jack London still
remains a puzzle to literary historians. A very few critics
have tried to analyze and explain his contradictions; none
have wholly succeeded." Reprinted: 1968.A3; 1974.A6.

1939 B SHORTER WRITINGS

1   DUNCAN, THOMAS W. "A Glance at Jack London." The University
     Review--A Journal of the University of Kansas City, 5,
     no. 3 (Spring), 219-21.
        Considered important in his own day, London is unjustly
     neglected by modern critics. "He wrote some dog stories,
     and therefore they have put him into the literary dog-
     house." Actually, he is "an excellent second-rater" who
     wrote a dozen "very good" books and thirty-eight "sound
     and workmanlike" ones. He failed to create individualized
     characters and to plumb the human soul; but he is a good

storyteller who takes your breath away "by the incisive-
ness, the lack of sentimentality, the lucid directness,
and often the glowing beauty of his paragraphs." His masterful irony, diversity of subjects and modernity are remarkable. London was a "romanticist"; his "lusty joy in
life" has discouraged intellectuals who will some day appreciate him as a "far better than average romantic writer."

2 EDWARDS, V. W. "The Jack London Myth." News Letter and Wasp,
  83, no. 51 (24 November), 7, 11.
   Recounts a debate in the Last Chance saloon over London's
  claim that Heinhold lent him $50 for college. For this and
  other biographical data, it is dangerous to quote "the Jack
  London myth in support of the Jack London myth."

3 FILLER, LOUIS. Crusaders for American Liberalism. New York:
  Harcourt Brace, pp. 124, 374, and passim.
   "Socialist, muckraker, romancer, London loved freedom as
  much as he hated injustice." The conflict between his proletarian origin and personal success led to his loss of
  faith in such ideals and motivated his suicide. Same, reprinted: Yellow Springs, Ohio: Antioch Press, 1961.

4 WALKER, FRANKLIN. San Francisco's Literary Frontier. New
  York: Knopf, pp. 352, 355, 360.
   Mentions London.

1940 A BOOKS

1 NOEL, JOSEPH. Footloose in Arcadia: A Personal Record of Jack
  London, George Sterling, Ambrose Bierce. New York: Carrick
  & Evans, pp. 15-53, 80-110, 119-60, 167-68, 174-98, 201,
  202-41, 251-59, 265-81, 325-30.
   Gives biography of London's early life from published
  sources and London's writings. Noel, a newspaperman and
  socialist, met London in 1898 in Cloverdale, California,
  and was associated with him until 1913. London's illegitimacy, his mother's rejection of him, the family's insta-
  bility, the "anti-social creed" of his wharf-rat companions,
  and London's belief that he was cheated of advantages by
  the social order determined his adult character: he was a
  hedonist and egoist who sought vengeance against society
  through socialist revolution and by living outside all
  codes. He asserted his right, as an immortal genius, to
  be first in fame and possessions, to win every argument
  and be absolute master of his own and all other peoples'
  lives. The Oakland socialists and other "self-centered

direct-actionists" helped develop London's intellect,
rhetorical skills, and his ego. Noel arranged his first
meeting with Sterling (1901); London took Sterling "into
sensualism" with frequent forays into the burlesque houses,
bordellos, gambling joints, dance halls, and prize fights
of the Barbary Coast. Together they investigated spiri-
tualism and Buddhism: London remained skeptical and declared the universe "mechanical." As he gained success,
London's anti-social behavior and greed grew. His Piedmont house "became the Mecca for women of many moods and
desires." He divorced Bess, an "ideal wife," because she
talked publicly about his illegitimacy, and he allowed
Anna Strunsky to be blamed for breaking up the marriage to
hide his extra-marital affairs from Bess. At Glen Ellen
with Charmian, who was hardworking, loyal, and wholly subservient to him, London acted "like Caesar," accumulating
land, things, and retainers as his "diseased egoism" grew.
He manipulated people to become rich in the Millergraph
venture, was disloyal to publishers, plagiarized often,
and resold old stories under new titles. Noel gave him a
novel, The South Sea Pearler, which was the source for The
Sea-Wolf. London sold the film rights to The Sea-Wolf
over Noel's head--Noel had dramatized it--and violated subsequent agreements with him, severing their friendship.
In later years, London and his friends were aware of his
mental deterioration to the borders of insanity. "Dis-
order was London's first law....He went in for private
wars when he couldn't get an official carnage to attend."
His life's tragedy was the frustration of an "internal
drive toward the unattainable." His death, according to
Sterling and Sinclair, was, predictably, a suicide.

1940 B SHORTER WRITINGS

1   CARNES, CECIL. Jimmy Hare, News Photographer: Half a Century
    With a Camera. New York: Macmillan, pp. 153, 154, 155,
    169, 227, 230.
        Mentions London as a friend of Hare's on the Russo-
    Japanese and Mexican War fronts.

2   CAUGHEY, JOHN WALTON. California: A Remarkable State's Life
    History. Englewood Cliffs, N. J.: Prentice-Hall, pp. 1,
    526.
        He was a "master storyteller,...Marxian socialist and
    revolutionist." His style lacks "restraint and polish"
    but won readers by its "spontaneity and forthrightness."
    Same, 3rd edition, 1970.

3   HINKEL, EDGAR JOSEPH, ed. Criticism of California Literature:
     A Digest and Bibliography. Volume 2. United States WPA
     Project. Oakland, California: Alameda County Library,
     502–47.
         Mimeographed. Offers excerpts of varying lengths from
     books and periodicals in English and foreign languages
     commenting on London's life and works.

4   HOWARD, ERIC. "Men Around London: Strawn-Hamilton, Tramp-
     Philosopher, and Sterling, Poet, Were Closest to Jack Lon-
     don in That Bohemian Group." Esquire, 13 (June), 62,
     183–86.
         London was a man of great mental and physical energy, a
     "sensitive" drinker, subject to depression and dominated
     by the desire to make his life beautiful to overcome the
     death impulse which haunted him. Sterling was his best
     critic; Hamilton "his favorite character" as well as his
     "guide, philosopher, and friend." London was unfailingly
     generous and well-liked by all. Although his "work was
     never truly popular with the great mass of magazine and
     novel readers," he had a profound influence on "youngsters"--
     radical writers--who idolized and emulated him. Gives
     biography.

5   JOHNSON, OSA. I Married Adventure: The Lives and Adventures
     of Martin and Osa Johnson. Philadelphia: Lippincott,
     pp. 41–64, 105–107, and passim.
         Describes Martin Johnson's experiences with the Snark
     (from Johnson's diary; see 1913.A1). On a visit to Glen
     Ellen, Osa won approval as Martin's wife; Jack named her
     "Snarkette."

6   PRESTON, WHEELER. "Jack London," in American Biographies.
     New York: Harper, pp. 628–29.
         Brief biography.

7   TEMPSKI, ARMINE VON. Born in Paradise. New York: Duell,
     Sloan & Pearce, pp. 198–99.
         Describes the Londons' visit to Paia, Hawaii.

1941 A BOOKS – NONE

1941 B SHORTER WRITINGS

1   BORDEN, CHARLES. "Jack London." Paradise of the Pacific, 53
     (January), 24–26.
         London enjoyed the strenuous life and wrote some "pot-

1941

boilers," but his Klondike tales had the "honest, gripping quality of first-hand experience and the gusto and punching power of an abundant vitality." He won popularity but not the critics' approval.

2   CARGILL, OSCAR. <u>Intellectual America: Ideas on the March</u>. New York: Macmillan, pp. 93, 95, 312, 332, 334, 336, 337, 338, 487.
    Norris's <u>Moran of the Lady Letty</u> and <u>A Man's Woman</u> "inspired" London. From London's tales, O'Neill "brought wholesale butchery and violence to contemporary primitivism." O'Neill's atavism in <u>The Emperor Jones</u> suggests London; Anna Christie resembles the "Amazon" in "The Night Born"; and the "rather witless radical talk of the type that London used to indulge in so handsomely" appears in <u>The Hairy Ape</u>.

3   CROSSMAN, R. H. S. "The Prophecies of Jack London." <u>New Statesman and Nation</u>, NS 19 (8 June), 723-24.
    <u>The Iron Heel</u>, "a unique mixture of wild-West thriller and Marxian sociology," accurately prophesied Japanese and Hitlerian Fascism. The exclusivity of the novel's redemptive socialists created a "profound kinship between the faith of revolutionary Christianity" and London's "myth of violence"; this, with London's "childish ecstasy in carnage, and secret conspiracy," gave <u>The Iron Heel</u> enormous popularity among simple people. It is thus "genuine proletarian literature."

4   DICKASON, DAVID H. "David Starr Jordan as a Literary Man." <u>Indiana Magazine of History</u>, 37:345-58.
    Mentions Jordan's intellectual influence on London. Expanded: 1942.B3; <u>see</u> 1922.B3.

5   FUNKHOUSER, RAY G. "Valley of the Moons." <u>Buick Magazine</u>, 6, no. 11 (February), 6.
    Describes ruins of Wolf House, ranch buildings.

6   HART, JAMES D. "London, Jack," in his <u>The Oxford Companion to American Literature</u>. New York: Oxford University Press, pp. 429-30.
    "His popularity, journalistic training, and eagerness for money caused him to write too prolifically, but his energy and ability as a storyteller gave even his worst writing a great appeal." Alternately championing the theories of Marx and Nietzsche in his life and writings, London's most convincing work depicted "individualistic struggle and primitive violence." Gives biography and

bibliography; discusses London's major works under their titles in this volume. Same, 4th edition, revised and enlarged, 1965.

7   SINCLAIR, UPTON. "Jack London Speaks to Us." The Psychic Observer, 58 (10 February), 1-2.
    Abridged version of 1930.B12 and 1931.B11.

1942 A BOOKS - NONE

1942 B SHORTER WRITINGS

1   ANON. "Jack London." Who Was Who in America. Volume 1. Chicago: A. N. Marquis, 742.
    Brief biography.

2   BOSWORTH, HOBART. "My Jack London." MTJ, 5 (Fall and Winter), 2-5, 24.
    An intimate friend who made movies of many of London's novels, Bosworth "loved him short of idolatry." London had a brilliant sense of humor, a pure mind, sincere love for people and animals, great self-control, "a mixture of manliness and of boyishness" that attracted women, and a "marvelous ability as a talker." He appreciated Charmian's care and help and understood his own career and degenerative illness. "He was frank and friendly, candid, playful, vital as few men I have ever met, and he retained his boyish charm until the end."

3   DICKASON, DAVID. "A Note on Jack London and David Starr Jordan." Indiana Magazine of History, 38 (December), 407-10.
    Probably, Jordan's popularizations (in lectures and essays) of the evolutionists "served as the most active influence in the building of Jack London's intellectual platform." Expansion of 1941.B4; see 1922.B3.

4   HINKEL, EDGAR JOSEPH, ed. Biographies of California Authors and Indexes of California Literature. Volume 1. United States WPA Project. Oakland, California: Alameda County Library, 129-31.
    Mimeographed. A biography of London with notations of sources.

5   IRWIN, WILL. The Making of a Reporter. New York: Putnam's, pp. 83-85.
    London's romantic and sincere Socialism was founded on Christian ethics. He was a brilliant talker and delighted in unconventional behavior to shock the bourgeoisie.

1942

6   JOHNSON, MERLE DEVORE. "Jack (John Griffith) London," in
     <u>American First Editions</u>. Fourth edition. Revised and en-
     larged by Jacob Blanck. New York: Bowker, pp. 318-22.
        Lists 52 volumes by London; 11 miscellaneous items; 11
     works about him. Revised and enlarged text of 1929.B6.

7   KAZIN, ALFRED. <u>On Native Grounds: An Interpretation of Modern</u>
     <u>American Prose Literature</u>. New York: Reynal & Hitchcock,
     pp. 86, 89, 92-93, 99, 110-16, 120, 274.
        The "greatest crusader" and "most unashamed hack" of his
     age, London was instinctively a romantic Socialist and "a
     prototype of the violence-worshipping Fascist intellectual."
     He failed at life and art because he grasped at many con-
     tradictory doctrines but committed himself to none except
     "revenge" on society for his early sufferings. He remains
     historically significant as the writer who best satisfied
     the public's taste for intense, unconventional, brutal and
     romantic adventures in fiction and in life. Same, in
     abridged edition: Garden City: Doubleday, 1956.

8   KUNITZ, STANLEY J. and HOWARD HAYCRAFT, eds. <u>Twentieth-Century</u>
     <u>American Authors: A Biographical Dictionary of Modern</u>
     <u>Literature</u>. New York: H. W. Wilson, pp. 843-45.
        Biography. "His beliefs were a mixture of Socialism,
     Haeckel's monism, Spencer's materialistic determinism, and
     Darwin's evolution."

9   MALONE, TED. See Russell, Frank Alden.

10   RUSSELL, FRANK ALDEN. "Jack London," in his <u>American Pilgrim-</u>
     <u>age</u>. New York: Dodd, Mead, pp. 234-52.
        His "peculiarly American" genius "was sure and penetrat-
     ing." Gives biography.

1943 A BOOKS - NONE

1943 B SHORTER WRITINGS

1   COFFMAN, R.[AYMOND] P.[EYTON]. and N. G. GOODMAN. <u>Famous</u>
     <u>Authors for Boys and Girls</u>. New York: A. S. Barnes,
     pp. 155-62.
        Juvenile biography.

2   FITZGERALD, BRASSIL. "Death at High Noon," in his <u>Never Sur-</u>
     <u>render</u>. Boston: Ginn, pp. 105-32.
        An instructive juvenile biography. "Poisoned by an un-
     happy childhood, by a sordid youth, he thought to cure

the world's ills by hating." Confused in mind and physically ill, London took "too many poisons" and died young.

3   KRUSKOPF, ANDERS. "Martin Eden of Sonoma." American Scandi-
       navian Review, 31:[347]-48.
          London named his hero after a Swede who emigrated to
       Sonoma and worked on London's ranch. He "just happened
       to like the name." The real Martin Eden died in 1943 in
       Santa Rosa.

4   STOVALL, FLOYD. American Idealism. Norman: University of
       Oklahoma Press, pp. 129-31, 132, 133-34.
          London was attracted to three "inharmonious" interpreta-
       tions of human life: evolutionary materialism, Nietzschean
       romanticism, and the class struggle. "So far as he has
       made his view known in his books, it ["moral idealism"]
       was subordinated to a materialistic philosophy of force."

5   WHIPPLE, THOMAS K. "Jack London--Wonder Boy," in his Study
       Out the Land. Berkeley: University of California Press,
       pp. 93-104.
          Reprint of 1938.B7.

1944 A BOOKS

1   GARST, DORIS SHANNON. Jack London: Magnet for Adventure.
       New York: Julian Messner, 217 pp.
          Juvenile biography.

1944 B SHORTER WRITINGS

1   ADAMS, J. DONALD. The Shape of Books to Come. New York:
       Viking, pp. 4, 50, 52.
          Mentions London in connection with naturalism.

2   WILLIAMSON, THAMES. Far North Country. New York: Duell,
       Sloan, & Pearce, pp. 73-74.
          London "apparently knew he was describing a non-existent
       Alaska." Mention of it made him "scowl and curse. It was
       a hell of a place; it had ruined his health"; but it was
       making gold for him in fiction.

1945 A BOOKS - NONE

1945

1945 B SHORTER WRITINGS

1   BAKER, RAY STANNARD. American Chronicle: The Autobiography
     of Ray Stannard Baker (David Grayson). New York: Scrib-
     ner's, pp. 137-41.
          Reminiscence of a visit to London in his "freak house"
     in Oakland in 1901. London tried to convert him to so-
     cialism; they read Ben Jonson's plays aloud and went
     sailing.

2   HOFSTADTER, RICHARD. Social Darwinism in American Thought,
     1860-1915. Philadelphia: University of Pennsylvania Press,
     pp. 34, 189.
          Mentions Spencer's influence and London's anti-Japanese
     feeling. Same, revised edition: New York: G. Braziller,
     1959.

1946 A BOOKS

1   McDEVITT, W[ILLIA]M. Jack London's First. "Limited to 500
     Copies." San Francisco: Recorder-Sunset Press, 32 pp.
          A collection of essays and items on London. "Jack Lon-
     don's First," pp. 3-5: his first professional publication
     was a story, "Two Gold Bricks," in the Owl (New York),
     September, 1897; he never knew it had been published
     (prints story, pp. 12-17). "His Travel is Cheap: An Oak-
     land Youth's Long Wanderings: Tours his own land as a
     tramp: Thousands of miles on the Brakebeam--Perilous ad-
     ventures," pp. 6-11: biography, reprinted from San Fran-
     cisco Chronicle (16 December, 1894), pp. 11-20. "Jack
     London--A Foreword (Written for a forthcoming biography),"
     pp. 18-20: a reprint of 1932.B13. "Scripter Unearths rare
     volume: autobiography of Professor Chaney, Jack London's
     Father, Found by Wm. McDevitt, LL.M.," pp. 20-24: Chaney's
     "Primer of Astrology" (1890). Both men were born under
     the same astrological sign, were sailors, gamblers, had
     similar illnesses, were socialistic, suicidal, aggressive,
     self-dramatizing and autobiographical writers; both were
     divorced, involved in lawsuits, served jail terms, and
     were handsome. "New Volume for London Collectors," p. 24:
     announcement of Jack London's First, reprinted from Coast
     Collector. "George Sterling's tribute to Jack London,"
     p. 25: poem (see appendix "Poems"). "Was Jack London a
     Journalist? (what Mrs. Jack says)," pp. 26-27: he was not;
     and there was mutual animosity between London and editors
     of California papers. "Addenda--Bibliographic Notes:
     Jack London Market Values," pp. 28-31: various partial

bibliographies, checklists, and sales records exist. Pamphlet reprinted: 1972.A4.

1946 B SHORTER WRITINGS

1   ATHERTON, GERTRUDE. My San Francisco: A Wayward Biography.
      Indianapolis: Bobbs-Merrill, pp. 96-98, 190, 284, 298-99.
      Author never knew London. Mrs. Oliver Remick (Laura)
      Grant writes an appreciation of him for this book: "His
      brilliant, restless mind, his craving for dangerous adventure, his natural kindliness, his unselfishness, his faith
      in his fellow man, his generosity--these....were the real
      Jack London."

2   FARRELL, JAMES T. "My Favorite Forgotten Book." Tomorrow, 6
      (November), 63-64.
      With imagination and profound insight, London "saw
      through the fallacies of reformism" to create The Iron Heel,
      "one of the most amazing prophetic works of the twentieth
      century."

*3 MONTGOMERY, ELIZABETH R. The Story Behind Great Books. New
      York: McBride, pp. 143-47.
      A juvenile. Cited in Woodbridge, 1966.A

1947 A BOOKS

1   FONER, PHILIP S. "Jack London: American Rebel," in Jack London: American Rebel; a Collection of His Social Writings
      Together with an Extensive Study of the Man and His Times.
      Edited by Philip S. Foner. New York: Citadel, pp. 3-130.
      Biography. "As a newsboy, sailor, mill-hand, stoker,
      tramp, and janitor, he came to know all there was to know
      about the life of the underdog....he took his heroes and
      heroines from the labor movement and wove his plots within
      their struggles." His writings expressed his "fierce
      hatred of the bourgeoisie" and conviction that the "exploited" must "take the management of society out of the
      hands of the exploiters." From his initial reading of the
      Communist Manifesto, London adopted and held all his life
      "the belief in the class struggle;...and confidence in the
      inevitable emergence of Socialism." The People of the
      Abyss, a "major sociological study of the underprivileged"
      and his "burning indictment against capitalism," brought
      him nationwide popularity among Party members. The Call
      of the Wild "is endowed with such magic and imagination,
      it moves so swiftly to its logical end, and recreates so

brilliantly the atmosphere appropriate to the moods of animals, that no reader could possibly be unmoved." The Sea-
Wolf conveys "a message which none of the critics grasped--
that under the present system the individualist must end in
self-destruction." Unanimously elected president of the
Intercollegiate Socialist Society (1905), London lectured
for them to capacity audiences at such schools as Harvard
and Yale where he "was the college man's idol." His socialist writings, based on news and government reports
from his clipping file, were "utilized by socialists and
trade unionists in their own talks and writings." The
Iron Heel, "a rare and prophetic novel," indicts conservative socialist leaders for their shortsightedness and
warns "that reformism would lead to world-wide disaster
for the working class." With few exceptions, the writings
based on his South Seas experience are "saturated with his
chauvinistic conceit of the supremacy of the Anglo-Saxon
race"; they added little to his stature as a writer and a
socialist. Martin Eden, although meant to be an attack on
individualism, fails to present socialism strongly in its
characters; it is "in many ways one of the least successful
of his works." Out of his need for money, and with the
"waning of his activity in the socialist movement," London
wrote "potboilers" in his later years. By the time he resigned from the party "he no longer fitted anywhere in the
movement," having denounced the conservative reformists
and alienated the left-wing forces by his militant posture
in World War I. Attacked by socialists for his defection,
he grew bitter and discouraged. "Like Martin Eden he now
had no reason to continue living....the final victory of
the 'white logic' was fulfilled." London "remains one of
America's most significant writers because he concerned
himself with the vital problems of his age....The spirit
of the common people of America, heroic, fiery and adventurous, will live forever in the pages of his rebel stories, novels, and essays." Includes a bibliography of
secondary sources. Revised edition: 1964.A1.

2   McDEVITT, W[ILLIA]M. Jack London as Poet and As Platform Man.
    Did Jack London Commit Suicide? San Francisco: Recorder-
    Sunset Press, 32 pp.
       A collection of essays and items about London. "Jack
    London as Poet," pp. 5-6: his poetry is not good; however,
    he had "all the fundamental qualities that conspire to the
    making of good poetry--emotion, sincerity in thought, in-
    tellectual reach as well as grasp, and withal a fine
    sense of critical judgment" (this essay reprinted:
    1970.B31). "The Discovery," pp. 6-7: a letter from

"Kenneth Richards" who found London's poem, "The Sea Sprite
and the Shooting Star" among the effects of Henry Meade
Bland in 1932 (prints this poem and "Sonnet," pp. 8-11).
"Did London Quote Himself," p. 12: a letter searching for
source of a line of poetry quoted in Martin Eden. "Jack
London--Soapboxer," pp. 13-16: London's lectures for the
Socialist party influenced many young men. He lost the
power to "speak extemporaneously and effectively in public"
after he became famous, and not wishing to expose this in-
capacity, he refused to make speeches. "Jack London on
the Platform," pp. 16-23: London's appearances for socialism in Oakland and San Francisco, 1905-1909, were arranged
and managed by McDevitt through the Socialist World, the
party organ whose longevity (some 22 years) "was due
largely to the generous money-aid and prestige-aid so
freely donated by" London. Never as fine a lecturer as
Sinclair, London attracted audiences by "the genius of personality." "Did Jack London Commit Suicide?" pp. 24-26:
he "committed virtual suicide by his meateating orgies and
the consequent toxic uremia, rendered more fatal by alcoholic excess...an overdose of sleeping powders may have
been a contributing factor. To me it is absolutely unbe-
lievable that he would commit the most dramatic action in
his life WITHOUR [sic] DRAMATIZING IT!" "Addendum to
Genealogy of Jack London," p. 27: "Earl Bertrand Russell
and Jack London have the same ancestry." Two additional
items, pp. 28-31, are Carl Browne's first-hand account of
Coxey's Army and a review of McDevitt, 1946.A1. Pamphlet
reprinted: 1971.A3.

3   STONE, IRVING. Jack London, Sailor on Horseback; A Biographi-
      cal Novel. Garden City: Doubleday, 337 pp.
          Reprint of 1938.A1; reprinted: 1960.A1.

1947 B SHORTER WRITINGS

1   ANON. "From Deed to Word: Jack London's Adventurous Life."
      Scholastic, 49 (13 January), 16-17.
          A life of high adventure, motivated by "a deep longing
      for beauty and grace" and for self-justification and
      money, did not bring London happiness. Gives biography.

2   CLELAND, ROBERT GLASS. California in Our Time (1900-1940).
      New York: Knopf, pp. 301-303.
          London was "an Ishmaelite of the stews and waterfront,
      whose hand was against every man as every man's hand was
      against him." Brief biography and criticism, derivative.

1947

3   LEARY, LEWIS, comp. Articles on American Literature Appearing
    in Current Periodicals, 1920-1945. Durham, N. C.: Duke
    University Press, p. 213.
        Lists seven items on London.

4   MORRIS, LLOYD. Postscript to Yesterday; America: The Last
    Fifty Years. New York: Random House, pp. 108, 115-21, 135,
    233, 265.
        The unresolved conflict between his ideals and ambition
    "left a deep fissure in his moral nature, and produced a
    startling inconsistency in his life and writing." London's
    revolutionary works woke the "social conscience" of the
    rich and gave the militant proletariat "a gospel and a
    program of action." However, his writing for money and
    portrayal of strong individualistic heroes indifferent to
    the masses soon alienated his working class and socialist
    audiences. London never realized that his own rise to
    fortune validated the myth of success he tried to discredit.
    In the 1940's his fame as a genius, "a precursor and
    prophet," endures only in Russia.

5   MOTT, FRANK LUTHER. Golden Multitudes. New York: Macmillan,
    pp. 234-35, 312.
        London was outstanding among "writers for he-men." He
    achieved success with The Call of the Wild, which has "a
    directness, a tonic quality of primal strength, and a
    fresh vividness." Call and The Sea-Wolf are assured
    lasting popularity.

6   PYLE, ERNIE. Home Country. New York: William Sloane, pp. 430-
    34.
        Reminiscence of a visit to London's ranch in 1939; de-
    scribes house, memorabilia, and library.

7   SNELL, GEORGE M. The Shapers of American Fiction, 1789-1947.
    New York: Dutton, 164, 187.
        Mentions London.

8   WITHAM, W. TASHER. Panorama of American Literature. New
    York: Stephen Daye, pp. 182, 217, 223-26, 256.
        London's "red-blooded naturalism" was a revolt against
    Victorian sentimentalism and prudery.

1948 A BOOKS - NONE

1948 B SHORTER WORKS

1   AMES, RUSSELL. "Jack London: American Radical." Our Time
    (London), 7 (July), 254-55.
        The fresh reformist content of his works "made him a
    hero to Socialists and workers"; the "poetical language...
    romantic settings...shocking violence; their Heroes and
    Villains--made him a hero of small boys and of the middle
    class." In his best novels, Martin Eden, The Sea-Wolf,
    and The Iron Heel, he offers for the first time in American
    literature "working-class heroes who attain great personal
    success despite monstrous obstacles, but are in the end
    defeated by natural and social forces too big for them."
    London's works are more important and "finer than his
    daily life." His best fiction has "done more to teach
    struggle and hope than a million times their wordage in
    editorials and texts."

2   ARNOLD, H. H. "My Life in the Valley of the Moon." National
    Geographic, 94 (December), 689-716.
        History of the Sonoma Valley. Mentions and illustrates
    London's ranch.

*3   CATALOGUE #1. San Francisco: El Dorado Bookstore.
        Illustrates 50 first editions of London's works and 6
    additional items. Cited in Tweney, 1974.B30.

4   COWIE, ALEXANDER. The Rise of the American Novel. New York:
    American Book Company, p. 746.
        London was inclined to "the cult of sturdy individualism
    and a love of primitive strength," and to Nietzsche's
    "power ethic." Yet he realized that socialism was the
    salvation of the proletariat.

5   [HOLMES, HAROLD C.]. A Descriptive & Priced Catalogue of
    Books, Pamphlets, and Maps Relating Directly or Indirectly
    to the History, Literature, and Printing of California &
    The Far West. Formerly the Collection of Thomas Wayne
    Norris, Livermore, California. Oakland, California:
    Holmes Book Company, pp. 106-11.
        Lists manuscript materials, letters, first editions,
    books by and about London; and whole issues of magazines
    with items by and about London.

6   LASK, THOMAS. "Jack London: American Rebel." New York Times
    Book Review (18 January), p. 24.
        A review of 1947.A1. "In the literature of protest in
    America....the writings of Jack London must occupy a place

very near the top." With "intensity and dialectical skill,"
sympathetic and realistic detail, he espoused the brotherhood of man, the class struggle and its preferred resolu-
tion in socialism. His finest indictments of society are
in the autobiographical Martin Eden, John Barleycorn, and
The People of the Abyss.

7   SPILLER, ROBERT E., et al., eds. Literary History of the
    United States. In three volumes. New York: Macmillan,
    Volume 2: 1033-37; Volume 3: 619-22.
       "London preached the more obvious radicalism of his day
    in romantic fiction that,...brought him all the rewards of
    adventure, love, learning, and worldly possessions that
    his insatiable body and mind craved, and led him to ego-
    centric despair and probable suicide....[He] left a small
    body of writing which, for sincerity and vitality, deserves
    to be rescued from the oblivion to which his artistic
    faults threaten to condemn it." His most powerful work is
    Martin Eden: "The chronicle of a sick ego, this thinly
    screened confession, with its fidelity, its misunderstand-
    ing of naked tragic forces, and its failure of resolution,
    is the central document of his career." The novel reveals
    the inconsistencies of London's beliefs in biological evo-
    lution, Anglo-Saxon supremacy, the Nietzschean superman,
    and socialism; these, with "an intense and inhibited ego-
    centricity" become one in Martin's struggle. In The Sea-
    Wolf, Larsen's awakening of Van Weyden "provides a magnifi-
    cent theme for a great novel"; but Maud's appearance "throws
    the whole plot off balance and turns a study in naturalism
    into a desert island romance." The Call of the Wild "is
    London's most satisfying work." His essays and tracts
    effectively convey his message "of social revolution."
    By the end of his life, London's unique "red-blooded
    eagerness and purity of the open life...had faded into a
    cynical negation." He had failed to realize the possibili-
    ties of naturalism.
       Volume 3 ("Bibliography") lists first editions and a few
    reprints, biographical and critical studies to 1945. Ma-
    terial in Volume 2 ("History") remains the same in the
    Second (1953), Third (1963), and Fourth (1974) editions;
    "Bibliography" is the same in the Second edition, is up-
    dated to 1958 in the Third edition, and updated to 1969
    in the Fourth edition. All bibliographies are superseded
    by Woodbridge, 1973.A7.

1949 A BOOKS - NONE

1949 B SHORTER WRITINGS

1　CHOMET, OTTO. "Jack London: Works, Reviews, and Criticism Published in German." In two parts. BB, 19 (January-April), 211-15.
　　Includes an index to this bibliography; 128 listings of translations of London's works and material on London. "Part II," BB, 19 (May-August), 239-40. Includes 145 listings of critical materials and book reviews.

2　DICKSON, SAMUEL. San Francisco Kaleidoscope. Stanford: Stanford University Press, pp. 114, 149-50, 185, 186, 241. Mentions London.

3　GINGER, RAY. The Bending Cross: A Biography of Eugene Victor Debs. New Brunswick: Rutgers University Press, pp. 182, 268, 339, 425-26.
　　Debs admired London but never met him. Debs said, "London was unquestionably a genius, an artist of the first water....a romantic mind, an adventuresome spirit." Debs was not surprised that London "endorsed the war." Same, reprinted (pagination changed): New York: Collier, 1962.

1950 A BOOKS

1　YOUNG, THOMAS. "Jack London and the Era of Social Protest." Ph.D. dissertation, Vanderbilt University.

1950 B SHORTER WRITINGS

1　COMMAGER, HENRY STEELE. The American Mind: An Interpretation of American Thought and Character Since the 1880's. New Haven: Yale University Press, pp. 111, 112-13, 114.
　　A romanticized Darwinism celebrating violence and animal power "riots unrestrained through twenty volumes" of London's. He naively drew on science and philosophy to explain life and justify his fiction, exhibiting in extreme form the confusions and contradictions of naturalistic literature. Same, reprinted: New York: Bantam Books, 1970.

2　HART, JAMES D. The Popular Book: A History of America's Literary Taste. New York: Oxford University Press, pp. 214-15, 222.
　　London attracted men and boys who admired Theodore Roosevelt and vicariously lived the "rugged-individualistic successes" and primitive passions of London's fiction.

1950

3 HUNT, ROCKWELL D. "Jack London," in his California's Stately
   Hall of Fame. Stockton, California: College of the Pacific,
   pp. [435]-40.
      Gives detailed biography. "Whatever he was and was not,
   whatever he did and failed to do, it may be truthfully declared that during his brief forty years he lived."

4 MAGNES, ISAAC D. "My Recollections of Jack London." Alf's
   Cat, 86 (October), p. [?].
      Everyone in Oakland (c. 1898-c. 1901) "considered Jack
   to be a fanatic" because of his Socialist speeches. He
   convinced Magnes to improve working conditions of employees
   in his uncle's department store. Reprinted: 1966.B22.

5 TOOTHAKER, CHARLES R. "'The Star Rover' and Daniel Foss's
   Oar." PBSA, 44:182-85.
      The story of Foss corresponds closely with a pamphlet
   printed in Boston in 1816, written by a man who claimed
   to be Daniel Foss; London read and used this source.

6 WECTER, DIXON. "Literary Lodestone." SatR, 33 (16 September),
   9-10, 37-41.
      "His virility, lavish spending, love of gorgeous trap-
   pings, sincerity, courage, determination, and passion for
   exact knowledge stamped him a true son of the West,...
   [He was] a kind of Tarzan in Marxist hand-me-downs,...a
   totalitarian, half-Communist, half-Fascist...who yearned
   by violence to make the world over." Reprinted: 1951.B10.

7 WILLIAMS, WILLIAM CARLOS. A Beginning on The Short Story
   (Notes). The Outcast Chapbooks no. 17. Yonkers, N. Y.:
   Alicat Bookshop Press, pp. 12-13.
      The best of London's stories mean "the terror and lone-
   someness of the wilderness in its impact on civilized
   man."

1951 A BOOKS

1 BASKETT, SAM S. "Jack London's Fiction: Its Social Milieu."
   Ph.D. dissertation, University of California (Berkeley).
   See also: 1955.B1; 1955.B2; 1956.B3; 1958.B2; 1966.B5.

2 HOLLAND, ROBERT B. "Jack London: This Thought and Art in Relation to His Time." Ph.D. dissertation, University of
   Wisconsin.

1951 B SHORTER WRITINGS

1 ANON. "The Sun-Dog Trail and Other Stories." Kirkus, 19
(1 June), 280.
"A dozen yarns, hewn out of the crudeness and rawness of
the West...and virile, lusty tales they are."

2 ANON. "London and Kyne." Oakland Tribune (22 July), p. 1C.
J. I. Thompson's recollections of teaching animal husban-
dry to London (and Peter B. Kyne) at the University of
California "Farm at Davis." London "liked to argue" and
often monopolized class time.

3 ANON. "Analyzing the Call of the Wild: The Sun-Dog Trail: And
Other Stories. New York Times Book Review (19 August),
p. 18.
"We can like Jack London or we can dislike him as a
writer, but we should not ignore him." In 1950, 43 London
titles were published abroad; Europeans admire the "great
élan and vigor" of his work. These stories include "his
best and his worst."

4 ANON. "London, Jack. The Sun-Dog Trail, and Other Stories.
ALA Booklist, 48 (1 December), 128.
Gives contents.

5 CLARK, BARRET H. Intimate Portraits. New York: Dramatists
Play Service, p. 15.
Maxim Gorky, interviewed in 1923, said: London "has been
tremendously influential" in Russia, moving new writers
"to exalt the will."

*6 GALLANT, JOSEPH. "A Proposal for the Reading of 'Scientific
Fiction.'" High Points, 33 (April), 20-27.
This new classification would include London's stories.
Cited in Clareson, 1972.B10.

7 HOFFMAN, FREDERICK J. The Modern Novel in America; 1900-1950.
Chicago: Regnery, pp. 32, 40.
Mentions London.

8 KNIGHT, GRANT C. The Critical Period in American Literature.
Chapel Hill: University of North Carolina Press, pp. 61,
128, 142, 150.
Mentions London.

9 QUINN, ARTHUR H., et al., eds. The Literature of the American
People: An Historical and Critical Survey. New York:

1951

Appleton-Century-Crofts, pp. 846-47, and passim.
The books which brought him popularity "celebrated the glory of stark violence and savage virility....London had little sense of the artistic sincerity of his work"; and he readily combined flashes of poetry with profitable sentimentality and red-blooded adventure.

10 WECTER, DIXON. Literary Lodestone: One Hundred Years of California Writing. Stanford: Stanford University Press, pp. 27-28.
Reprint of 1950.B6.

1952 A BOOKS

1 ROTHBERG, ABRAHAM ALAN. "The House That Jack Built: A Study of Jack London: The Man, His Times, and His Works." Ph.D. dissertation, Columbia University.
Excerpted and revised: 1963.B17.

1952 B SHORTER WRITINGS

1 BEVAN, ANEURIN. In Place of Fear. New York: Simon and Schuster, p. 19.
The Iron Heel had a "profound" effect on the minds of Bevan and other British workingclass readers.

2 BROOKS, VAN WYCK. "Frank Norris and Jack London," in his The Confident Years, 1885-1915. New York: Dutton, pp. 227-37.
London broke away from the genteel tradition "for he detested false culture" and despised "the weak and the tender-minded." His Alaskan stories vehemently affirm life while insisting life is a struggle for survival "in which the fighting will has a chance to triumph." Such themes, with an imperialist and racist bias taken from Kipling, appealed to popular audiences as well as to socialists, Roosevelt-followers, and intellectuals. London "made battles of the mind as actual and thrilling" as physical adventure. Later, "confusion of ideas led to his undoing, while his own thirst for money and power destroyed the artist in him." The Call of the Wild was "written directly from his unconscious," and Buck, beating his way upward without moral scruples, was London himself, as were all his heroes. London's suppression of his spiritual nature perhaps brought on the final depression that killed him. Gives biography.

3   DARGAN, MARION. Guide to American Biography; Part II--1815-
     1933. Albuquerque: University of New Mexico Press,
     pp. 463-65.
         Lists 21 sources of London biography, some critically
     annotated.

4   MILLS, GORDON H. "American First Editions at Texas University--
     VIII. Jack London (1876-1916)." Library Chronicle, 4
     (Fall), 189-92.
         Gives biography. He has a "simple, forceful prose style"
     and "an exuberance and a vitality that demand admiration,"
     but he indulges in "melodramatic attitudinizing."

5   ROOSEVELT, THEODORE. Letters. Edited by Elting E. Morison.
     Volume V. Cambridge: Harvard University Press, pp. 41,
     617, 1081, 1221-23, 1343.
         Objects to London's claim in "The Other Animals" [Col-
     lier's, 41 (5 September, 1908), 10-11] that Roosevelt said
     animals can't reason. London "deliberately invents state-
     ments" and makes misstatements and unsupportable denials.
     Concerning the bulldog and lynx episodes in White Fang:
     "Now mind you, I have not the slightest intention of en-
     tering into any controversy on this subject with London.
     I would as soon think of discussing seriously with him any
     social or political reform." Collier's should be more
     careful about what it prints. For articles in this con-
     troversy, see 1907.B22; 1907.B34; 1907.B35; 1907.B44.

6   SCHERMAN, DAVID E. and ROSEMARY REDLICH. Literary America: A
     Chronicle of American Writers from 1607-1952 with 173 Photo-
     graphs of the American Scene That Inspired Them. New York:
     Dodd, Mead, pp. 104-105.
         "An erratic writer who later turned out frequently melo-
     dramatic potboilers, London is remembered for his adventure
     yarns, for brilliant, intense short stories, and as one of
     the earliest writers dealing with the lives of working
     people and major problems of his age." Same, reprinted as
     America: The Land and Its Writers (1956).

7   WAGENKNECHT, EDWARD. "Jack London and the Cult of Primitive
     Sensation," in his Cavalcade of the American Novel. New
     York: Henry Holt, pp. 218, 222-29, 232, 355, 368, 531-32.
         "Temperamentally he was closest to Nietzsche, as his
     supermen and superdogs attest,...he rejected the ideal of
     universal brotherhood in favor of a passionately-held
     Anglo-Saxon racism." Marxism appealed to his "humanitar-
     ianism and love for the underdog...and his passion for sen-
     sation." Although London gave "the most extreme expression

to "the cult of raw meat and red blood," his "natural tone
was wholesome and manly." His dog novels are "eloquent,
impassioned, and spontaneous; they represent daring and
successful use of the imagination." Overall, his style is
simple, occasionally eloquent, but seldom polished; and
his characters are usually undeveloped. By writing for
money, he "betrayed his art" which thereby failed to sustain him. London was "a hack writer of genius, and,...the
faults of his work were the faults of his life" which was
deliberately suicidal.

8   WEST, RAY BENEDICT, JR. The Short Story in America, 1900-1950.
Chicago: Regnery, pp. 10, 12, 30, 31-34, 81.
The bulk of his tales "are vitiated by conformance to
the timid requirements of his commercial markets, but a
strong interest in nature, a background of wide experience
as a traveler, and a consistent point of view gave his
work a substance lacking in most popular fiction of his
time." Neither an influence on nor in the mainstream of
naturalism, London was closer to Crane and part of the
movement because of his (limited) professional craftsman-
ship--"some form of literary discipline"--which added a
"sense of values" or control to the material. Wilbur
Daniel Steele wrote "in the dramatic tradition" of London.

1953 A BOOKS - NONE

1953 B SHORTER WRITINGS

1   GEISMAR, MAXWELL. "Jack London: The Short Cut," in Rebels and
Ancestors: The American Novel, 1890-1915. Boston: Houghton
Mifflin, pp. 139-216.
"Under a program of denial his life, his writing [the
"short cut to satisfaction"], his modes of feeling, even,
were to become a strictly mechanical or at best a well-
regulated chemical process." London's success story became a case history "of thwarted ambition and moral corruption." He lived by false values and his sin was that
he knew their falsity. The origin, form and texture of
his work is the "world of dream and fantasy and desolate,
abnormal emotion....his best work was often a transcript
of solitary nightmares" in which he identified the terrors
of primitive life with his childhood fears, cannibalism
with Darwinian survival, love with meat; and the archetypal quest for the lost father-rescuer became an analog
of his own search for a legitimate father, for affection,
security, and fame. Related to these were his fear of

woman's domination, disdain for lower class women's animal
sexuality, and the "sexual narcissism" of some of his
heroes. Although refreshingly original, the early Klondike tales were "circumscribed by a shallow set of moral
values." The Call of the Wild exhibited "the brilliance
of London's own intuitions of animal instincts and the
mythical buried night-life of the [human] race." Sadism
and horror dominate The Sea-Wolf, "the study of a cruel
and to a large degree corrupt 'natural man.'" London's
socialistic writings were bold and insightful. The Iron
Heel eloquently satirizes middle class ethics and American
society, and it blueprints dehumanization of the masses
through terrorism. Martin Eden derives its power from the
sustained authentic tone of the hero's struggle and the
stress on class conflict, although its focus is too narrow
to be novelistic and the conclusion is ambiguous. After
the failure of the Snark voyage, London "capitulated
cynically" and completely to the vulgar lower middle class
taste for savagery, horror, and barbaric racism, as in his
South Sea tales. John Barleycorn, "a fascinating study of
the alcoholic ego at its highest point of desperate and
fatal superiority," suggests that his self-destructive
drinking and squandering of wealth were modes of taking
revenge on his father. In The Valley of the Moon, on the
theme of "race, blood and soil," London identifies his
personal defeat with "the decline of the superior white
race itself." Finally, in "an incredibly bad novel," The
Star Rover, the strait-jacketed "Last Superman" exemplifies London's futile defiance; "the Loony Protagonist was
the last phase of the monomaniac as hero....the final triumph was that of invincible, untouchable paranoia." The
many failures and fears of his later years convinced London there was no escape from the "walled-in" self, and he
committed suicide. Same, reprinted: New York: Hill and
Wang, 1963. Revised and abridged version: 1960.B7.

2   WALKER, FRANKLIN. "Jack London's Use of Sinclair Lewis Plots,
     Together with a Printing of Three of the Plots." HLQ, 17,
     no. 1 (November), 59-74.
        Lewis and London met only once, but through correspon-
     dence (18 letters, September 18, 1910-November 15, 1911)
     they arranged for London to buy 27 plots for $137.50 out
     of the 55 plots Lewis submitted to him. London used 3
     plots for short stories, one for The Abysmal Brute, and
     one for The Assassination Bureau, Ltd., which he could not
     complete.

1954

1954 A BOOKS

1 LANE, FREDERICK A. The Greatest Adventure; A Story of Jack
       London. American Heritage Series. New York: Aladdin
       Books, 192 pp.
          Juvenile biography.

1954 B SHORTER WRITINGS

1 BURTON, HOWARD A. "The Human Bondage of Martin Eden and the
       Literary Bondage of the Modern Reader." The Annotator
       (Purdue University), No. 4 (November), 10-15 [Mimeographed].
          Compares and contrasts Martin Eden with Maugham's Of
       Human Bondage. Although London's novel is superior in
       many ways to Maugham's, it has been neglected because of
       London's "sub-literary" reputation, the college readers'
       difficulty in identifying with a hero who thinks, and the
       novel's "political explosiveness." It is firmly structured
       by various logical patterns, by Martin's relations to women
       and his reading of Swinburne. The characters "tend to be
       walking embodiments of ideas," but London plumbs psychologi-
       cal-Freudian depths and challenges the reader by dramatiz-
       ing, with subtlety, the ideas, primarily "the failure of
       the Nietzschean philosophy." The novel's style is uneven
       but "adequate, even good, and occasionally it is excellent."
       Notes the humor, irony, and effective descriptions. For a
       response, see 1954.B2.

2 CORDELL, RICHARD. "Quid Pro Quo." The Annotator (Purdue
       University), No. 4 (November), 16-19 [Mimeographed].
          A response to Burton, 1954.B1. Martin Eden is not read
       because of London's "hyperthyroid style," the "phony
       literary quality" of his dialogue, the lack of subtlety
       in presenting ideologies and characters, and the "half-
       baked intellectual swagger" of the hero. "The novel has
       heat and fire (much of it ignus [sic] fatuus), but little
       light."

3 CUNLIFFE, MARCUS. The Literature of the United States. Bal-
       timore: Penguin Books, pp. 196, 203, 215, 220-21, 223,
       227, 309, 360.
          "The Superman and the underdog, the class war and the
       law of the wolf-pack, the mission of the Nordic peoples
       and the doom of capitalism: he handles these seemingly
       ill-assorted themes with an irresistible bounce, like
       some dexterous and strident Barnum of the printed word."
       The "crudest of writers,...he is remarkably readable."
       Same, 3rd edition, 1967.

4 EDMONDSON, ELSIE F. L. "The Writer as Hero in Important American Fiction Since Howells." Ph.D. dissertation, University
   of Michigan.

5 KNIGHT, GRANT C. The Strenuous Age in American Literature,
   1900-1910. Chapel Hill: University of North Carolina
   Press, pp. 32-34, 80-85, 131-33, 192-93, 222-23, and passim.
      London "was a primitive bard, a scald who sang of valor-
   ous men who fight and kill and surmount hunger and pain."
   [Discusses stories]. The Call of the Wild, "one of the
   few classics about a dog," may owe something to Alfred
   Ollivant's Owd Bob. The Sea-Wolf is "a monument to the
   fierceness and frankness of the Will to Power." A Daughter
   of the Snows has many flaws; but it is better than London
   thought it was. The Game "degenerates into a potboiler
   with only a simmering humor and pathos." The Mutiny of
   the Elsinore is "one of the best sea stories in our literature." Before Adam "can be quickly discarded in favor of
   White Fang of the same year." Burning Daylight and Martin
   Eden "combined social criticism with narrative and each
   was an admission of disillusionment and dejection." London "could not take the long leap over the gap separating
   American romanticism from French naturalism....London's
   instinct was to feel life as chaos and battle...but his
   intelligence, which was not of the most acute, tried to
   rationalize instinct" by imposing order-giving laws on it.
   Torn between discipleship to Nietzsche and Marx, "he com-
   promised a narrative gift originally distinguished by
   vigor, freshness, and dramatic proficiency, and eventually
   wrote some of the poorest novels of the day."

6 LEARY, LEWIS, comp. Articles on American Literature Appearing
   in Current Periodicals, 1900-1950. Durham, N. C.: Duke
   University Press, pp. 186-88.
      Lists 59 articles about London and 2 by him.

7 O'CONNOR, RICHARD. High Jinks on the Klondike. Indianapolis:
   Bobbs-Merrill, pp. 121-29.
      Describes London in the Yukon. Material revised some-
   what and reprinted: 1964.A2.

1955 A BOOKS - NONE

1955 B SHORTER WRITINGS

1 BASKETT, SAM S. "A Source of The Iron Heel." AL, 27 (May),
   268-70.

1955

London used the "views on socialist theory and practice"
of William McDevitt and Austin Lewis, printed in the Socialist Voice, 1905-1907. He "borrowed" ideas and sometimes actual phrasing of articles on religion and news
events. See dissertation, 1951.A1.

2   BASKETT, SAM S. "Jack London on the Oakland Waterfront." AL,
     27 (November), 363-71.
        London's self-portrayal as an oyster thief and member of
     the Fish Patrol in John Barleycorn is uncritically accepted
     by biographers. Other evidence, including documented
     chronology, contemporary accounts, London's attitudes
     towards money, family, and law, and his failure to exploit
     such experiences in his fiction "sharply contradicts" his
     version of events. John Barleycorn cannot be trusted as
     autobiography. See dissertation, 1951.A

3   BLOTNER, JOSEPH. The Political Novel. Garden City: Doubleday,
     pp. 12, 97.
        The Iron Heel is "clearly meant to be a political instru-
     ment."

4   HIGHAM, JOHN. Strangers in the Land: Patterns of American
     Nativism, 1860-1925. New Brunswick: Rutgers University
     Press, pp. 172-75.
        London "came gradually to a fully nativistic position
     via an ingrained sense of white supremacy and an extensive
     education in imperialistic race-thinking." His warnings
     about the "Yellow Peril" and mongrelism, and his glorifica-
     tion of "the ruthlessness of supermen and master races"
     strengthened popular xenophobia throughout the United
     States in the early 1900's. Same, reprinted: New York:
     Atheneum, 1963.

5   LYNN, KENNETH. "Jack London: the Brain Merchant," in his The
     Dream of Success: A Study of the Modern American Imagina-
     tion. Boston: Little, Brown, pp. 75-118.
        The "success mythology" of Horatio Alger dominated Lon-
     don's socialism which attracted him as an avenue for per-
     sonal social and cultural advancement. The value of so-
     cialism is at best ambiguous in his early novels which con-
     vey the message "absolute wealth corrupts absolutely and
     competition is the health of the state." The Sea-Wolf,
     his "most fully realized novel," condemns the American
     capitalist system for destroying a superior individual,
     Larsen, "the natural-born fighting aristocrat." In The
     Iron Heel, London insures the defeat of Everhard and "the
     intellectual Alger heroes who became revolutionary

socialists when they failed to become millionaires." London here acknowledges that the "financial oligarchy" of America is impregnable, that Alger and Marx are incompatible, and that socialism would bring a "hellish paradise," stultifying and degenerative. The autobiographical <u>Martin Eden</u> "says a plague on both socialism and success." From 1908, London's enormous appetite for high living bound him even more firmly to writing for money. When his plan to escape by returning to the land (in <u>Burning Daylight</u>) failed, he embraced the final "dream of escape,...now unmistakably associated with death" in <u>The Little Lady of the Big House</u>. "Jack London's last dream of escape did not fail him."

6   MILLS, GORDON. "Jack London's Quest for Salvation." <u>AQ</u>, 7 (Spring), 3-14.
    The concepts of individualism and socialism fuse, rather than contradict one another in London's novels. He saw individualism "as simply a romantic desire for intense experience," as exemplified by Van Weyden, Larsen, Martin Eden, and others. The elements of socialism which attracted him were "its potential force"; "the cult of the leader"; "the idea of atavism"; the "concept of social evolution"; and "the ideal of brotherly love." Everhard typifies the fusion; and all London's writings sustain "two desires: one, the desire for adventure, combat, power; the other, the desire for friendship, justice, and a serene intellectuality." In a socialistic society where brotherly love prevails, individualistic impulses can be harmlessly expressed. London supports this ideal by attacking capitalistic society's hypocrisy though his frank, unconventional heroines and with dual plot structure in five novels, which move from violence to a "love theme."

7   SHANNON, DAVID A. <u>The Socialist Party of America: A History</u>. New York: Macmillan, pp. 6, 34, 38, 55, 56-57.
    The eccentric dress and Korean valet of the "anarchosyndicalist Jack London" did not advance the cause during his lecture tour.

8   SPILLER, ROBERT E. <u>The Cycle of American Literature: An Essay in Historical Criticism</u>. New York: Macmillan, pp. 201, 205-206, 218, 224.
    "By accepting all the new radicalism [Nietzsche, Darwin, Marx] with uncritical enthusiasm, London put power into his tales but lost control of the forces he had unleashed."

1955

9   WYKES, ALAN. A Concise Survey of American Literature. New
        York: Library Publishers, pp. 106-107.
        London "had a much more durable success than Norris"
        because he offered violent physical action, anti-middle
        class sentiments, and belief in the "ultimate triumph of
        the proletariat." When he became an "agitator," however,
        he was boring.

1956 A BOOKS - NONE

1956 B SHORTER WRITINGS

1   ANON. "The Dog Beneath the Skin." Time, 68 (24 December), 62.
        "Much of the fascination of London's work and life lay
        in the fact that he could never decide, for himself or his
        characters, which footprints of what gigantic hound to fol-
        low--the wolf of the wilderness or the Saint Bernard of
        civilization." We can still read London for his "raw vi-
        tality and a real storytelling gift."

2   BAIRD, JAMES. Ishmael: A Study of the Symbolic Mode in Primi-
        tivism. Baltimore: Johns Hopkins Press, pp. 37n, 207.
        London's Oceanic narratives [South Sea Tales and A Son of
        the Sun]...are minor allegories of Nietzchean will in de-
        fiance of adversity." The friendship of David Grief and
        Mauriri illustrates the Oriental custom of tayo. Same,
        reprinted: New York: Harper, 1960.

3   BASKETT, SAM S. "Introduction," in Martin Eden. New York:
        Holt, Rinehart and Winston, pp. v-xxvi.
        London's "most considerable work" is "a fictionalized
        autobiography" with examination of "the wider significance
        of the experience." Author and hero isolated themselves
        from their class and human companionship; they had in com-
        mon "intellectual pessimism and personal despondency."
        Martin's death "was quite likely a reflection of a con-
        scious suicidal impulse" of London's "which probably led
        to his death by an overdose of morphine." A principal
        theme of the novel is the conflict between individualism
        and socialism. Martin was the "unmitigated individualist"
        who fails; but some reviewers, confused by the weak so-
        cialist characters and incompetent working class in the
        novel, mistook it for an attack on socialism. Martin's
        abrupt change of mood from "animal verve and gusto" to
        "boredom and despair" is the "weakest part of the book."
        Other weaknesses are its subjectivity, lack of a single
        strong point-of-view, excessive emphasis on Martin who

1956

finds no challenger among the "flat and insipid" other
characters, flawed diction, and inconsistencies arising
from a combination of romanticism, realism and naturalism.
Martin Eden is not an artistic success, but it does portray
the serious and significant problems of the failure to find
values and the awareness of inadequacy. On the whole it
reflects "American intellectual experience of the last half
of the ninettenth century." Same, reprinted in 1963 edition. See dissertation, 1951.A1.

4   BROOKS, VAN WYCK and OTTO L. BETTMANN. Our Literary Heritage:
    A Pictorial History of the Writer in America. New York:
    Dutton, pp. 187, 199, 214-15, 230, 231.
        London "was a success until his own thirst for money and
    power destroyed the artist in him....His will to power
    destroyed his will to live....he ended in suicide."

5   CANTWELL, ROBERT. Famous American Men of Letters. New York:
    Dodd, Mead, pp. 161-70.
        Juvenile biography.

6   DUNN, ROBERT. World Alive: A Personal Story. New York: Crown,
    pp. 105, 117-19.
        Reminiscences of London in Seoul, Korea.

7   JOHNSTONE, ARCHIE. "Why Russians Love Jack London." World
    News (London), 3 (7 January), 27-28.
        His works are more popular than any other writer's.
    Since "he relies more on the power and beauty of content
    than on form," he loses little in translation. London's
    work is "typically" American. Russians admire his heroes'
    strong will to live and the autobiographical quality of his
    writing.

8   LEWIS, OSCAR. Bay Window Bohemia: An Account of the Brilliant
    Artistic World of Gaslit San Francisco. Garden City:
    Doubleday, pp. 186-87, 192-96, 217, and passim.
        Describes the meeting and feud of London and Bierce;
    gives biography. London's home was the gathering place
    for writers and reformers.

9   [MORTIMER, JAMES E.]. "The Inspiration of Jack London: Man of
    Adventure, Writer of Genius, Militant Socialist." The
    Draughtsman (January), pp. 18-20, concluding page unnumbered.
        London became a socialist as a result of his childhood
    poverty, experiences as a manual laborer, vagrant, and
    prisoner, reading of the Communist Manifesto, and difficult
    apprenticeship as a writer. To the movement he contributed

"his greatest work," The Iron Heel, his aid in getting The Jungle published, and his lectures. London's ties to the "cult of the superman" and his racism were unworthy of him; his later writings estranged him from the party. Reprinted: 1974.B23.

10 RIDEOUT, WALTER. The Radical Novel in the United States, 1900-1954: Some Interrelations of Literature and Society. Cambridge: Harvard University Press, pp. 30, 38-46, 47, 111, and passim.

London was of the lower middle class by birth. From his experiences as a manual laborer and hobo, and from his readings, he formed an image of "society as a struggle in the Pit," and he was drawn to Marxism for its "vision of a better world" and for "the violence of the class war" which reproduced his own upward strivings. "His creative imagination always functioned increasingly well the more it was able to disintegrate the fabric of social life or the civilized responses of the individual personality, reducing that life, that personality to its simplest level, a condition of complete violence. His concern is with the struggle, which horrifies and fascinates him, rather than with the achievement." In view of his commitment to making money, it is admirable that he "put a considerable amount of energy, money, and writing into the Socialist cause at the risk of his reputation and his royalty checks."

11 SHEPARD, IRVING. "Introduction," in his edition of Jack London's Tales of Adventure: Illustrated. Garden City, N. Y.: Hanover House, pp. [vii]-xii.

London's "exuberant, unfettered imagination and a boundless lust for life," with his unique combination of realism and romanticism characterizes these writings. Gives detailed biography; volume contains articles, stories, and selections from seven novels.

12 SINCLAIR, UPTON. The Cup of Fury. Great Neck, N. Y.: Channel Press, pp. 11-12, 43, 50-55, 71, 160-66, and passim.

Idolized by the public and "equally admired by serious literary critics, sociologists, and philosophers," London was a story-teller and social philosopher "of the first rank." He began drinking at the age of five and continued all his life for the excitement of the saloons, to prove his manhood and gain prestige, and for relief from boring labor. He drank heavily and in secret. Alcoholism made his work deteriorate and turned him into an intolerant, quarrelsome, nervous man whose "humor was crude horseplay, or crazily complex practical jokes." His friends deserted him; he took his own life.

JACK LONDON: A REFERENCE GUIDE

13   WALCUTT, CHARLES CHILD.   "Jack London: Blond Beasts and Super-
        men," in American Literary Naturalism: A Divided Stream.
        Minneapolis: University of Minnesota Press, pp. 87-113.
           Revised text of 1938.B6.   Gives less emphasis to the
        theoretical and historical concepts of the superman and of
        naturalism; offers somewhat enlarged discussion of London's
        fiction, previously contained in footnotes.

1957 A BOOKS - NONE

1957 B SHORTER WRITINGS

1   ALEXANDER, SIDNEY.   "Jack London's Literary Lycanthropy."
        Reporter, 16 (24 January), 46-48.
           London "was a potentially good artist who was spoiled by
        trying to be a thinker."   Some of his fiction reveals an
        admirable "blend of realism and romanticism,...love-hate
        for nature as the magnificent enemy," skillful irony, and
        clean prose style resembling Hemingway's.

2   ANDERSON, CARL L.   "Swedish Criticism Before 1920: the Recep-
        tion of Jack London and Upton Sinclair," in his The Swedish
        Acceptance of American Literature.   Stockholm: Almquist &
        Wiksell; Philadelphia: University of Pennsylvania Press,
        pp. 33-44.
           London "set new bookselling records in Sweden."   Working-
        class readers appreciate his "action, adventure, and sunny
        romance," and exposure of the evils of capitalism.   Critics
        admire his "socialistic bias," the "primitive" spirit of
        adventure, and interpretation of the simple, outdoors life
        in his undemanding books.   From 1907 for twenty years, his
        popularity was undiminished; in 1951 he was "still very
        far ahead of all" other American authors.   He influenced
        two Swedish authors.

4   CHASE, RICHARD.   The American Novel and Its Tradition.   Garden
        City: Doubleday, p. 198.
           Mentions London.

5   WHEELER, D.[ANIEL] E.[DWIN].   "As I Remember Them."   American
        Mercury, 85 (August), 112-18.
           Wheeler wrote friendly notes on London's rejection slips
        from Cosmopolitan and Collier's which turned down seriali-
        zation of The Call of the Wild and The Sea-Wolf.   Gives
        biography.

175

1958

1958 B SHORTER WRITINGS

1   ANON. "Jack London," in <u>Cyclopedia of World Authors</u>.   Edited
    by Frank Nothen Magill. New York: Harper and Row,
    pp. 663-65.
        Brief biography and criticism.

2   BASKETT, SAM S. "Jack London's Heart of Darkness." <u>AQ</u>, 10
    (Spring), 66-77.
        London read and greatly admired Conrad; his "In a Far
    Country" (1899) has the same "situation and theme" as
    Conrad's "An Outpost of Progress" (1898). The "two most
    personal of London's books"--<u>Martin Eden</u> and <u>John Barley-
    corn</u>--explore the motif of Conrad's "Youth" and "Heart of
    Darkness": "an individual's attempt to achieve self-identi-
    fying values in a tragic and ironic universe." London was
    inferior to Conrad "as a prose writer and thinker." <u>See</u>
    dissertation, 1951.A1.

3   BERTON, PIERRE. <u>The Klondike Fever: The Life and Death of the
    Last Great Gold Rush</u>. New York: Knopf, pp. 69, 156, 203,
    339, 425.
        Mentions and quotes London.

4   HEINEY, DONALD. "Jack London," in his <u>Recent American Litera-
    ture</u>. Great Neck, N. Y.: Barron's Educational Series,
    pp. 65-68.
        "London is a pulp-writer of genius; the quality of his
    work far transcends his technique and content....His sub-
    jectivity and enthusiasm lend a sincerity to his work which
    raises it far above the level of ordinary magazine fiction."
    Brief biography and plot summaries.

5   LERNER, MAX. "Introduction," in <u>The Iron Heel</u>. Library Edi-
    tion. New York: Macmillan, pp. vii-xiii.
        It has grown in relevance over the years as the charac-
    ter and repressions of the Oligarchy became realities in
    World War I. London foresaw "the reality of class con-
    flict," the tenacity of both capitalists and working-class
    leaders, and "the depth of possibility in human sadism on
    both sides." The novel is autobiographical in the sense
    that the war of the classes in the external world is the
    struggle within London between Nietzsche and Marx which
    he could not resolve. "I think he died of it." He pro-
    jects the "Brotherhood of Man" as the peace he sought but
    never achieved.

6 PETERSON, C.[LELL] T. "The Jack London Legend." <u>ABC</u>, 8,
     no. 5 (January), 13-17.
        London generally falsified, distorted or exaggerated the
     facts of his experiences in his fiction while creating
     imaginative realities. Biographers have too readily ac-
     cepted the legend as truth. London's "drive for success"
     and belief in the myth of an "American boy's heritage"
     motivated his frequent blurring of the "distinction between
     truth and fiction."

7 PETERSON, CLELL. "Jack London's Sonoma Novels." <u>ABC</u>, 9,
     no. 2 (October), 15-20.
        London first establishes a set of values: "belief in a
     return to the land and to nature, in freedom and individu-
     alism, in the possibility of the good life, and in the re-
     ality and worth of human love." Then, he progressively
     undermines these values by debasing their symbolic equiva-
     lents: the horse, symbol of freedom; and "feminine under-
     garments, nudity, and references to Venus," symbols of
     physical love. In <u>Burning Daylight</u> and <u>The Valley of the
     Moon</u>, "the horse symbolizes escape from a complex and hos-
     tile urban civilization; it stands for the good life and
     suggests also the "mysteries of sex and love." In <u>The
     Little Lady of the Big House</u>, the horse becomes "a play-
     thing" and a cheapened parody of the frontier spirit;
     while sex and love "become corrupted to a striptease" and
     the sterility and death of Paula. London's artistic
     failures in his late work reflect his personal "intellec-
     tual and idealistic failure."

8 ZAVALISHIN, VYACHESLAV. <u>Early Soviet Writers</u>. New York:
     Praeger, pp. 83, 174, 312.
        Mayakovski's screenplay of <u>Martin Eden</u> (1918) bears
     little resemblance to the novel. London was "practically
     worshipped by many of the Proletariat writers."

1959 A BOOKS - NONE

1959 B SHORTER WRITINGS

1 BYKOV, VIL. "Jack London in the Soviet Union." <u>QNL</u>, 24
     (Summer), 52-58.
        London's writing is "more popular in the U.S.S.R. than
     that of any other foreign author." Russians admire his
     "incomparable atmosphere of heroism and inspired struggle"
     against nature and society, the "optimistic tone, a life-
     asserting force," and his "romanticism and vigor." Such

qualities reflect both the revolutionary history of Russia
and its "classical tradition as articulated by Tolstoy and
Chekov." London helps Russians understand "the national
traits of the American people" common to the two cultures.
He "merits the recognition of his homeland."

2 CALDER-MARSHALL, ARTHUR. "The Prince of Oyster Bay." The
   Listener, 62 (30 July), 178-79.
      Biography. London was "Hemingway's literary uncle" and
   "a wonderful storyteller, as fresh as D. H. Lawrence, as
   sensitive and as crude; the one great natural genius of
   American literature in this century, and the most fertile
   influence." Throughout the world, London symbolized "the
   emergent twentieth-century man, romantic, tough, courageous,
   ...who put heart back into the exploited earth and hope into the hearts of the exploited workers."

3 FRAKES, JAMES R. "Comment [on] 'The White Silence,'" in his
   edition of Short Fiction: A Critical Collection. Englewood Cliffs: Prentice-Hall, pp. 21-23.
      It represents the typical "action" story with an omni-
   scient observer, inner and external conflicts, and suspenseful narrative.

4 MILLS, GORDON. "The Symbolic Wilderness: James Fenimore
   Cooper and Jack London." NCF, 13 (March), [329]-40.
      Parallels in their fiction include similar codes of
   gentility; using the form of the sentimental novel; asso-
   ciating the wilderness with "freedom, purity, and strength"
   as well as crudity, and civilization with "refinement" as
   well as decadence. However, as a materialist and individualist, London was "both insincere and confused" in his
   romantic primitivism, particularly in Burning Daylight.
   His liberated heroine, materialistic hero, and "the spiritual barrenness of the wilderness all imply that the wilderness as a symbol placed in opposition to civilization
   must have little force in London's fiction.

5 PETERSON, CLELL T. "Jack London's Alaskan Stories." ABC, 9,
   no. 8 (April), 15-22.
      Parallel to London's personal conflict between individ-
   ualism and socialism runs the tension in his fiction between nature and civilization. In his Klondike diary
   this tension takes the form of contrast between white men
   who go native and those who remain Anglo-Saxon. In the
   early Alaskan tales, the energy of civilization drives
   the action; later, Nature competes with civilization and
   the latter wins; but in A Daughter of the Snows, Nature

"is the source of real values," and this weakens the fiction. London resolved the conflict only in The Call of the
Wild.

6   SPRINGER, ANNE MARIE. "The American Novel in Germany: A Study
     of the Critical Reception of Eight American Novelists Be-
     tween the Two World Wars." Ph.D. dissertation, University
     of Pennsylvania.
     Published: 1960.B16.

7   ZIRKLE, CONWAY. Evolution, Marxian Biology, and the Social
     Scene. Philadelphia: University of Pennsylvania Press,
     pp. 301-304, 318-37, 349, 350.
        London, an "orthodox Marxian socialist," was "the most
     logical and intellectually honest of the few Marxians" who
     openly expressed belief in racial inequality, which is "the
     real Communist doctrine of race." Although generally ill-
     informed, London influenced "the intelligentsia" of his
     time by spreading the idea that Darwinian and Marxian
     theories were harmonious. "His biological world was self-
     consistent," true to his knowledge of evolutionary theories
     and his experience of life. He accepted, as did Marx and
     Engels, Lamarck's theory of inherited acquired characteris-
     tics, and combined this in his fiction with belief in "ra-
     cial memory" (Samuel Butler) and the biology of Darwin,
     Huxley, Spencer, and Haeckel. Lamarck's theory justified
     socialism, since, as London shows in The People of the
     Abyss, capitalism degrades the individual, thus deteriora-
     ting the race; only a good environment (of the "well-inte-
     grated group") generates superior races which are fittest
     to survive through natural selection. London believed in
     the eventual progress of "many different superior stocks."
     Laborers would provide raw material for "aristocracy";
     "the labor leader was his aristocrat par excellence," a
     man like Everhard, highly-developed mentally and physically,
     "a natural leader of his fellows."

1960 A BOOKS

1   STONE, IRVING. Jack London, Sailor on Horseback: A Biographi-
     cal Novel. Giant Cardinal Edition. New York: Pocket
     Books, 314 pp.
     Reprint of 1938.A1.

1960 B SHORTER WRITINGS

1   ANON. "Introduction," in The Call of the Wild. School

1960

edition, Literary Heritage Series. New York: Macmillan,
pp. v-x.
Gives historical background, comment on the novel, and
biography.

2 ANON. "Rebel Writer." MD Medical Newsmagazine (September),
pp. 175-80.
"From the first London declared himself in rebellion
against the falsely optimistic, sentimental and bloodless
fiction of the day;...He was the first American writer to
portray the working class sympathetically;...to incorporate
in his fiction the scientific attitudes of the twentieth
century....London became the most radical as well as the
most successful writer in the country."

3 BERTON, PIERRE. "Gold Rush Writing." CanL, no. 4 (Spring),
59-67.
The Call of the Wild "is a classic of sorts....It seems
curiously naive and sentimental today." The Smoke Bellew
tales "are simply true anecdotes masquerading under the
guise of fiction."

*4 BOGGS, W. ARTHUR. "Looking Backward at the Utopian Novel,
1888-1900." BNYPL, 64 (June), 329-36.
Bellamy influenced London. Cited in Clareson, 1972.B10.

5 BYKOV, VIL. "On the Trail of Jack London: Among Those Who
Knew Him." SovL, 2 (1960), 133-43.
Describes Bykov's visits to Oakland, Glen Ellen, London's
ranch study, library, and Wolf House ruins; his interviews
with Joan London and Anna Strunsky, and research in the
Huntington Library. Translated by Ralph Parker.

6 DURHAM, PHILIP and TAUNO F. MUSTANOJA. American Fiction in
Finland. Helsinki: Société Néophilologique, pp. 37-41,
and passim.
Although London "had his principal vogue in the 1920's,
he still places sixth in popularity in a poll of contemporary writers of fiction." Some sixteen of his translated
works received a great deal of critical attention early in
the century. His work "presents a valuable picture of the
American man and the American scene."

7 GEISMAR, MAXWELL. "Introduction: Jack London: The White
Logic," in his edition of Jack London: Short Stories.
American Century Series. New York: Hill and Wang,
pp. ix-xix.
Discusses life and works. London's "best work remains,

ironic, macabre, mordant, but fixed in the record of
national letters." Revised and abridged version of
1953.B1.

8   HAYDOCK, JAMES. "Jack London: A Bibliography of Criticism."
     BB, 23 (May-August), 42-46.
         Lists 27 books and pamphlets, 109 parts of books, and
     94 articles about London, published 1900-1955. All but a
     few are subsequently included in Woodbridge, 1966.A6.

9   HOWARD, LEON. Literature and the American Tradition. Garden
     City: Doubleday, pp. 247-48.
         London "was basically an escapist, a he-man Lafcadio
     Hearn or a Cro-Magnon Henry Adams, whose primary impulse
     was to go over the horizon or revert to primitivism be-
     cause his hatred of the existing order was more real than
     his hope for changing it."

10   JONES, EVAN, ed. The Father: Letters to Sons and Daughters.
     New York: Rinehart, pp. 73-74.
         There were strained relations between London and his
     daughters. Gives excerpts from a letter to Joan.

11   LORD, WALTER. The Good Years: From 1900 to the First World
     War. New York: Harper, pp. 122, 136, 138, 140.
         Mentions London in relation to the San Francisco fire.

12   MODERN LANGUAGE ASSOCIATION OF AMERICA, AMERICAN LITERATURE
     GROUP, COMMITTEE ON MANUSCRIPT HOLDINGS. American Literary
     Manuscripts. Austin: University of Texas Press, pp. 228-29.
         Identifies 30 repositories holding from one to an unde-
     termined large number of letters, documents, manuscripts,
     books with marginalia, and memorabilia by and about London.

13   NICHOLS, LUTHER. "The Book Corner: London's Novel is Still
     Pertinent." San Francisco Examiner (9 November), sec. 3,
     p. 3.
         No other novel "is more deeply rooted in our folk-myth."
     Martin Eden has much to tell young writers. "In Eden's
     disafiliation, he foreshadowed many of the heroes of
     modern fiction--....who equally reject bourgeois, grey-
     flanneled values and organized political action."

14   SALOMON, LOUIS B. "Introduction," in The Call of the Wild and
     Other Stories. New York: Dodd, Mead, pp. v-viii.
         His writing "reflects both his own inner conflicts...
     and some of the chief literary and intellectual currents
     of his time." Gives biography.

1960

15   SINCLAIR, UPTON. My Lifetime in Letters. Columbia: University
     of Missouri Press, pp. [see below].
        Letters from London to Sinclair, pp. 20-30. London men-
     tioned in letters to Sinclair from Sterling, pp. 33, 35,
     36, 37-38, 39, 45, 47, 49, 248; from Frank Harris, pp. 175,
     178, 180; from H. L. Mencken, pp. 239, 328; from Charmian
     London, pp. 30-31. Sinclair's comments on London, pp. 21-
     22, 240-41, 333, and elsewhere.

16   SPRINGER, ANNE M. "Jack London and Upton Sinclair," in her
     The American Novel in Germany: A Study of the Critical
     Reception of Eight American Novelists Between the Two World
     Wars. Hamburg: Cram, de Gruyter, pp. 31-39.
        London's popularity in this period "with the young of all
     ages" surpassed that of any American author. The freshness,
     energy, New World robustness and masculinity of his adven-
     ture tales; the colorful, exotic aspects of his life as
     described in The Road; his "predilection for Nietzschean
     philosophy"; his socialistic message in entertaining form--
     all appealed "to the diversified tastes and demands of the
     mass of the German reading public" as well as to critics
     and university professors. Published form of dissertation,
     1959.B6.

17   STRUNSKY, ANNA. "Memories of Jack London." Greenwich Village
     Lantern, 1, no. 1 (December), 8-9.
        "He was youth, adventure, romance. He was a poet and a
     thinker. He had a genius for friendship. He loved greatly
     and was greatly beloved." London was an idealist without
     illusions and a passionate man who systematized his life by
     a creed of "Law, Order and Restraint." His success in at-
     taining power, fame, and wealth "was the tragedy of his
     life. He mortgaged his brain in order to meet the market
     demands," saw the failure of truth and justice, and suf-
     fered from melancholia and suicidal impulses. London's
     genius and sincerity, his love of life and of mankind are
     memorable. Prints excerpts from London's letters to her.
     Reprinted: 1962.B17.

18   THORP, WILLARD. American Writing in the Twentieth Century.
     Cambridge: Harvard University Press, pp. 10, 116, 151,
     161-64.
        The conflicts between socialism and evolutionism, and
     producing hack-work for money or fine literature, added
     to "disappointments as a lover and a father" led to Lon-
     don's suicide. His fictional theme is the struggle for
     survival, led by "the blond beast, the superman." Gives
     biography.

19   WOODWARD, ROBERT H. "The History of a Sea Sprite." London
     Lore (San Francisco; for United Amateur Press Association
     of America--Jack London Amateur Press Club), Arm and Torch
     Series, no. 3 (1960), 3 pp. unnumbered.
          A history of London's poem, "The Sea Sprite and the
     Shooting Star" (1899), privately printed in 1932. Ex-
     panded: 1964.B19.

1961 A BOOKS

1   CALDER-MARSHALL, ARTHUR. Lone Wolf: The Story of Jack London.
    London: Methuen, 188 pp.; New York: Duell, Sloan & Pearce,
    1962, 167 pp.
         Juvenile biography.

2   CARLSON, ROY WERNER. "Jack London's Heroes: A Study of Evo-
    lutionary Thought." Ph.D. dissertation, University of New
    Mexico.

3   HENDRICKS, KING, ed. Creator and Critic: A Controversy Between
    Jack London and Philo M. Buck, Jr. Monograph Series vol-
    ume 8, no. 2 (March). Logan: Utah State University Press,
    47 pp.
         Gives biographical sketches of London and Buck, pp. 6-17;
    reprints Buck's "The American Barbarian" (1912.B13),
    pp. 20-29; prints letters exchanged by London and Buck in
    response to the essay, November 5, 1912, to July 19, 1913,
    pp. 30-44. London denies he is an individualist, claims
    belief in culture and socialism, and pits his passion and
    faith in man against the dry, "too well balanced" critic.
    Buck replies: an author can be judged only by his works.
    London's barbarian individualists have confidence only in
    themselves, in luck, and in "rash, inconsequential, brute
    action." Moreover, socialism denies liberty to all, re-
    duces men to a dead level, rules "by the iron rod of ef-
    ficiency and social service," and paralyzes the heart and
    brain. London's blind individualism severs humanity from
    "the traditions of the past" and his socialism is "false
    to human nature."

4   LABOR, EARLE GENE. "Jack London's Literary Artistry; a Study
    of His Imagery and Symbols in Relation to His Themes."
    Ph.D. dissertation, University of Wisconsin.
         Excerpted and revised: 1962.B8; 1970.B28. Revised and
    expanded: 1974.A3.

1961

1961 B SHORTER WRITINGS

1   AARON, DANIEL. Writers on the Left. New York: Harcourt,
        Brace and World, pp. 38, 55-56, 104, 113, 168, 233, 322.
            Mentions London. Same, reprinted: New York: Avon, 1969.

2   ANON. "London, Jack," in Chamber's Biographical Dictionary.
        New edition. New York: St. Martin's, p. 805.
            Biography.

3   BERTON, PIERRE. "Introduction," in The Call of the Wild. New
        York: Heritage Press, pp. vii-xv.
            Discusses London and other writers in the Klondike.
        Since London was in the "advance guard" rather than the
        "mainstream" of the gold rush, he deals "only sketchily
        with the specifics of the great stampede" but concretely
        and accurately with the great outdoors and animals he knew
        well.

4   BUXTON, FRANCES and SUMIRA YAMASHITA. "Oakland: A Literary
        Retrospect." California Librarian, 22 (October), 215-18.
            Describes London's early years in Oakland. Brief.

5   BYKOV, VIL. "Jack London." Soviet Woman, no. 11 [November],
        26-27.
            Describes his visit to London's ranch and library; gives
        biography. When London abandoned his work for the "Ameri-
        can working-class movement" which had "fired his creative
        energies," his writing became "an irksome chore" and he
        took his life. London "was a child of his age and his
        country and he could not surmount the barriers erected by
        contemporary American conditions."

6   GERSTENBERGER, DONNA and GEORGE HENDRICK. The American Novel,
        1789-1959: A Checklist of Twentieth-Century Criticism.
        Volume 1. Denver, Colorado: Swallow, 174-76.
            Lists 41 articles and books.

7   GILLIGAN, EDMUND. "Introduction," in The Sea-Wolf. New York:
        Heritage Press, pp. v-ix.
            London draws from himself the characters of Larsen and
        Van Weyden and dramatizes the physical and philosophical
        truth of Larsen's decline and Van Weyden's "ascent into
        manhood."

8   LANGFORD, GERALD. Richard Harding Davis Years: A Biography
        of a Mother and Son. New York: Holt, Rinehart, Winston,
        pp. 239-40, 287.

Davis helped London out of some difficulties in Tokyo
and later in the Mexican War.

9 OPPEWALL, PETER. "The Critical Reception of American Fiction
    in the Netherlands, 1900-1953." Ph.D. dissertation, Uni-
    versity of Michigan.

10 RUGGLES, MELVIN J. "American Books in Soviet Publishing."
    American Slavic and East European Review, 20, no. 3
    (October), 419-35.
        London was the most popular foreign author in the U.S.S.R.
    in 1918-1957 with 18,588,000 copies of 662 titles and edi-
    tions. Among American authors he surpasses the second-
    place Twain by two to one. Russians value London's social
    protest, stories of frontier life, and science fiction.

11 SEIDLER, MURRAY. Norman Thomas: Respectable Rebel. Syracuse:
    Syracuse University Press, pp. 42, 52, 73.
        Mentions London.

12 SHIVERS, SAMUEL A. "The Demonaics in Jack London." ABC, 12,
    no. 1 (September), 11-14.
        A demonaic is "a being of tremendous energy and determi-
    nation who at the same time is possessed of an intensely
    evil quality." Such characters are Larsen, David Rasmun-
    sen, Dan Cullen, and Batârd, the devil incarnate in a dog.
    All are personifications of instincts or passions whose
    acts "proceed from a biological basis" or a driving power
    of will.

13 SHORER, MARK. Sinclair Lewis: An American Life. New York:
    McGraw-Hill, pp. 164-66, 171, 186-87, 219, and passim.
        London's The Valley of the Moon is "an extended, if
    fictionalized, account of life in the Carmel Colony."
    Lewis offered some fifty-seven plots to London, who paid
    him for twenty-six and used five. The relationship be-
    tween them "jogged to an end in 1915." Same, reprinted:
    New York: Crest, 1963.

14 SNELL, GEORGE. The Shapers of American Fiction, 1898-1947.
    Second edition. New York: Cooper Square, pp. 164, 287.
        Mentions London in relation to Hemingway's A Farewell
    to Arms and Vardis Fisher's The Golden Rooms.

15 SWANKEY, BEN. "Jack London--Working Class Rebel: January 12,
    1876-November 22, 1916." The Dispatcher (International
    Longshoreman's and Warehousemen's Union, San Francisco),
    19, no. 1 (13 January), 6-7.

1961

"He was a worker, he wrote for workers, and he was read by workers." The fresh vigor and truthful realism of his fiction revolutionized American literature.

16   WOODBRIDGE, HENSLEY C. "Variants in the American and English Editions of the War of the Classes by Jack London." ABC, 12 (November), 43-44.
     At the insistence of his British publishers, London changed four passages in "The Scab" to make them "more palatable to the English public." Prints the variants.

1962 A BOOKS

1   FRANCHERE, RUTH. Jack London: The Pursuit of a Dream. New York: Crowell, 264 pp.
    Juvenile biography; includes a bibliography.

2   SHIVERS, ALFRED SAMUEL. "Romanticism in Jack London: A Study of Romantic Qualities in His Life and in Selected Short Stories and Novels." Ph.D. dissertation, Florida State University.
    Revised: 1961.B12; 1962.B13; 1963.B20.

1962 B SHORTER WRITINGS

1   ANON. "London, Jack." The Encyclopedia Americana. Volume 17. New York: Americana Corporation, 712-13.
    Biography. Much of his popularity "was gained because of the utter baseness and brutality in his stories which shocked and at the same time thrilled the reader."

2   ANON. "London (John Griffith)," in British Museum General Catalogue of Printed Books. Volume 144. London: Trustees of the British Museum, 61-69.
    Bibliography to 1955. Lists 144 editions (in English and foreign languages) of works by London; 9 works about him.

3   BROWN, DEMING. "Jack London and O. Henry," in his Soviet Attitudes Toward American Writing. Princeton: Princeton University Press, pp. 219-38.
    From 1905 until the 1950's, London "has been read more widely than any other non-Russian author." Russian readers "deeply respect the elemental vigor of his writing, his hearty temperament, and his love of violence and brute force....[his] ability to dramatize simple, fundamental virtues such as courage, perseverance, and strength of

will....his hardihood, expansive love for humanity, large-
ness of heart, forthrightness, and healthy aspiration."
Russian critics deem his strongest trait the inspiring
mood of optimism conveyed by his heroes; they see as major
defects "his all-pervasive individualism" and "racial
chauvinism." After 1927 critics recognized "that London
was an ideologist of the petty bourgeoisie" and nearly all
his characters seek personal independence. He lost "ideological respectability" but is published "as a critical
realist." London shares popularity with O. Henry for their
criticism of the United States and suspenseful stories
which make little demand upon readers.

4   BURDICK, EUGENE. "Introduction," in The Best Short Stories of
    Jack London. Premier Book. New York: Fawcett, pp. v-viii.
       London often wrote "with the power of the marlinspike,
    but he could also write with the delicacy of a whaler doing
    scrimshaw on a whale's tooth." His stature has grown be-
    cause he can make the "lost and savage world" come alive
    for us. "For this reason, if for no other, he will not
    soon be forgotten. It is the mark of the master writer."
    Discusses tales.

5   GURIAN, JAY. "The Romantic Necessity in Literary Naturalism:
    Jack London." OJES, 2:1-11.
       London's heroes are ambiguous because they struggle to
    survive in "a causative naturalist universe" while simul-
    taneously striving to overcome it and to realize a private
    vision or ideal. Thus Larsen accepts and fights to master
    a Darwinian universe while he worries about his philosophy.
    Martin Eden succeeds as an individualist in a causative
    world but finds "intellectual morality" empty and ideal
    "spiritual morality" unattainable. The Call of the Wild
    "is a perfect parable of a biologically and environmen-
    tally determined universe," and Buck, as an animal, is
    London's only unambiguous hero. London is "a romantic in
    his exultation of private visions" without which no human
    can be a hero. Reprinted: 1966.B16.

6   HART, JAMES D. "Californians on Soviet Best-Seller Lists."
    QNL, 27 (Summer), 61-63.
       A response to (and reiteration of) 1961.B10. Claims
    the reasons for London's popularity are more complex
    than Ruggles indicates.

7   HERZBERG, MAX J., ed. "London, Jack (John Griffith)," in The
    Reader's Encyclopedia of American Literature. New York:
    Crowell, pp. 649-50.

1962

> Gives biography and description of works; see additional
> scattered references throughout. "Within the context of
> his time, he dealt with timeless themes: man's struggle
> against hostile nature and against hostile society for a
> better world and the nobility of the human spirit. His
> universal idiom still evokes a universal response."

8 LABOR, EARLE. "Jack London's Symbolic Wilderness: Four Ver-
    sions." NCF, 17 (September), 149-61.
      London's portrayals of the wilderness reveal his life-
    long "quest for Elysium" and "progressive disillusionment"
    with the American Dream. In the earliest version, the
    White Silence of the Northland, insignificant man battles
    hostile Nature, is ignored by the presiding god of natural-
    ism, and he adapts or escapes through imagination, courage,
    brotherly love, and personal integrity. In the second
    version, the "hot, putrid, and malign" jungles of Melanesia
    are a wasteland ruled by Satan, where man is physically and
    morally corrupted. In the third version, Polynesia is a
    "Paradise Lost" ruled by a benevolent god but despoiled by
    the white man's "commercialism and civilization." The
    fourth version, the Valley of the Moon in the American
    West, is where heroic and spiritually pure men can create
    a new Eden. This pastoral wilderness appears in four
    novels; however, the autobiographical The Little Lady of
    the Big House "reveals the collapse of his faith in the
    restorative powers of this wilderness." Excerpted and
    revised from 1961.A4; revised: 1974.A3.

9 LEY, WILLY. "Introduction: Jack London, the Man and His work,"
    in Before Adam. New York: Macmillan, pp. v-xiv.
      Gives detailed biography; discusses reception of the
    novel. Epilogue by Loren Eisley: "No writer has since
    produced so moving and vivid a picture of man's primordial
    past....The great swamp...I as a man now mentally perceive
    as a symbol of man's long journey, harried by his own
    ferocity from age to age." Both reprinted: New York:
    Bantam, 1970.

10 LONDON, JOAN. "Jack London Wrote of the People, Spoke with
    the Voice of a Worker." The Dispatcher (International
    Longshoreman's and Warehousemen's Union, San Francisco)
    (24 August), p. 4.
      Gives biography; describes London's contributions to
    organized labor.

11 MICHELMORE, PETER and AL STUMP. "Wild Life of the Iron Wolf."
    True, 43, no. 299 (April), 122-37.

Gives biography, from various sources. "Love, war,
liquor and rebellion: those were the four delights in the
life of John Griffith London--the greatest action writer-
adventurer America has ever produced."

12   ST. JOHNS, ADELA ROGERS. Final Verdict. New York: Doubleday,
      pp. 352-63, and passim.
          The author frequently visited the Glen Ellen ranch where
      London entertained a steady flow of guests. Such stimula-
      tion was demanded by "the insatiable mind, the loving heart,
      the deep understanding and restless spirit" of London. He
      adopted "Nora" [Adela] as his godchild seemingly to re-
      place his daughter Joan who refused to be with him. Earl
      Rogers was London's drinking buddy.

13   SHIVERS, SAMUEL A. "Jack London: Author in Search of a Biogra-
      pher." ABC, 12, no. 7 (March), 25-27.
          London's autobiographical works cannot be trusted; secon-
      dary materials are generally sentimental, hero-worshipping,
      one-sided, naive, or undocumented. A definitive objective
      biography is needed.

14   SIGAL, CLANCY. "Good Old East End." New Statesman, 64
      (13 July), 50.
          In The People of the Abyss London produced "an immortal
      job of polemical reporting," much of which is "splendid,
      full-blooded stuff, remarkable in its controlled passion"
      and pleading for social justice. London, "one of the
      world's natural aristocrats, an autodidact Nietzchean,"
      felt both pity and contempt for the weak, animal-like poor.

15   SINCLAIR, ANDREW. Prohibition: The Era of Excess. Boston:
      Little, Brown, pp. 59, 232, 326-27.
          John Barleycorn is an "honest and moving" book. Lon-
      don's melancholia, pessimistic nature, and belief in the
      destructive degenerative effects of alcohol poison made
      this work "marvelous dry propaganda."

16   SINCLAIR, UPTON. The Autobiography of Upton Sinclair. New
      York: Harcourt, Brace and World, pp. 44, 113-14, 169, 182,
      248, 252.
          London and the Sterlings "took poison to escape the
      claws of John Barleycorn." London found "he could not have
      his wife and another woman at the same time, and so he
      voluntarily removed himself from the world."

17   STRUNSKY, ANNA. "Memories of Jack London." The Bowery News,
      69 (c. June), 8-9.
          Reprint of 1960.B17.

1962

18 WAUGH, ALEC. <u>The Early Years of Alec Waugh</u>. New York: Farrar,
    Strauss, pp. 248, 272.
        Mentions London.

19 WOODRESS, JAMES. <u>Dissertations in American Literature, 1891-
    1955, with Supplement, 1956-1961</u>. Durham, N. C.: Duke
    University Press, pp. 30, 95.
        Lists thirteen items, including three in German.

<u>1963 A BOOKS</u>

1 ASIMOV, ISAAC. <u>Two Out-of-Print Masterpieces by Jack London</u>.
    N.p.: The Library of Science [Book Club, Extra Selection
    for March], unpaged [2-4] folder.
        Cited in 1966.A6; reprinted: 1971.B2. Reviews <u>Before
    Adam</u>: London uses the "device of racial memory" to convey
    the thoughts and emotions of "sub-men with a feeling of
    authenticity." Reviews <u>The Star Rover</u>: a "blend of fan-
    tasy and historical fiction" in London's vivid and vital
    style.

<u>1963 B SHORTER WRITINGS</u>

1 ADAMS, A. K. "Introduction," in <u>White Fang and Other Stories</u>.
    New York: Dodd, Mead, pp. v-ix.
        London lived and wrote with "unbounded gusto and unre-
    strained energy." Gives biography.

2 ALEXANDROVA, VERA. <u>A History of Soviet Literature</u>. Trans-
    lated by Mirra Ginsburg. Garden City: Doubleday, pp. 95-96.
        Mentions London.

3 ANON. "The Cruise of the Dazzler: A Plea." <u>The Courier</u>
    (Syracuse University Library Associates), 3, no. 4 (Decem-
    ber), 15.
        Requests a copy of this book for the library.

4 BARNES, L. "The Proletarian Novel," <u>Mainstream</u>, 16 (July),
    51-57.
        "London's reputation, where he has a good one, rests
    solidly on four novels in three of which working-class
    heroes of stature engage in epic struggles to make their
    mark in the world."

5 BOUCHER, ANTHONY. "Ethical Killers: <u>The Assassination Bureau,
    Ltd</u>." <u>New York Times Book Review</u> (8 December), p. 49.
        "The join [of London and Fish] is imperceptible. The

book is one unified delight--the grandest thriller in
years."

6   BROOKS, VAN WYCK. The Writer in America. New York: Dutton,
    pp. 64, 67.
        London is one of the "overgrown exuberant boys" among
    American writers, and one of those who committed suicide
    because he was thwarted as a writer.

7   CALDER-MARSHALL, ARTHUR. "Introduction," in his edition of
    The Bodley Head Jack London. Volume 1. London: Bodley
    Head, pp. 7-16.
        London was the "New Twentieth Century Man." Gives biog-
    raphy; discusses London's wide-ranging subjects, his style,
    social and political concerns, and the sources and themes
    of the stories in this volume [The Call of the Wild and 17
    tales]. "In the stream of American literature Jack London
    appears as a lake....a writer of genius who denied even
    the nature of genius, an artist who thought of himself as
    a great politician, a great reformer, a great farmer, a
    great almost anything except writer....[It is] as Prome-
    theus I see him, Prometheus Vinctus, the deliverer bound
    in the chains of materialistic monism."

8   CARROLL, LAVON B. "Jack London and the American Image." ABC,
    13, no. 5 (January), 23-27.
        London "exemplifies in his life and work the restless,
    naive, and romantic temperament of our culture." His
    rough but fresh writings, idealistic and materialistic like
    the nation, are unified by "his vivid journalistic style"
    and his "obsession" with contemporary ideologies. London's
    best writing is personal imaginative journalism. The cen-
    tral conflict in his work is between the Old Testament God
    and the Devil, for him a primitive brute force which both
    energizes and threatens man, a force like Larsen or indus-
    trialized society. The "love of the Ideal in the form of
    a woman" helps his heroes overcome evil. All the novels
    affirm life, "the dignity of man, and the power of love."

9   FADIMAN, CLIFTON. "An Afterword," in The Call of the Wild.
    Classics Series. New York: Macmillan, pp. 127-28.
        "To me this is the most powerful dog story ever written."
    London believed in force and survival of the fittest. "At
    bottom I think he hated civilization."

10 FOX, R. M. "Red Eye the Atavism." A.E.U. Journal (Amalgamated
    Engineering Union, London), (January), p. 9.
        There are "links of conduct and temperament" between the

1963

apes of <u>Before Adam</u> and modern man. Our "breast-beating
egoists," members of Tory clubs and certain industrialists,
like Red Eye, oppose the security and happiness of the
masses.

11 GANNETT, LEWIS. "Introduction," in <u>The Sea-Wolf</u>. Pathfinder
edition. New York: Bantam, pp. v-xvii.
A detailed biography showing London as a representative
American of his era. This introduction also appears in
the Bantam "Classic" edition of 1960.

12 GLANCY, DONALD R. "Socialist with a Valet: Jack London's
'First, Last, and Only' Lecture Tour." <u>QJS</u>, 49 (February),
31-39.
Lecturing on behalf of Socialism, London's "desire was
to jar the complacency of America's bourgeoisie." He identified himself with the workingman but wore silk shirts
and traveled with a Korean valet. For his speeches, he
made effective use of sociological studies, government and
periodical reports. "A contrapuntal interweaving of boyish
appearance, lively appealing personality, slashing thoughts,
brutal words, and shocking views startled audiences which
at first were captivated by the speaker and at last were
antagonized."

13 KATONA, ANNA. "American Belles Lettres in Hungarian Translation." <u>HSE</u>, 1:65-86.
In 1949-1955, London "grew into an American classic in
Hungary," and in succeeding years he remained a leading
figure. From 1956-1961, fourteen of his books were translated and published.

14 MORIARTY, MARY O'C. "London, Jack. <u>The Assassination Bureau,
Ltd.</u>" <u>Best Sellers</u>, 23 (15 December), 334.
A "suspenseful and fast-moving story."

15 MURPHY, GARDNER. "Jack London on Transmigration," in <u>The Star
Rover</u>. New York: Macmillan, pp. 317-21.
Although London's concepts of transmigration, the com-
monality of soul principles, and the unity of physical and
spiritual continuity lack scientific validity, his use of
these ideas enriches "a brilliant story and superb piece
of science fiction." This volume includes a bibliography
of works by and about London, reprinted from the Macmillan
edition of <u>Before Adam</u> (1962).

16 RICHLER, MORDECAI. "Dogs and Wolves." <u>Spectator</u>, 211 (5 July),
28.

"London was for real....a man of enviable size." As a
militant socialist, "at best his ideology was muddled, at
worst, it was condescending, arrogant, and ridden with
bigotry." His most enjoyable works are The Call of the
Wild and some Alaskan stories.

17   ROTHBERG, ABRAHAM.   "Introduction," in The Call of the Wild
     and White Fang. Pathfinder Edition. New York: Bantam,
     pp. 1-17.
        London's life combines the American myths of Horatio
     Alger, the anti-Establishment rebel, "the red-blooded
     writer and war-correspondent," "the alcoholic who destroyed
     his own talent," and the artist who fails in business. His
     life and work both mirror and criticize these myths and the
     virtues and vices of his era. London's individualism and
     socialism, his love of the soil, drive for success, and
     racism derive from aspects of his childhood. Personal pri-
     vations and miseries encountered in his youthful wanderings
     haunted him, and when he saw these duplicated in the London
     slums, he lost much of his faith in the working class and
     in civilization. To escape, he fled from cities to the
     Sonoma ranch, he traveled world-wide, and he chose primi-
     tive materials for his fictions.
        The Call of the Wild, his "most perfectly realized"
     novel, and White Fang are autobiographical and allegories
     of human life. They have three levels: the narrative,
     biographical, and political-philosophical. Despite the
     bathetic regeneration of White Fang, both dog novels re-
     veal that "eat or be eaten" is the law of wilderness and
     society, and both exalt "violence, romanticism, killing,
     and 'wine-of-life' intensity in savagery." London's "so-
     called revolutionary stories reveal a perverse nihilism,
     a sadistic syndicalism, a tremendous joy in burning so-
     cieties to the ground and going native." His sympathy for
     the working poor and oppressed natives, although genuine,
     was always "tinged with contempt"; he cared less for social
     justice than for "the bloodletting of the revolutionary
     process itself" through which he could "master the masters
     of society." "Ultimately London failed in what he wanted
     to be and to do." His failure is an instance "of the
     failure of success in America." Gives biography. Excerpted
     and revised from 1952.A1.

18   SALISBURY, HARRISON E. "Books of the Times: A Literary Curi-
     osity." New York Times (19 December), p. 31.
        Discusses the history of the London-Lewis-Fish collabora-
     tion and the plot of The Assassination Bureau, Ltd. The
     work has "a genuine fascination, a curious blend of

1963

suspense and pseudo-philosophy." Although popular in
Europe, London is almost unknown here; perhaps this book
"may stimulate a new generation of readers to discover the
great London novels of man and his eternal struggle with
the elemental forces of nature."

19 SEELYE, JOHN. "The American Tramp: a Version of the Pica-
      resque." AQ, 15 (Winter), 535-53.
        In The Road, the "struggle between tramp and trainmen is
      given an epic dimension." The hobo as a rugged "revolu-
      tionary hero" is London himself, and the tramp's life
      takes on mythic proportions. The novel "established the
      tradition in which Kerouac has been writing," and Dean
      Moriarty is "London's modern equivalent."

20 SHIVERS, ALFRED S. "The Romantic in Jack London: Far Away
      Frozen Wilderness." Alaska Review, 1, no. 1 (Winter),
      38-47.
        London gives "a new twist to several romantic qualities"
      in his Alaskan fiction: settings are remote and strange;
      the spirit of romance is a saving virtue; primitivism and
      "noble stoicism" in the face of danger are endorsed;
      "exoticism and sense of the wonderful exist side by side
      with cruelty and brutality." In The Call of the Wild,
      which may be read "as a misanthropic allegory in the form
      of a beast fable," there is "glorified atavism" and "the
      addition of strangeness to beauty" in poetic passages.
      Excerpted and revised from 1962.A2.

21 STANLEY, DONALD. "The Book Corner: A Finishing Touch." San
      Francisco Examiner (5 December), p. 39.
        "There is reason to suppose that even so muddled an in-
      tellect as London's had grasped the hopeless unintellec-
      tuality of the story." The Assassination Bureau, Ltd. be-
      comes "a kind of dilute James Bond."

22 WRIGHT, DAVID. "Book Reviews: The Bodley Head Jack London"
      [Volume 1]. The Listener, 70 (4 July), 27.
        London had the essential "imaginative apprehension of
      the nature of reality," enabling him to produce a stag-
      gering variety of high quality work. The day is coming
      when he will be recognized "as one of the three master-
      writers of American fiction in the first half of the
      twentieth century" [with Fitzgerald and Crane].

JACK LONDON: A REFERENCE GUIDE

1964 A BOOKS

1 FONER, PHILIP S. <u>Jack London: American Rebel</u>. Revised edi-
    tion. New York: Citadel, 159 pp.
        Reprints title essay of 1947.A1 and omits London's
    writings. Adds "Supplementary Material," explanatory and
    historical footnotes to the essay, drawn principally from
    dissertations, articles, and books written since 1947 and
    from London's own works. Also includes a new analysis of
    racism in <u>The Little Lady of the Big House</u>, and a bibliog-
    raphy, slightly enlarged. Revised edition of 1947.A1.

2 O'CONNOR, RICHARD. <u>Jack London: A Biography</u>. Boston: Little,
    Brown, 440 pp.
        London was the son of Flora Wellman, an enigmatic neurotic
    who dabbled in spiritualism, and, probably, of William H.
    Chaney, a "fascinating" bigoted, arrogant astrologer, law-
    yer, and editor. His step-father, John London, was an
    "earnest, hard-working but luckless...mild, passive, toler-
    ant man." Jack created for himself a "salable personality.
    ...as a carefree, venturesome, uncomplicated man of action,
    though underneath the picaroon was a man tormented by the
    act of his illegitimate birth, the lovelessness of his up-
    bringing, his need to gain recognition, his almost desper-
    ate longing for a son, his conviction that he had been de-
    prived of the joys of boyhood." He never forgot the "bar-
    renness and poverty" of childhood and his harsh life as a
    factory worker, sailor, hobo, and prisoner. London en-
    joyed the "haphazardness, the variety, the comradeship,
    the romantic squalor of life on the Road"; and, attracted
    by this irresponsible "Man's world" and a possible quick
    fortune, he joined the gold rush to the Klondike. In one
    year he made $1000 by taking "120 boats through dangerous
    rapids" and accumulated materials for his fiction in which
    he wove "a legend, creating a Klondike that never existed
    except in his imagination." In later years, London spent
    six months in Japan, Korea, and Manchuria, covering the
    Russo-Japanese War for the <u>Examiner</u>; he "took hundreds of
    photographs," was the first to send back a detailed account
    of the first clash, and came away with his "anti-Oriental
    prejudices" and "fear of 'the Yellow Peril'" heightened.
    He endeavored to create a "self-sufficient barony" on
    1000 acres of California land, where he bred animals,
    farmed scientifically, entertained hundreds of friends and
    strangers, and built Wolf House for $80,000. He sailed
    the <u>Snark</u> to the South Seas and contracted yaws, malaria,
    a "mysterious skin ailment," and a "nervous condition"
    while losing "his dream of a primitive paradise." In

business ventures--color lithography, a Mexican land deal,
a grapejuice company--"he was gypped, hoodwinked, over-
charged and outbargained wherever he went." London helped
organize the Authors League of America and secure changes
in the copyright law. During the Mexican War, he identified with the revolutionaries but switched support to
United States armed intervention; as a war correspondent,
he "spent most of his time drinking" in Vera Cruz. In the
last two years of his life, London revisited Hawaii, where
he "fell in love again" with an unknown woman. He suffered
from nephritis, pyorrhea, uremia, rheumatism, dysentery,
edema of the ankles, headaches, obesity, and great mental
strain; his gluttonous eating and drinking, irritability
and belligerency drove his friends away; yet he continued
to generously aid young writers and causes. In 1916, he
resigned from the Socialist party, but he had never been
a committed Socialist, believing in it "as an actor believes
in the lines he is declaiming." Although London's letter
to his daughter on the eve of his death "was clear evidence
that he had not intended--until the unendurable pain be-
gan--to make an end of his life," he committed suicide with
an overdose of narcotics. "He had lived as he pleased,...
had taken what he wanted out of life, and now he had no
more use for it....His only choice was to live as Jack
London, a hedonist enjoying life to the hilt, or to die,
quite shamelessly, at the moment of his choosing."

London, the man and legend, was argumentative, opinion-
ated, and self-centered, needing to outdo and surpass all
other men. The women in his life were Mabel Applegarth--
"Her fragility, her cultivated voice and delicate manner
made her seem like a goddess to Jack"; Anna Strunsky, who
valued him "for his gusto, his appetite for living, his
vitality and customary high humor"; Bessie Maddern, "the
eternal homemaker"; and his "Mate-Woman" Charmian Kittredge,
who "with ruthless cunning" and Jack's complicity wrecked
his first marriage. With a "lusty, unrestrained attitude
toward sex," London had "his marital cake and his illicit
frosting" in many "catch-as-catch-can romances." "Momen-
tary pleasure was the only consideration with him....he
did tend to glory in and embellish his reputation as the
Stallion of the Piedmont Hills." London's "'Man-Comrade'"
was George Sterling. The friendship of "Wolf" and "Greek"
was "probably as harmful to both men as it was touching.
Each, in his immaturity, encouraged the profligate, the
self-destructive boyishness in the other."

London, the writer, pursued money. "The motive force
that drove him to produce fifty books in sixteen years of
his professional career, was an unquenchable desire for

success and all its rewards....The joys of creation, by
his own account, escaped him completely....Nothing was
worth doing if it didn't succeed on its merits in the mar-
ketplace." However, London "was filled with disgust and
resentment," which corrupted his life and work, at the
necessity of writing for money. While his publisher sent
him an ever-escalating monthly income, he churned out
A Daughter of the Snows, whose heroine was the "mouth-
piece" for Jack's sociological and political theories; The
Call of the Wild in which "all of the finest and purest
elements of Jack's talent happened to crystalize"; The
Sea-Wolf, meant to show that "the Nietzschean hero was
doomed by his inevitable imperfections," a novel that
"breaks in half" and lapses from realism into false and
insipid sentimentality; The Iron Heel, "largely an un-
tempered melodrama," propagandistic and artificial; three
collections of stories about the South Seas--"It was evident from their content that Jack was more at home as a
writer in the sub-Arctic than in the tropics"; Martin Eden,
"a sort of guidebook, inspiration, and Sacred Writ" to
young writers; John Barleycorn, "credited with being an
important factor in the campaign [for] Prohibition"; The
Valley of the Moon, "a fervent statement of the mystic
bonds of 'race, blood, and soil,'" and of London's "disgust
with the world" and humanity; and The Little Lady of the
Big House, a "hymnal on the back-to-the-land theme," conveying his "urge to break away from the modern world."
During his last six years or so, London concentrated on
magazine writing, buying story plots from Sinclair Lewis
and others, caring more for "his growing list of possessions" than for "the quality of his work." His "last
several major efforts" met "comparative indifference from
critics and book-buyers alike" because, having "isolated
himself from the main current of American life" for ten
years, London "was trapped in nostalgia."
   "He survives today chiefly as a storyteller with a vigor
and freshness that carries over, with a recurring sense of
discovery, to each new generation of readers. Undoubtedly
that appeal will increase....His own life story, his consciously created legend, was an even greater artistic work
than any he committed to paper."

1964 B SHORTER WRITINGS

1   BRUCCOLI, MATTHEW J. "Introduction" and "Textual Note," in
       his edition of The Sea-Wolf. Boston: Houghton Mifflin,
       The Riverside Press, pp. v-xv; 1-2.
       The novel has memorable scenes, suspenseful action, and

the magnificent character Wolf Larsen. Larsen is Nietzsche's "higher man, intermediate between man and superman," whose indomitable will to live and to gain power as
an end in itself can be defeated only by death. The absence of conflict between "Larsen's materialism and Van
Weyden's idealism" and of a worthy collectivist voice among
other characters weakens the novel. From Chapter XXVI, it
degenerates into "romantic fantasy" because of the disap-
pearance of Larsen, "lack of personal conflict," and London's "fear of Mrs. Grundy" and his editor. The Sea-Wolf
supports civilized values of "courage, strength, adapta-
bility, and high standards of conduct," exemplified by the
matured Van Weyden and by Maud. By combining these with
glorification of individualism, London gave readers "adventure and virtue masquerading as naturalism" to be enjoyed
in good conscience.

2   CALDER-MARSHALL, ARTHUR. "Introduction," in his edition of
The Bodley Head Jack London. Volume 2. London: Bodley
Head, pp. 7-27.
     John Barleycorn, "a literary masterpiece," is London's
"greatest book....one of the most poignant documents of
our century, a fortuitous work of inhibited and tortured
genius." As autobiography and confession, it dramatizes
the themes of suicide, illegitimacy, and psychological
conflicts arising from the lack of love and continuity in
London's childhood. He wrote it "to reassure himself that
he was not an alcoholic." Discusses in detail London's
life, reading, marriages, friendships, etc. in relation to
John Barleycorn and the two other works in this volume:
The Cruise of the Dazzler, The Road.

3   DEUTSCH, ANDRÉ. "Limited Thrills." TLS (3 December), p. 1101.
     The Assassination Bureau, Ltd. is "something of a thriller
of the Stevensonian kind....a thoroughly poor novel."

4   FEIED, FREDERICK. No Pie in the Sky: The Hobo as American Cultural Hero in the Works of Jack London, John Dos Passos,
and Jack Kerouac. New York: Citadel, pp. 15, 18, 23-40,
41, 43, 44, 45, 56, 57-58, 75, 81-85, 87, 88, 89, 91.
     London was "the first American writer of any signifi-
cance to speak of the tramp or hobo from intimate knowledge
and understanding." His hobo is "a social fact, a phenomenon of economic determinism under capitalism," necessary
to capitalism's existence. London's treatment of the hobo
in several essays, stories, and The Road demonstrates his
"generous human sympathies," belief in the need for socialism, and conviction "that all life was a struggle for

personal or biological supremacy" in which survival was
the test of superiority. With all its harsh realism, The
Road's dominant note is "one of humor, high spirits, and
pride" of endurance; its "positive and optimistic" tone
conveys London's confidence in inevitable social change;
and the style "is vigorous and powerful, working under
bunchéd muscle."

5   FULLER, EDMUND. "Reading for Pleasure: Logical Lunatics."
    Wall Street Journal (14 January), p. 12.
        The Assassination Bureau, Ltd. is a slight but enter-
    taining "crude quasi-Dostoyevskian cautionary tale about
    overweening intellectual pride." Into it London has woven
    "a web of paradoxes about the integrity, responsibility,
    and the mystique of the superior person above the law."
    Gives plot summary.

6   FULLER, JOHN. "Almighty Aposiopesis." New Statesman, 68
    (24 July), [126]-27.
        Review of The Bodley Head Jack London, volume 2. The
    pieces convey London's source of energy but not the
    "social conscience of his best work." John Barleycorn is
    ironic "in the conflict between the claims of his ethical
    message and his desire to apotheosise his swash-buckling
    adolescence." The Cruise of the Dazzler "is dry and honest
    and readable still."

7   GORDON, DUDLEY C. "Charles F. Lummis and Jack London: An Evalu-
    ation." Southern California Quarterly, 46 (March), 83-88.
        In 1905, Lummis invited London to join the Southwest
    Society of Los Angeles (an art-Indian preservation group);
    London declined, saying he had his own cause, the socialist
    revolution. Prints five brief letters exchanged; compares
    the lives, influences on, war-correspondent and hobo
    careers, writings, and accomplishments of the men. Lon-
    don's work made no tangible contribution to the betterment
    of society.

8   JAHER, FREDERIC COPLE. "Jack London: 'The Stone the Builders
    Rejected,'" in his Doubters and Dissenters: Cataclysmic
    Thought in America, 1885-1918. London: Free Press of
    Glencoe, Collier-Macmillan, pp. 188-216.
        London was one of several writers who felt cut off from
    society and focused on its destruction. A rootless man,
    living "in a world of conflict, deprivation, and persecu-
    tion," London as "the arch-individualist" was more alien-
    ated and paranoid than most other "cataclysmists." He
    responded to alienation by trying to either escape from

or destroy present reality. He posed as a romantic adventurer and created characters like Everhard, the dominating
Darwinian-Nietzschean hero, who were projections of his
ego; and he continually fled and returned to responsibility.
In his thought London linked the "cataclysmic themes" of
"race war and class revolution." Anglo-Saxon supremacy
would civilize savages and prevent foreigners' domination
of America. Socialism promised him freedom and satisfied
his need for companionship. Marxism provided him with a
rationale for his sense of alienation--he was a member of
an ostracized group betrayed by capitalism--and an outlet
in violent revolution for the vengeful hostilities he felt.
In The Iron Heel, London loathes the masses, distrusts
human nature, hates the rich, and admires the master class;
here he vicariously takes revenge on society while destroying himself (Everhard). The total despair, brutalization,
and death in The Scarlet Plague shows London's own loss of
hope and deep depression; and his suicide is the final
"cataclysmic act" which "offered the only relief from ir-
reversible degeneracy and unresolvable contradiction."

9   JENNINGS, ANN S. "London's Code of the Northland." Alaska
     Review, 1, no. 3 (Fall), 43-48.
          The code is based on the premise that Nature, ruling by
     laws inflexible and absolute, opposed "all which is not
     nature" in the Klondike. The points of the code are: "the
     ascendancy of the cold"; survival of the strongest; loss
     of civilized morality; "the glory of the struggle accom-
     panying the blood lust." "In the end, it was London's very
     code which destroyed itself, and the reign of Nature, when
     it taught men the necessity of cooperation for survival."

10   JOHNSON, B. S. "Jelly-Cats." Spectator, 213 (18 December),
     849-50.
          Review of The Assassination Bureau, Ltd. "This is the
     sort of plot which is too much of a plot...and the ratio-
     nalist, humanist and anarchist smatterings of knowledge in-
     corporated are unconvincing and badly assimilated." A
     disservice has been done to London's reputation; the "book
     should never have been allowed to get further than a thesis-
     writer's footnote."

11   LABOR, EARLE. "The Assassination Bureau, Ltd." SSF, 1, no. 4
     (Summer), 303-305.
          A fascinating literary curiosity and "a well-made mystery
     thriller." The "thematic ambivalence" of London's work
     appears in Dragomiloff, "a hybridized caricature of the
     blond superman and the Marxist."

12   _____. "A Dedication to the Memory of Jack London: 1876-1916."
      Arizona and the West, 6, no. 2 (Summer), 92-96.
          London captured the spirit of the West in his life as a
      "hard-hitting, hard-drinking, hard-living individualist."
      His "mythopoeic genius" and "talent for telling a surpass-
      ingly good story" give force to his works. London envi-
      sioned the creation of a new Eden in California. Gives
      brief biography and history of works.

13   LOWNDES, ROBERT A. W. "Introduction," in The Call of the Wild.
      Classics Series. New York: Airmont, pp. 1-5.
          Biography.

14   _____. "Introduction," in White Fang. Classics Series. New
      York: Airmont, pp. 1-6.
          Biography.

15   RANSOM, M. A. and E. K. ENGLE. Sea of the Bear. Annapolis:
      U. S. Naval Institute, p. 96.
          Mentions The Sea-Wolf in connection with the old days of
      seal-hunting.

16   SHIVERS, ALFRED S. "Jack London's Mate-Women." ABC, 15,
      no. 2 (October), 17-21.
          His women and men share the traits of "grit, energy,
      homage to the Anglo-Saxon racial line, resourcefulnes
      [sic], admiration for bodily perfection and prowess." Lon-
      don sympathizes with the loyal, self-sacrificing Indian
      women; his white heroines become progressively more domes-
      ticated, and they range widely in plausibility and person-
      ality. He modeled the fictional women on a combination of
      real women in his life. Excerpted and revised from
      1962.A2.

17   WALKER, FRANKLIN. "Afterword," in Jack London: The Sea-Wolf
      and Selected Stories. Signet Classic. New York: New
      American Library, pp. 337-48.
          Discusses the Sophie Sutherland voyage, the sealing in-
      dustry, and prototypes of characters and incidents in the
      novel.

18   _____. "Foreword," in The Call of the Wild and Selected
      Stories. Signet Modern Classic. New York: New American
      Library, pp. vii-xii.
          Biography.

19   WOODWARD, ROBERT H. "Jack London's Lost Poem." MTJ, 12,
      no. 3 (Winter), 6-7.

1964

"The Sea Sprite and the Shooting Star" "is a hopeful
vision of a love not to be [London's for Mabel Applegarth]
and is sadly and strangely prophetic. Prints poem. Revised version of 1960.B19.

1965 A BOOKS - NONE

1965 B SHORTER WRITINGS

1   ANON. "London, Jack," in The Reader's Encyclopedia. Second
     edition. Edited by William Rose Benét. Volume 1. New
     York: Crowell, 596-97.
     "His work is marked by sympathy with the poor; prophecies
     of world revolution and a future socialist state; emphasis
     upon the primitive, the powerful, the cruel; and a predi-
     lection for the violent, usually embodied in an animal or
     a superman." Gives biography and bibliography.

2   ANON. "Man Behind the Legend." Newsweek, 66 (13 December),
     106E, 106F, 109.
     A review of Letters from Jack London. He was a legendary
     American--"Leatherstocking at the typewriter, Hemingway
     before the fact," and a rags-to-riches success. If these
     letters "help to kindle interest in this lamentably neg-
     lected writer, they will have served a valuable purpose."
     Gives biography.

3   BERCOVICI, ALFRED. "Death Drive." Argosy (August), pp. 38-39,
     104.
     Fictionalized biography of "the Prince of the Drunkards"
     and his attempted suicide by drowning.

4   BERTHOFF, WARNER. The Ferment of Realism: American Literature,
     1884-1919. New York: Free Press, pp. 244-47, and passim.
     "Perhaps the most gifted prose talent of his generation,
     certainly the most prodigally squandered, belonged to Jack
     London." "An element of charlatanism" informs his work
     and the "glare of mass notoriety" in which he lived. He
     appealed to the common man's prejudices and dreams of con-
     quest; at the same time his work conveyed "the spreading
     panic and emptiness of modern life." His "emphatic no-
     nonsense colloquialism" became the "basic idiom of the
     straight-talking mass-market fantasy-realists" in the
     1950's and 1960's. At times, London could write natural,
     strong prose and well-structured narratives. He could not
     manage novels. His best works are The Road and The People
     of the Abyss.

5   CALDER-MARSHALL, ARTHUR. "Introduction," in his edition of
    The Bodley Head Jack London. Volume 3. London: Bodley
    Head, pp. 5-18.
        London wrote Martin Eden to assure himself "that he was
    not a manic-depressive." Martin, London's "scapegoat," is
    a vital, fully-realized character, but Ruth, a "parody" of
    Mabel Applegarth, is not individualized. Discusses the
    composition of the novel and its relation to London's biog-
    raphy, particularly the women in his life. Martin's sui-
    cide is "clinically" justified but "artistically indefen-
    sible"; London "just killed Martin for money." Volume con-
    tains Martin Eden.

6   DANIELS, ROGER. "Racism in London." SatR, 48 (16 October),
    44.
        A letter in response to 1965.B14. London "shared the
    racist views of most American Socialists." See also
    1965.B8; 1965.B15.

7   DIEKMANN, EDWARD, JR. "From London to Peking in Fifty-one
    Years." American Opinion, 8, no. 2 (February), 79-89.
        Douglas MacArthur was the "same kind of man as Jack";
    both were in Vera Cruz to see things at first hand. "The
    Unparalled Invasion" (1914) showed the expansionist peril
    of China, and this "carefully ignored and suppressed" tale
    resembles MacArthur's "The Vision of Douglas MacArthur."
    It is "strange and illuminating" that both men came up with
    similar plans. London's "China of 1908 is the whole of the
    Communist world today." Socialists attacked London for
    writing the truth about Mexico, and "a Socialist workman"
    set fire to Wolf House; London "was murdered by the vin-
    dictiveness of those [Socialists] who had called him their
    friend."

8   FONER, PHILIP S. "Racism in London." SatR, 48 (16 October),
    44
        A letter in response to 1965.B14. London's "magnificent
    cause was weakened by his white supremacist ideology."
    See also 1965.B6; 1965.B15.

9   FRIEDMAN, RALPH. "Jack London's Valley of the Moon." Main-
    liner (United Airlines Magazine), 9 (July), 14-16.
        "The intimate brush strokes of the artist are here in
    this chapter [8 of Burning Daylight], disclosing the keen
    eyes, the razor edge sense, and the bountiful nature of....
    the literary conquistadore, mounted on a good steed and
    glory." Describes London Park, museum, Wolf House ruins.

1965

10   GALL, MORRIS. "Jack London: Introduction," in The Sea-Wolf.
     Classics Series. New York: Airmont, pp. 1-4.
         Larsen "perhaps best represents London's admiration for
     brute strength--the Nietzschean superman," and he exempli-
     fies London's fascination with "the predatory wolf."
     Gives biography.

11   HILLMAN, SERRELL. "Jack London--Transitory Egoist." TamR,
     35 (Spring), 86-90.
         Like Fitzgerald, London was a drunk who led a glamorous
     life and died young. But he did not write "a tenth as well
     as Fitzgerald." London was "a violent, unabashed egocen-
     tric....an individualist, with the rather crazed ideas...
     of Nordic supremacy and Jewish insufficiency....a very
     mixed-up man." His colorful life is far more interesting
     than his work which was "for the most part, trash."

12   LABOR, EARLE. "Introduction," in his edition of Great Short
     Works of Jack London. New York: Harper and Row, pp. vii-
     xvii.
         Major themes of the Far North fictions are "primitivism,
     atavism, environmental meliorism, stoicism and humanism."
     The White Silence dominates these writings which reveal
     London's "mythopoeic genius." Gives biography.

13   _____. "Paradise Almost Regained." SatR, 48 (3 April), 43-44.
         Stories of Hawaii deal with race relations, London's
     personal problems, and the ecological corruption of people
     and land by civilization. London takes a variety of sym-
     pathetic approaches to the Hawaiians and reveals his pre-
     occupation with the myths of Freud and Jung. "The best of
     him is more than a handful of dust."

14   _____. "Life was Always Worth the Living." SatR, 48 (25 Sep-
     tember), 38-39.
         Review of Letters from Jack London. They reveal his
     heroic "courage and talent," sensitivity, generous spirit,
     humanism, and professionalism. He was a "myth-hero for
     his generation" and an influence on his successors. A
     controversy stemmed from Labor's remark here: "London was
     a crusading socialist with enough common sense to perceive
     inequalities among races as well as in individuals." See
     1965.B6; 1965.B8; 1965.B15.

15   _____. "Denotations of Inequality." SatR, 48 (30 October),
     42.
         By considering London's work and life in total context,
     critics "may revise the labels 'hack' and 'racist' to read

'craftsman' and 'humanist.'" A response to 1965.B6, B8;
see also 1965.B14.

16 LYNN, KENNETH S. "Disturber of Gentility." New York Times
    Book Review (14 February), pp. 18, 20.
        Review of O'Connor, 1964.A2. Biographers of London fail
    to account for the development of his "superb narrative
    drive and the delicate feeling for words...sensitive re-
    sponsiveness to the tragedy of man's fate and his apocalyp-
    tic nightmares of war and social upheaval." London "de-
    cisively changed the course of American fiction."

17 McLEAN, ALBERT F., Jr. American Vaudeville as Ritual. Lexing-
    ton: University of Kentucky Press, pp. 149-51.
        Some one hundred pages of Michael, Brother of Jerry seem
    "adapted directly from the humane society literature."
    The novel spurred the American Humane Education Society to
    form Jack London Clubs (against exploitation of animals on
    the stage).

18 MILLER, F. DeWOLFE. "Whitman Bibliography in Russia." WWR,
    11, no. 3 (September), 77-79.
        London is the third most popular American author in
    Russia.

19 RATHBONE, CHARLES. "A Word to the Reader," in Jack London's
    Stories of the North. Selected by Betty M. Owen. Scholas-
    tic Library Edition. New York: Scholastic Book Services,
    pp. iv-viii.
        London's heroes find their true selves by actively chal-
    lenging environments. Through their lives London answers
    important questions about men under stress and about sur-
    vival values.

20 SILLITOE, ALAN. "The Boy Revolutionary." New Statesman, 69
    (18 June), 972-74.
        London rose to literary success from a life of poverty.
    Socialism strengthened his self-image by making him feel
    superior to "those he wanted to ape" while remaining loyal
    to his proletarian roots. His self-destructive response
    to success was in many ways like that of D. H. Lawrence.

21 SIMPSON, CLAUDE M. "Jack London: Proletarian or Plutocrat."
    Stanford Today, series 1, no. 13 (Summer), 2-6.
        These conflicting value systems inform London's life and
    works. In The Call of the Wild, "his best-controlled and
    most consistent piece of work," he combines in Buck bru-
    tality and "the simplistic biological drives" with love,

1965

loyalty, and unselfishness. A theme of The Sea-Wolf is "the problem of survival in primordial surroundings," and Larsen celebrates the physical and intellectual side of London. Here and in Martin Eden, London's intentions are "blurred." In practice, London "is a thoroughgoing individualist" and overall an "unstable mixture of contending forces from which he escaped only into death."

22   STRAUMANN, HEINRICH. American Literature in the Twentieth Century. Third edition, revised. New York: Harper and Row, p. 32.
     London's stress on "brute instincts" attracted an enormous reading public.

23   TANNER, TONY. "The Call of the Wild." Spectator, 215 (16 July), 80-81.
     Review of several volumes by and about London. His two dog books, some stories, and Martin Eden reveal London's "own ambivalent attitudes towards the call of the camp and the call of the wild." Related to these "twin pulls-- towards culture and social achievement, and again to the savage freedom of the wild"--is the struggle between "energy and inertia" or the energies of life and death. The attractions of drink and death are "subtly intermingled" in John Barleycorn, his greatest work along with The People of the Abyss. "Perhaps he was not a great writer (though he is underrated),...But much of what he called his 'impassioned realism' still has an amazing power, and there are moments when he seems to have a hold on profound elemental issues."

24   VON SZELISKI, JOHN. "Jack London: Return from the Yukon. Scenes from a Scenario." Berkshire Review, 1, no. 2 (Autumn), 15-23.
     A dramatization of London's return from Alaska to his mother in Oakland.

25   WALKER, FRANKLIN. "Jack London: Martin Eden," in The American Novel From James Fenimore Cooper to William Faulkner. Edited by Wallace Stegner. New York: Basic Books, pp. 133-43.
     London's first choice for the novel's title was "Success," and the second "Stardust." He creates "a number of excellent minor figures" to help dramatize Martin's quest, which he had conceived of as a proletarian's attainment of and disillusionment with middle class values. Until he neared the end, however, he was uncertain how he would complete it, although he "always insisted that Martin's suicide was

the logical outcome of his experiences." London's reason
for the suicide--Martin's individualism and failure to
adopt Socialism--"is not very persuasive." London's "admiration for Martin as an individualist" is never in doubt.
The suicide is foreshadowed throughout, until it seems
Martin reaches "the depressive stage of a manic-depressive
existence." This is London's best book, but like all of
them "it is uneven in structure, sometimes clumsy in expression, at times mawkish in tone. Yet it possesses great
lasting power." It portrays truthfully urban life in California in its time, the feelings of an adolescent chal-
lenging adult society, the conflict of class values, and
"the joys and depressions of a neurotic temperament."
Summarizes plot.

26   WARE, JUDGE WALLACE L.   "The World of Jack London," in his The
     Unforgettables. Hertford, London: Mimram Books, pp. 67-77.
        When London neared the Santa Rosa Courthouse in his
     "Tally-ho, with four-in-hand, attired in a cowboy regalia,"
     Courts declared a recess so all could welcome him. On the
     walls of a lean-to alongside the Southern Pacific tracks,
     London painted: "BEWARE OF CAPITALISTS / HUMAN BLOOD-
     SUCKERS / JACK LONDON." On the evening of his death, the
     Elks Club of Santa Rosa was gathered to initiate him into
     the Order. Expresses admiration for London's works and
     recounts a Tong War and trial "worthy of a Jack London
     Mafia-style gangster plot."

1966 A BOOKS

1   HENDRICKS, KING. Jack London: Master Craftsman of the Short
     Story. Logan: The Faculty Association, Utah State Uni-
     versity (April), 28 pp.
        London kept painstakingly accurate records of his maga-
     zine submissions and rejections [prints some facsimile
     records with analyses]. For his early work, he earned as
     little as $5 a story. In 1912, he signed a five-year
     contract with Cosmopolitan at $24,000 annually to write
     twelve stories and a novel per year. In his stories, Lon-
     don "had the ability to create a strong narrative, to
     create marvelous story atmosphere, to infuse into it
     graphic descriptions...[and] develop an ironical situa-
     tion." "To Build A Fire," his "short story masterpiece,"
     and "Love of Life" share a theme London often used: the
     determination to live. "The Law of Life" is "almost a
     picture poem" which reveals "the depth of human tragedy."
     "The Chinago" is "the greatest story of London's career

and one of the great stories of all time." He wrote 149 short stories.

*2   NORTON, MARGARET. Dear Comrades. Sonoma, California: Sonoma Co., 100 pp.
      A play based on the life of London. Produced by the Sonoma County Theater Guild, and directed by Dan Norton, it opened June, 1966, at the Sebastiani Theater in Sonoma. Cited in Woodbridge, 1966.A7; authorship cited as Daniel and Margaret Norton in Woodbridge, 1973.A7.

3   WALCUTT, CHARLES CHILD. Jack London. Pamphlets on American Writers no. 57. Minneapolis: University of Minnesota Press, 48 pp.
      Summarizes London's life and writings, offers plot summaries and analyses of several stories and novels, and a selected bibliography. London belongs to the "naturalistic movement, which embraces scientific determinism, Darwinism, the Spencerian philosophy of evolution, and Marxism." He resembles such writers as Twain, Fitzgerald, and Hemingway who "tried to live several lives at once and in the attempt sacrificed their lives, their art, or their peace to the excess they attempted."
      His best works, the Alaskan stories, The Call of the Wild, White Fang, and The Cruise of the Snark, compel attention by their vigorous new ideas, intense and concrete language, the energy of a "fierce commitment to life," and strong, suspenseful narrative line. Buck and White Fang enact "London's own myth" of the unloved, fatherless, poverty-stricken child whose innate strengths enable him to survive. Martin Eden, "among his worst" novels, "turns into a daydream of sulky spite, of childish pique." Reprinted: 1974.B31.

4   WALKER, FRANKLIN DICKERSON. Jack London and the Klondike: the Genesis of an American Writer. San Marino, California: Huntington Library; London: Bodley Head, 288 pp.
      A detailed examination of London's year in the Klondike (1897-98) and the uses he made of this experience in his fiction give "a vivid and valid picture of the famous rush," an accurate view of the "most important segment" of London's biography, and insight into his writing methods and "creative talent." His rebellious and adventurous youth and his frontier background contributed to the "restlessness, independence, resourcefulness, exaggeration, [and] crudity" so strong in his character and writings.
      On July 25, 1897, he boarded the Umatilla, with his brother-in-law, J. H. Shepard, staked by his stepsister,

Eliza, for the Klondike. The diary of Fred C. Thompson, one of their party, and "excerpts from London's fiction" furnish details of his trip from San Francisco to Dawson; his fiction gives London's reaction to Dawson City; and London's diary of June 8-June 30, 1898, "detailed and directed toward the articles and stories he wished to write," records his homeward journey on the Yukon.

In the fifteen months after his return from Alaska, London earned only $150 from his writing; but in 1900, publication of "An Odyssey of the North" in Atlantic Monthly and of The Son of the Wolf established him as a writer. "His writing methods, together with his attitudes towards the several phases of his craft, developed and became fixed during the five years he spent primarily on Klondike materials." He consulted rhetorics, guides, professional journals on writing, experimented with various forms and styles, and searched for "situations to illustrate the conflicts faced by man [in the Klondike]--man against nature, the white man against the Indian, the weak against the strong." In 6 volumes of Klondike tales, 5 novels, a play, and several articles he dramatized his true experiences and impressions: debarking at and leaving Dyea; packing over the Chilkoot Pass; life in the camps and breaking trail; the trip on Lake Lindeman in the Yukon Belle; running Box Canyon and White Horse Rapids--"the only boat other than his own which Jack ran through was taken through for kindness rather than gain....he never piloted for money at White Horse"; navigating Lake Laberge; wintering on Split-Up Island; discoveries of gold and stampedes of prospectors; life in Dawson City; treacherous natural forces; and the Indians, whom he gave "sympathy but little genuine understanding" [Walker locates these materials in London's fictions]. Real persons became models for his fictional ones: Louis Bond (Stanley Price) and his dog (Buck); Emil Jensen (Malemute Kid); Father William Judge and St. Mary's Hospital (in Burning Daylight).

Uneven in quality, the Klondike tales are unified by London's "joy in conflict, his feeling that the persecuted must fight, his admiration for the fighter that could win." He was a humanist with faith in the natural progress of man. Although London's "naturalism,...jingoism,... [and] historical determinism" are now seen as inaccurate or out-dated, "there is a very important place in our sophisticated and often tired world for London's hero who fights even while he is falling, and he by no means always falls." Includes a bibliography of London's Klondike writings.

1966

5   WILCOX, EARL JUNIOR. "Jack London and the Tradition of Ameri-
      can Literary Naturalism." Ph.D. dissertation, Vanderbilt
      University, 1966.
        Excerpted and revised: 1969.B29; 1970.B48; 1973.B53.

6   WOODBRIDGE, HENSLEY C., JOHN LONDON, and GEORGE H. TWENEY,
      comps. Jack London: A Bibliography. Georgetown, Cali-
      fornia: Talisman Press, 423 pp.
        The only book-length London bibliography, with materials
      in English and some 70 foreign languages. Major areas are:
      Writings by London--books (first editions, reprints, trans-
      lations); collections and anthologies; short stories sepa-
      rately published; contributions to periodicals and news-
      papers; ephemera; motion pictures based on his works.
      Writings about London--books and pamphlets; parts of books;
      articles; reviews; theses and dissertations. Revised and
      enlarged: 1973.A7.

1966 B SHORTER WRITINGS

1   ANON. "London, Jack. Letters from Jack London." ALA Book-
      list, 62 (1 January), 429.
        "A vivid and revealing self-portrait."

2   ANON. "London, Jack. Letters from Jack London. Choice, 3
      no. 3 (May), 210.
        They "illustrate his firm belief in the rights of all
      men and his just as firm stand in favor of racial superi-
      ority. They show him as part anarchist, part revolutionist,
      part capitalist, and all man."

3   ANON. "London Fog." TLS (15 September), pp. 849-50.
        Letters do not illuminate "the obscure or controversial
      episodes in London's life." Gives excerpts.

4   ANON. "Klondike Jack." TLS (10 November), p. 1021.
        A review of The Bodley Head Jack London and 1966.A4.
      London, "the American Gorky, a true vagabond and man of
      the people," was America's "recording angel of the struggle
      between savage and civilized man, between the wilderness
      and the advancing camp and city." He misunderstood the
      Indian mind but recognized "the savage in the civilized
      American" and his driving need to "glut his greed" in the
      Yukon.

5   BASKETT, SAM S. "Letters from Jack London." AL, 38 (Novem-
      ber), 404-405.
        "Nothing could more clearly indicate the plight of

London biography than the fact that fifty years after his
death they constitute a significant document."

6   BLOTNER, JOSEPH. The Modern American Political Novel, 1900–
     1960. Austin: University of Texas Press, pp. 150–53.
         The Iron Heel, "the first apocalyptic novel of the cen-
     tury....became proof for generations of radicals that a
     proletarian could write popular and vigorous fiction....
     it is London's fierce partisanship which accounts for the
     best and worst in this novel." Finds weakness in its
     characterizations--Everhard is "too much the superman" and
     Avis is a "disembodied character"--and its didacticism.
     Gives summary.

7   BUBKA, TONY. "Jack London's Definition of a Scab." ABC, 17,
     no. 3 (November), 23–26.
         The "definition," published in many versions from at
     least 1936 through 1966 and attributed to London, was
     definitely not written by him.

8   BYKOV, VIL. "Jack London in the U.S.S.R." ABC, 17, no. 3
     (November), 27.
         Excerpts from Bykov's "Jack London's American Critic,"
     Voprosy Literature (Moscow: September, 1965); translated
     by Boris Schiel.

9   CALDER, JENNI. "Dollar Signs." New Statesman, 72 (30 Septem-
     ber), 484.
         Letters "reveal his shrewd confidence, his unerring grasp
     of his own abilities in relation to public taste, and his
     severe, at times cruel, criticisms of aspiring writers."
     Although deeply concerned for his art, London wrote for
     money. "The rolling, reckless, unconfined style of his
     letters is the style of his novels."

10   CALDER-MARSHALL, ARTHUR. "Introduction," in his edition of
     The Bodley Head Jack London. Volume 4: The Klondike Dream.
     London: Bodley Head, pp. 7–18.
         London's tales and stories of the Klondike "sprouted
     haphazardly" over the course of his career; they are re-
     arranged here "in historical sequence" to show his prog-
     ress from fact to fiction. The early tales evince Kip-
     ling's influence (Anglo-Saxon superiority) on a foundation
     of Spencer's survival of the fittest. London blends first-
     hand experience, readings, and hearsay, and real people
     whom he transforms into heroic figures: he "was a Homer of
     the Gold Rush." He is "at his best in describing inaction,
     especially the decline into death." Discusses the stories
     in this volume.

1966

11 CHAPMAN, ARNOLD. "Curwood and London: Lords of the Frozen
    Wild," in his The Spanish-American Reception of United
    States Fiction, 1920-1940. Publications in Modern Philol-
    ogy no. 77. Berkeley: University of California Press,
    pp. 42-56.
        Sixteen London titles were published in Spanish in 1925-
    1930 in Spain. London and Curwood entered South America
    "arm-in-arm" in 1925-26, and London reached his height of
    popularity there in 1930-40 with The Call of the Wild,
    White Fang, and The Sea-Wolf. Most critics linked him to
    Kipling; they appreciated his romantic Socialistic defense
    of the working-class poor and Alaskan and South Seas na-
    tives, his ability to combine realism and adventure, and
    his political theorizing. Gives bibliography.

12 FONER, PHILIP S. "Jack London: An Appreciation." ABC, 17,
    no. 3 (November), 9-10.
        London was "a new voice in American literature," lively,
    defiant, vigorous, and realistic in depicting the injustice
    he knew first-hand. In subject and expression, he was "a
    supreme artist....[and] spokesman for a new concept of so-
    ciety."

13 FRENCH, ROBERTS W. "A Sustained Distance." Humanist, 26
    (July-August), 134.
        These "uniformly tedious" Letters give us "primarily a
    picture of the professional author at work." Their "emo-
    tional deficiency" suggests a similar lack of conviction
    in London.

14 FULLER, FRANK A. "'Martin Eden' and Critical Realism." ABC,
    17, no. 3 (November), 19-21.
        In this "penetrating analysis of the dilemma of the in-
    dividual," the Morse family's character defects and the
    falseness of Martin's aspirations to middle-class status
    are conveyed by the plot structure and expressed through
    London's authorial voice and Martin's characterization.

15 GHINSBERG, SAMUEL. "The Horses Knew the Way..." San Francisco
    Sunday Examiner and Chronicle (6 March), "This World" sec-
    tion, pp. 33, 37.
        Describes a visit to London's ranch in 1915. "He was
    the most likable character I have ever met."

16 GURIAN, JAY. "The Romantic Necessity in Literary Naturalism:
    Jack London," AL, 38 (March), 112-20.
        Reprint of 1962.B5.

212

17 HACKER, DAVID W. "The Legend and Legacy of Jack London: A
    Hack Writer, But With Flashes of Brilliance." National
    Observer (3 January), p. 10.
        He "was an enormous puppy,...who somehow bounded through
    40 years of life" and wrote "50 books--most of them worth
    no more than a handful of fool's gold." The Call of the
    Wild and Martin Eden do offer flashes of poetic and narra-
    tive power. London has influenced American literature and
    remained popular with the public perhaps because of his
    "robustness in tale and life." Discusses Letters, "another
    curiosity of the London life."

18 HOLMAN C. HUGH. "Fiction: 1900-1930," in American Literary
    Scholarship: An Annual/1964. Edited by James Woodress.
    Durham, N. C.: Duke University Press, pp. 142-43.
        An essay-review of major work on London.

19 _____, comp. "London, Jack (John Griffith) (1876-1916)," in
    his The American Novel Through Henry James. Goldentree
    Bibliography. New York: Appleton-Century-Crofts, 54-56.
        Lists 33 biographical and critical items.

20 LONDON, JOAN. "W. H. Chaney: A Reappraisal." ABC, 17, no. 3
    (November), 11-13.
        Gives biography of Chaney. The "probability is very
    strong" that he was London's father, although Chaney de-
    nied it.

21 _____. "The London Divorce." ABC, 17, no. 3 (November), 31.
        Gives Anna Strunsky's account of London's divorce from
    Bess Maddern, as told to Joan in 1928.

22 MAGNES, ISAAC D. "My Farewell Recollections of Jack London,"
    in his The Amateur Bohemian. Anaheim, California: Isaac D.
    Magnes (October), pp. [1]-[4].
        Reprint of 1950.B4.

23 MALONE, G. P. "Hobo Americanus: Jack London." Contemporary
    Review (London), 209 (December), 322-24.
        "Many of his works skimmed the margin of potboilers.
    The Lady of the Snows [sic] is a tedious example of the
    pitfalls he stumbled into." The faults of his writing are
    brutality, sadism, "hodge-podge philosophy," racism, and
    bombastic style. His virtues are, like Hemingway's, "sim-
    plicity, directness, dignity," sympathy with nature and
    with "the inarticulate." In both writers "a rare nobility
    of spirit was coupled with a curiously primitive intelli-
    gence." Gives biography.

1966

24   MENTON, WILLIAM. "Letters from Jack London." Journal of the
     West, 5 (April), 291-93.
          They reveal his "courage and power as a man, as well as
     a writer" and his extraordinary commitment "to his private
     world of thought and emotion." They should be read for
     "fun and insight [and] some invaluable instruction to
     writers."

25   NEWELL, GORDON, ed. The H. W. McCurdy Marine History of the
     Pacific Northwest. Seattle: Superior Publishing Company,
     pp. 203-204, 212, 248-49.
          Briefly describes several ships associated with London's
     career and with Captain Alexander McLean, model for Larsen.

26   PETERSON, CLELL T. "The Theme of Jack London's 'To Build a
     Fire.'" ABC, 17, no. 3 (November), 15-18.
          The journey of the nameless hero suggests the "archetypal
     theme of rebirth"; but London's Everyman is "modern, sen-
     sual, rational man" who fails to achieve illumination be-
     cause he lacks imagination and "has ceased to feel the
     primitive pulse beat of his own life." Whiteness and ab-
     sence of daylight symbolize the unknowable world where
     reason fails. Variations on two motifs--"the struggle of
     man against nature and 'love of life'"--in "To Build a
     Fire" (1902 and 1908) and "Love of Life" (1905) show the
     maturing of London's thought and artistry and his movement
     "from comic to tragic vision."

27   PRICE, LAWRENCE MARSDEN. The Reception of United States Litera-
     ture in Germany. Chapel Hill: University of North Carolina
     Press, pp. 57, 121, 123, 124, 130-32, 133, 148, 185, 221.
          London's works have been popular in Germany since before
     World War I. His adventure tales are most prized, and
     Martin Eden and The Iron Heel are "valuable propagandist
     works for the Socialists." London was blacklisted by the
     Nazis. Lists 8 works about London written in German,
     1924-1960.

28   SAVOLAINEN, ERKKI. "Helsinki is Talking About: Jack London
     Fans." San Francisco Chronicle (1 December), p. 10.
          Since 1907, London has been popular with the Finns for
     his devotion to the outdoors and his social commentary.
     Criticism has been generally favorable, and London has in-
     fluenced several Scandinavian writers.

29   SHIVERS, ALFRED S. "Jack London Letters." ABC, 16, no. 5
     (January), 3-4.
          They help us appreciate his "world-wide popularity" and

great generosity. "One learns to like London very much as a person of amazing courage, forthrightness, gusto, and heart."

30 TANNER, TONY. "London Calling." Spectator, 217 (19 August), 234.
    Letters reveal "a sort of classic 'progress' of the young self-made American writer."

31 TWENEY, GEORGE H. "Letters from Jack London." WAL, 1 (Spring), 66, 68.
    London's "rugged realism" paved the way for Lewis, Dreiser, Hemingway, Faulkner, and Steinbeck. His life and thought have "generally been greatly misunderstood," and the letters reveal him speaking for himself.

32 WALCUTT, CHARLES CHILD. Man's Changing Mask: Modes and Methods of Characterization in Fiction. Minneapolis: University of Minnesota Press, pp. 240-41.
    London's popularity depends on his ideas, on his dramatization of "the popular image of Darwin and Spencer forcibly conglomerated into a structure of rebellious socialism."

33 WALKER, FRANKLIN. The Seacoast of Bohemia. Book Club of California Publication no. 122. San Francisco: Book Club of California, pp. 34-52, 84-94, 115-19, and passim.
    London and Sterling met in 1901, remained lifelong friends and companions in philandering. The Londons visited the Sterlings in Carmel in 1906 for a "frenetic party which lasted for five days." A second visit, for two weeks in February, 1910, is partly described in The Valley of the Moon. Jim Hopper is the "Carmelite" and Sterling is Mark Hall. On March 11, 1910, London bought 14 plots from Lewis [see Walker, 1953.B2]. Sterling also sold plots to London and read proof for him. Sterling sold him a completed play, "The First Poet," for $25; London published it in Cosmopolitan (1911) and in The Turtles of Tasman (1916) without crediting Sterling. Revised edition: 1973.B50.

34 _____. "To Keep the Pot Boiling: Letters from Jack London." Nation, 202 (24 January), 105-107.
    London is seen by ordinary folk "as a rebel with stamina, an Alger boy who made good, a spirited adventurer whose life was as exciting as his books."

35 _____. "Frank Norris and Jack London." Mills College Magazine, series 56, no. 4 (Spring), 15-23.

They never met or corresponded; their origins and lives differed radically. Both, however, were special students at the University of California, disliked their English courses, and earned poor grades. Both were "apostles of adventure," admired Kipling, "extolled frontier life and the Anglo-Saxon fighting spirit" in fiction with mingled romantic and realistic elements. In July, 1902, they published stories identical in plot to one another and to two stories, based on a newspaper article, published in 1901. Where Norris concentrated on creating atmosphere through local color, London emphasized the obsession of the murderer, in the style of Poe.

36 WARNER, RICHARD H. "A Contemporary Sketch of Jack London." AL, 38 (November), 376-78.
A memoir (of 1916) by Marshall Bond, who met London in Dawson in 1897 and visited him in Oakland later. "During his period of development the man was leonine in courage, brilliant in speech, loyal and independent. The impression lasts over all these years that 'Here was a man.'"

37 WATERS, HAL. "Anna Strunsky and Jack London (Based on Exclusive Interviews in 1963 and 1964)." ABC, 17, no. 3 (November), 28-30.
Describes Strunsky's involvement with the London divorce; reprints a newspaper article on the subject; and quotes Strunsky's impressions of London.

38 WINGFIELD, WILLIAM. "Jack London's Forlorn Dream: The Wolf House Ruins Stand as His Real Memorial, the Legacy and Monument to the Great Writer, Just as He Predicted." The West, 5, no. 2 (July), 10-13, 49-50.
"Wyatt Earp was a close friend" of London's in the Yukon. In Santa Rosa London discussed agriculture with Luther Burbank and went on drinking sprees with Earl Rogers. He tried to establish a "private dukedom" in Sonoma "to create his own name and have his own family." Gives biography, describes the Ranch and London's death. Reprinted: 1974.B34.

39 WOODBRIDGE, HENSLEY C. "Jack London: A Bibliography: A Supplement." ABC, 17, no. 3 (November), 32-35.
Additions to Woodbridge, 1966.A6 of materials to September 1, 1966.

40 YOUNG, PHILIP. Ernest Hemingway: A Reconsideration. University Park: Pennsylvania State University Press, pp. 199-200.

The Sea-Wolf "came without a blush from" Moran of the
Lady Letty "but introduced Hemingway's Harry Morgan in a
character called Wolf Larson [sic]."

1967 A BOOKS

1   GILES, JAMES RICHARD. "A Study of the Concept of Atavism in
    the Writings of Rudyard Kipling, Frank Norris, and Jack
    London." Ph.D. dissertation, University of Texas.
    Revised: 1969.B15; 1969.B16; 1970.B17.

2   McMILLAN, MARILYN JOHNSON. "Jack London's Reputation as a
    Novelist: An Annotated Bibliography." Master's thesis,
    Sacramento State College.
        Entries are arranged alphabetically by title of the
    novel. Annotates articles and reviews (no titles given).
    93 leaves. Abridged text, in part: 1967.B14.

3   PRICE, STARLING WORTH. "Jack London's America." Ph.D. disser-
    tation, University of Minnesota.

1967 B SHORTER WRITINGS

1   ALLSOP, KENNETH. Hard Travellin': The Hobo and His History.
    New York: New American Library, pp. 105, 202-203, 212,
    255-59.
        London was "the first American writer of stature to
    write about hobo life from the inside." Resembling Gorky
    in many ways, he defined and himself symbolized the new
    man, tough, independent, and sympathetic to the lower class
    struggle. Gives excerpts from The Road and essays.

2   ANON. "London, Jack," in Websters Biographical Dictionary.
    First Edition. Springfield, Massachusetts: G & C Merriam,
    p. 914.
        Brief biography.

3   BULLEN, JOHN S., ed. "Annual Bibliography of Studies in
    Western American Literature." WAL, 1 (Winter), 327.
        Lists secondary items on London. This bibliography
    appears regularly in the Winter (or February) issues of
    WAL, volumes 1-10 (1967-1976); it lists an average of 3
    London items per issue.

4   COAN, OTIS W. and RICHARD G. LILLARD. America in Fiction.
    Fifth edition. Palo Alto, California: Pacific Books,
    pp. 96, 152.
        A bibliography; mentions The Iron Heel.

1967

5   COREN, ALAN. "A Weakness for Strength." Punch, 252 (22 March), 435.
    London's four "most autobiographical" books (John Barleycorn, Revolution, The Road, The Abysmal Brute) expose the contradictions and paradoxes of his life: socialism vs. his "mad reactionary dream" of return to frontier innocence and primitive savagery; Marxism vs. Nietzschean racism. London was "a sentimental bully, a libertinous puritan, and an alcoholic advocate of prohibition." He managed to work out such conflicting principles only through his dog heroes.

6   ELLIS, JAMES. "A New Reading of The Sea-Wolf." WAL, 2 (Summer), 127-34.
    Larsen's headaches symbolize the tension "between his intellectual allegiance to a materialistic world and his aesthetic sense of the impossibility of living joyfully in such a world." Through a "Doppelgänger" relationship with Humphrey (later joined by Maud), Larsen is "fragmented by the incursion of idealism." He is "animal-man in the process of becoming human"; and his attempt to refute Humphrey's idealism provides the novel's central conflict. Larsen fails to destroy the idealists or his own idealistic part--the "human heart."

7   HAHN, EMILY. Romantic Rebels: An Informal History of Bohemianism in America. Boston: Houghton Mifflin, pp. 108-18, 119, 124, 292.
    "His ambition was to strike a blow for mankind and make the world a fit place for the underprivileged." Conservative socialists considered him "an impertinent radical," his own comrades questioned his money-making and high living, and others criticized his morals. No longer a rebel when he died, London had pioneered the rapprochement of Bohemia "with the forces of political revolution." Gives biography.

8   HOLMAN, C. HUGH. "Fiction: 1900-1930," in American Literary Scholarship: An Annual/1965. Edited by James Woodress. Durham, N. C.: Duke University Press, pp. 163, 174-75.
    Essay-review of major work on London.

9   HORTON, ROD W. and HERBERT W. EDWARDS. Backgrounds of American Literary Thought. Second edition. New York: Appleton-Century-Crofts, pp. 230, 239, 259.
    Mentions London.

10 HORVÁTH, ANTAL. "Jack London's Checkered Career in Hungary."
      HSE, 3 (December), 55-70.
      His first work in book form was Before Adam (1918), fol-
    lowed by The Call of the Wild (1921). A "veritable cult
    of Jack London" flourished from 1921-1930, with transla-
    tions in several editions of some 29 titles. The public
    "and even a handful of critics" admired his "narrative
    talent," settings, and heroes, and (for socialists) "his
    revolutionary tendencies." "London was unable to break in-
    to the inner sanctum of the Hungarian literary world." To
    1934 he remained the most popular foreign author; his repu-
    tation then dropped, enjoyed a "mild revival" in 1940-1944
    and after 1948 when his socialist ideas, critical realism,
    and exposure of evils in American society were emphasized
    as part of the nation's anti-capitalist campaign. From
    1954-1960, new editions, accurate biographies, and objec-
    tive critical estimates appeared. After 1960, "a dropping-
    off could be observed," but his "classic novels of adven-
    ture" still interest Hungarian readers.

11 HUTCHENS, JOHN K. "Penmen of the Golden West: 1. Heritage of
      the Frontier." SatR, 50 (23 September), 34-35, 97-98.
      London "may be the most popular of all native California
    authors." He left "a permanent mark on American litera-
    ture--...as the rugged, life-hungry forerunner of Heming-
    way in the cult of courage, violence, and the revolt
    against the genteel tradition."

12 LABOR, EARLE. "Jack London's Mondo Cane: The Call of the Wild
      and White Fang." JLN, 1 (July-December), 2-13.
      London deliberately wrote to entertain his readers and
    not tax their brains. His seemingly effortless work "is
    difficult for the critics because he is so easy for his
    reader." But in his "beast fables," London actually dealt
    with forbidden subjects of human sexuality and unscrupulous
    behavior. In "Bâtard," an "anatomy of hatred," the dog
    symbolizes "man's unconscious brute impulses." The Call of
    the Wild is "a projection of the reader's essential mythic
    self, a dynamic symbol of libido, elan vital, the life
    force." It is a redemptive human allegory. In contrast,
    White Fang, more intellectualized and artificial, remains
    a memorable dog story and an "initiation story." Excerpted
    and revised from 1961.A4; revised: 1974.A3.

13 LABOR, EARLE and KING HENDRICKS. "Jack London's Twice-Told
      Tale." SSF, 4 (Summer), 334-41.
      London wrote two versions of "To Build a Fire," one for
    The Youth's Companion (1901), the other for Century

<u>Magazine</u> (1908). The first is a "well-made boys' story" with autobiographical elements, direct narrative, and an "<u>exemplum</u>" form. The second employs imagery and symbolism to create a "somber and sinister" atmosphere and ironic tone. The dog as "'reflector'" and foil points up the man's lack of imagination and wisdom. The story has been anthologized 49 times.

14   McMILLAN, MARILYN, comp. "Unrecorded Contemporary Reviews of London's Novels." <u>JLN</u>, 1 (July-December), 14-17.
     Lists periodical reviews of 15 novels (without titles or annotation). Abridged text of 1967.A2.

15   MARTIN, JAY. <u>Harvests of Change: American Literature, 1865-1914</u>. Englewood Cliffs, N. J.: Prentice-Hall, pp. 62, 208, 234-39.
     London "wrote in a philosophical tradition rather than a literary one"; he imaginatively transforms ideologies and ideas into action. He tried "to abolish the mythical supports of conventional social, economic, and philosophical attitudes by confronting these with the actualities of human aspiration and frustration." His works did not support individualism or "enact Roosevelt's Strenuous Life or Nietzsche's Superman"; rather, as suggested in <u>The Iron Heel</u>, he foresaw the eventual triumph of group strength, cooperative endeavor, and socialism as "the health of the state and the cure for the alienated individual." The balance of social commitment and celebration of individual force in <u>Martin Eden</u> and <u>The Sea-Wolf</u> provides "the basic tension of the tragedy in psyche and society." London's life and mind demonstrate "the multiplicity of the modern mind" predicted by Charles and Henry Adams.

16   REES, DAVID. "Clear, White Light." <u>Spectator</u>, 218 (24 March), 343-44.
     "The true interest of his books lies in the tension between the life of action and the life of acceptance" exposed with "terrible precision" in <u>John Barleycorn</u>. Drink is "the true Prince of Darkness of Jack London's life," and he succumbs to its self-destructive lure.

17   VANDERBEETS, RICHARD. "Nietzsche of the North: Heredity and Race in London's <u>The Son of the Wolf</u>." <u>WAL</u>, 2 (Fall), 229-33.
     Six of the nine tales reveal London's doctrine of supremacy of the white man and his contempt for the Alaskan Indian.

18 WALKER, DALE L. "Jack London (1876-1916)." ALR, 1 (Fall),
        71-78.
            A bibliography of writings about London, many critically
        annotated. Describes areas of work needed on London.

19 WALKER, FRANKLIN. "Ideas and Action in Jack London's Fiction,"
        in Essays on American Literature in Honor of Jay B. Hubbell.
        Edited by Clarence Gohdes. Durham, N. C.: Duke University
        Press, pp. 259-72.
            Ignored by critics, London remains alive as a folk hero,
        "the poor boy who made good, the radical who successfully
        challenged the Establishment, the hyperthyroid extrovert
        who lived dangerously and adventurously for all of his
        forty years." His best works are the Klondike escapist
        adventure yarns. The Iron Heel, in which Everhard--who
        is Jack London--prophetically advances a variety of ideas,
        is "ineptly done"; it has a "derivative and tenuous" plot,
        artificial narrative, and pervasive "tone of unreality."
        The Valley of the Moon is unconvincing since London's own
        back-to-the-land ventures failed. The Scarlet Plague,
        which presents ideas "quietly and without distortion....
        merits a wider reading public."

20 WALKER, WARREN. Twentieth-Century Short Story Explication:
        Interpretations, 1900-1966, of Short Story Fiction Since
        1800. Hamden, Connecticut: Shoestring Press, pp. 442-43.
            Lists thirteen London items. Supplements: 1970.B45;
        1973.B51.

21 WOODBRIDGE, HENSLEY C., comp. "Additional Reviews." JLN, 1
        (July-December), 18-19.
            Additions to 1966.A6; lists 36 reviews (without titles)
        in English and Italian.

1968 A BOOKS

1 BUBKA, TONY. "A Jack London Bibliography: A Selection of Re-
        ports Printed in the San Francisco Bay Area Newspapers:
        1896-1967." Master's Thesis, San Jose State College.
        330 leaves.
            Lists articles by and about London with full titles and
        (for most) annotations. Arranged topically in twenty-
        five sections. Discusses bibliographical procedures,
        sources, published work on London; and gives a biographi-
        cal chronology. Complete table of contents printed:
        1968.B19 and 1973.A7; sections printed, 1969.B4.

1968

*2   FAIRBANKS, ROLLIN J. "The Impact of the Wild on Henry David
        Thoreau, Jack London, and Robinson Jeffers." Ph.D. disser-
        tation, University of Otago (Dunedin, New Zealand).
        Cited in 1975.B29.

3   LONDON, JOAN. Jack London and His Times: An Unconventional
        Biography. Americana Library Series no. 9. Seattle:
        University of Washington Press, 402 pp.
        Reprint of 1939.A1 with a new introduction by the author.
        Same, in paperback edition, 1969. Reprinted: 1974.A6.

4   McCLINTOCK, JAMES IRVIN. "Jack London's Short Stories."
        Ph.D. dissertation, Michigan State University.
        Revised: 1970.B30; 1972.B25; 1975.A1.

1968 B SHORTER WRITINGS

1   ALLATT, EDWARD. "Jack London and Upton Sinclair." JLN, 1
        (January-June), 22-27.
        They knew one another for a dozen years, corresponded,
        but met only three times. Sinclair disapproved of Lon-
        don's drinking and life style, and London disliked Sin-
        clair's sexual puritanism. Prints London's endorsement
        of The Jungle.

2   ANON. "London (John Griffith)," in British Museum Catalogue
        of Printed Books: Ten-Year Supplement, 1956-1965. Volume
        28. London, pp. 358-61.
        Lists 29 London titles and 6 works about him.

3   ANON. "Wild and Tame." TLS (14 March), p. 263.
        Review of The Call of the Wild. London's dog novels
        survive because in writing them he was not handicapped by
        a lifelong "difficulty in understanding human beings."
        Parallels in his life and works to Hemingway are clear:
        "the mystique of manhood, the pride in toughness, the
        sense of life as a game or fight, and of nature as some-
        thing to pit oneself against."

4   BENOIT, RAYMOND. "Jack London's The Call of the Wild." AQ,
        20 (Summer), 246-48.
        In theme, structure, and style it is "a ritual enactment
        of the American wish to turn back to simplicity," a signi-
        ficant "pastoral protest" in the tradition of Thoreau,
        Twain, and their successors.

5   BYKOV, VIL. "The Traditions of Jack London." JLN, 1 (July-
        December), 62-66.

Harte, Kipling, Twain, Poe, Melville, Stevenson, Conrad, Norris, and Gorky influenced London's writing. Later writers whom he influenced are O'Neill, Lewis, Hemingway, Dos Passos, Kerouac, and several Russian authors.

6   DEANE, PAUL. "Jack London: The Paradox of Individualism." EngR, 19, no. 2 (1968), 14-19.
The unresolved conflict in London's work is between the individual and society. Buck submits his individualism to society, but civilization continually fails him and forces him to reassert his self-sufficient nature. White Fang is degraded when he becomes subservient to society. The Sea-Wolf synthesizes these themes: Larsen, the heroic individualist, dies; and Van Weyden regresses to a more primitive state of individuality but gains the understanding to apply his new strength for the betterment of society. Martin Eden's admirable individuality isolates him from society and brings him to suicide. The "balance of attitudes" in such works perhaps "speaks for itself."

7   FRENCH, WARREN. "Fiction: 1900-1930," in American Literary Scholarship: An Annual/1966. Edited by James Woodress. Durham, N. C.: Duke University Press, pp. 155-56.
Essay-review of major work on London.

8   GIBBS, JAMES A. Shipwrecks off Juan de Fuca. Portland, Oregon: Binfords & Mort, p. 142.
London found inspiration for The Sea-Wolf in the North Pacific sealing fleet.

9   GROSS, DALTON, ed. "Seventeen George Sterling Letters." JLN, 1 (July-December), 41-61.
Prints letters to "Wolf," November 11, 1910-October 29, 1915, and three to other persons after London's death. Sterling claimed London died "of twelve grains of morphine" because he was in love with both Charmian and an unidentified "white woman living in Hawaii."

10   KENYON, NINA NAOMI. "Self-Hatred as a Basis for Criticism of American Society." Ph.D. dissertation, St. Louis University.

11   LABOR, EARLE. "Notes: Jack London: An Addendum." AL, 2 (Spring), 91-93.
Addition of sixteen items, annotated, to 1966.A6.

12   McCARTHY, MARY. "Hanoi II." New York Review of Books (6 June), pp. 5-7.

1968

> Quotes a Vietnamese: "We have started to translate your
> progressive writers: Jack London and Mark Twain."

13   MARTÍ-IBÁÑEZ, FELIX. "The Poetry of Conduct and the Poetry of
      Circumstance." MD Medical Newsmagazine (December), pp. 9-
      16.
>   Gives plot summary of "To Build A Fire" (printed here,
> pp. 172, 174-80). "This is a perfect story" of a death
> struggle between cold and man. "Never was Jack London
> more successful in making us live through such tragic hours
> as these in which cold, ice, snow, solitude, and silence
> permeate the printed page." Reprinted: 1972.B26.

14   ORWELL, GEORGE. "Introduction to Love of Life and Other Sto-
      ries by Jack London," in The Collected Essays, Journalism
      and Letters of George Orwell: In Front of Your Nose.
      Edited by Sonia Orwell and Jan Angus. Volume 4. New York:
      Harcourt, Brace and World, pp. 23-29.
>   London was a complex man, "a Socialist with the instincts
> of a buccaneer and the education of a nineteenth-century
> materialist." He felt and exhibited a natural urge towards
> brutality, Nordic supremacy, and the triumph of the strong;
> but his experiences and sympathies lay with the working
> class, and "he hated exploitation and hereditary privi-
> lege." The Iron Heel, on which his reputation mainly
> rests, "is not a good book, and on the whole its predic-
> tions have not been borne out." However, London did for-
> see some aspects of totalitarianism, and he understood
> the mind of the ruling class. The theme of his fiction
> is "the cruelty of Nature. Life is a savage struggle,
> and victory has nothing to do with justice." Many of his
> best stories are objective presentations of this theme in
> an urban setting where his "glorification of brutality"
> is curbed by awareness of the sufferings caused by indus-
> trial capitalism. London is "a very uneven writer....
> Even his best stories have the curious quality of being
> well told and yet not well written." At least six of his
> works "deserve to stay in print": the stories in this
> volume and a few more; The Iron Heel, The Road, The Jacket,
> Before Adam, and The Valley of the Moon. This essay was
> written November, 1945 and originally published in the
> 1946 edition of Love of Life, London: Paul Elek.

15   SCHNECK, JEROME M. "Hypnotic and Non-Hypnotic Revivification
      with Special Reference to Jack London's 'Martin Eden.'"
      Psychiatric Quarterly, 42 (July), [504]-507.
>   The episode of Martin's intense re-living of the Cheese
> Face fight and his fainting ("revivification"), with his

subsequent confusion and gradual reorientation, is remarkably similar to some "hypnotic revivification experiences in clinical settings." Martin's experience illustrates "the overlap of waking and hypnotic behavior....Whether or not Jack London was familiar with such hypnotic behavior is a question that cannot be answered."

16　SINCLAIR, UPTON. "Is This Jack London?" in The First Occult Review Reader. Edited by Bernhardt J. Hurwood. New York: Award Books, pp. 13-26.
　　Reprint of 1930.B12 and 1931.B11; abridged version: 1941.B7.

17　WAGER, WILLIS. American Literature: A World View. New York: New York University Press, pp. 168, 172-74, 179.
　　London was "one of our first internationally famous Californians and earliest writers of proletarian literature." Gives biography.

18　WALKER, DALE L. "Note to the Next London Biographer." JLN, 1 (January-June), 28.
　　London met Robert ["Believe it or Not"] Ripley in 1911 when he covered the Johnson-Jeffries fight.

19　WOODBRIDGE, HENSLEY C. "More References Concerning Jack London." JLN, 1 (January-June), 34-40.
　　Additions to 1966.A6; lists books, parts of books, articles, and theses about London.

20　ZIFF, LARZAR. The American 1890's: Life and Times of a Lost Generation. New York: Viking, pp. 219, 253, 265, 274.
　　Mentions London.

1969 A BOOKS

1　BAMFORD, GEORGIA LORING. The Mystery of Jack London. Folcroft, Pennsylvania: Folcroft Press, 255 pp.
　　Reprint of 1931.A1.

2　[LIVINGSTON, LEON RAY]. From Coast to Coast With Jack London by A-No. 1. Grand Rapids, Michigan: Black Letter Press, 135 pp.
　　Reprint of 1917.A2.

3　[SCHLOTTMAN, DAVID H.], comp. "The Jack London Checklist." Olympia, Washington: Author (December). Typescript.

1969

Alphabetizes by titles of periodicals the English language materials listed in Woodbridge, 1966.A6.

1969 B SHORTER WRITINGS

1   ALLATT, EDWARD. "Upton Sinclair on Jack London in 1963."
    JLN, 2 (September-December), 77-78.
        Prints transcripts of two tape-recorded interviews with
    Sinclair.

2   BARRETT, ARTHUR. "[Introduction]," in his Jack London and Walt
    Whitman. New York: Odyssey, pp. 3-11.
        Fictionalized biography (for young readers). The rest
    of the volume contains selections by the two authors.

3   BLANCK, JACOB, comp. Bibliography of American Literature:
    Washington Irving to Henry Wadsworth Longfellow. Volume 5.
    New Haven: Yale University Press, 431-67.
        Lists first editions and locations; reprints; books con-
    taining materials by London.

4   BUBKA, TONY. "Introduction, Review of Literature, Summary and
    Conclusions as well as the Section: Death, Cremation and
    Burial from A Jack London Bibliography." JLN, 2 (January-
    April), 26-42.
        Describes procedures and problems of research; assesses
    published biographies of London, their inaccuracies re-
    vealed by data from newspapers. Lists articles about Lon-
    don in San Francisco Bay Area newspapers, with full nota-
    tion and some descriptive annotation. This is a section
    of Bubka's thesis, 1968.A1. Complete table of contents:
    1968.B19 and 1973.A7.

5   COLIN, VERA. "Book Review." JLN, 2 (September-December),
    105-13.
        Reviews Vil Bykov, Dzhek London (Izdatelstvo Saratskogo
    Univesiteta, 1968). Bykov attempts to analyze London's
    creative work in the context of his biography, socio-
    political opinions, and historical milieu. London's
    loyalty to socialism and faith in the masses endured. He
    paved the way for "socialist-realist literature in America."
    Rejoinder by Bykov: 1970.B5.

6   CONGER, LESLEY. "Off the Cuff: London Revisited." The Writer,
    82 (November), 6-8.
        Martin Eden, a once-favorite book, now embarrasses the
    reader with the "overwhelmingly nauseating" Ruth and Mar-
    tin's many enthusiasms. Thirty-five years ago it was up-
    lifting and revealing for the aspiring writer.

Jack London: A Reference Guide

7   CURLEY, DOROTHY NYREN, comp. "London, Jack," in her edition
    of A Library of Literary Criticism: Modern American Litera-
    ture. Fourth enlarged edition. Volume 2. New York:
    Ungar, 223-29.
        Gives excerpts from periodical articles, books, and
    introductions to London's works.

8   DAVIS, WILLIAM H. L. "My 1916 Visit to Jack London." JLN, 2
    (May-August), 55-65.
        Memoir of a meeting at the Sacramento Hotel, a drive back
    to Glen Ellen with London, and a stay at his ranch.

9   DEANE, PAUL. "Jack London: Mirror of His Time." LHR, 11
    (1969), 45-50.
        His work reflects the main ideas of his period: a pure
    attitude towards sex and man-woman relations; "naturalistic
    ethics and values"; Darwinian and Nietzschean theories;
    pessimism; sympathy for the underdog. Torn between social-
    ism and individualism, he never achieved "a consistent in-
    tellectual position," a failure which makes him representa-
    tive of his time.

10 DEKLE, BERNARD. "Jack London: The Call of the Wild," in his
    Profiles of Modern American Authors. Rutland, Vermont:
    Chas. E. Tuttle, pp. 25-31.
        Gives biography and criticism, derivative.

11 DHONDT, STEVEN T. "Jack London's When God Laughs: Overman,
    Underdog and Satire." JLN, 2 (May-August), 51-57.
        London's early poverty influenced these stories con-
    cerned with "the condition of the uneducated, unwashed,
    unfortunate underdog." The title story and "The Chinago,"
    in particular, show that man is generally controlled by
    societal or cosmic forces and must actively work to change
    oppressive institutions. Satire and irony inform both
    stories.

12 FINDLEY, SUE. "Naturalism in 'To Build a Fire.'" JLN, 2
    (May-August), 45-48.
        The protagonist is the force of nature. In "true Freu-
    dian fashion," London reveals the insignificance and help-
    lessness of man against a "consciously evil" active Nature.

13 FRENCH, WARREN. "Fiction: 1900-1950," in American Literary
    Scholarship: An Annual/1967. Edited by James Woodress.
    Durham, N. C.: Duke University Press, pp. 167, 174-75.
        Essay-review of major work on London.

1969

14   FURNAS, J. C. The Americans--A Social History of the United
      States, 1587-1914. New York: Putnam's, pp. 678, 680, 726,
      782, 871, 876, 915.
         Mentions London.

15   GILES, JAMES R. "Beneficial Atavism in Frank Norris and Jack
      London." WAL, 4 (Spring), 15-27.
         Norris, in Moran of the Lady Letty, and London, in The
      Son of the Wolf, The God of His Fathers, and A Daughter of
      the Snows, offer the concept of beneficial atavism: "be-
      lief in the healthful influence of a life of violence,
      emphasis on the ideal of an individual becoming a man by
      struggling with a hostile environment, and a complete ac-
      ceptance of Anglo-Saxon racism." Such atavism is bene-
      ficial when it occurs on a "frontier" or at sea; in con-
      trast, atavism occurring in an industrialized and civilized
      city environment is destructive. Excerpted and revised
      from 1967.A1.

16   _____. "Thematic Significance of the Jim Hall Episode in White
      Fang." JLN, 2 (May-August), 49-50.
         Environment has the power to mold animals and humans "in-
      to distinct personalities." Hall's prison experiences re-
      duce him to a bestial level; thus, the novel, and The Call
      of the Wild by extension, are brought "to the level of
      social commentary." Excerpted and revised from 1967.A1.

17   _____. "Jack London 'Down and Out' in England: The Relevance
      of the Sociological Study People of the Abyss to London's
      Fiction." JLN, 2 (September-December), 79-83.
         London shows that "the machinations of laissez faire
      capitalism" cause physical and mental dehumanization and
      debasement of the East Enders. Similarly, in other works,
      atavism occurring in urban environments is bad, but in
      wilderness areas it is beneficial. Excerpted and revised
      from 1967.A1.

18   JESPERSON, B. MOSBY. "Fifty Years Since Jack London Died."
      JLN, 2 (January-April), 1-4.
         Biography. Translated from the Danish by Henry A.
      Clausen; reprinted from Svendborg Avis (November, 1966).

19   JODY, MARILYN. "Alaska in the American Literary Imagination.
      A Literary History of Frontier Alaska with a Bibliographi-
      cal Guide to the Study of Alaskan Literature." Ph.D.
      dissertation, Indiana University.

20   LIBMAN, VALENTINA, comp. <u>Russian Studies of American Litera-</u>
       <u>ture: A Bibliography</u>. Translated by Robert V. Allen.
       Edited by Clarence Gohdes. Chapel Hill: University of
       North Carolina Press, pp. 118-28.
         Lists works by and about London published in Russian,
       1910-1963.

21   MARTINEZ, ELSIE WHITTAKER. "Jack London," in her <u>San Francisco</u>
       <u>Bay Area Writers and Artists</u>. Berkeley: University of
       California Bancroft Library, Regional Oral History Office.
       Bound Typescript, pp. 122-54.
         An interview conducted by Franklin D. Walker and Willa
       Klug Baum. Reminiscences by the daughter of London's
       friend Herman "Jim" Whittaker who was the wife of another
       friend, Xavier Martinez. Discusses London's personality
       and views; his philosophical conflicts; enthusiasm for
       socialism; relations with Anna Strunsky, his two wives,
       other women, and the Carmel writers group; the <u>Snark</u> voyage
       and Valley of the Moon ranch; London's disillusionment with
       life and suicide.

22   NICHOL, JOHN W., comp. "Jack London: A Bibliography, Addenda
       I." <u>JLN</u>, 2 (September-December), 84-87.
         Lists parts of books, articles, reviews (some with brief
       annotations).

23   ODESSKY, MARJORY H. "The Death of Jack London: Accident or
       Intent?" <u>Journal of Historical Studies</u>, 2:204-207.
         "The shape of London's personality, the overall pattern
       of his life, is not inconsistent with the classic psycho-
       sociological explanation of some suicides....the actual
       evidence so far publicly adduced leaves the question open."
       Gives biography and account of London's death (derivative).

24   PEARSALL, ROBERT BRAINARD. "Elizabeth Barrett Meets Wolf Lar-
       sen." <u>WAL</u>, 4 (Spring), 3-13.
         Although Maud Brewster resembles Anna Strunsky in some
       respects, she "is mostly Miss Barrett of Wimpole Street."
       London read the Brownings and refers to them throughout
       <u>The Sea-Wolf</u>. Maud has Elizabeth's physical and spiritual
       qualities, she is rich, well-educated, socially aware, a
       writer of sonnets and essays, and she believes that love
       is "passionate, spiritual, and intuitive." The relation-
       ship of Maud and Humphrey follows the love-legend of the
       Brownings.

25   POWELL, LAWRENCE. "California Classics Re-Read: <u>Martin Eden</u>."
       <u>Westways</u> (Automobile Club of Southern California), 61,
       no. 9 (September), 10-13, 45.

London is in the "mainstream of American literature": he was like Steinbeck in his deeply rooted love for California, and like Hemingway in their "celebration of the virile life," fascination with "their own maleness," and destruction by success. London's "tragedy was that he was never able to gear a manic-depressive nature to an ordered existence." Offers biography (from published sources and London's letters and essays); and briefly evaluates the novels. Revised: 1971.B29.

26   SCHMITT, PETER J. Back to Nature: The Arcadian Myth in Urban America. New York: Oxford University Press, pp. 125, 127-28, 135-37.
    Only in The Call of the Wild did London "raise the wilderness theme to serious art." His other Klondike tales seemed to many inaccurate or superficial. In later novels, the heroes seek escape from evils of urban life, worldly wealth, or poverty in simple Arcadian suburbs.

27   SHIVERS, ALFRED S. "Jack London: Not a Suicide." DR, 49 (Spring), 43-57.
    Presents evidence against the verdict of suicide: London's medical history, the impossibility of calculating a lethal dose of morphine, the very survival of notation pads and of the vials, the presence of a gun he did not use, and testimony of London's personal physician. He died of "uraemic poisoning," possibly complicated by "an innocent overdose" of morphine, combined with the alcohol he drank that evening.

28   STONE, IRVING. "Jack London's Klondike." Travel and Camera, 32, no. 8 (August), 45-57.
    London was a "flawed genius" who had everything a man could want. His flaw was his illegitimate birth and his life-long attempts to "repatriate his mother and father in his own mind." When London's "imagination ran out" and he wrote desperately for money, he perished. For a rebuttal, see Earle Labor, "An Open Letter to Irving Stone," JLN, 2 (September-December), 114-16.

29   WILCOX, EARL J. "Jack London's Naturalism: The Example of The Call of the Wild." JLN, 2 (September-December), 91-101.
    The novel is a "Darwinian or Spencerian allegory directly applicable to human existence," combined with elements of naturalistic theory. Analyzes plot. Excerpted and revised from 1966.A5.

30   [WOODBRIDGE, HENSLEY C.]. "Jack London: A Bibliography—A
      Supplement." JLN, 2 (January-April), 5-25.
         Additions to 1966.A6; lists works by and about London in
      English and foreign languages.

31   _____. "Foreign Language Collections and Anthologies." JLN,
      2 (May-August), 67-69.
         Additions to 1966.A6.

32   _____. "Material in English on London." JLN, 2 (May-August),
      71-72.
         Additions to 1966.A6; lists books and articles, some an-
      notated.

33   WOODBRIDGE, HENSLEY C. "Book Review." JLN, 2 (May-August),
      73-74.
         Describes Dzek London, a bibliography compiled by the
      All Soviet State Library of Foreign Literature (Moscow:
      Kniga, 1969), 147 pp. It lists 1327 items in Russian and
      English by and about London.

34   WOODWARD, ROBERT H., comp. "Jack London: A Bibliography,
      Addenda II." JLN, 2 (September-December), 88-90.
         Lists materials by and about London, and motion pictures
      based on his works.

1970 A BOOKS

1   COLLINS, BILLY GENE. "The Frontier in the Short Stories of
      Jack London." Ph.D. dissertation, Kansas State University.

2   GAER, JOSEPH, ed. Jack London: Bibliography and Biographical
      Data. Bibliography & Reference Series 383; American
      Classics in History & Social Science 161. New York: Burt
      Franklin, 45 pp.
         Reprint of 1934.A1.

3   GOWER, RONALD ALLAN. "The Creative Conflict: Struggle and
      Escape in Jack London's Fiction." Ph.D. dissertation,
      University of New Mexico.
         Excerpted: 1970.B19; 1971.B17.

1970 B SHORTER WRITINGS

1   ANON. "Introduction to the Poems." The London Collector, 1
      (July), 3-7.

231

1970

In his early years London wrote over thirty poems in various verse-forms to sharpen his writing skills and to make money. Prints four poems.

2 ANON. "A Long Distance Interview with Jack London." The London Collector, 1 (July), 7-8.
Reprint of 1916.B34.

3 BRAYBROOKE, NEVILLE. "The Hero Without a Name: B. Traven's 'The Death Ship.'" Library Review (Scotland), 22 (Autumn), 371-73.
The theme of the fight "against mammon" or the dictatorial power which money gives is also treated in London's The Iron Heel.

4 NO ENTRY.

5 BYKOV, VIL. "A Comment on Vera Colin's Review of Bykov's Dzhek London." JLN, 3 (January-April), 35-36.
Response to 1969.B5.

6 CHAPMAN, ARNOLD. "Between Fire and Ice: A Theme in Jack London and Horacio Quiroga." Symposium, 24 (Spring), 17-26.
Describes similarities in their lives. The stories, "To Build a Fire" and "La Isolación" (both 1908) share a theme: "the downfall of a man who, exposed to the wilderness fatally overlooks his body's limitations." Other resemblances include plot line; linking sense qualities of heat and cold to dramatic tension; protagonists who are selfish Anglo-Saxon outsiders driven by "blind will"; instinctively-wise dogs who provide ironic contrast and choric observation. Both writers "felt themselves participants in the huge American drama, where the sons and grandsons of Europe fling themselves against the last virgin lands,...to face another rejection and death."

7 DAY, MARTIN S. History of American Literature from the Beginning to 1910. Garden City: Doubleday, pp. 259-60.
Summarizes London's life and four works and indicates his debt to Spencer, Marx, and Nietzsche.

8 DeGRUSON, GENE. "Jack London and E. Haldeman-Julius." JLN, 3 (January-April), 1-7.
Describes their interview (See 1913.B41); quotes a letter to Joan London (1937); lists Haldeman-Julius pamphlets and articles on London, and his "Little Blue Book" issues of London's works. See also: 1970.B27; 1972.B20.

9 DHONDT, STEVEN T. "'There is a Good Time Coming': Jack London's Spirit of Proletarian Revolt." JLN, 3 (January-April), 25-34.
     London's youthful experience of poverty and hard work haunted him. The spirit of revolt is strong in "the Apostate," a satire on the ruling class of modern industrial society, and in "A Curious Fragment," a satire on ignorance.

10 DILLON, RICHARD H. "Jack London," in his Humbugs and Heroes: A Gallery of California Pioneers. Garden City: Doubleday, pp. 214-18.
     London was "touched with genius." His best works are the outdoor adventure tales; he failed to make the most of his talents. Gives biography.

11 ERBENTRAUT, EDWIN B. "The Intellectual Undertow in Martin Eden." JLN, 3 (January-April), 12-24.
     London's and Martin's conflict between individualism and socialism is compounded by a conflict of realism and materialism vs. mysticism, idealism, and sentimentality. The name "Eden" "symbolizes Paradise" and blissful ignorance. Martin is the "perfect man," combining physical, intellectual, and "spiritual, aesthetic power," who lives "in a world that doesn't measure up to his ideals." London's own melancholy and the parallels in the novel to the Christ story also illuminate the action and inevitablity of Martin's death.

12 _____. "The Symbolic Triad in London's The Little Lady of the Big House." JLN, 3 (September-December), 82-89.
     The novel reveals pressures London endured: Dick and Evan are the warring physical and psychical elements of his nature; Paula symbolizes "the sensitive, enveloping, cohesive element of London's psyche." The novel seeks a balance among these; and its value lies in "a number of glistening passages of description and dialog, in the exuberance...of London's presentation, and in the shining symbolism; life (Jack London's life, especially), is revealed by the book."

13 FRENCH, WARREN. "Fiction: 1900-1930," in American Literary Scholarship: An Annual/1968. Edited by J. Albert Robbins. Durham, N. C.: Duke University Press, pp. [177], 183-84.
     Essay-review of major work on London.

14 FUJIWARA, SAKAE. "A Summary of One Chapter From Jack London in Connection with the American Dream." JLN, 3 (September-December), 73-81.

London shows his lack of commitment to equality, true
Socialism, and the welfare of the weak in his roles as
muckraker; spokesman for evolutionary beliefs; admirer of
individualism, the Horatio Alger myth, Anglo-Saxon superiority, and supermen. His Socialism is not an ideology but
"the outlet of the twisted and frustrated American Dream."
From the writer's dissertation, Keio Gijyuku University,
Japan (1970).

15 GEISMAR, MAXWELL. "The Shifting Illusion: Dream and Fact," in
American Dreams, American Nightmares. Edited by David
Madden. Carbondale: Southern Illinois University Press,
p. 49.
London "started his fabulously successful career as a
popular fiction writer who embraced the cause of revolutionary socialism, only to end up as a disenchanted hack
writer, a paranoid alcoholic, an early advocate of fascism
and the superman."

16 GERSTENBERGER, DONNA and GEORGE HENDRICK. The American Novel,
1789-1959: A Checklist of Twentieth-Century Criticism:
II. Criticism Written 1960-1968. Denver: Swallow,
pp. 230-32.
Lists 51 articles and book references for London. A
supplement to 1961.B6.

17 GILES, JAMES R. "Some Notes on the Red-Blooded Reading of Kipling by Jack London and Frank Norris." JLN, 3 (May-August),
56-62.
London read Kipling superficially. He admired Kipling's
glorification of violence, Anglo-Saxon virility, and im-
perialism; he overlooked the "respect and basic humanity"
Kipling showed towards lesser races and the relation of
brutality and atavism to maintenance of the British Empire
and law. Excerpted and revised from 1967.A1.

18 GOLDSTEIN, JACK J. "Learning the Hard Way?" Serif, 7 (June),
36-37.
Notes a mysterious edition of The Call of the Wild.

19 GOWER, RONALD. "The Creative Conflict: Struggle and Escape
in Jack London's Fiction." JLN, 3 (September-December),
118-19.
Abridged version of 1971.B17.

20 GROSS, DALTON H. "George Sterling: The King of Carmel." ABC,
21, no. 2 (October), 8-16.
London did not influence Sterling's behavior, philosophy,

or artistic values, which were already formed by the time
they met in 1901. They had many beliefs in common. Their
life-long friendship "was the most important emotional relationship in the poet's adult life, a relationship so intense that it was very nearly erotic."

21 GUNN, DREWEY WAYNE. "Three Radicals and a Revolution: Reed,
    London, and Steffens on Mexico." SWR, 55 (Autumn), 393-
    410.
       In 1911 London expressed support for the Mexican revo-
    lutionaries in an open letter and his hatred of Diaz in
    "The Mexican." But as correspondent for Collier's in 1914,
    he sat out the war in the cafes of Vera Cruz. The effects
    of the Mexican venture were: he got dysentery; and he wrote
    "inferior" articles showing contempt for Mexican culture
    and the "chicken thief" revolutionists, indicating "to the
    socialists that he had sold out." "Ironically, in the
    twenties he became one of the most popular American writers
    in all Latin America." Revised: 1974.B15.

22 HAIGHT, ANNE LYON. Banned Books. Third edition. New York:
    Bowker, pp. 73, 110.
       London's works were banned in Italy and Yugoslavia in
    1929 and burned in Germany in 1932.

23 HAMBY, JAMES A. "Note on Jack London: A View in Oil." JLN,
    3 (September-December), 102-103.
       Describes two oil paintings by Maya Kelman (Charmian's
    dressmaker), painted after London's death.

24 HENDRICKS, KING. "Introduction," in The Road. Santa Barbara,
    California: Peregrine Smith, pp. i-xvi.
       The Road preserves "the emotions, the personality" of
    London and conveys "the youthful wanderlust spirit of the
    road." It records his reminiscences of travels over the
    Sierras to Reno and back, to Michigan, Nebraska, and
    Missouri, following and then deserting Kelly's Army, and
    to several places on the East Coast. These experiences
    made him decide to get an education and become a socialist.
    Gives biography and excerpts from London's road diary and
    essays.

25 HENDRICKS, KING and IRVING SHEPARD. "Introduction," in their
    edition of Jack London Reports: War Correspondence, Sports
    Articles, and Miscellaneous Writings. Garden City: Double-
    day, pp. [vii]-xix.
       London is now seen "as an interpreter of the ideals and
    desires of mankind." A complex, generous, honest man, an

outspoken critic of injustice and cruelty, "his genius was universal" as were his experiences. Gives biography; discusses records London kept of magazine submissions and rejections.

26 HENRY, JAMES L. "A Proposed Chronology of Editions of The Son of the Wolf." JLN, 3 (January-April), 8-11.
   Describes first editions and first states of this book. See 1970.B32.

27 JOHNSON, RICHARD COLLES and G. THOMAS TANSELLE. "The Haldeman-Julius 'Little Blue Books' as a Bibliographical Problem." PBSA, 64 (1970), 29-78.
   Lists eleven London works in this series, pp. 66-67, 74. See 1972.B20.

28 LABOR, EARLE. "'To The Man on the Trail': Jack London's Christmas Carol." JLN, 3 (September-December), 90-94.
   London's Northland Code teaches the need for physical hardiness tempered by compassion, respect, and love for one's fellow man. Revised and enlarged: 1974.A3.

29 LEARY, LEWIS, comp. Articles on American Literature, 1950-1967. Durham, N. C.: Duke University Press, pp. 345-46.
   Lists 56 items on London.

30 McCLINTOCK, JAMES I. "Jack London's Use of Carl Jung's Psychology of the Unconscious." AL, 42 (November), 336-47.
   For stories in On The Makaloa Mat, London drew on Jung's concepts of the libido, oedipal myths, and archetypal symbols of death and rebirth. The Jungian system was the last of many scientific theories through which London sought values and salvation; his search again ended in "enervating disillusionment." Revised and enlarged: 1975.A1.

31 McDEVITT, WILLIAM. "Jack London as Poet." The London Collector, 1 (July), 13-19.
   Reprint of essay in 1947.A2; reprinted: 1971.A3.

32 McNEEL, LAIRD. "More on The Son of the Wolf." JLN, 3 (September-December), 135-36.
   Additions to 1970.B26.

33 NASH, RODERICK. The Call of the Wild (1900-1916). American Culture Series. New York: Braziller, pp. 1-2.
   The Call of the Wild appealed as an allegory summoning overcivilized, confused Americans to return to Buck's

1970

"simple, vigorous, unrestrained life in the North." This
mood and message of primitivism is evident in the arts,
literature, and popular culture of the era.

34 NICHOL, JOHN. "The Role of 'Local Color' in Jack London's
Alaska Wilderness Tales." WR, 6 (Winter), 51-56.
London brought the techniques of the local color tradition to a new level of perfection by rejecting sentimentality and using environmental detail to create atmosphere
that intensifies the action, characterization, and a universal theme.

35 PAVESE, CESARE. American Literature: Essays and Opinions.
Translated by Edwin Fussell. Berkeley: University of
California Press, pp. 4, and passim.
In certain London novels, drinking is "a protest against
a social system which suffocates and denies life." This
myth is perpetuated in later American literature.

36 REXROTH, KENNETH. "Jack London's Native Sons," in his With
Eye and Ear. New York: Herder and Herder, pp. 167-70.
"His memory and his literary set,...represent a bygone
despotism of mediocrity,...At the name of Jack London I
bristle like a hedgehog at the sight of a hairbrush." His
career as "a provincial Walter Scott" brought him "nothing
but financial disasters and heart-break....He quite simply
drank himself to death." London never grew up or learned
from experience. His immaturity shows in "his relations
with George Sterling [which] were as homosexual as could
be"; and in his "refusal to accept woman as anything but
a deformed boy." London could not portray adults or adult
conflicts in his fiction: his heroes "behave like newsboys,
playground bullies and Eagle Scouts." His style is "nause-
ating, dated journalese," and his storytelling is of commercial quality, done "incomparably better" today in magazines and comic books. "So London's best stories are
about dogs. I, as a man, think they're better, but maybe
if dogs could read, they'd think they were kind of silly."

37 SHERKO, ARTHUR. "An Analogue for Lost Face." JLN, 3 (September-December), 95-98.
Canto twenty-nine of Ludovico Ariosto's Orlando Furioso
tells an age-old story which resembles in some details
London's idea.

38 SISSON, JAMES E., comp. "Jack London's Published Poems: A
Chronological Bibliography." The London Collector, 1
(July), 20-21.
Lists twelve poems.

237

1970

39 SLOANE, DAVID E. E. "David Graham Philips, Jack London, and
    Others on Contemporary Reviewers and Critics, 1903-1904."
    ALR, 3 (Winter), 67-71.
        Prints London's brief remarks on reviewers solicited by
    Bookman. London repeats the comment in Martin Eden "as a
    criticism of middle class readers." For rebuttal and
    response, see Cook, 1973.B12; Sloane, 1973.B42.

40 SPINNER, JONATHAN H. "Jack London's Martin Eden: The Develop-
    ment of the Existential Hero." MichA, 3,1:43-48.
        The novel "breaks through ["the westering myth and the
    Horatio Alger legend"] as one of the first fictional state-
    ments of American existentialism." Martin believes in the
    dream of success; urged by his Eve, he gains education,
    develops "introspective self-awareness," and success at
    tests of physical endurance. But lacking "mental tough-
    ness" and "emotional strength," he finds that hard work
    brings only "spiritual and intellectual" death in modern
    society. Martin responds to "his existential reality"--
    loneliness, alienation from his class, disillusionment with
    bourgeoisie values, and rejection of socialism--by escaping
    to the dream of paradise in the South Seas. He "kills him-
    self physically on route to his spiritual death....Suicide,
    from this desert of emotions, from this spiritual hell,
    becomes a positive act for Eden."

41 TILLETT, JEFFERY. "Introduction: Jack London, Son of the
    Wild," in Jack London: Twelve Short Stories. New York:
    St. Martin's, pp. 7-16.
        His writing is uneven because of "his inability to be
    selective in what he read,...his chequered education,"
    and his rigid writing schedule which left little time for
    revision. The fictions' great qualities include imagina-
    tion, theme of struggle, physical energy, and savage humor.
    Gives a detailed biography.

42 TROTSKY, LEON. "Jack London's The Iron Heel," in Leon Trotsky
    on Literature and Art. Edited by Paul N. Siegel. New
    York: Pathfinder Press, pp. [221]-24.
        An excerpt from Trotsky's letter (October 16, 1937) to
    Joan London. In its social analysis, vivid expression of
    the evils of capitalism, and unique prophetic vision, Lon-
    don's novel attests to the courageous "powerful intuition
    of the revolutionary artist."

43 WALKER, DALE L. "Jack London, Sherlock Holmes, and the Agent."
    The Baker Street Journal, NS 20, no. 2 (June), 79-85.

London never met Doyle, but he probably read his work in 1899-1903. He "wrote no detective fiction" but there are "several touches of Holmes" in such novels as Jerry of the Islands, The Mutiny of the Elsinore, and the first part of The Assassination Bureau, Ltd. London shows familiarity with Holmes's deductive method in "A Goboto Night." "London was a conscious Sherlockian....at least a fascinated follower" of the Holmes stories. Enlarged: 1974.A8.

44 _____. "How Sinclair Lewis Sold Jack London the Idea for 'Tarzan of the Apes'; Or Twoupmanship in the Game of Literary Antecedents." ERB-dom, 37 (August), 12-16.
Burroughs may have gotten the inspiration for Tarzan from London's "When the World Was Young" (1910), whose plot London purchased from Lewis; or from other London novels and stories published before 1911.

45 WALKER, WARREN. Twentieth-Century Short Story Explication: Supplement I, 1967-69. Hamden, Connecticut: Shoestring Press, p. 158.
Additions to 1967.B20; Supplement II: 1973.B51.

46 WARD, A. C. "London, Jack," in Longman's Companion to Twentieth-Century Literature. London: Longman, p. 371.
His "spendthrift habits, ostentatious hospitality, and alcoholism...led to the dwindling of his creative abilities." Once dismissed by critics, "he has now returned as literature." Most of his fiction is "unlikely to attain academic repute," but The Call of the Wild and White Fang are of "classic rank." Gives biography.

47 WESTON, ROGER. "'Before I Die,--I'll Have 1,000 Women!'" in The World's Greatest Lovers. Edited by Phil Hirsch. New York: Pyramid Books, pp. 94-108.
Fictionalized biography of London's adventures with the whores of the world.

48 WILCOX, EARL. "Le Milieu, Le Moment, La Race: Literary Naturalism in Jack London's White Fang." JLN, 3 (May-August), 42-55.
This novel and Before Adam "constitute the high water mark of London's blatant use of evolutionary concepts in two tawdry pieces of naturalistic fiction." White Fang is "hack work in its artistry and uninspiring in its philosophy." Its importance lies in its full-blown naturalism modified somewhat by Spencerian evolutionary doctrine and in its parallels and contrasts to The Call of the Wild. Excerpted and revised from 1966.A5.

JACK LONDON: A REFERENCE GUIDE

1971

1971 A BOOKS

1   ANON. Jack London: A Sketch of His Life and Work; With Por-
     trait. Cedar Springs, Michigan: Wolf House Books.
     Facsimile reprint of 1905.A1.

2   DAY, A. GROVE. Jack London and the South Seas. New York:
     Four Winds Press, 169 pp.
     Juvenile biography.

3   McDEVITT, W[ILLIA]M. Jack London as Poet and as Platform Man.
     Did Jack London Commit Suicide? Cedar Springs, Michigan:
     Wolf House Books.
     Facsimile reprint of 1947.A2; part reprinted in 1970.B31.

4   What's New About London, Jack? 1, no. 1 (10 July), 5 pp.; 1,
     no. 2 (14 August), 9 pp.; 1, no. 3 (25 September), 7 pp.;
     1, no. 4 (13 November), 4 pp.; 1, no. 5 (25 December),
     6 pp.
     Mimeographed. All issues offer annotated primary and
     secondary bibliography, news items, and notes; occasionally
     prints stories or essays by London.

1971 B SHORTER WRITINGS

1   ANON. "London and the Daily Worker." JLN, 4 (January-April),
     54-55.
     A query about London's works published in this paper
     after his death.

2   ASIMOV, ISAAC. "Two Out-of-print Masterpieces by Jack London."
     The London Collector, 2 (April), 27-28.
     Reprint of 1963.A1.

3   BAIRD, NEWTON D. and ROBERT GREENWOOD. An Annotated Bibliogra-
     phy of California Fiction, 1664-1970. Georgetown, Cali-
     fornia: Talisman Literary Research, pp. 276-80.
     Briefly describes and evaluates 19 London novels and
     gives, for each, a few locations of reviews and critical
     comment.

4   BOGARD, WILLIAM JUDDSON. "The West as A Cultural Image at
     the End of the Nineteenth Century." Ph.D. dissertation,
     Tulane University.

5   BOLL, T. E. M. "The Divine Fire (1904) and Martin Eden (1909)."
     ELT, 14:115-17.
     London congratulated May Sinclair on her novel, whose

hero-poet Rickman is a dynamic monist, inspired by a woman
to rise to great social and creative heights. "It seems
quite possible" that this work inspired London's novel,
although London, devoted to his own truth, saw "a different
outcome with a different writer meeting a different woman."

6   BOWEN, JAMES K.   "Notes: Jack London's 'To Build a Fire':
     Epistemology and the White Wilderness."   WAL, 5 (Winter),
     287-89.
        Animals, but not men, may rely on instinct for survival.
     The traveller "of limited mental capacity" fails; but the
     old-timer who uses "good judgment, tempered with emotional
     insights" survives.

7   BRIGGS, JOHN E.   "Comment by the Editor: An Impulsive Youth."
     Palimpsest, 52 (June), 347-52.
        London's "character was scarred and his judgment warped
     by what he saw of social injustice" on the road; but it
     was here he learned the art of storytelling.   Gives biog-
     raphy.   Comment follows reprint of "Tramping with Kelly
     Through Iowa: A Jack London Diary," pp. 316-46.

8   BYKOV, VIL.   "Memorable Dates: New Facts About Jack London."
     JLN, 4 (January-April), 47-48.
        Describes literary activity on London in Russia.   Trans-
     lated by Samuel Sorgenstein; reprinted from Literaturnaia
     Rossia, 3, no. 419 (15 January).

9   CADY, EDWIN H.   The Light of Common Day: Realism in American
     Fiction.   Bloomington: Indiana University Press, pp. 47,
     48, 51.
        Mentions London.

10   DeJOVINE, F. ANTHONY.   The Young Hero in American Literature:
     A Motif for Teaching Literature.   New York: Appleton-
     Century-Crofts, pp. 36-37, 65, 86, 102-103, 118-19, 134.
        Compares Martin Eden with other fictional young men.
     Briefly analyzes paradox and symbolism in Martin Eden.

11   DODSON, MARY KAY.   "Naturalism in the Works of Jack London."
     JLN, 4 (September-December), 130-39.
        London demonstrates that heredity and environment de-
     termine one's fate through his animal characters and men
     who resemble beasts: Buck, Diable, Black Leclere, Captain
     Decker, Wolf Larsen.

12   EICHELBERGER, CLAYTON L., comp.   A Guide to Critical Reviews
     of United States Fiction, 1870-1910.   Metuchen, N. J.:
     Scarecrow Press, pp. 203-205.

241

1971

Lists locations of 78 reviews (without titles) of London's works. For Supplement, see 1974.B9.

13   ERBENTRAUT, EDWIN B. "'A Thousand Deaths': Hyperbolic Anger."
      JLN, 4 (September–December), 125–[129].
      In this story (1899), "clear indications are found of
      London's anger and anxiety arising from the clouded father-
      question." Analyzes biographical parallels.

14   FLINK, ANDREW. "The Three Faces of the Wolf House." JLN, 4
      (September–December), 151–55.
      London's favorite boyhood book was Irving's The Alhambra.
      Wolf House, the Big House in The Little Lady of the Big
      House, and the Alhambra are similar in location and archi-
      tectural style.

15   FRENCH, WARREN. "Fiction: 1900–1930," in American Literary
      Scholarship: An Annual/1969. Edited by J. Albert Robbins.
      Durham, N. C.: Duke University Press, pp. 206–207.
      Essay-review of major work on London.

16   GLANCY, DONALD R. "Jack London and 'Billy the Kid.'" ABC,
      22, no. 3 (November–December), 5.
      This play, ascribed to London, was in fact written by
      Walter Woods, copyrighted August 14, 1903.

17   GOWER, RONALD A. "The Creative Conflict: Struggle and Escape
      in Jack London's Fiction." JLN, 4 (May–August), 77–114.
      Among many reasons for London's poor literary reputation
      are the unevenness of his work and critics' emphasis on
      his flamboyant life style, Socialism, ideological incon-
      sistencies, and historical era. London's continued popu-
      larity with the public, however, rests on such qualities
      as his strength of style, vitality of autobiographical
      works, convincing portrayals of humanity, and quest for
      meaning in the struggles—for survival, love, power, jus-
      tice—among men and between man and society. His central
      theme is "that all of life is a battle, that action, con-
      flict, and struggle are the essence of life." His work
      moves through three phases in a cyclical pattern which
      parallels his life. First, he deals with physical battles,
      simple emotional experiences, and direct action; this is
      his best work. Second, he dramatizes philosophical con-
      flicts which brings complexity and self-consciousness to
      the work. Third, in his late and poorest writing, he re-
      turns to "nature and love" for the meaning of the struggle
      but finds only confusion, despair, and suicide. Represen-
      tative of a transitional period, London was influenced by

the movement from frontier to civilization, Roosevelt's
"American work-ethic," philosophies of Spencer, Marx, Darwin, and Nietzsche, and literary-societal tensions of his
era. Gives biography. This article is the "Introduction"
and chapters 1 and 6 from dissertation, 1970.A3. Abridged:
1970.B19.

18 GRENANDER, M. E. <u>Ambrose Bierce</u>. TUSAS. New York: Twayne,
pp. 71, 163.
Bierce detested London's socialism and his involvement
with George Sterling.

19 HAVLICE, PATRICIA PATE. <u>Index to American Author Bibliogra-
phies</u>. Metuchen, N. J.: Scarecrow Press, p. 105.
Lists ten items for London.

20 JOHNS, FRANCIS A. "Addendum to Woodbridge: Jack London: A
Bibliography." <u>PBSA</u>, 65 (First Quarter), 74.
Notes a variant edition of <u>The Strength of the Strong</u>.

21 JONES, HOWARD MUMFORD. <u>The Age of Energy: Varieties of American Experience, 1865-1915</u>. New York: Viking, pp. 147, 163,
252, 414.
Mentions London.

22 LACHTMAN, HOWARD. "<u>Daughters of the Rich</u>: A New Jack London
Play." <u>JLN</u>, 4 (January-April), 11-15.
The theme is "the moral penalty of worldly success."

23 LEITHEAD, J. EDWARD. "The Klondike Stampede in Dime Novels."
<u>ABC</u>, 21, no. 4 (January), 23-29.
Mentions London: his tales "are still among the best of
their kind."

24 MOTTRAM, ERIC. "London, Jack," in <u>The Penguin Companion to
American Literature</u>. Edited by Malcolm Bradbury, et al.
New York: McGraw-Hill, pp. 156-57.
"In many ways London is the archetypal popular twentieth-
century novelist; his conflicts are still central." Gives
biography and notes works.

*25 NEWELL, GORDON. "Way of the Sea Wolf," in his <u>Sea Rogues'
Gallery</u>. Seattle: Hangman Press, pp. 38-47.
Story of Captain Alex McLean, the model for Wolf Larsen.
Cited in <u>What's New About London, Jack?</u>, 2, no. 2
(11 March 1972), p. 13.

1971

26   NOTO, SAL. "Jack London as Social Critic." <u>JLN</u>, 4 (September-
      December), 145-50.
          London's writings express his concern for the problems
      of society and his faith in the workingman. <u>The People of
      the Abyss</u> shows anger at the results of English capitalism;
      <u>Martin Eden</u> reveals how society stifles the individual; and
      "The Dream of Debs" is a "crusade in itself for organized
      labor."

27   PARKAY, FORREST WINSTON. "The Influence of Nietzsche's <u>Thus
      Spoke Zarathustra</u> on London's <u>The Sea-Wolf</u>." <u>JLN</u>, 4
      (January-April), 16-24.
          Both heroes assert the will to power and the will to
      live, they stress the physical and deny the existence of
      good and evil. Larsen "fails as the Nietzschean overman,
      and Zarathustra fails in his quest to find his supreme
      being." London ultimately found Nietzsche "disillusioning
      and sterile."

*28   PHILLIPS, GARY JAMES. "Moonface the Murderer." <u>WN</u>, 8 (Febru-
      ary), 13.
          This label applied to Earwicker in <u>Finnegans Wake</u> is a
      reference to London's "Moonface." Cited in <u>Abstracts of
      English Studies</u>, 15:334.

29   POWELL, LAWRENCE CLARK. "<u>Martin Eden</u>: Jack London," in his
      <u>California Classics: The Creative Literature of the Golden
      State</u>. Los Angeles: Ward Ritchie, pp. 185-95.
          "His biography should be required reading in writing
      classes to encourage persistence against the obstacles of
      poverty and lack of education, as well as to warn against
      the perils of unbridled success in the form of money and
      fame." A slightly enlarged version of 1969.B25.

30   REDLIKH, FYODOR. "Lake Jack London." <u>Soviet Life</u>, 2 (Febru-
      ary), 51-53.
          In the 1930's, geologists accidently dropped a book of
      London's into this lake in the Kolyma Range and named
      the lake after him.

31   RICHARDSON, KENNETH RIDLEY. "London, Jack," in his edition of
      <u>Twentieth-Century Writing: A Reader's Guide to Contemporary
      Literature</u>. Levittown, N. Y.: Transatlantic Arts, p. 380.
          London is "now read in the English-speaking world chiefly
      for his extravert and often brutal adventure stories,"
      and the Communist world admires his Socialistic work.

32 SILET, CHARLES L. P. and SHARON SPERRY SILET, eds. "Charmian
    London to Upton Sinclair: Selected Letters." JLN, 4 (Janu-
    ary-April), 25-46.
        Letters exchanged, 1916-1941. Reprints Charmian's and
    summarizes Sinclair's. Letters include biographical com-
    ment on and interpretation of London, his views on spiri-
    tualism and telepathy, his purchase of plots from Sinclair
    Lewis.

33 SISSON, JAMES E., comp. "Jack London's Plays: A Chronological
    Bibliography," in his edition of Jack London. Daughters of
    the Rich. Oakland, California: Holmes Book Co., pp. [17-
    20].
        Lists seventeen plays.

34 SISSON, JAMES E. "Introduction," in his edition of Jack Lon-
    don's Articles and Short Stories in The (Oakland) High
    School Aegis. The London Collector, No. 3 (1971), pp. 1-
    [8] (Whole issue, 44 pp., contains facsimile reprints of
    London's stories and sketches); also published, Grand
    Rapids, Michigan: Wolf House Books.
        In these early writings, published January 18 to Decem-
    ber 18, 1895, "one recognizes imagery, characters, themes,
    and stylistic devices that would reach full maturity" in
    the later fiction. Gives chronological list of Aegis
    publications.

35 _____. Review of The Road. JLN, 4 (January-April), 49-52.
        Describes contents. "A vital document in understanding
    the man and the writer." It is a fresh and vivid record
    of London's insights and America's optimism.

36 SOLENSTEN, JOHN. "Richard Harding Davis' Rejection of 'The
    Call of the Wild.'" JLN, 4 (May-August), 122-23.
        Davis, in "The Nature Faker" (1911), repudiates the
    values of primitive natural life in the novel.

37 STANSKY, PETER and WILLIAM ABRAHAMS. The Unknown Orwell. New
    York: Knopf, pp. 135-36, 139-40, 160, 230-33, 277-78.
        The book that most affected Orwell while at Eton was The
    People of the Abyss. It moved him to later explore the
    East End and write Down and Out in Paris and London.

38 WALKER, DALE L. "The Famous Fantastic Jack London." The Lon-
    don Collector, 2 (April), 24-26.
        Describes London contributions in Famous Fantastic
    Mysteries [magazine] of 1947, 1948, 1949.

1971

39   WEIDERMAN, RICHARD. "Jack London: Master of Science Fiction."
     The London Collector, 2 (April), 14-23.
       Four novels, thirteen stories, and an unpublished play
     are "concerned with man's present and future life in so-
     ciety." They show the influence of Wells, Darwin, and
     Marx. The Star Rover evinces the prison life of Ed Morrell
     and London's own experience with hasheesh. Lists 17 pub-
     lished items of science fiction by London.

40   _____. "Scorn of Women: Jack London's Rarest First Edition."
     JLN, 4 (May-August), 119-21.
       Lists all first editions with number of copies published.

41   ZIEGENFUSS, ALAN JOHN. "Jack London: The 'Kipling of the
     Klondike'--His Historic Life and Times." Pacific Traveler,
     55:8-12, 26-27, 34.
       His basic themes were "greed and avarice, fidelity and
     loyalty, personal and social revenge, personal and racial
     conquest, and mental aberrations under extreme conditions."
     London reached peak power in 1910; thereafter, unhappy and
     bitter, he became an alcoholic and committed suicide.
     Since 1916, "he has become the most popular American author
     in the world." Gives biography, discusses works.

42   ZINN, HOWARD. "Introduction," in The Iron Heel. New York:
     Bantam Books, pp. vii-xiii.
       London confronted the evils of his time and ours: the
     "rule of corporate wealth"; governments' lawlessness,
     thievery, and suppression of dissent; and the "psychic and
     material insecurity" of modern man. London's solutions,
     the ballot box, then violent revolution, now seem inade-
     quate; but the novel still forces us to focus on present
     evils and seek their remedies.

1972 A BOOKS

1   ANON. Jack London: Who He Is and What He Has Done. Cedar
     Springs, Michigan: Wolf House Books, 16 pp.
       Facsimile reprint of 1908.A1

2   [IRVINE, ALEXANDER]. Jack London at Yale. Cedar Springs,
     Michigan: Wolf House Books, 28 pp.
       Facsimile reprint of 1906.A1.

3   JOHNSON, MARTIN E. Through the South Seas with Jack London.
     Cedar Springs, Michigan: Wolf House Books, 380 pp.
       Reprint of 1913.A1.

4   McDEVITT, W[ILLIA]M. Jack London's First. Cedar Springs,
        Michigan: Wolf House Books, 32 pp.
        Facsimile reprint of 1946.A1.

5   MOSBY, C. V. A Little Journey to the Home of Jack London.
        Cedar Springs, Michigan: Wolf House Books, 20 pp.
        Facsimile reprint of 1917.A4.

6   WALKER, DALE L., comp. The Fiction of Jack London: A Chrono-
        logical Bibliography. Research and editing by James E.
        Sisson, III. El Paso: Texas Western Press, 67 pp.
        Lists 229 items with publication data, critical annota-
        tions, and reference sources. Offers a chronology of Lon-
        don's works and life and an introduction describing this
        volume and its value.

7   What's New About London, Jack? 2, no. 1 (14 February), 10 pp.;
        2, no. 2 (11 March), 9 pp.; 2, no. 3 (15 April), 9 pp.;
        2, no. 4 (11 May), 9 pp.; 2, no. 5 (10 June), 11 pp.; 2,
        no. 6 (15 July), 13 pp.; 2, no. 7 (2 September), 11 pp.;
        2, no. 8 (14 October), 12 pp.; 2, no. 9 (25 November),
        11 pp.; 2, no. 10 (30 December), 3 pp.
        Mimeographed. All issues offer annotated primary and
        secondary bibliography, news items, and notes; occasionally
        prints stories or essays by London.

1972 B SHORTER WRITINGS

1   ANON. "London (John Griffith)," in British Museum General
        Catalogue of Printed Books: Five-Year Supplement, 1966-
        1970. Volume 15. London, 635-37.
        Lists 18 London titles and 6 works about him.

2   ANON. "Book Review." Pacific Traveler, 56 (1972), 5.
        Daughters of the Rich is "a nicely fashioned hymn to
        Socialism." Although at times melodramatic and didactic,
        it captures the atmosphere of the 1910's "with delicious
        accuracy."

3   ANON. "Jack London News." CEA, 34 (May), 29-30.
        Describes journals devoted to publishing materials on
        London.

4   BECK, WARREN A. and DAVID A WILLIAMS. California: A History
        of the Golden State. Garden City: Doubleday, pp. 475-76.
        London's writings "reveal a Darwinian glorification of
        brute force. He was a Nietzschean who was interested in
        power and its manipulation....a social critic of the first
        order....a restless and tumultuous soul."

1972

5   BLAKE, FAY M. The Strike in the American Novel. Metuchen,
        N. J.: Scarecrow Press, pp. 65-66, and passim.
            The Valley of the Moon offers an "authentic picture of
        working class life" and a realistic account of a strike.
        The Iron Heel is "a disturbingly prescient description of
        the rise of a Fascist-like dictatorship in the United
        States....[it] delivers a still shocking impact."

6   BOUWMAN, FRED. "George Sterling and Jack London: A Literary
        Friendship." JLN, 5 (May-August), 108-10.
            Gives biography of each man and describes their relation-
        ship, 1901-1916.

7   BRIDGWATER, PATRICK. "Fictional Supermen: Jack London and
        Theodore Dreiser," in his Nietzsche in Anglosaxony: A
        Study of Nietzsche's Impact on English and American Litera-
        ture. Leicester, England: Leicester University Press,
        pp. 163-70.
            London read Nietzsche "in c. 1903" and was the first to
        introduce the Superman into American literature. However,
        his heroes--Larsen, Martin Eden, Daylight--are "merely
        biological" Supermen, lacking "Nietzsche's essentially
        spiritual ideal." London was emotionally and aesthetically
        attracted to Nietzsche, but rationally "his values were
        given by the Socialism to which he was dedicated."

8   BURKE, WILLIAM J. and WILL D. HOWE. American Authors and
        Books, 1640 to the Present Day. Third edition, revised
        by Irving Weiss and Anne Weiss. New York: Crown, p. 387.
            Brief biography.

9   The Chaney Chronical [sic]. Edited by David H. Schlottman.
        No. 1 (31 October), 3 pp.
            A mimeographed newsletter, published irregularly, de-
        voted to the study of the life and works of William H.
        Chaney (London's father).

10   CLARESON, THOMAS. Science Fiction Criticism: An Annotated
        Checklist. Kent, Ohio: Kent State University Press,
        pp. 36, 45, 56, 87.
            Four articles, briefly annotated, which include London.

11   CLAYTON, LAWRENCE. "The Ghost Dog, a Motif in The Call of the
        Wild." JLN, 5 (September-December), 158.
            The folk-literature of the Bering Strait Eskimos records
        a legend of ghost dogs.

12   DONER, DEAN. "London, Jack," in The World Book Encyclopedia.
       Volume 12. Chicago: Field, 394.
       Brief life and works.

13   DUNN, N. E. and PAMELA WILSON. "The Significance of Upward
       Mobility in Martin Eden." JLN, 5 (January-April), 1-8.
       To understand the novel "the reader's orientation must
       be to the psycho-sociological patterns of real life rather
       than to the literary conventions of the well-made plot."
       London's own "upward mobility striving" structures the
       novel, provides form and theme, and accounts for Martin's
       search for identity, his restlessness, sacrifice of present
       for long-term good, and high energy level. Later, when
       frustrated, "his mobility moves downward" and suicide is
       inevitable. Martin is an "intellectual moralist defeated
       by class morality,...an individualist defeated by herd-
       psychology."

14   ERBENTRAUT, EDWIN B. "The Protean Imperative." JLN, 5 (Sep-
       tember-December), 153-57.
       London was "protean," and the endings of his stories,
       with "variety, change, multiplicity" and compelling in-
       tellectual and emotional impact, are "protean imperatives."

15   _____. "Jack London, D. Litt." JLN, 5 (September-December),
       159-63.
       London's respect for learning and his critical abilities
       appear in his essays, letters, and fictional portraits of
       professors.

16   ETULAIN, RICHARD W. Western American Literature: A Bibliogra-
       phy of Interpretive Books and Articles. Vermillon, S. D.:
       Dakota Press, pp. 90-92.
       Lists 43 articles and books about London.

17   FRENCH, WARREN. "Fiction: 1900-1930," in American Literary
       Scholarship: An Annual/1972. Edited by J. Albert Robbins.
       Durham, N. C.: Duke University Press, pp. 233-34.
       Essay-review of major work on London.

18   GLANCY, DONALD R. "'Anything to Help Anybody': The Authorship
       of Daughters of the Rich." JLN, 5 (January-April), 19-26.
       The play is "a vaudeville sketch, written by a sometime
       Glen Ellen neighbor, Hilda Gilbert." For rebuttal, see
       Sisson, 1972.B33.

19   HOFFMEISTER, CHARLES C. "A Short Note on Alexander Kuprin and
       Jack London." JLN, 5 (May-August), 135-38.

1972

Describes biographical parallels. Kuprin admired <u>Martin Eden</u> and other London heroes driven by "an insatiable passion for adventure, a noble protest against claustrophobia, cynicism, self-love, cowardliness, and deterioration of capital cities."

20 JOHNSON, RICHARD COLLES and G. THOMAS TANSELLE. "BAL Addenda: Haldeman-Julius Little Blue Books." <u>PBSA</u>, 66:67-71.
Corrections and supplements to BAL 11897; London references on pp. 68-69. <u>See</u> 1970.B27.

21 LABOR, EARLE. Review of <u>Gold</u>. <u>JLN</u>, 5 (September-December), 169-71.
"Readable and fast-moving" but far inferior to London's fiction.

22 LACHTMAN, HOWARD. "All That Glitters: Jack London's <u>Gold</u>." <u>JLN</u>, 5 (September-December), 172-78.
"One of his best efforts to write for the stage despite the inherent defects and flaws of melodrama." Describes sources and history of the play; analyzes it in relation to London's fiction. Reprinted: 1973.A1.

23 _____. "Man and Superwoman in Jack London's 'The Kanaka Surf.'" <u>WAL</u>, 7 (Summer), 101-10; published as "The Little Lady of the Big Surf: Man and Superwoman in Jack London's 'The Kanaka Surf.'" <u>Pacific Historian</u>, 16 (Fall), 35-46.
The story features a provocative subject; an anti-romantic "epic battle" of husband and wife which establishes "a satiric naturalism"; London's intrusions to explain critics' misinterpretation of his attacks on the Nietzschean superman; a close resemblance of the fictional couple to the Londons, and of the domestic conflict to the one in <u>The Little Lady of the Big House</u>. London attempts "to internalize the adventure story in order to explore the more unknown frontier of the human psyche."

24 LEIPOLD, EDMOND L. <u>Famous American Fiction Writers</u>. Minneapolis, Minnesota: T. S. Denison, pp. 53-59.
Juvenile biography.

25 McCLINTOCK, JAMES I. "Jack London: Finding the Proper Trend of Literary Art." <u>CEA</u>, 34 (May), 25-28.
London's fiction combined romanticism and realism. He affirmed the possibility of human dignity and progress through the use of imagination, courage, compassion, and intelligence, while he revealed the truth about human limitations and the brutal natural world. Excerpted and revised from 1968.A4. Revised and enlarged: 1975.A1.

26 MARTÍ-IBÁÑEZ, FELIX. "Man and Cold," in his The Mirror of
Souls and Other Essays. New York: Clarkson N. Potter,
pp. 139-41.
Reprint of 1968.B13.

27 PROFFER, CARL R., ed. and trans. Soviet Criticism of American
Literature in the Sixties: An Anthology. Ann Arbor, Michi-
gan: Ardis, pp. 116, 166, 203.
Mentions London.

28 RATHER, LOIS. Encounters: Some Incidents of Literary History.
Oakland, California: The Rather Press, pp. [31], 34-38,
40-42, 58-59.
Discusses London's relations with Ina Coolbrith, Sterling,
and Frederick Bamford.

29 ROSENZWEIG, PAUL JONATHAN. "The Wilderness in American Fiction: A Psychoanalytic Study of a Central American Myth."
Ph.D. dissertation, University of Michigan.

30 SANDBURG, CHARLES A. [CARL]. "Jack London: A Common Man."
JLN, 5 (January-April), 14-18.
Reprint of 1906.B46.

31 SILET, CHARLES L. P., ed. "Upton Sinclair to Jack London: A
Literary Friendship," JLN, 5 (May-August), 49-76.
Prints letters from Sinclair, 1905-1916. The bond between them was socialism. Sinclair also shows "a feeling
for Jack himself, as the boyhood hero,...a romantic figure,
the original leader of the Revolution."

32 SISSON, JAMES E. "Jack London and the Daughters of the Rich."
Evidence of London's authorship of this play includes:
the manuscript (Huntington Library) and U. S. copyright
bear only London's name; the play was produced under his
name and credited to him by contemporary reviews. Rebuttal of 1972.B21.

33 _____. "A Letter from Jack London to Miss Blanche Partington,
Written April 9, 1913." JLN, 5 (May-August), 77-97.
London met this music and drama critic of the San Francisco Call in 1902. She aided his dramatic ventures and
favorably reviewed his plays. Although at the height of
his career in 1913, London was plagued with problems at
the Ranch, a lawsuit, business failures, an appendectomy,
and the burning of Wolf House. Explains and expands the
details of London's letter to create a biography of the
year 1913; offers an "Appendix" of data on London's cattle,
and a "Selected Bibliography."

1972

34 STERN, JEROME H. "London, Jack," in <u>The Encyclopedia Ameri-
    cana International Edition</u>. Volume 17. New York, 700–
    701.
        Life and works. London was a "naturalist" and an indi-
    vidualistic Marxist writer of "exciting, well-detailed and
    vividly told fiction." The struggles of his human and
    animal heroes "embody a recognition of primal forces,
    which make London's works timeless literature." Much of
    his work remains "readable and valuable."

35 SWEENEY, BEN. "London's The Way of War: When? Where? Why?"
    <u>JLN</u>, 5 (January–April), 9–13.
        Describes a search for the facts about this poem.

36 _____. "Jack London's Noble Lady." <u>JLN</u>, 5 (May–August), 111–
    22.
        Biography of Ina Coolbrith; discusses her influence on
    London and his participation in tributes to her. Re-
    printed: 1973.B45.

37 TARKHOVA, YELENA. "What They Read." <u>Soviet Life</u> (September),
    pp. 56–57.
        In a sociologist's poll of young Russian factory workers'
    reading habits, London was named one of the most popular
    American writers.

38 WALKER, DALE L. "Jack London in Tahiti." <u>Otahiti</u> (September),
    pp. 8–11.
        Gives biography and describes the voyage of the <u>Snark</u>.

39 _____. "Jack London and Maurice Magnus: An Annotation on a
    Strange Correspondent." <u>JLN</u>, 5 (September–December),
    149–52.
        Discusses the career of Magnus and London's letter to
    him in 1911.

40 _____. "William Tum Suden Bahls Remembers Jack London: Three
    Letters." <u>JLN</u>, 5 (May–August), 98–104.
        As a child of ten, Bahls knew London. The letters give
    his recollections and evaluation of London.

41 WEIDERMAN, DICK. "Jack London as a Wester[n] Writer." <u>The
    Zane Grey Collector</u>, 18 (April), 11–12.
        In his fiction set in Alaska, the Northwest, and northern
    California, as well as by his life on the Beauty Ranch,
    London showed his love for the West and "tried to preserve
    its romance and luster."

42   WILLIAMS, RAYMOND. "Social Darwinism." The Listener, 88
        (23 November), 696-700.
        Briefly notes London's application of this theory in
        White Fang and The Iron Heel, pp. 699-700.

1973 A BOOKS

1   ANON. World Premiere Performance of Gold by Jack London and
        Herbert Heron. Jackson, California: Jackson High School
        Drama Class, 32 pp.
        Souvenir booklet. Offers essays on Gold and on this
        production, including James E. Sisson III, "The Search for
        Jack London's Lost Works and the Discovery of Gold,"
        pp. 15-19: describes his research since 1962 to locate
        London's plays, stories and articles. A table of contents
        for this booklet is printed in JLN, 6 (January-April),
        pp. 29-30. See also Pure Gold and Curtain Raisers, 1973.A5;
        1973.B41; and 1972.B22.

2   AUFDERHEIDE, LAWRENCE RICHARD. "American Literary Primitivists:
        Owen Wister, Stewart Edward White, and Jack London." Ph.D.
        dissertation, University of Michigan.

3   FREEMAN, A. W. A Search for Jack London. Chicago: Adams
        Press, 81 pp.
        A personal interpretation based on thirty-five years of
        studying London. Offers biography and criticism excerpted
        or derived from many published sources with Freeman's
        evaluations of these. "Jack's Yukon-Klondike books do not
        compare, except for certain descriptive passages, with
        his later books with socialistic and mythic motifs." He
        was a "Humanist" and writer of the "Common People....He
        will remain an enigma through the ages."

4   WALKER, DALE L. The Alien Worlds of Jack London. Wolf House
        Books Monograph Number One. Grand Rapids, Michigan: Wolf
        House Books, 47 pp.
        London's "fantasy fiction" reflects his "sense of won-
        der," his lifelong "flight from reality" and attraction
        to the unknown. It includes his early "weird" tales;
        "science fiction" involving revival of the dead, rejuvena-
        tion, invisibility, or a craft from outer space; "pre-
        history" tales; and "futuristic" fiction in which terrorism
        or blackmail threatens the normal scheme of living. Ad-
        ditionally, The Star Rover concerns reincarnation and
        transmigration, and "War" contains elements of "eldritch
        fantasy." Wells and several lesser writers influenced

1973

London. Includes analyses of individual works, detailed
notes and a chronological bibliography of 26 primary items.
See 1973.B33.

5   What's New About London, Jack? 3, no. 1 (22 February), 7 pp.;
        3, no. 2 (10 March), 10 pp.; 3, no. 2 [sic] (28 April),
        12 pp.; 3, no. 3 [sic] (9 June), 11 pp.; 3, no. 5 (28 July),
        12 pp.; 3, no. 6 (25 August), 26 pp.--this is a special
        issue, Pure Gold and Curtain Raisers, with bibliography
        and essays devoted to London's plays and the 1973 per-
        formance of Gold [See 1973.A1; 1973.B41]; 3, no. 7 (31 Oc-
        tober), 9 pp.; 3, no. 8 (22 November), 8 pp.; 3, no. 9
        (6 December), 8 pp.
           Mimeographed. All issues offer annotated primary and
        secondary bibliography, news items, and notes; occasionally
        prints stories or essays by London.

6   The Wolf--'73. Edited by "d. Henry S." [David H. Schlottman].
        Olympia, Washington: London Northwest, 25 pp.
           Mimeographed. Distributed at the Third Annual Jack
        London Banquet, January 12, 1973, Oakland, California.
        Contains eight essay-tributes on the theme "What Jack Lon-
        don Means to Me" and three essays on London events and
        publications of 1972.

7   WOODBRIDGE, HENSLEY C., JOHN LONDON and GEORGE H. TWENEY,
        comps. Jack London: A Bibliography. Enlarged edition.
        Millwood, N. Y.: Kraus reprint, 554 pp.
           Contains a "Supplement" of 119 pages plus a new inclu-
        sive index, both compiled by Woodbridge. Lists additions
        through 1970 to all categories of 1966.A6.

1973 B SHORTER WRITINGS

1   ALDISS, BRIAN W. Billion Year Spree: The True History of
        Science Fiction. Garden City: Doubleday, pp. 117, 149-52,
        313.
           London's place in science fiction "is secured by three
        books." The Iron Heel, "most eminent in reputation,"
        clothes "honest sympathies with the poor...in clichés,
        with alternate spates of denunciation and sentimentality.
        ...London had no real vision of a future; his future is
        just the present and the past, only more so." The Star
        Rover, influenced by Ouida, "is an uneven book"; and Be-
        fore Adam "has a sort of wild lyric truth."

2   ANATER, FRANCES. "Jack London." California Highway Patrolman,
        37 (March), 17-18, 46-48.
           Gives biography.

3   ANON. "London, Jack," in <u>Cassell's Encyclopedia of World</u>
    <u>Literature</u>. Revised and enlarged. New York: Morrow,
    p. 67.
        Brief biography.

4   ANON. "London, Jack," in <u>Chamber's Encyclopaedia</u>. New Revised
    edition. Volume 8. London: International Learning Systems,
    657.
        Brief biography.

5   ARMOUR, RICHARD. "Jack London," in his <u>It All Started with</u>
    <u>Freshman English</u>. New York: McGraw-Hill, p. 130.
        Brief note on <u>The Call of the Wild</u>.

6   AULD, LARRY. "London on London--A Last Word." <u>Book Collecting</u>
    <u>& Library Monthly</u>, 60 (April), 100-101.
        London regretted that his attempt in <u>The Star Rover</u> to
    expose prison conditions and celebrate "the Spirit Tri-
    umphant" missed fire. Gives excerpts from reviews and
    London's comments.

7   BERRY, JEFF. "Monsieur Londre and the Pearl Buyer." <u>JLN</u>, 6
    (January-April), 13-22.
        "The House of Mapuhi" fictionalizes an incident told to
    London in Tahiti by Alexandre Drollet. London names and
    describes Emile Lévy, a pearl buyer and ship's chandler
    with whom he quarreled in Papeete, as the villainous
    "thief who cheated natives." Reprinted from <u>Otahiti</u> (Sep-
    tember, 1972).

8   BROOKS, CLEANTH, R. W. B. LEWIS, and ROBERT PENN WARREN.
    "Jack London (1876-1916)," in their <u>American Literature</u>:
    <u>The Makers and the Making</u>. New York: St. Martin's,
    pp. 1632-34.
        London's reading "gave a context for his writing," and
    the ideas he gleaned "became the fuel for a projected
    melodrama" in his fictions; but London was not personally
    involved with these ideas. He projected his own contra-
    dictions into heroes like Larsen, "the Nietzschean super-
    man and apostle of materialism,...[and] the narrator, a
    civilized man of spiritual sensitivity." London's intended
    emphasis (on individualism <u>or</u> social cooperation) remains
    ambiguous in <u>The Sea-Wolf</u> and <u>Martin Eden</u>. "The drama of
    a class war fulfilling his own need for apocalyptic vio-
    lence" attracted London to Marxism. Instructive contrasts
    may be drawn between his life and works and those of Davis,
    Crane, Dreiser, and Sinclair. "The ideas of his time as
    caught in his fiction have long since lost meaning. He

remains a splendid writer of books for boys....His temperament triumphed over all his ideas, and the world he
created never seemed quite real." Gives biography.

9 BUTTERWORTH, KEEN. "Gold/A Play in Three Acts." ALR, 6
(Spring), 156-58.
A "neat little tragi-comedy full of coincidences and
improbabilities,...It is thoroughly enjoyable reading;...
although its value as drama is insignificant."

10 The Chaney Chronical [sic]. Edited by David H. Schlottman.
No. 2 (1 May), 7 pp.
A mimeographed newsletter, published irregularly, de-
voted to the study of the life and works of William H.
Chaney (London's father).

11 CLARESON, THOMAS D. "Notes [to] 'The Red One,'" in his edition
of A Spectrum of Worlds. Garden City: Doubleday, pp. 87-90.
The fabric is naturalistic with action motivated by
"instincts of survival and sexuality" and an intellectual
drive. Irony is created by placing Bassett, a scientific
idealist, in a violent, savage world and then revealing
him to be as brutal as this world. The story is modern
in its sense of wonder and "cosmic loneliness."

12 COOK, GEORGE. "London's Bookman Letters." JLN, 6 (May-August),
81-87.
A rebuttal to Sloane, 1970.B39 and 1973.B42. London
suggests that reviewers' misunderstandings might arise
from his failure to make his meanings clear. He insists
"that a writer does not have time to be both a writer and
a literary agent." The letters reveal a "complex person"
who is "torn between truth, friendship, charity, and personal needs and goals."

13 DAVIDSON, MARSHALL B. and THE EDITORS OF AMERICAN HERITAGE.
The American Heritage History of the Writers' America.
New York: American Heritage, pp. 242-44.
A writer of widespread and enduring popularity, London's
romantic fiction stressed brute force; but he was also
dedicated to socialism and humanitarianism. His work expressed "the struggle and revolt" in "a changing world of
ideas." Gives biography.

14 DAY, DOUGLAS. Malcolm Lowry: A Biography. New York: Oxford
University Press, pp. 90, 96, 102, 469.
Lowry's reading of London and O'Neill influenced his
character and life.

15 DUC, DO DUC. "Jack London's Dream at the Turn of the Century,"
    JLN, 6 (September-December), 133-45.
        London's works describe class and racial conflicts as
    they existed "in the ruthless and inhuman world of the
    American capitalist system" of his time. He "was on the
    side of the oppressed, the conquered and exploited." The
    class struggle is central to The Iron Heel, "a dream of
    the socialist ideology," which predicts "the coming of
    Hitler, Mussolini, McCarthyism, and the Taft-Hartley laws
    in America." The novel shows the "gigantic oppressive
    machinery" and "iron heel of imperialism" of today's Ameri-
    can leaders. Translated from the Vietnamese by N. T.
    Ngoc-Phuong; originally published in Tap-chi Van-hoc, 2
    (1966), 19-29.

16 ELDER, JAY. "American Renewal in the London Legend." The
    London Collector, 4 (February), [12]-17.
        London's "thrusting untame delight in life and being,"
    his perennial youthfulness, rebelliousness, and questing
    for truth, seem integral to American literature and his-
    tory. "Had we a living whole shape about Jack London on
    stage or on film," our "great Myth" might be born.

17 ERBENTRAUT, EDWIN B. "The Key to Complexity: Jack London and
    the Theory of Complementarity." JLN, 6 (September-Decem-
    ber), 119-22.
        Niels Bohr's theory as applied to literature by Norman
    Rabkin provides a key to London. His mind "was a unity
    of strange alliances"; contradictions "acted as comple-
    ments to each other, and as catalysts to the London psyche.
    Those contradictions developed symbiotic relationships,
    and became the dynamos of the pulsing power that was
    Jack's mind."

18 EVERSON, WILLIAM. "Archetype West," in Regional Perspectives:
    An Examination of America's Literary Heritage. Edited by
    John Gordon Burke. Chicago: American Library Association,
    pp. 257-58, 259.
        In London "the primitivistic element in the Western
    archetype drives down to its archaic root....his reduc-
    tionist onslaught on nuclear experience is in its very
    simplicity a more effective literary method than any save
    the most superior aesthetic formality....he is a better
    writer than conventional highbrow criticism allows."

19 FARMER, PHILIP JOSÉ. Doc Savage: His Apocalyptic Life. Gar-
    den City: Doubleday, pp. 184-85.
        Wolf Larsen, "a Danish-born Norwegian," was the maternal

257

1973

grandfather of Doc Savage; Larsen "was a human wolverine. ...a genius who had never arrived." Probably, he was also the grandfather of J. P. Marquand's Mr. Moto.

20 FRENCH, WARREN. "Fiction: 1900-1930," in American Literary Scholarship: An Annual/1971. Edited by J. Albert Robbins. Durham, N. C.: Duke University Press, pp. 218-19. Essay-review of major work on London.

21 GIDLEY, M. "Notes on F. Scott Fitzgerald and the Passing of the Great Race." JAmS, 7 (August), 171-81. Mentions London's racism, p. 173.

22 HENRY, JAMES L. "'The First Poet': Jack London or George Sterling?" JLN, 6 (May-August), 60-65. A recently-found manuscript of this play in Sterling's hand plus historical facts indicate that Sterling wrote it. Notes changes in the text between the manuscript and printed versions.

23 HINDMAN, KATHLEEN B. "Jack London's The Sea-Wolf: Naturalism with a Spiritual Bent." JLN, 6 (September-December), 99-110. Larsen, the materialist, isolated egoist, and aggressive primitivist is a foil to Van Weyden, an idealist and defensive primitivist who is driven by the force of "spirit." Love for Maud divides Larsen against himself and destroys him; but love humanizes and further spiritualizes Van Weyden.

24 HOFFMEISTER, CHARLES CHRISTIAN. "Recent Soviet Attention to Jack London--I." JLN, 6 (January-April), 23-24. Describes editions of The Call of the Wild and White Fang published in English with Russian introductions, and a translation of "Stranger than Fiction."

25 _____. "Recent Soviet Attention to Jack London--II." JLN, 6 (May-August), 57-59. Notes an enlarged version of Vil Bykov's Dzhek London: Ia Mnogo Zhil, and reprints one chapter in English.

26 _____. "Recent Soviet Attention to Jack London--III." JLN, 6 (September-December), 131-32. Examines two translations of London's review of Sinclair's The Jungle.

27 HOWARD, PATSY C., comp. and ed. Theses in American Literature, 1896-1971. Ann Arbor, Michigan: Pierian Press.

Lists doctoral and master's theses, items 3754-3774, on London. Reprinted in part: 1974.B38.

28 ISANI, MUKHTAR ALI. "Jack London on Norris' The Octopus."
    ALR, 6 (Winter), 66-69.
    Reprints London's review of 1901.

29 KAPLAN, JUSTIN. Lincoln Steffens: A Biography. New York:
    Simon and Shuster.
    Numerous scattered references to London; page numbers
    are in his index.

30 LABOR, EARLE. "Portrait of the Artist as Professional." JLN,
    6 (September-December), 93-98.
    Excerpt from Labor, 1974.A3.

31 LACASSIN, FRANCIS. "A Classic of Revolt." JLN, 6 (May-August),
    71.78.
    Introduction to the French edition (1973) of The Iron
    Heel. London's "most fascinating" novel is a convincing
    Marxist "propaganda instrument of remarkable simplicity";
    it is autobiographical in many respects. Translated by
    Annie Woodbridge, with notes by Hensley C. Woodbridge.

32 LACHTMAN, HOWARD. Review of Gold. Pacific Historian,
    17:94-95.
    "One of London's best plays, a glittering romp on the
    stage of adventure."

33 LEIBER, FRITZ. Review of The Alien Worlds of Jack London.
    JLN, 6 (September-December), 151-53.
    Supplies a table of contents for Walker, 1973.A4.

34 LYNN, KENNETH. "Violence in American Literature and Folklore,"
    in his Visions of America: Eleven Literary Historical
    Essays. Westport, Connecticut: Greenwood, pp. 189-205.
    The defeat of Everhard and socialism in The Iron Heel
    may be explained in three ways: "London was interested in
    violence for violence's sake"; or, he was committed to a
    competitive capitalistic economy and realized that so-
    cialism would bring society's decay; or, his "socialist
    hopes" were overwhelmed by contemporary failures of other
    radical movements. The novel's violent (and realistic)
    conclusion "enabled a philosophically troubled writer to
    resolve his ambivalence....[it] may well have been the
    sign of London's sanity as a social prophet, rather than
    of his psychological imbalance."

1973

35   MEHL, R. F., JR.   "Jack London, Alfred Henry Lewis, and Primi-
      tive Woman."   JLN, 6 (May-August), 66-70.
         "The Wit of Porportuk" (1906) resembles Lewis's "The
      Mills of Savage Gods" (1902) in theme, plot, and protago-
      nist. London's story "is by far the better written, the
      more interesting and the more readable."

36   MOSS, MERTON.   "Kurt Vonnegut's 'Piano Player' [sic] and Jack
      London's 'Iron Heel.'"   Industrial Worker, 70 (November),
      10.
         In both novels, the working class fails in its revolt,
      and both inspire intensified "efforts in the Struggle."
      Through a figure of a priest, the novels offer the same
      moral: "Don't be a trafficker in symbols." Describes dif-
      ferences between the novels.

37   QUISSELL, BARBARA CAROLYN.   "The Sentimental and Utopian Novels
      of Nineteenth Century America: Romance and Social Issues."
      Ph.D. dissertation, University of Utah [The Iron Heel].

*38   RHODEHAMEL, JOSEPHINE DeWITT and RAYMOND FRANCIS WOOD.   Ina
      Coolbrith--Librarian and Laureate of California. [Provo,
      Utah]: Brigham Young University Press, pp. 119, 150-51,
      162, 183, 185-86, 266, 269, 312, 334, 382, 427, 431, 482.
         Discusses London's relationship with Coolbrith. Data
      courtesy of James E. Sisson.

39   SEYMOUR-SMITH, MARTIN.   Funk & Wagnalls' Guide to Modern World
      Literature. New York: Funk and Wagnalls, pp. 44-45.
         London is not a great writer, but he is "a remarkable
      one, with a gift for story-telling unsurpassed in his
      time....[He] is not only still readable, but still worth
      reading (a different matter)."

40   SHULSINGER, STEPHANIE C.   "Jack London in the Klondike."   Real
      West, 16 (June), 13-15, 68.
         Gives biography and an account of London's year in Alaska,
      condensed from published sources.

41   SISSON, JAMES E.   "Jack London's Curtain Raisers."   What's New
      About London, Jack? 3, no. 6 (25 August), 75-78.
         London felt "an almost desperate desire for fame as a
      dramatist, but he had only a limited success." Five of
      his one-act plays were produced in his lifetime. Discusses
      plots, history of composition and early performances of the
      plays, and reviews the 1973 productions of them. See
      1973.A1.

42   SLOANE, DAVID E. E.   "Jack London on Reviewing: An Addendum."
        ALR, 6 (Winter), 70-72.
        Prints a 1905 letter by London.   He "rejects the idea of
     truth-telling in commenting on other people's writing,
     falling back apologetically on a Darwinist conception of
     competition."   London's pessimistic view of friendship and
     family security is later expressed in Martin Eden and John
     Barleycorn.   Since such views seem to contradict other evi-
     dence of his concern for young writers, this letter is
     either "a consciously contrived role,...or London himself
     was deeply confused" about the novelist's responsibilities.
     This is an addition to Sloane, 1970.B39; for a rebuttal,
     see 1973.B12.

43   STARR, KEVIN.   "The Sonoma Finale of Jack London, Rancher,"
        in his Americans and the California Dream, 1850-1915.   New
        York: Oxford University Press, pp. 210-238 (and many scat-
        tered references).
        London was neurotically concerned with his health and
     physique and obsessed with his supposedly mean origins,
     loveless childhood, and his family's failure to make good
     in California.   From these fantasies, he created a personal
     myth and identified it with an historical myth of the An-
     glo-Saxon Americans' failure to triumph gloriously in Cali-
     fornia.   To explain and redeem both myths, first he acted
     out "a variety of fantasies--socialist revolutionary, war
     correspondent, sportsman, brawler, drinker, womanizer."
     Neither these roles nor socialism proved redemptive.
     Second, he drew fictional alter egos with superb physical
     strength, others, "drunks who sober up," and heroines who
     reflected his obsessions; he also adopted a "blatant,
     schizoid Anglo-Saxonism," and created heroic pre-Revolu-
     tionary War ancestries for himself and his heroes.   Lon-
     don's attempt to define himself and salvage his dream
     through the Ranch, Wolf House, and business ventures, be-
     gun in earnest in 1909, is depicted in his fiction.
     Burning Daylight was "a fantasy of recuperation" of the
     London family and the Golden West.   Themes of The Valley
     of the Moon were the mythical element of his dream as a
     rancher.   When his Ranch ventures failed, all wish-fulfill-
     ment went into The Little Lady of the Big House, which
     "stank of madness and decay" and showed people "dead in
     spirit and in appetites."   By killing off Paula, "London
     admitted the falsity and weariness of his dream."   The
     "psychological facts" of London's life (paralleling "Cali-
     fornia's own internal social tensions")--his interest "in
     the literature of perversion," sado-masochistic tendencies,
     lust for violence, hatred of women, latent homosexuality,

and sense of inferiority—compelled him to construct re-
demptive personal and historical dream-worlds; but these,
in turn, prevented fulfillment of his ideals and drove him
into a "pattern of self-destruction."

44   ST. JOHN, JEFFREY. "Most Modern Fiction Pales in Light of
     Jack London." National Observer (10 February), p. 10.
        London's work is rooted in reality and charged with his
     "lust for life," making it substantial and enduring.

45   SWEENEY, BEN. "Jack London's Noble Lady." Pacific Historian,
     17 (Fall), 20-31.
        Reprint of 1972.B36.

46   UPTON, ANN. "The Wolf in London's Mirror." JLN, 6 (September-
     December), 111-18.
        London consistently identified with the name, symbol,
     and actuality of the wolf. The "archetypal image of the
     wolf as both preserver and destroyer," contemporary "com-
     petitiveness of business and the gold rush," and his "in-
     nate perceptiveness" made him see the two sides of his
     nature in the wolf's two faces: the aggressive, adventurous
     face of the "lone wolf" and the cooperative, brotherhood-
     seeking face of "the wolf when he ran in the packs." The
     journeys of the wolf-dogs Buck and White Fang "are an at-
     tempt at vicarious atavism, and a mirror image of London's
     two faces."

47   VOSS, ARTHUR. The American Short Story: A Critical Survey.
     Norman: University of Oklahoma Press, pp. 167-71.
        Only The Call of the Wild and a few stories such as
     "Love of Life" and "To Build a Fire" "have real distinc-
     tion," for in these London depicts "vividly and dramati-
     cally" man's struggle against nature. In some South Sea
     tales he portrays "the white man's exploitation of the
     natives" but generally fails "to explore moral ambigui-
     ties." None of the proletarian stories "rises much above
     the level of propaganda except for 'The Apostate.'" If
     London had not written so much so fast "he might well have
     produced a body of work of more enduring merit." Gives
     brief biography.

48   WALKER, DALE L. "Jack London: The Unmined Gold." The London
     Collector, 4 (February), [5]-11.
        The "formidable legend" of London's life and the uneven
     quality of his work have hindered serious criticism.
     Attention should be paid to "the creator of literature."

49   WALKER, FRANKLIN. "London, Jack," in Encyclopaedia Britannica.
        Volume 14. Chicago: Encyclopaedia Britannica, 263.
        Biography.

50   _____. The Seacoast of Bohemia. New and enlarged edition.
        Santa Barbara, California: Peregrine Smith.
        Revised edition of 1966.B33; material on London is the
        same.

51   WALKER, WARREN. Twentieth-Century Short Story Explication:
        Supplement 2, 1970-72. Hamden, Connecticut: Shoestring
        Press, pp. 90-91.
        Additions to 1967.B20.

52   WIEDERMAN, RICHARD. "Editorial." The London Collector, 4
        (February), [1]-2.
        With Crane and Twain, London will be recognized as "one
        of the three literary giants of his time."

53   WILCOX, EARL. "'The Kipling of the Klondike'; Naturalism in
        London's Early Fiction." JLN, 6 (January-April), 1-12.
        Three themes dominate his first three volumes of stories:
        "survival of the fittest, the deterministic orientation of
        the universe, and the superiority of the inevitable white
        man." The women in these tales are often central charac-
        ters, strong, courageous, and faithful prototypes of his
        later "Amazon-like women." Excerpted and revised from
        1966.A5.

54   WIRZBERGER, KARL-HEINZ. "Jack London and the Goldrush." JLN,
        6 (September-December), 146-47.
        Smoke Bellew most clearly parallels London's Klondike
        experience. Martin Eden is his masterpiece. Article trans-
        lated from the German by Ruby Susan Woodbridge; originally
        published in Die Buchgemeinde (May, 1967).

55   WOLFE, HILTON JOHN. "Alaskan Literature: The Fiction of Ameri-
        ca's Last Wilderness." Ph.D. dissertation, Michigan State
        University.

56   WOODBRIDGE, HENSLEY C., comp. "WLT^2: First Supplement." JLN,
        6 (January-April), 31-54.
        Additions to 1973.A7; lists articles and stories by Lon-
        don, English and foreign editions; material about London.

57   _____. "WLT^2: Supplement 2." JLN, 6 (September-December),
        123-30.
        Additions to 1973.A7; lists articles and stories by

1973

London; anthologies and collections; English and foreign
editions; material about London.

58 YARDLEY, JONATHAN. "Reconsideration: Jack London." New Republic, 168 (2 June), 31-33.
Reviews reprints of Martin Eden. It is a novel about
"the creative passion," "a glorification of Eden's individual genius," and it powerfully exposes the "hypocrisy
and emptiness" of the middle class.

1974 A BOOKS

1 COOPER, JAMES GLENNON. "The Womb of Time: Archetypal Patterns
in the Novels of Jack London." Ph.D. dissertation, Texas
Tech University. Printed in part, 1975.B3.
Printed in part, 1975.B3.

2 HARPHANN, GEOFFREY GALT. "Cultural Degeneration and the Gro-
tesque in H. G. Wells and Jack London." Ph.D. dissertation, University of California (Los Angeles).
Printed in part, 1975.B9.

3 LABOR, EARLE. Jack London. TUSAS. New York: Twayne, 179 pp.
A true child of America's "Age of Adolescence" and "a
twentieth century man," London's nature and writings were
marked by inconsistencies and contradictions: he was a
money-hungry hack writer and a disciplined, well-trained
professional craftsman; he was loyal to friends, "generous
to the verge of bankruptcy," compassionate to the underdog,
and "the manliest of men," but he was also a quick-tempered,
petty and vindictive egoist, a racist, childish practical
joker, and self-destructive hedonist. Considering himself
a great thinker, London culled from the works of Nietzsche,
Marx, Haeckel, Spencer, and Kidd only those ideas which
suited him, distorting and combining their thoughts at
will. He was a swashbuckling individualist who preached
Socialism and an "American folk hero" who epitomized the
myths of the frontier and of success.
London's life-style and writings were shaped by such
early experiences as shame of bastardy, grinding poverty,
minimal formal education, extensive reading, harsh physical
toil, and adventures as an oyster pirate, seaman, hobo, and
prison inmate. In 1895-98, he graduated from Oakland High
School, joined the Henry Clay Debating Society and Socialist
Labor Party, spent a term at the University of California,
and a year with gold-hunters in the Klondike. In later
years London was a Socialist lecturer; an unsuccessful can-
didate for Mayor of Oakland; a rancher-farmer; and the

builder and skipper of the <u>Snark</u> on a two-year voyage
through the South Seas.

From 1898 to 1916, London produced fifty books, thousands
of letters, and countless periodical articles and essays.
He typed 1000 words a day, six days a week, and never re-
wrote a page. Chronic technical weaknesses of his work
are: "his longer plots tend to be episodic and disjointed;
his dialogue is strained; and his characters often degen-
erate into caricature." On the other hand, his immediate
and lasting world-wide popularity derives from his work's
"human interest, romantic imagination, sympathetic understanding," robustness and truthfulness-to-life; also, his
"clear, straightforward, uncluttered, imagistic" style,
and portrayals of "archetypal tensions between civilization
and the wilderness, the machine versus the garden," all ani-
mated by a "mythopoeic force."

A moral idealist, London's work reflects "the human yearn-
ing to recapture the perfection of Eden." His "quest for
Paradise" informs the fiction of the Northland, the South
Seas, and the California wilderness. He is an artist in
the "visionary mode," deriving materials from "'racial
memories'" and expressing them in symbols and myths. The
Klondike writings express "universal dreams"; here, the
"laws of the White Silence" give order to the cosmos, and
heroes survive by adapting to the Northland code of "co-
operation, sympathy, and brotherhood...integrity, courage,
forbearance, and--above all--imagination." The Myth of the
Hero animates the plot of <u>The Call of the Wild</u>; the novel
follows a "richly symbolistic form" of four movements as
the style shifts from the naturalistic and literal to the
symbolic and lyrical. <u>White Fang</u>, an initiation story, is
a "sociological fable" in which the death-principle is set
against a cluster of life-values. <u>The Sea-Wolf</u> offers a
"universal, timeless motif of initiation" and an archetypal setting of ship and sea. Larsen is "the Captain Ahab
of literary Naturalism"; and Van Weyden's "growth from
effete snobbery into dynamic manhood constitutes the main
plot." The novel exemplifies the need for a "sensible
equipoise" between the animalistic and civilized worlds.
<u>Martin Eden</u> combines the archetypal themes and structure
of "the Dark Fall" and the American myth of success. "Martin's is also the universal sickness of modern man caught
in the Naturalistic trap."

In his South Seas fiction, London sought "to recapture
the simple maternal security of nature," but in Polynesia
he found "Paradise Lost"; and in Melanesia, "the wilder-
ness-as-Eden symbol is wholly inverted." The California
wilderness, however, becomes a pastoral haven, a place of

salvation through love. Among many "overtly propagandistic"
books, The Iron Heel, "his bravest novel," is "the fictional
articulation of his private dreams of revolutionary glory."
London's fantasies, Before Adam, The Scarlet Plague, and
The Star Rover, resemble Poe's work, "woven within a frame-
work of violence and death; they are textured metaphors of
darkness, chaos, pain, and terror.
    Reappraisal of London should focus on his "palpable
achievements" as a "social crusader," "folk writer" com-
parable to Mark Twain, and "literary craftsman," whose
"ultimate greatness derives from his 'primordial vision'--
the mythopoeic force which animates his finest creations."
Includes notes and references, primary sources, and an
annotated bibliography. Incorporates in revised form
dissertation, 1961.A4; 1962.B8; 1964.B13; 1967.B13;
1970.B28; 1973.B30.

4   LACHTMAN, HOWARD LAWRENCE. "The Wide World of Jack London."
      Ph.D. dissertation, University of the Pacific.
      Partially printed: 1972.B23.

5   LEWIS, SINCLAIR. Sinclair Lewis on the Valley of the Moon.
      Grand Rapids, Michigan: Wolf House Books, 1 foldout page.
      Reprint of 1932.A1.

6   LONDON, JOAN. Jack London and His Times: An Unconventional
      Biography. Washington Paperback edition. Seattle: Uni-
      versity of Washington Press, 402 pp.
      Reprint of 1968.A3.

7   RATHER, LOIS. Jack London, 1905. Oakland, California: The
      Rather Press, 133 pp.
        A detailed account of London's life in this year. He
      lectured and wrote for the Socialists; lost the Mayoralty
      election in Oakland; spent the summer with Charmian at
      Wake Robin and married her in November; wrote "The Great
      Interrogation" and was romantically linked to his co-
      author, Ida Lee Bascomb. He attended prize-fights which
      inspired The Game; became the first president of the Inter-
      collegiate Socialist Society; and his White Fang was
      serialized.

8   WALKER, DALE L. Jack London, Sherlock Holmes and Sir Arthur
      Conan Doyle. Amsterdam, N. Y.: Alvin S. Fick, 39 pp.
      Revised and enlarged text of 1970.B43

9   What's New About London, Jack? 4, no. 1 (1 June), 7 pp.; 4,
      no. 2 (31 December), 10 pp.

Mimeographed. Annotated primary and secondary bibliography, news items, and notes.

10   The Wolf '74. Edited by David H. Schlottman. Olympia, Washington: London Northwest, 21 pp. and insert, London's "A Northland Miracle."
        Distributed at the Fourth Annual Jack London Banquet, January 12, 1974, Oakland, California. Contains ten essay-tributes on the theme "I Remember Jack"; and comments on publications by and about London in 1973.

1974 B SHORTER WRITINGS

1   ANON. "London, Jack," in Webster's American Biographies. Edited by Charles Van Doren. Springfield, Massachusetts: G & C Merriam, p. 646.
        Brief biography.

2   BUKOSKI, ANTHONY. "Jack London's Wolf Larsen: Nietzschean Super Man at All?" JLN, 7 (September-December), 109-10.
        In several letters London claimed The Sea-Wolf attacked Nietzsche's "super-man idea."

3   BURTON, LOU. "'Some Monstrous Worm.'" JLN, 7 (September-December), 117-21.
        Bill's partner in "Love of Life" survives dehumanization by assertion of a primordial "will or compulsion that... caused the first atoms to combine themselves into living organisms. The man's behavior was motivated by that same force that caused an amoeba to reproduce or a worm to seek food."

4   CHICOREL, MARIETTA, ed. Chicorel Index to Short Stories in Anthologies and Collections. Chicorel Index Series. Volume 12B. New York: Chicorel Library, 1139-42.
        Lists 85 London stories.

5   COOK, GEORGE. "Meeting Jack London's Bishop." JLN, 7 (January-April), 42-43.
        M. A. Ransom recorded meeting a man in Alaska who may have known London. See 1964.B

6   DAVIS, JOSEPH ADDISON. "Rolling Home: The Open Road as Myth and Symbol in American Literature, 1890-1940." Ph.D. dissertation, University of Michigan [The Road].

7   DeVORE, LYNN. "The Descent of White Fang." JLN, 7 (September-December), 122-26.

1974

A structural interweaving of a "biblical theme," color imagery, and movement from North to South, chart the downward journey of White Fang: he first lives by "a primitive natural law"; then "emerges as a kind of Nietzschean superdog," living by the Old Testament law; then he learns the "law of hate"; and finally he is "regenerated through love," emerging as the "true New Pauline man." Ironically, he thus becomes "a corrupted canine with eyes half shut and patient." The novel shows London's disillusionment with the American dream.

8   FLINK, ANDREW. "'Call of the Wild'--Parental Metaphor." <u>JLN</u>, 7 (May-August), 58-61.
        John Thornton is "the symbol of parental love," standing in relation to Buck as John London did to Jack.

9   EICHELBERGER, CLAYTON L., comp. <u>A Guide to Critical Reviews of United States Fiction, 1870-1910</u>. Volume 2. Metuchen, N. J.: Scarecrow Press, 173-74.
        Lists 35 additions to 1971.B12.

10   ERBENTRAUT, EDWIN B. "The Balanced Vision: Missionaries and the Test of Spirit in Two Jack London Stories." <u>ABC</u>, 24, no. 4 (March-April), 31-32.
        In "The God of His Fathers" and "The Whale Tooth," "<u>grace under pressure</u> is the touchstone London uses to test the ring of a man's spirit."

11   _____. "Glowing Meteor, Deathless Light: Jack London and George Sterling." <u>The London Collector</u>, [whole issue] no. 5 (August), [1]-11.
        They were "great artists" who "reverenced each others' artistic achievement." London used Sterling as a character in three novels and trusted him to read proof of his works. London's "philosophical pessimism" and socialism informed Sterling's poetry.

12   FLEMING, BECK LONDON. "Memories of My Father, Jack London." <u>Pacific Historian</u>, 18 (Fall), 5-10.
        Reminiscences of childhood and appreciative comment.

13   FORREY, ROBERT. "Male and Female in London's <u>The Sea-Wolf</u>." <u>L&P</u>, 24:135-43.
        The Van Weyden-Larsen conflict may resemble London's own conflict between his inner secret self--the "sissy" he feared he might be and the homosexual "longing for love and male companionship"--and his "public self"--the virile, animal-like "proto-fascistic ego ideal." The "effete

intellectual" Van Weyden progresses from a womanly role to manhood through scenes of "sexual significance." After Larsen's death, he re-directs the homosexual desire he apparently felt for Wolf towards Death Larsen, thus coupling his forbidden sexual wishes with his "self destructive" impulse for death by drowning. He longs for and fears both of these desires; but the connection between them "is not something of which Van Weyden (and perhaps London) was aware."

14 FRENCH, WARREN. "Fiction: 1900-1930," in <u>American Literary Scholarship: An Annual/1972</u>. Edited by J. Albert Robbins. Durham, N. C.: Duke University Press, pp. 244-46.
    Essay-review of major work on London.

15 GUNN, DREWEY WAYNE. <u>American and British Writers in Mexico, 1956-1973</u>. Austin: University of Texas Press, pp. 55-57, 64-69.
    Revised text of 1970.B21. Discussion of London is essentially the same.

16 HENRY, JAMES. "Give a Man a Boat He Can Sail." <u>JLN</u>, 7 (January-April), 23-29.
    Prints four letters from George Sterling to Herbert Peet and Opal Heron describing a yachting trip (1909) on upper San Francisco Bay with London and others.

17 HICKS, GRANVILLE. "The Superman and the Socialist," in <u>Granville Hicks in the New Masses</u>. Edited by Jack Alan Robbins. Port Washington, N. Y.: Kennikat, pp. 352-57.
    A review of Stone, 1938.A1, written October 11, 1938. London clung to contradictory humanitarian and egotistical ideas. "Individualism predominated in his writings.... One could compile from his letters either a Socialist or an anti-Socialist anthology." Socialism was the only "curb upon his extravagant temperament." If he had been a better Socialist, he would have been a "more integrated person" and thus a better writer.

18 KAYE, FRANCES W. "Jack London's Modification of Herbert Spencer." <u>JLN</u>, 7 (May-August), 67-72.
    In <u>White Fang</u> "the rule of tooth and claw" is modified by love. Martin Eden adopts Spencer, and London unjustly punishes him for the sin of individualism. <u>The Iron Heel</u> "is an artistically unsuccessful attempt at a socialist critique of contemporary capitalism." In <u>Burning Daylight</u>, London shows concern for social justice and compassion; and <u>The Valley of the Moon</u> "defines the good life" with "nothing identifiably Marxist, and very little of Spencer."

1974

19 KETTERER, DAVID. <u>New Worlds for Old: The Apocalyptic Imagination, Science Fiction, and American Literature</u>. Bloomington: Indiana University Press, pp. 118, 126-33, 161-63.
Offers a detailed analysis of <u>The Iron Heel</u>, a "classic
dystopia." Everhard is the personal embodiment of the
"driving evolutionary force" of Socialism. Moral and
philosophical ambiguities arise from the essentially simi-
lar humanity and morality of the Socialists and Oligarchy,
the "metaphysical" vision of the materialistic hero, and
other conflicts, creating chaos in the novel. Chaos also
results when the reader attempts to distinguish among
eight "apocalyptic reorientations to reality" suggested
in the novel. London could not convey the historical reality of a Socialist utopia; therefore, this writer "can
only conceive of a reality in which the dystopian situation
continues indefinitely."

20 LONDON, JOAN. "A Tribute to My Father." <u>JLN</u>, 7 (September-
December), 94-95.
Written in 1966, this is similar to statements in her
"Introduction" to 1968.A3.

21 MONTEIRO, GEORGE. "Jack London: An Unrecorded Parody." <u>JLN</u>,
7 (May-August), 65-66.
Prints "Evaporated Fiction: <u>The Game</u>" from <u>The Touch-
stone</u> (January, 1906), p. 7.

22 MORRILL, SIBLEY S. "Jack London: UC Rebel of '96." <u>JLN</u>, 7
(September-December), 100-106.
Recounts London's experiences at the University of California. Article is reprinted from <u>East Bay Magazine</u> (Oakland) (December, 1966).

23 [MORTIMER, JAMES E.]. "The Inspiration of Jack London: Man
of Adventure, Writer of Genius, Militant Socialist." <u>JLN</u>,
7 (January-April), 34-41.
Reprint of 1956.B9.

24 POWNALL, DAVID E. <u>Articles on Twentieth-Century Literature:
An Annotated Bibliography, 1954-1970</u>. Volume 4. New
York: Kraus-Thomson, 2360-66.
Lists and briefly describes 31 articles on London.

25 PRAKKEN, SARAH L. <u>The Reader's Advisor: A Layman's Guide to
Literature</u>. Twelfth edition. Volume 1. New York: Bowker, 561-62.
Biographical sketch; lists London's books in print (11
titles) and six books about him.

26 SIEGEL, PAUL N. "Jack London's Iron Heel: Its Significance
    for Today." International Socialist Review (July-August),
    pp. 18-29.
        It belongs to the genre Frye calls the "'anatomy,' a
    dissection or analysis of ideas in a loosely narrative
    form." Thus Everhard is "a powerful cartoon figure un-
    bending in his iron determination to liberate his class
    and all mankind"; and "a series of colloquies" conveys the
    arguments. The theme is "the magnitude of the task of
    conquering capitalism, the power and ferocity of the ruling
    class....there is no doubt that the workers will finally
    perform their historic mission." Prevailing ideas in the
    work include London's commitment to "proletarian fraternity,
    solidarity, and internationalism"; his "belief in the bio-
    logical inferiority of women" and in "biological determin-
    ism" (but here emphasizing the transcendence of animal na-
    ture through cooperation); an anticipation of Keynesian eco-
    nomics; a mixed attitude of "compassion, repulsion, and
    dread" towards the people of the abyss and outrage against
    the society which created their plight. There is "signifi-
    cant confusion in London's mind as to how the revolution
    will triumph." Discusses the relation of London's "remark-
    able Marxist prognostication" to economic and anthropologi-
    cal theories, and to contemporary business, labor, working-
    class, middle-class, and military conditions.

27 SPINNER, JONATHAN H. "A Syllabus for the 20th Century: Jack
    London's 'The Call of the Wild.'" JLN, 7 (May-August),
    73-78.
        London "describes an education, spiritually as well as
    physically, of a being suffering through the dilemma of
    existence of the modern world." Buck breaks the "North-
    land dog's three great laws: fear of man; no quarter among
    themselves; and hard work" as he learns that "violence,
    not love" is the only way to survive.

28 TAYLOR, J. GOLDEN. "The Western Short Story," in Western
    Writing. Edited by Gerald W. Haslam. Albuquerque: Uni-
    versity of New Mexico Press, pp. 96-97, 100.
        Briefly discusses "All-Gold Canyon" and "To the Man on
    the Trail."

29 TUCK, DONALD H., comp. The Encyclopedia of Science Fiction
    and Fantasy Through 1968. Volume 1. Chicago: Advent,
    278-79.
        Gives brief biography; lists ten volumes of London's
    fiction with publication data and prices of several edi-
    tions in English and foreign languages; gives the contents
    of volumes (collections) or brief plot summaries (novels).

1974

30   TWENEY, GEORGE H. "Jack London: Bibliographically and Bio-
        graphically Speaking." JLN, 7 (January-April), 9-22.
           Reviews bibliographical problems of London first editions;
        comments on the quality and contents of published and un-
        published bibliographies and biographies, and offers a
        checklist of 63 such items.

31   WALCUTT, CHARLES CHILD. "Jack London," in his edition of
        Seven Novelists in the American Naturalist Tradition: An
        Introduction. Minneapolis: University of Minnesota Press,
        pp. 131-67.
        Reprint of 1966.A3.

32   _____. "London, Jack (pseudonym of John Griffith)," in Ency-
        clopedia of American Biography. Edited by John A. Garraty.
        New York: Harper and Row, pp. 683-84.
        Biography and criticism.

33   WEITZEL, ROY L. "Toward a 'Bright White Light'; London's Use
        of Swinburne in Martin Eden." JLN, 7 (January-April), 1-8.
           Allusions to Swinburne and his poetry shape the plot and
        two "major motifs: the relationship between art and life,
        and the role of the artist in the society of the novel."
        Martin, "the innocent artist" intuitively appreciates Swin-
        burne's sensuality, freedom, and truth-to-experience; but
        Ruth, "an incomplete woman," objects to indelicacy, fails
        to understand "the complexity of life," and drives Martin
        into paralyzing conventionality. Swinburne, Brissenden,
        and Martin, who recognized the oneness of "true living and
        true literature," failed to survive in bourgeoise society.

34   WINGFIELD, WILLIAM. "Jack London's Forlorn Dream." The West,
        17 (March), 38-41, 63.
        Reprint of 1966.B38.

35   WOODBRIDGE, HENSLEY C. "L'Appel de la vie Series Directed by
        Francis Lacassin." JLN, 7 (January-April), 30-33.
           Describes the current reprints of "French standard trans-
        lations of London's works with introductions, notes of
        various kinds, and explanatory matter," including several
        texts and much secondary material not available in English.

36   _____, comp. "WLT^2: Supplement 3." JLN, 7 (January-April),
        49-54.
           Additions to 1973.A7; lists stories and letters by Lon-
        don; collections; English and foreign editions; materials
        about London.

1975

37 ____. "Into What Language Has London Been Translated?" JLN,
7 (May-August), 84.
Book-length translations in 68 languages are documented
in 1973.A7.

38 ____, comp. "WLT^2: Supplement 4." JLN, 7 (May-August),
85-89.
Additions to 1973.A7; lists stories and ephemera by London; foreign editions; materials about London.

39 ____. "WLT^2: Supplement 5." JLN, 7 (September-December),
127-31.
Additions to 1973.A7; lists collections and anthologies;
English and foreign editions; materials about London.

40 WOODRESS, JAMES L. "Jack London," in his American Fiction,
1900-1950. A Guide to Information Sources. Volume 1.
Detroit: Gale Research, 145-48.
Lists bibliography and manuscripts; works of fiction;
editions and reprints; biography; criticism.

41 WOODWARD, ROBERT H. "Collector Creates 'The World of Jack
London.'" Hobbies, 78 (January), 49-50.
Describes the museum of London's works, photographs,
maps, and memorabilia developed by Russ Kingman in Glen
Ellen.

1975 A BOOKS

1 McCLINTOCK, JAMES I. White Logic: Jack London's Short Stories.
Wolf House Books Monograph Number Two. Grand Rapids,
Michigan: Wolf House Books, 222 pp.
In 1898-1902, London established the forms, techniques,
and style of all his later stories by studying other
writers, particularly Kipling, successful magazine fiction, and Herbert Spencer's Philosophy of Style. He moved
from "formula" stories to the "essay-exemplum form," to
greater reliance on dialogue and action in "frame" stories;
and finally to his most dramatic form with a limited third-
person narrator and powerful central scenes. From Spencer
and Haeckel he derived a philosophy of life and a rationale
for rooting his fiction "in an expanding reality of harsh
facts" while imbuing it with idealism.
Men who "undertake a romantic quest for identity (ideals)"
confront the Northland, which is the harsh actuality of
life and a cosmic realm of death. In the early Alaskan
tales, London's ideal man is the Malemute Kid, who pits

his life-giving values--"common sense, intelligence, ingenuity, integrity, loyalty, love and active strength,"
and imagination--against the naturalistic universe. But
his attempts to affirm man's significance and dignity fail;
"the message is that man is limited." Other protagonists
find reason and logic, like ideals, useless weapons in the
"uncharted land of the spirit," the mythical Northland.
They must move beyond these to violence and death to deal
with nature on its own "supra-rational" level and perhaps
define themselves. In his best Alaskan fiction, and in
better stories throughout his career, the mood is pessimistic: London depicts deficient, limited men, inhibited
or destroyed by "indifferent or even sadistically irrational forces." His concerns are modern: "alienation,
disenchantment, ironic ambivalence, and impotence."

London's best work appears in the six volumes of Alaskan
tales (1898-1908): The Son of the Wolf; The God of His
Fathers; Children of the Frost; The Faith of Men; Love of
Life; and Lost Face. Stories of 1906-1911 show "a growing
loss of literary vitality" and "a retreat into the inconsequential." In a few socialist stories he moves to themes
of "social mastery" in an attempt to affirm positive
values; the best of these are in The Strength of the
Strong (1914). South Sea Tales (1911) and The House of
Pride (1912) are distinctly "second-rate"; they reveal
London's "philosophical pessimism turning into artistic
cynicism." With their "collective hero" the brutal, exploitative white man, all but a few of these tales are
marred by racism, "perverse sensationalism," an unsuitable
"comic tone" or "mechanical sadism," and sentimentality.
Tales in the 1912 collections, Smoke Bellew and A Son of
the Sun are "potboilers." Those in Moon-Face (1906), When
God Laughs (1911), The Night Born (1913), and The Turtles
of Tasman (1916) are "relatively inconsequential fiction."
Occasional excellent tales do appear in some of these volumes, but generally they are characterized by emphasis on
"the merely sensational" and "irrational man's abnormal
psychology"; a tone of grim or slapstick humor; "techno-
logical trickery"; dependence on pathos, propaganda, or
prejudice to move the reader, and the airing of "personal
grievances."

Seven stories in London's last collections, The Red One
(1918) and On the Makaloa Mat (1919) show the influence
of Jung's Psychology of the Unconscious and of Freud.
These tales return to the themes of "death, the conflict
between primitive and modern culture, and the struggle
between optimism and pessimism." Overall, London's best
stories offer "a protagonist who is possessed both by

demons and a compelling intuition, which he must struggle
to verify, that a saving illumination is the reward for
agony....London intuitively, at first, and deliberately,
at last, evoked the mythopoeic." Analyzes and evaluates
many individual stories. Volume includes notes and a primary and secondary bibliography. Includes revised texts
of 1970.B30; 1972.B25; and dissertation, 1968.A4.

2   PANKAKE, JON ALAN. "The Broken Myths of Jack London: Civiliza-
     tion, Nature, and the Self in the Major Works." Ph.D.
     dissertation. University of Minnesota.

3   What's New About London, Jack? 5, no. 1 (20 June), 10 pp.;
     5, no. 2 (20 September), 10 pp.; 5, no. 3 (18 September),
     10 pp.
        Mimeographed. All issues offer annotated primary and
     secondary bibliography, news items, and notes.

4   The Wolf--'75 [Edited by David H. Schlottman]. Olympia,
     Washington: London Northwest, 21 pp.
        Mimeographed. A Jack London Birthday Annual, distributed
     January 12, 1975, Oakland, California. Contains obituaries
     and tributes, accounts of London's cremation, burial, and
     will, reprinted from Bay Area newspapers of November, 1916.

1975 B SHORTER WRITINGS

1   BURSTEIN, HAROLD M. "Bibliographical Assistance Solicited."
     JLN, 8 (January-April), 20-21.
        Believes that three stories ("In Gold Time," "A Cala-
     veras Hold-Up," "Frazer's Find") were written by London
     in 1895, submitted to a Black Cat contest, and published
     there in October, November, and December, 1895, under the
     pseudonym "Roberta Littlehale."

2   CLAYTON, LAWRENCE. "The Sea-Wolf: London's Commedia." JLN,
     8 (May-August), 50-54.
        Among parallels to Dante's work are use of a first per-
     son retrospective narrator, Humphrey's journey on "a water-
     borne Inferno or Hell," and his growth to awareness as he
     moves upward to redemption by the pure Maud-Beatrice.
     Larsen functions as guide, judge, tormentor, and suffering
     demon; he is like "the three-headed Satan and Cerebus."

3   COOPER, JAMES GLENNON. "The Womb of Time: Archetypal Patterns
     in the Novels of Jack London: Excerpts." JLN, 8 (January-
     April), 1-5.
        In such novels as Martin Eden and The Sea-Wolf, London's

1975

"conscious intention and unconscious accomplishment" conflict; his worshipful attitude toward the heroes makes the
novels "heroic tragedies on the death of individualism"
although he claimed otherwise. Recurrent themes in his
works, "such as the abyss and the summit, the White Silence,
and atavism,...are archetypal elements" in his private myth.
His characters, mostly self-portraits, are "symbols of unconscious 'characters' in the collective psyche of the
race....themselves archetypes" over and above their significance in the fiction. Excerpted from dissertation, 1974.A1.

4   DAGHLIAN, CARLOS. "Jack London in Brazil and Portugal." JLN,
       8 (January-April), 22-27.
         Lists 28 translations of 19 London titles, and 2 col-
       lections of stories; also stories in general anthologies
       and magazines, material about London in Portugese, and re-
       views of motion picture adaptations of his novels.

5   FARMER, PHILIP JOSÉ. "Foreword," in Curious Fragments; Jack
       London's Tales of Fantasy Fiction. Edited by Dale L.
       Walker. Port Washington: Kennikat, pp. vii-x.
         Qualities of London's fantasy fiction which influenced
       many later writers include: "awe of the vastness, harsh-
       ness, and indifference of nature set against a fierce ad-
       miration of man's fighting spirit and intellect"; affirma-
       tion of life and human effort to transcend animality; be-
       lief "that character determines destiny"; blending of fan-
       tasy with reality and using concrete detail to exemplify
       philosophical views. Before Adam and The Star Rover are
       "science fiction classics." Comments on the stories in
       this collection. Volume includes an "Introduction" and
       "A Note on the Selections," pp. 3-10, by the editor, who
       notes London's affinity for fantastic elements in his
       other works; includes also a London chronology and "Sug-
       gested Readings."

6   FORTIER, EDWARD J. "Views of America: VIII: Jack London's
       Far North." National Observer (21 June), p. 22.
         London is considered "the most influential of Far North
       authors" by several modern writers and Alaskan readers
       (who are quoted here).

7   FRENCH, WARREN. "Fiction: 1900-1930," in American Literary
       Scholarship: An Annual/1973. Edited by James Woodress.
       Durham, N. C.: Duke University Press, pp. 233-34.
         Essay-review of major work on London.

8   HAIRE, DAVID B. and DENNIS E. HENSLEY. "A Comparative Look at
     W. S. Maugham and Jack London." JLN, 8 (September–December), 114–18.
         They "focused upon the average man" and dealt with themes
     of "marital infidelity, miscegenation, justified murder,
     class struggle, and mass poverty."

9   HARPHANN, GEOFFREY. "Jack London and the Tradition of Super-
     man Socialism." AmerS, 16 (Spring), 23–33.
         With other literary socialists like Shaw, Sinclair, and
     Wells, London operated within the popular tradition of
     "Group Individualism." He adopted the evolutionary princi-
     ples and contempt for the bestial masses of De Casseres,
     and the idea of the "superior man" of Osias L. Schwarz.
     His socialism was exclusive: he believed in Nordic domi-
     nance, that the fit would survive and the unfit perish.
     The Iron Heel reveals London's ambiguous vision of the
     mob as both apocalyptic agents and degenerate sub-humans.
     With Martin Eden, he abandoned the ideals of superman so-
     cialism by portraying Brissenden as "the prophet of higher
     truth." Brissenden, the "artist-degenerate" popularized
     by Max Nordau, carries the message "that knowledge leads
     to nihilism; that perception means only consciousness of
     decay and degeneration; and that the will to intenser life
     means the will to suicide." Excerpted and revised from
     1974.A2.

10   HATCHEL, LINDA. "Animal Imagery in London's 'A Piece of Steak.'"
     JLN, 8 (September–December), 119–21.
         Tom King is like a lion in name, physical appearance,
     motivation, actions, and fighting techniques. The law of
     survival of the fittest is shown governing animal and hu-
     man behavior.

11   HAVLICE, PATRICIA PATE, comp. Index to Literary Biography.
     Volume 2. Metuchen, N. J.: Scarecrow Press, 730.
         Cites eight references to London.

12   HENSLEY, DENNIS E. "A Note on Jack London's Use of Black
     Humor." JLN, 8 (September–December), 110–13.
         In fiction from 1895, he incorporated morbid and absurd
     elements for comic relief and comic effects.

13   _____. "Sherlock Holmes and Smoke Bellew." JLN, 8 (September–
     December), 129–32.
         For "The Mistake of Creation," London borrowed the false
     fire alarm trick from Doyle's "A Scandal in Bohemia."

1975

14 JØRGENSON, JENS PETER. "Jack London's 'The Red One'; A
    Freudian Approach." JLN, 8 (September-December), 101-103.
        Bassett, like Conrad's Kurtz, is "possessed, crippled,
    and finally killed" by his "uncontrollable libido." The
    story "is loaded with sexual symbolism," primarily phallic.

15 KING, FRANCES. "Treatment of the Mentally Retarded Character
    in Modern American Fiction." BB, 32 (July-September), 113.
        Briefly describes "Told in the Drooling Ward."

16 KINGMAN, RUSS. "Introduction," in The Valley of the Moon.
    Jack London Centennial Series, no. 1. Santa Barbara,
    California: Peregrine Smith, pp. v-x.
        Gives biographical background of events and characters
    in the novel. Valley advocates "a life style based on a
    closeness to the soil, a rejection of urban values and
    problems, and an appreciation for the pleasures of 'the
    road.'"

17 LABOR, EARLE. "Jack London in Denmark." JLN, 8 (September-
    December), 95-100.
        Account of a seminar on London taught at Aarhus Univer-
    sity. London remains popular in Denmark, where "something
    like 2,000,000 copies" of his works have been sold since
    1913.

18 LACASSIN, FRANCIS. "Jack London Between the Challenge of the
    Supernatural and the Last Judgment." JLN, 8 (May-August),
    59-65.
        The Iron Heel and London's other fiction set in the
    future lie "just outside of the science fiction genre" be-
    cause his concern is more the study of social relations,
    presaging "an aggravation of social inequalities" in the
    future, than a vision of the benefits of scientific progress.
    London's pessimism, socialism, and challenge to the super-
    natural links him with the school of Wells. In London's
    works, a violent apocalypse with vengeance wreaked on the
    privileged classes precedes the possible advent of a so-
    cialist utopia. Article is translated by Jack Hockett,
    with notes by Hensley C. Woodbridge.

19 LACHTMAN, HOWARD. "Another Look at 'The Vally of the Moon.'"
    San Francisco Chronicle (20 July), "This World" section,
    p. 20.
        In spite of structural flaws, dated dialogue, and senti-
    mentality, the novel is a meaningful and readable presen-
    tation of "modern man's quest for meaning through urban
    ordeal and rural odyssey." Revised: 1975.B20.

20 ____. "Reconsideration: The Valley of the Moon by Jack London." New Republic, 173 (6 September), 27-29.
"A minor masterpiece of proletarian fiction...[and] an
important milestone in the literature of nostalgia," the
novel contrasts the sterile "dissension-torn city" and its
working poor with "the life-sustaining country" that promises
personal and national redemption. Discusses London's ranch-
ing and farming activities. Expanded text of 1975.B19.

21 LEITZ, ROBERT C. "Jack London in 'Rhymed Reviews' and 'Impu-
dent Interviews.'" JLN, 8 (September-December), 122-28.
Reprints six poems by Arthur Guiterman from Life, 1910-
1914. See appended "Poems."

22 MOHAN, CHANDRA. "Jack London's Humanism." JLN, 8 (May-August),
40-49.
He loved mankind and optimistically trusted man's nobility
and goodness to triumph over hostile nature and social
evils. His revolutionary Marxist Humanism, strongest in
The Iron Heel and "The Mexican," promises "a just society
on the basis of economic equality" and universal brotherhood.

23 MONTEIRO, GEORGE. "Jack London: Additions to the Bibliography,"
JLN, 8 (May-August), 78-79.
Lists principally reviews of London's novels.

24 NIELSEN, J. O., trans. "Jack London--Lone Wolf and Social
Critic." JLN, 8 (September-December), 107-109.
A sketch of his life and works from History of World
Literature (Copenhagen, 1973).

25 ORECHWA, OLGA P. "[Review of] Jerzy Szkup, Recepcja Prozy
Amerykanskiej W Polsce Ludowej W Latach 1945-1965. War-
szawa: Universytet Warszawski, Instytut Filologii Angiel-
skiej, 1972." JLN, 8 (January-April), 6-7.
In this twenty-year period, 81 London works were published in Poland. Among foreign writers, London ranked
sixth in 1944-55, second in 1950-55, third in 1956-60, and
first in 1955-65. The author regrets that London's popularity was not reflected in the work of Polish literary
critics during these years.

26 POWERS, RICHARD GID. "Introduction," in his edition of The
Science Fiction of Jack London: An Anthology. Gregg
Press Science Fiction Series. Boston: Gregg, pp. vii-xxiv.
Gives brief biography, analyzes individual stories, and
discusses literary influences. London adopted "revolutionary

socialism and scientific racism" to escape his "cultural
poverty," to give order to his life and provide a "master
formula" for his art. He read widely but uncritically and
never explored his own inner being; thus his mind remained
unintegrated with his personality and the larger culture.
In a sense, all his work was science fiction, for it was
"fanciful rather than imaginative, speculative rather than
introspective." His fictional theme was that uncomprehen-
sible, uncontrollable natural laws dominate man's life.
He used the laws, discoveries, and ideologies of science
in various ways for plot and thematic development in his
fiction. London saw science as "an abstract substitute
for culture" rather than a part of culture. His work was
"filled with pain and sense of limitation growing out of
this cultural isolation."

27   RIBER, JØRGEN. "Archetypal Patterns in 'The Red One.'" JLN,
      8 (September–December), 104–106.
         Bassett journeys into his subconscious in quest of wis-
      dom and dies "as a result of his hubris." Archetypes
      noted include two negative aspects of "the Great Mother":
      the siren and the vagina dentata, and the positive "Sophia"
      aspect.

28   SCHLOTTMAN, DAVID HENRY. "To Build Yet Another Fire." JLN, 8
      (January–April), 11–14.
         London published two versions of "To Build a Fire." The
      ideas of both appear in a later story, "The Match" by Cur-
      wood; and another variation occurs in a comic strip, Mark
      Trail (1974), by Ed Dodd.

29   SKIPP, FRANCIS E. "Guide to Dissertations on American Literary
      Figures, 1870–1910: Jack London." ALR, 8 (Autumn), 299–306.
         Describes and evaluates nineteen dissertations (1935–
      1970) wholly or in part on London; and briefly discusses
      five German-language dissertations (1927–1960).

30   TSUJII, EIJI. "Jack London Items in the Japanese Press of
      1904." JLN, 8 (May–August), 55–58.
         Reprints accounts of London's arrest by the Moji Water
      Police for taking pictures in a war zone.

31   UMPHLETT, WILEY LEE. The Sporting Myth and the American Ex-
      perience. Lewisburg, Pennsylvania: Bucknell University
      Press, pp. 101–102, 109.
         Boxing in "A Piece of Steak" symbolizes man's life-
      struggle against great odds. King is crushed by organized
      boxing as London's other competitive individualists are

crushed by "superior forces." The contrast between King's
dream and American reality is a pervasive theme in modern
fiction.

32 WINGFIELD, WILLIAM. "Jack London and the Occult." Fate:
True Stories of the Strange and Unknown (July), pp. 70-75.
London "thought he was being driven toward some ultimate
foreordained goal." His heroes are predestined to doom;
and his works show "prophetic" or "psychic" qualities.

33 WINNICK, DAVID. "What Jack London (or Allende) Knew About the
Enemies of Democracy." Tribune (London; a Labour Weekly)
(17 January), p. 6; and JLN, 8 (January-April), 8-10.
A review of The Iron Heel. It is a "brilliantly imaginative" novel that exposes the plight of industrial workers,
the indifference of the upper class, and the relation of
capital to "law, press, and universities." It is still
worth reading.

34 WOODBRIDGE, HENSLEY C., comp. "WLT^2: Supplement 5." JLN, 8
(January-April), 28-31.
Additions to 1973.A7; lists stories and articles by Lon-
don; English and foreign editions; materials about London.
[The number (5) of this supplement repeats 1974.B39.]

35 _____. "WLT^2: Supplement 6." JLN, 8 (May-August), 80-82.
Additions to 1973.A7; lists editions, stories, collections, anthologies; materials about London.

36 _____, comp. "WLT^2: Supplement 7." JLN, 8 (September-December),
133-37.
Additions to 1973.A7; lists editions and anthologies;
materials about London.

1976 A BOOKS

1 ANON. Jack London Centennial Pieces. Olympia, Washington:
What's New About London, Jack? Cedar Springs, Michigan:
The London Collector, 32 pp.
Commemorative pamphlet for the London Centennial dinner,
January 12, Oakland, California. Contains an essay, Russ
Kingman, "What About the Second Hundred Years?" which re-
views London's status; and five previously uncollected
selections by London, written 1897-1917.

2 What's New About London, Jack? 6, no. 1 (1 April), 12 pp.
Annotated primary and secondary bibliography, news
items and notes about London.

1976

1976 B SHORTER WRITINGS

1   AIGNER, HAL. "The Jack London Legacy." San Francisco Examiner
    and Chronicle (11 January), California Living Magazine,
    pp. 22, 24-27.
    London represented his restless era of transition and
    remains significant today. His remarkably diverse works,
    sustained by "autobiographical vibrancy," include "adven-
    ture, science fiction, political fiction, sports fiction,
    murder mysteries, war correspondence, psychological horror,
    the first 'Beat' novel, and what has recently been labeled
    'new journalism.'" Qualities which continue to generate
    worldwide admiration for his work are his devotion to the
    common man's dignity and power, his "mystical reverence
    for life," and his "commitment to love, companionship and
    justice."

2   BENNETT, RAINE EDWARD. "The Intimate Jack London." San Fran-
    cisco (18 March), pp. [46]-49, 100-101, 108.
    Personal reminiscences of Jack's deep love for Charmian,
    their guests and friends, daily activities, and Jack's
    generosity.

3   DeMARCO, GORDON. "Jack London: A Century of Labor Advocacy."
    Classroom Teacher (Oakland) (30 January), p. 6.
    "London devoted a significant share of his literary
    craft and personal energy to advance" the socialist move-
    ment.

4   FORREY, ROBERT. "When Jack London Came to Yale." Yale Alumni
    Magazine, 39 (May), 26-28.
    Reviews accounts of London's talk at Yale (1906) and
    articles generated by it. Although London preached "life"
    he was preoccupied with death; and "if on a political level
    London rejected Yale and Yale men as products of a moribund
    capitalist system, on another level he may have admired
    them as archetypal Anglo-Saxons. Apparently his racism
    went deeper than his socialism....he remained for the rest
    of his life an incurably romantic collegian, particularly
    about athletics and the opposite sex....No Yale man could
    have been more committed to material success and less
    alive on occasion to moral or spiritual values." See
    Irvine, 1906.Al.

5   KAPLAN, BERNARD D. "Greatest American Author? Europe for
    Jack London." San Francisco Examiner and Chronicle
    (8 February), section A, p. 20.
    France, Germany, Britain, and Russia celebrate London's

centenary with reissues of his works, critical studies and a film. His conflicting ideologies, radicalism, and Americanism attract European critics.

6   LINDSAY, JACK. "Born in Poverty 100 Years Ago, His Contradictions Tore Him Apart...Jack London." Morning Star (London) (10 January), p. 4.
     "His work remains a great achievement, an enduring monument of working-class struggle."

Poems about Jack London

*1 HEINEY, E. B. The Call of the Wild. A Tribute in Verse.
     Huntington, Indiana (22 May, 1905), 4 pp. folder.
     Cited in Woodbridge, 1966.A8.

*2 METCALFE, SADIE BOWMAN. "A Farewell Shot." Western World, 2,
     no. 1 (April, 1907), 30.
     Cited in Woodbridge, 1966.A8.

3   GUITERMAN, ARTHUR. "Jack London." Life, 55 (31 March, 1910),
     576.

4   _____. "Burning Daylight." Life, 56 (10 November, 1910), 833.

5   _____. "Adventure." Life, 57 (8 June, 1911), 1131.

6   _____. "John Barleycorn." Life, 62 (25 September, 1913), 540.

7   _____. "The Valley of the Moon." Life, 63 (19 February,
     1914), 327.

8   _____. "The Mutiny of the Elsinore." Life, 64 (5 November,
     1914), 829.
     [All Guiterman poems cited and reprinted in 1975.B21].

9   BURROUGHS, JACK. "Dead?" San Francisco Bulletin (24 November,
     1916), p. 8.

10 LOWE, GEORGE N. "Good-by Jack London." San Francisco Bulletin
     (24 November, 1916), p. 8.

11 PERRY, STELLA GEORGE STERN. "'A Man Has Just Passed By.'"
     San Francisco Bulletin (24 November, 1916), p. 8.

12 STERLING, GEORGE. Untitled tribute, read by Edward B. Payne
     at London's funeral. San Francisco Chronicle (25 November,
     1916), p. 8.
        Reprinted as "Farewell! Farewell!" California Writers
     Club Quarterly Bulletin, 4 (December, 1916), 1 and 1975.A4.

Poems about Jack London

Reprinted as "To Jack London." <u>Overland Monthly</u>, 69 (May, 1917), 360; and frequently elsewhere.

13 NETHING, RICHARD. "A Tribute to Jack London." <u>The World</u> (Oakland) (1 December, 1916), p. 3.

14 LEWIS, LUCIEN M. "Jack London." <u>Out West</u>, NS 44 (December, 1916), 242.

15 GARRETT, W. B. "Jack London." <u>Bohemia</u> (San Francisco), 1, no. 6 (15 December, 1916), 172.

16 RICHARDSON, FLORENCE. "His New Adventure: A Tribute to Jack London." <u>Bohemia</u> (San Francisco), 1, no. 6 (15 December, 1916), frontispiece.

17 McBOYLE, A. M. "Jack London: As He Lived." <u>Silhouette</u>, 1, no. 4 (December 1916–January 1917), 73.

18 COLE, VERA HEATHMAN. "Jack London." <u>Overland Monthly</u>, 69 (February, 1917), 160.

19 ANON. "Jack London (In Memoriam)." <u>International Socialist Review</u>, 17 (April, 1917), 624.

20 BRALEY, BERTON. "Jack London: An Appreciation." <u>Overland Monthly</u>, 69 (May, 1917), 415.

21 GORDON, CARL. "Jack London--A Little Journey." <u>The Fra</u>, 19 (May, 1917), 63-64.

22 SLOAN, BESSIE I. "At Jack London's Home, April Twenty-second, 1917." <u>California Writers Club Monthly Bulletin</u>, 1 (May, 1917), 7.

23 MILLER, J. CORSON. "The Last Trail." <u>Current Opinion</u>, 62 (June, 1917), 431.

24 McGIMSEY, GROVER C. <u>A Son of the Gods</u>. Ukiah, California: Northern Crown Publishing Company, 1918. 25 pp.

25 DAVIS, GRACE MONROE. "To Jack London." <u>Overland Monthly</u>, 90 (May, 1932), 108.

26 _____. "The Rebel." <u>Overland Monthly</u>, 90 (May, 1932), 118.

27 KELLY, SARAH HAMMOND. "Martin Eden." <u>Overland Monthly</u>, 90 (May, 1932), 108.

28   WILSON, NELL G. "Adventuring (In Memory of Jack London)."
         Overland Monthly, 90 (May, 1932), 120.

29   GORDON, W. D. "The Eagle." Overland Monthly, 90 (July, 1932),
         159.

30   GWIN, IRMA A. "In the Valley of the Moon (Dedicated to Jack
         London)." The Snark (Jack London Amateur Press Club,
         UAPAA), 2, no. 1 (February, 1944), [5].

31   STAFFORD, WILLIAM. "Jack London." Poetry, 106 (August, 1965),
         323.

*32   DAVIS, WILLIAM HOWARD LEE. "Apostrophe to Jack London," in
         his The Wheel of Life and Other Poems. Hermiston, Oregon:
         Author, 1968, pp. 12-14.
            Cited in Woodbridge, 1973.A7.

33   WOODWARD, ROBERT H. "Martin Eden." JLN, 4 (September-Decem-
         ber, 1971), [160].

34   LACHTMAN, HOWARD. "Elegy for Jack London." Pacific Historian,
         15 (Fall 1971), 92-93.

35   MARTIN, JAY. "Wolf House in the Spring." CEA, 34 (May, 1972),
         22-24.

36   KNIGHT, ARTHUR WINFIELD. "The Wolf House." Poetry Newsletter,
         23 (October, 1973), 11.

37   BELLMAN, SAMUEL I. "Am Lit Symmetrics (4) Jack London." CEA,
         36 (May, 1974), 26.

      [An additional 22 poems to London are listed in Bubka, 1968.A1;
      and see note 1 to my "Introduction"].

Master's Theses on Jack London*

1   ANDREW, LLOYD D. "Jack London, Pioneer Naturalist." Texas
    Western College of the University of Texas, 1956.

2   BACKUS, JOHN E. "Jack London, His Works and His Philosophy."
    Fordham University, 1936.

3   BARNEY, DANFORD. "La Bete Humaine: A Study of the Bestial
    Imagery in Frank Norris and Jack London and Conflicts
    Which are Illuminated by Such a Study." University of
    Colorado, 1966.

4   BIERNE, THOMAS F. "A Comparative Study of the Novels of the
    Sea of Jack London." St. John's University, 1952.

5   BOUCHER, JAMES J. "The Political and Economic Opinions of
    Jack London." University of Kentucky, 1936.

6   BRAGIN, MOSES. "The Superman in Jack London's Works." Colum-
    bia University, 1929.

7   CAMPBELL, HARLAN SHELDON. "Jack London's Principles of Writing:
    A Critical Appraisal." Stanford University, 1950.

8   CARROLL, JOSEPH P. "Jack London: Socialist Writer." Univer-
    sity of Kansas, 1967.

#9 CARROLL, LAVON B. "Woman in the Novels of Jack London." Utah
    State University, 1963.

10 COLLEY, NELLIE M. "The Romanticism and Realism in Jack Lon-
    don's Works." Louisiana State University, 1939.

11 COST, CHARLES C. "The Darwinian Thought of Jack London." New
    York University, 1965.

#12 DHONDT, STEVEN T. "Jack London's Satire in When God Laughs."
    Utah State University, 1967.

JACK LONDON: A REFERENCE GUIDE

Master's Theses on Jack London

13   DISHINGER, MARY L. "Jack London's Indictment of Capitalism." Illinois State University, 1966.

14   DOZIER, MARY DEAN. "The Conflict Between Individualism and Socialism in the Life and Novels of Jack London." North Texas State College, 1948.

#15   FEIED, FREDERICK J. "The Hobo in the Works of Jack London, John Dos Passos and Jack Kerouac." Columbia University, 1961.

16   FINDLEY, EMMA S. "The Dichotomy of Jack London." Baylor University, 1967.

17   FRANK, JEANETTE. "Naturalism in Selected Novels and Stories of Jack London." Texas Woman's University, 1970.

18   FRAUENGLASS, ETTIE. "Jack London as a Socialist." New York University, 1939.

19   FREEMAN, H. A. "Jack London and the Problem of Poverty." State University of Iowa, 1932.

#20   FUJIWARA, SAKAE. "Jack London in Connection with the American Dream." Keio Gijyuku University (Japan), 1970.

21   FULKERTH, ROBERT C. "Naturalism in the Works of Jack London." Chico State College, 1969.

22   FULLER, FRANK A. "Jack London and Critical Realism." Roosevelt University, 1965.

23   GLEASON, EDWIN P. "Jack London and Socialism." Columbia University, 1947.

24   GRANT, NORMAN. "Social Consciousness in Selected Works of Jack London." University of Maine, 1965.

25   GREEN, E. CAROL. "Social Aspects of Some of Jack London's Novels." Utah State University, 1959.

26   HALL, VIVIAN HALPERN. "Jack London: Superman and Socialist." University of Colorado, 1947.

27   HEWICK, WALTER E. "An Analysis of Jack London's Naturalism." Howard University, 1967.

JACK LONDON: A REFERENCE GUIDE

28 HORTON, ARTHUR L. "Jack London's Reputation as a Novelist."
    Auburn University, 1951.

29 JUDD, RICHARD. "Revolution and White Silence: Emotional Con-
    siderations in Jack London's Social Philosophy." Cali-
    fornia State College (Fullerton), 1972.

30 KAYS, MAJORIE. "Jack London's The Valley of the Moon: A
    Textual and Critical Study." Ohio State University, 1948.

31 KOLAR, MILDRED MARGUERITE. "Jack London's Unstandardized
    Mastery of Description and Narration." University of
    Nebraska, 1927.

32 LANDIS, JOAN SELBY. "Narrative Techniques in Jack London's
    Alaskan Short Stories." Mills College, 1956.

33 LEVITT, MORTON P. "The Social and Economic Writings of Jack
    London." Columbia University, 1960.

34 MASIELLO, ARTHUR. "Darwinism in the Works of Jack London."
    Seton Hall University, 1960.

35 NEAL, CURTIS M. "Jack London's Alaskan Fiction: A Study of
    Epic Characteristics." North Carolina State University,
    1971.

#36 NICHOL, JOHN WILLIAM. "Local Color in the Alaskan Stories of
    Jack London." Ohio State University, 1948.

37 NICHOLS, THOMAS W. "The Social Philosophy of Jack London."
    Louisiana State University, 1931.

#38 PETERSON, CLELL THOMPSON. "Jack London and the American
    Frontier." University of Minnesota, 1951.

39 SCHMEDAKE, DOROTHY MAY. "Dichotomy in the World of Jack Lon-
    don." Washington University, 1944.

40 SHAW, EDWARD A. "Jack London: Social Critic." University of
    Oklahoma, 1956.

41 SHEAR, WALTER LEWIS. "A Study of the Morality in the Novels
    of Three Modern American Novelists." State University of
    Iowa, 1957.

#42 SHIVERS, ALFRED SAMUEL. "The Characters of Jack London."
    University of Florida, 1959.

Master's Theses on Jack London

43 SPARKS, EVA C. "The Quiet Ones: A Study of Jack London's
    Lesser Heroes." Mississippi State University, 1967.

44 SPENCER, ARTHUR FRANK. "Jack London: Nietzchean Socialist and
    Agrarian." University of Washington, 1933.

45 TUDOR, STEPHEN H. "Reversion in Jack London's Novels." State
    University of Iowa, 1960.

46 WINSOR, WILLIAM T. "Nature and Naturalism in the Works of
    Jack London." Columbia University, 1957.

47 YOUNG, THOMAS DANIEL. "The Political and Social Thought of
    Jack London." University of Mississippi, 1948.

---

*Cited in Woodbridge, 1966.A6; Woodbridge, 1973.A7; Howard, 1973.B27;
Woodbridge, 1973.B57; Woodbridge, 1974.B38.

#Excerpted and revised for articles; see author's name in the Index.

Manuscript Collections

These descriptions of Jack London materials were supplied by the persons named in each annotation. In most cases, I have summarized the detailed information they generously provided. Repositories are listed alphabetically by city.

Berkeley, Calif. University of California. Bancroft Library. Jack London Collection (Irene Moran).
    Manuscripts of 2 sketches.
    Correspondence: letters by London to 10 persons (number unspecified); 4 letters to or about London.
    Photographs.

Bloomington, Ind. Indiana University. The Lilly Library (Saundra Taylor).
    Correspondence: 10 memoranda/letters to publishers and 16 personal letters by London (including 13 to Upton Sinclair); 2 letters about London.

Cambridge, Mass. Harvard University. The Houghton Library (Rodney G. Dennis).
    Correspondence: 10 letters by London (1899–1915).

Charlottesville, Va. University of Virginia. Clifton Waller Barrett Library. Jack London Collection.
    Manuscripts: typescript synopses, page proofs, and preliminary copy of The Sea-Wolf (with holograph corrections); typescripts of 3 essays/stories.
    Correspondence: c. 130 letters by London (1900–1916); c. 62 letters by Charmian London and London's associates.
    Miscellaneous: photographs, memorabilia, receipts, checks, clippings.

Logan, Utah. Utah State University. Merrill Library. Special Collections and Archives. Jack and Charmian London Collection (Manuscript Collection 10).
    The description below concentrates on Jack London materials and is summarized from a 164-page Register published by USU in

Manuscript Collections

> June, 1976. In addition to original correspondence and manu-
> scripts, this collection includes photographic and microfilm
> copies of several thousand London letters held by six other
> libraries.
>
> I. Correspondence
>   A. Of Jack London with publishers, periodicals, and individuals,
>   1898–1916: letters by London, 1162 pieces; letters to Lon-
>   don, 1551 pieces.
>   B. Of Charmian London, Jack Byrne, Executors of the London
>   Estate, Ninetta Payne, Eliza Shepard, and others.
> II. Manuscripts
>   A. Record Books and Journals: includes records of magazine
>   sales; Japanese-Russian War Notebook; Logs, accounts, and
>   notes of the <u>Snark</u> voyage; Tramp Diary.
>   B. Typescript and Holograph Materials: manuscripts of <u>The
>   Abysmal Brute</u>, <u>The Acorn Planter</u>, <u>Adventure</u>, <u>The Assassina-
>   tion Bureau</u>, <u>Martin Eden</u>; some 50 stories, articles, and
>   poems; notes on novels, plays, stories, autobiographies.
> III. Fiction, Articles, and Letters Separately Published in Periodi-
>   cals, c. 224 items.
> IV. Miscellaneous: contracts; accounts; wills; photographs; writings
>   about London; Sinclair Lewis plots, typescripts with Lewis's
>   notes; London's clipping files.

Los Angeles, Calif. University of California. A1713 University Re-
  Search Library. Special Collections (Brooke Whiting).
  Manuscripts: holograph of "Up the Peking Road."
  Correspondence: 8 letters by London.

Los Angeles. University of Southern California. The Library. Ameri-
  can Literature Collection. The Jack London Collection (incorpo-
  rating the Cresmer Collection) (Heddy A. Richter).
  Manuscripts: holograph notes for lectures, articles; typescripts
    of 7 essays, 6 sketches, 4 stories, 5 plays, 1 poem; notes for
    fiction and essays; first draft of <u>The Assassination Bureau</u>
    (with corrections by London and George Sterling).
  Correspondence: 38 letters by London; 26 letters to and about
    London.
  Works by London: 74 books, including all first editions (some
    signed); 37 articles and stories published in periodicals;
    pamphlets and leaflets (some from the Harvey Taylor collec-
    tion).
  Materials about London: 21 books; pamphlets and brochures; manu-
    scripts, including Harvey Taylor, "The Jack London Bibliography"
    (350 leaves); biographical clippings, articles, and typescripts.
  Miscellaneous: publishers' contracts, royalty statements, and
    correspondence; publication announcements.

JACK LONDON: A REFERENCE GUIDE

Madison, Wis. The State Historical Society of Wisconsin. Division of Archives and Manuscripts (Joanne E. Hohler).
 Correspondence: 1 letter by London; letters about London by Joan London and Ernest Untermann, by George N. Caylor and Richard O'Connor.

New York, N. Y. New York Public Library.
 1) Berg Collection of English and American Literature (David Pankow).
 Manuscripts: typescripts of the play The Sea-Wolf (by Guy Bolton and Joseph Noel), with agreements, correspondence.
 Correspondence: 12+ pieces--receipts, letters, telegrams, agreements by and about London.
 2) Manuscripts and Archives Division. Jack London Survey [of materials in various collections].
 a. Macmillan Co. Records. c. 1000 items: letters from London to George Brett (1899-1916); letters (from Brett and Macmillan) to Charmian London (1916-1958); photographs, pamphlets, promotional materials.
 b. Macmillan Letterbooks. c. 200 letters from Brett (and other Macmillan persons) to London; c. 50 letters to Charmian London (all, 1901-1907).
 c. Hayden Carruth Papers. c. 8 letters by and to London; c. 7 letters concerning London by and to Ninetta Eames (all, 1906-1908); photographs.
 d. Miscellaneous collections: c. 7 letters by London and others concerning him.

Oakland, Calif. Main Library. California Room (Frances H. Buxton).
 Correspondence: 14 letters by London (holograph and typescript).
 Works by London: 30 books inscribed by London; copies of all London works, including first editions.
 Miscellaneous: clippings, articles, pamphlets by and about London; books about London; photographs.

Princeton, N. J. Princeton University. The Library (Agnes B. Sherman).
 Correspondence: 3 letters by London.

San Francisco, Calif. Public Library. Special Collections (Anne E. Englund).
 Manuscripts and Works: manuscript notes for 5 novels and stories; typescripts with notes of The Acorn Planter and "A Good Woman"; London's books, including first editions.
 Correspondence: 3 letters by London; 5 about him.
 Miscellaneous: photographs; news clippings.

JACK LONDON: A REFERENCE GUIDE

Manuscript Collections

San Marino, Calif. The Huntington Library. The Jack London and
Charmian (Kittredge) London Collections (William Ingoldsby).
These two collections of personal and professional papers contain
some 15,000 pieces covering the years 1888-1932. The data be-
low, summarized from a 29-page description, concentrates on
materials by and about Jack London.
I. Jack London Collection (in boxes 1-137).
A. Personal Papers.
1. Business papers [regarding the ranch, business ventures, lawsuits], 1142 pieces.
2. Correspondence, 247 pieces [includes c. 143 letters by
London, 9 to him].
B. Professional Papers.
1. Agreements, assignments, contracts [for dramatizations,
film productions, publications, translations of London's works], 160 pieces.
2. Correspondence, 6315 pieces [includes c. 55 letters by
London; others are principally to London concerning
his works and socialism from friends, fans, translators,
adaptors, editors].
3. Lawsuits, 122 pieces.
4. Manuscripts: c. 550 pieces by London, including typescripts and holograph articles, stories, essays, and
notes for these. Boxes 107-136 contain "Manuscripts
of Jack London's Books," number unspecified.
5. Notebooks: 7 notebooks [kept by London, 1904-1916;
include records of magazine sales, ideas for plots].
II. Jack London and Charmian (Kittredge) London Collection: Addenda
(19 boxes).
1. Manuscripts by London: 4 holograph letters/sketches;
diary-datebooks for 1904-1905; typescripts of 30
stories, 6 novels, non-fiction books, and plays; 54
items (multiple pages) of notes on plots, subjects,
lists of names for stories.
2. Correspondence: c. 35 letters by London; c. 58 letters
to London; other family and miscellaneous correspondence.
3. Miscellaneous: London documents, bills, receipts, and
memorabilia; poems and recollections about London, 12
items; Sinclair Lewis plots, 12 items; diaries, manuscripts, and letters of Charmian London.

Stanford, Calif. The Stanford University Libraries. Special Collections, Fe77 (Blodwen Tarter).
Papers of Jack London, 182 items: correspondence with Mabel and
Edward Applegarth and James B. Pinker; poems; manuscripts;
scraps and facsimiles.
Collection Fe80 mentions London; Felton Vertical File contains
some London ephemera.

Stockton, Calif. University of the Pacific. Stuart Library of
Western Americana (Robin Lampson).
Works by London: all first editions to 1916 inscribed by London
to members of his family; 25 volumes (including all first
editions since his death) signed by Joan or Becky London.
Works about London: books, some inscribed; complete files of the
three London periodicals; periodical clippings.

Index

299

INDEX

Conrad, Joseph, 1927.B4; 1958.B2
A CONCISE SURVEY OF AMERICAN
    LITERATURE, 1955.B9
CONTEMPORARY AMERICAN LITERATURE,
    1922.B4
A Contemporary Sketch of Jack
    London, 1966.B36
Contrast as Device, 1929.B12
Cook, George, 1973.B12; 1974.B4
Cook, May Estelle, 1906.B36
Cool, Una H. H., 1906.B37;
    1908.B26-B27; 1909.B11;
    1910.B20-B21; 1911.B31-B32;
    1912.B14
Coolbrith, Ina, 1972.B36;
    1973.B38
Cooper, Frederic Taber, 1904.B32-
    B33; 1905.B40; 1906.B38-B39;
    1907.B38; 1909.B12; 1914.B22-
    B23
Cooper, James Fenimore, 1959.B4
Cooper, James Glennon, 1975.B3
Cordell, Richard, 1954.B2
Coren, Alan, 1967.B5
Corey, William A., 1931.B3-B5
Coryn, Sidney G. P., 1907.B39;
    1908.B28; 1910.B22
Cottrell, George, W., 1930.B2
Cowie, Alexander, 1948.B4
Cowley, Malcolm, 1936.B2
CREATING THE MODERN AMERICAN
    NOVEL, 1935.B2
The Creative Conflict: Struggle
    and Escape in Jack London's
    Fiction, 1970.B19; 1971.B17
CREATOR AND CRITIC, 1961.A3
CRITICAL GUIDE, 1930.B2
THE CRITICAL PERIOD IN AMERICAN
    LITERATURE, 1951.B8
The Critical Reception of American
    Fiction in the Netherlands,
    1900-1935, 1961.B9
CRITICISM OF CALIFORNIA LITERA-
    TURE, 1940.B3
Criticism--Foreign, 1917.B7;
    1918.B13; 1934.B2; 1949.B1;
    1957.B2; 1959.B6,B16;
    1961.B10; 1962.B3; 1963.B13;
    1965.B11; 1966.B11,B27;
    1967.B10; 1969.B20; 1971.B8;
    1973.B24-B26; 1975.B18,B25

Criticism--General, 1907.B41;
    1912.B13; 1916.B44; 1917.B28-
    B29,B42,B47; 1919.B4-B6;
    1920.B9,B16; 1922.B5,B6;
    1925.B4; 1926.B7; 1929.B6;
    1933.B4; 1936.B5; 1937.B1;
    1938.B6,B7; 1939.B1; 1940.B3;
    1942.B7; 1947.A1; 1948.B7;
    1952.B2,B7; 1953.B1,B2;
    1954.B5; 1955.B5-B6; 1956.B10;
    1958.B7; 1959.B7; 1962.B8;
    1963.B17; 1964.B8; 1966.A1,A4,
    B10; 1967.B15; 1968.B14;
    1969.B15; 1971.B17; 1972.B13;
    1973.A4, B8,B46; 1974.A3;
    1975.A1, B3,B9,B26,B29
Crossman, R. H. S., 1941.B3
The Cruises of Bay-Pirate Jack,
    1917.B34
CRUSADERS FOR AMERICAN LIBERALISM,
    1939.B3
Cultural Degeneration and the Gro-
    tesque in H. G. Wells and
    Jack London, 1974.A2
Cunliffe, Marcus, 1954.B3
THE CUP OF FURY, 1956.B12
CURIOUS FRAGMENTS: JACK LONDON'S
    TALES OF FANTASY FICTION,
    1975.B5
Curley, Dorothy Nyren, 1969.B7
The Curse of Sociability, 1913.B49
THE CYCLE OF AMERICAN LITERATURE,
    1955.B8
CYCLOPEDIA OF WORLD AUTHORS,
    1958.B1

Daglian, Carlos, 1975.B4
Dale Carnegie's 5-Minute Biogra-
    phies, 1938.B3
Dall, William H., 1902.B13-B14;
    1903.B42
Daniels, Roger, 1965.B6
Dargan, E. Preston, 1917.B29
Dargan, Marion, 1952.B3
Darwin, Charles, 1959.B7
DAUGHTERS OF THE RICH, 1971.B22;
    1972.B18,B32-B33
David Graham Phillips, Jack Lon-
    don, and Others on Contempo-
    rary Reviewing, 1970.B39

Gurian, Jay, 1962.B5

Hacker, David W., 1966.B17
Hahn, Emily, 1967.B7
Haight, Anne Lyon, 1970.B22
Hail and Farewell to Jack London, 1916.B37
Haile, Margaret, 1903.B45
Haire, David B., 1975.B8
Haldeman-Julius, Emanuel, 1913.B41; 1917.A1; 1970.B8, B27; 1972.B20
The Haldeman-Julius Little Blue Books as a Bibliographical Problem, 1970.B27
Hale, Edward E., 1908.B29; 1916.B41-B43
Hall, Gifford, 1903.B46
Hamby, James A., 1970.B23
Hamilton, Fannie K., 1903.B47
Haney, John Louis, 1923.B1
Hanoi II, 1968.B12
HARD TRAVELLIN': THE HOBO AND HIS HISTORY, 1967.B1
Harkins, Edward F., 1903.B48-B49
Harris, Frank, 1909.B13-B15
Harphann, Geoffrey, 1974.A2; 1975.B9
Hart, James D., 1941.B6; 1950.B2; 1962.B6
Hart, Jerome A., 1931.B8
Hartwick, Harry, 1934.B1
HARVESTS OF CHANGE: AMERICAN LITERATURE, 1865-1914, 1967.B15
Hatchel, Linda, 1975.B10
Hatcher, Harlan, 1935.B2
Haunts of Jack London, 1905.B41
Haverland, Stella, 1938.B4
Havlice, Patricia Pate, 1971.B19; 1975.B11
Hawkes, Edith Granger, 1932.B8
Hawthorne, Julian, 1903.B50
Haycraft, Howard, 1942.B8
Haydock, James, 1960.B8
Hearts are Trumps, 1920.B14
Heiney, Donald, 1958.B4
Helsinki is Talking About: Jack London Fans, 1966.B28
Hendrick, George, 1961.B6; 1970.B16

Hendricks, King, 1961.A3; 1966.A1; 1967.B13; 1970.B24-B25
Henry, James, 1970.B26; 1973.B22; 1974.B16
Hensley, Dennis E., 1975.B8,B12-B13
The Hero Without a Name: B. Traven's The Death Ship, 1971.B3
Hervey, John L., 1917.B36
Herzberg, Max J., 1962.B7
HE WAS A MAN, 1925.A1
Hicks, Granville, 1933.B4; 1974.B17
Higham, John, 1955.B4
HIGH JINKS ON THE KLONDIKE, 1954.B7
HIGH SPOTS OF AMERICAN LITERATURE, 1929.B8
Hill, Murray, 1920.B11
Hillman, Serrell, 1965.B11
Hindman, Kathleen B., 1973.B23
Hindus, Maurice G., 1924.B5
Hinkel, Edgar Joseph, 1938.B5; 1940.B3; 1942.B4
A HISTORY OF AMERICAN LETTERS, 1936.B6
A HISTORY OF AMERICAN LITERATURE, 1930.B1
HISTORY OF AMERICAN LITERATURE FROM THE BEGINNING TO 1910, 1970.B7
The History of a Sea Sprite, 1960.B19
A HISTORY OF SOVIET LITERATURE, 1963.B2
Hobo Americanus: Jack London, 1966.B23
Hodder, Alfred, 1904.B35
Hoffman, Frederick J., 1951.B7
Hoffmeister, Charles C., 1972.B19; 1973.B24-B26
Hofstadter, Richard, 1945.B2
Holland, Robert B., 1951.A2
Holliday, Robert Cortes, 1920.B12
Holly, F. M., 1913.B42
Holman, C. Hugh, 1966.B18-B19; 1967.B8
Holmes, Harold C., 1948.B5
Homans, James E., 1918.B9
HOMECOMING, 1933.B3
HOME COUNTRY, 1947.B6
Horacio Quiroga, Literary Kin of Kipling and Jack London, 1925.B1

INDEX

INDEX

INDEX

INDEX

INDEX